A Concise History of History

This short history of history is an ideal introduction for those studying or teaching the subject as part of courses on the historian's craft, historical theory and method, and historiography. Spanning the earliest known forms of historical writing in the ancient Near East right through to the present and covering developments in Europe, Asia, Africa and the Americas, it also touches on the latest topics and debates in the field, such as 'Big History', 'Deep History' and the impact of the electronic age. It features timelines listing major dynasties or regimes throughout the world alongside historiographical developments; guides to key thinkers and seminal historical works; further reading; a glossary of terms; and sample questions to promote further debate at the end of each chapter. This is a truly global account of the process of progressive intercultural contact that led to the hegemony of Western historiographical methods.

DANIEL WOOLF is Professor of History at Queen's University, Ontario. He is the author of several books, including *A Global History of History*, the award-winning *The Social Circulation of the Past, Reading History in Early Modern England* and *The Idea of History in Early Stuart England*. He is a Fellow of the Royal Historical Society, of the Society of Antiquaries of London, and the Royal Society of Canada.

A Concise History of History

Global Historiography from Antiquity to the Present

DANIEL WOOLF
Queen's University, Ontario

CAMBRIDGE
UNIVERSITY PRESS

CAMBRIDGE
UNIVERSITY PRESS

University Printing House, Cambridge CB2 8BS, United Kingdom

One Liberty Plaza, 20th Floor, New York, NY 10006, USA

477 Williamstown Road, Port Melbourne, VIC 3207, Australia

314–321, 3rd Floor, Plot 3, Splendor Forum, Jasola District Centre, New Delhi – 110025, India

79 Anson Road, #06–04/06, Singapore 079906

Cambridge University Press is part of the University of Cambridge.

It furthers the University's mission by disseminating knowledge in the pursuit of education, learning, and research at the highest international levels of excellence.

www.cambridge.org
Information on this title: www.cambridge.org/9781108426190
DOI: 10.1017/9781108550789

First published 2019

Printed in the United Kingdom by TJ International Ltd. Padstow, Cornwall

A catalogue record for this publication is available from the British Library.

Library of Congress Cataloging-in-Publication Data
Names: Woolf, D. R. (Daniel R.), author.
Title: A concise history of history : global historiography from antiquity to the present / Daniel Woolf, Queen's University, Ontario.
Description: Cambridge : Cambridge University Press, 2019. | Includes index.
Identifiers: LCCN 2018035148 | ISBN 9781108426190
Subjects: LCSH: Historiography – History.
Classification: LCC D13 .W687 2019 | DDC 907.2–dc23
LC record available at https://lccn.loc.gov/2018035148

ISBN 978-1-108-42619-0 Hardback
ISBN 978-1-108-44485-9 Paperback

In memory of Georg G. Iggers (1926–2017) and Hayden White (1928–2018)

... History may be servitude,
History may be freedom ...
T. S. Eliot, 'Little Gidding' (1942)
Four Quartets

Contents

Preface and Conventions

This book is a revised and abridged version of my 2011 work entitled *A Global History of History* (*GHH*). That book aspired to a coverage of the history of historical thought and writing – and historical representation in non-alphabetic and oral forms – that was, if not encyclopedically comprehensive, at least global in intent. It was quite lengthy, and pitched at the graduate student/academic market. It appeared at nearly the same time as *The Oxford History of Historical Writing* (2011–12), a multivolume series under my general editorship, devoted to the same subject and similarly global in reach. Neither of these titles was especially suited to undergraduates in need of a more concise survey of the history of history – hence the present volume.

In the preface to *GHH* I wrote the following, which still serves adequately to explain the general aim in writing such a book:

Many years of teaching courses on historiography, and the prescription of several different textbooks for the students in those courses, convinced me that a further work was needed … There are several books covering very long time spans, and one or two with a global reach, but none in English, of which I am aware, that do both. A conviction that students ought to be exposed to the 'historical cultures' of other civilizations than their own has thus informed my choice of subject; a strong sense that there is a story to be told about the development of historical thought, historical writing and the modern historical discipline, and that it relates directly to some of the larger movements of world history (in particular the global engagement of different peoples and cultures over several millennia), provides the 'plot', if a work on historiography can be said to have a plot.

My overall perspective has not changed in the intervening time, though naturally my thinking about particular historians/historical thinkers and about the connections between historical cultures has, necessarily, evolved with further reading, especially of works that had not appeared by mid-2010 when *GHH* went to press (for example Frederick C. Beiser's comprehensive study of the origins and development of

German historicism, Dipesh Chakrabarty's intellectual biography of Indian historian Jadunath Sarkar, and several recent works on global history), or of which I was previously unaware. The process of abridgement has also been useful to me (though often quite challenging) in considering what aspects and examples to keep and which to jettison, and in revising or refining certain points made in the longer work. While the abridgement remains global in scope, it is by design less comprehensive than the former book, and some historical traditions discussed at some length in *GHH* have had to be left aside altogether, or mentioned only in passing. My hope is that those readers who have their curiosity whetted by this *Concise History* might be inclined to consult its bigger, older sibling for further detail.

However, this is not simply an abridgement. I have also taken the opportunity in the current book, which is about 60 per cent the length of *GHH*, to rearrange the contents of most chapters and to reorganize the whole. Thus, while a great many passages appear here verbatim and unchanged from the former work, there are many sections that have been rewritten in part or whole, and in particular the periods covered by particular chapters have been changed. The opening chapter on antiquity is the least changed, though shorter, but from that point on chapters from the earlier book have been combined, shrunk extensively, and, in several cases, rewritten with different periodization in mind. Thus the two early modern chapters of *GHH* have become one; the chapter on the eighteenth century now extends through the Revolutionary and Romantic periods up to the first decades of the nineteenth century; and the two *GHH* chapters on the nineteenth century have here become a single one extending from the second third of the century to the end of the Second World War. Most significantly, I have very heavily revised the last two chapters and added material on recent and prospective future developments in the field that a few readers of *GHH* felt had been given shorter shrift than I intended (though even here many sentences from the former book are repeated verbatim). This re-periodization has been intellectually helpful insofar as it has exposed some continuities and transitions that did not appear as clearly in the previous book, the chapter divisions of which were a little more conventional.

In the interest of remaining concise and accessible, I have also abandoned, with some regret, a few features of the former book that were well received, such as its specialized 'subject boxes' (sidebars on particular topics mentioned in passing in the main text), the extensive offset 'text boxes' containing examples of historical writing (especially many from non-European cultures), and the illustrations, which are a 'nice-to-have' rather than a necessity. I have, however, retained the 'timeline' feature of each chapter (reduced and rearranged to reflect the reorganization of chapters), though here retitled 'Milestones'. These list significant dates of developments or particular works in the history of historical writing. I have added, as an aid to readers, a selective glossary of terms that will likely be unfamiliar to many readers. Finally, I have been somewhat selective in providing birth or death dates within the text, especially in Chapters 6 and 7 where a great many persons mentioned are still living. Many of those mentioned principally as authors of secondary works in historiography do not have their vital dates included, a space-saving choice that does not reflect my gratitude for what I have gleaned from their work.

The very lengthy Further Reading section at the conclusion of *GHH* has been reduced into a few suggestions (linked to specific chapter sections) which here appear at the end of each chapter, and there are no footnotes or endnotes. In most instances where direct quotation is used, the book or author quoted is listed in the relevant further reading section, without specific page reference. The precise citation of many of these quotations can be found more precisely in *GHH*; for some others, I shall beg the reader's indulgence given that they are taken from reasonably accessible works. (Quotations from the 'primary' sources of the book, past great historians or historical thinkers, are generally given parenthetical edition and page references immediately following the extract.) I have not listed works in languages other than English unless, as some do, they include essays or chapters in English. A much fuller bibliography (though obviously without works published in the past eight years) can be found in *GHH*. Works listed once in a further reading section are not listed again in that chapter even if relevant to subsequent sections; they are, however, re-itemized in later chapters if relevant.

As the hope is that the book may be useful in a classroom setting, I have added, for the benefit of instructors, something *not* contained in *GHH*, namely a series of questions for class discussion or essay assignment. Historiography is not an easy subject to teach, even by specialists, and I hope that these questions will ignite conversations even if they by no means exhaust all topics that ought to be or might be discussed.

Diacritics and Transliteration

Even more than in *GHH*, again in the interest of making the book more 'reader-friendly', I have adopted a 'minimal-diacritical' approach to the transliteration of titles and names. Thus the dots, bars and underlined characters that featured in *GHH* (for languages such as Arabic) have disappeared, doubtless to the discomfort of my Islamicist or Arabist friends, though the characters ' ('ayn) and ' (hamza) remain in certain instances. With familiar proper or family names that are frequently used in English (such as 'Muhammad', in Arabic), diacritics have been dispensed with altogether. Japanese words and names have lost their macrons. All foreign words are rendered in the Latin alphabet. Most historical works are cited exclusively by an English translation of their actual title, in some instances with the original title also included and transliterated – this permits me, for instance, to refer to Ibn Khaldun's *Muqaddimah* by its familiar name and, on occasion, to give the reader a sense of the original title. For Latin-alphabet languages (e.g. French, Spanish, Turkish) I have retained conventional accents, most of which will be familiar to even monoglot English-language readers.

Chinese names and words remain as in *GHH* rendered according to the pinyin system, which has supplanted the older Wade-Giles system as the standard protocol for transliteration: thus Mao Zedong not Mao Tse-tung. Certain exceptions to this rule apply for historians with established Western names, such as Confucius, whose Chinese name was either Kong Qiu or Kong Zi (Master Kong). The names of Chinese historians publishing in Western languages, and the titles of books originally issued in those languages, follow the actual spelling of the author or title, whether Wade-Giles or pinyin.

Chinese, Korean and Japanese names appear with the family name first, followed *without a comma* by the given name. This is a well-known and common practice for Chinese and Korean, but in the case of Japanese, Western journalistic practice has tended to invert the name order according to North American usage, a practice that I have not followed: thus a reference to Kume Kunitake denotes a historian whose family name is Kume. Occasional exceptions, mainly historians whose names appear Western-style on their English-language publications, are indexed *with* commas to avoid confusion; a few Japanese historians (Motoori Norinaga and Hayashi Razan for instance) are by convention referred to by their given names, e.g. Norinaga.

Dates

A multitude of calendars have been used by various peoples in the course of the past five thousand years. Full compliance with the non-Eurocentric principles of this book would suggest that dates be recorded as the authors being described recorded them, for instance using the Hijri year of the Muslim calendar. However, this would be far more confusing than helpful. The compromise often used of Common Era (CE) or Before the Common Era (BCE) seems to me simply to replicate the conventional Western calendar under a different name. I have therefore, as in *GHH*, stuck with BC and AD.

Vital dates (where known) for most historians (and many who were not historians but nonetheless figure in the narrative) are provided in the main text. In some cases alternative dates are used either because of lack of agreement in scholarship as to a single date, or in some instances because the date itself is tied to a particular chronological scheme which itself is ambiguous. In the final chapters, certain vital dates have, sadly, had to be revised owing to the deaths of individuals still living when the first book went to press. Certain abbreviations for dates have been used:

b. = born, in the case of historians still living as of mid-2018.

c. = *circa*, approximate year where no firm year is known or agreed upon.

cent. = century or centuries.

d. = died, used where there is a firm death year (or approximate, in which case noted as 'd. *c.*').

est. = established, for instance, a journal or historical society.

fl. = *floruit*, that is 'flourished', generally used in relation to authors for whom birth and death dates are entirely unknown or highly obscure; indicates active period.

r. = reigned. When a monarch is noted, his or her regnal years, not years of birth and death, are noted in parentheses.

Acknowledgements

It is my pleasure to repeat here the acknowledgements I made in the *Global History of History* and to add a few more individuals who have either joined me on various historiographical projects going back to the early 1990s (when I first ventured outside my home turf of early modern England) or sharpened my thinking on particular issues. I thank in this respect Guido Abbattista, Michael Aung-Thwin, Donald Baker, Michael Bentley, Stefan Berger, Jeremy Black, the late Ernst Breisach, Adam Budd, Peter Burke, the late John Burrow, Fernando Cervantes, Dipesh Chakrabarty, Eileen Ka-May Cheng, Youssef Choueiri, William Connell, Antoon De Baets, Ewa Domańska, Richard Evans, Sarah Foot, Grant Hardy, Bruce Janacek, Donald R. Kelley, Newton Key, Tarif Khalidi, Ann Kumar, the late Joseph M. Levine, Fritz Levy, Chris Lorenz, Juan Maiguashca, Stuart Macintyre, Allan Megill, Matthias Middell, Mark Salber Phillips, J. G. A. Pocock, Attila Pók, José Rabasa, Anthony Reid, Chase Robinson, Jörn Rüsen, Dominic Sachsenmaier, Masayuki Sato, Zachary Sayre Schiffman, Axel Schneider, Baki Tezcan, Romila Thapar, Edoardo Tortarolo, Aviezer Tucker, Markus Völkel, Peer Vries and Q. Edward Wang. Many others have provided encouragement or assistance, such as my long-suffering team in the Principal's Office at Queen's University, who have tolerated with good grace my occasional absences for half-days or summertime weeks of writing. I will not mention them all, given the length of this list, but they, too, have my deepest appreciation.

Michael Watson at Cambridge University Press provided the impetus for *GHH* over a decade ago and more recently suggested this abridgement as a way of updating the original book and bringing it to a wider audience; I am grateful, too, for the press's anonymous readers for helpful feedback on the initial proposal and the penultimate text. Ian McIver supervised the publication process with a firm hand. Rose Bell, who copy-edited *GHH* in 2010, undertook the present book also. I am again grateful for her meticulous attention to detail and helpful suggestions. Among my past doctoral students, I thank Dr Matthew Neufeld, Dr Sarah Brand, and Dr Jane Wong Yeang-Chui. Other graduate students assisted in other ways with the original book (including summarizing for me books in languages which I do not read), in particular (at the University of Alberta 2002–9) Tanya Henderson, Carolyn Salomons, Tony Maan and Nina Paulovicova. The experience of teaching historiography to many students at varying levels has added immeasurably to my sense of what I liked in other textbooks and what I did not, which was not always the same as what the students liked. Current Queen's University graduate students David White, Kimberley Bell, Virginia Vandenberg, Megan Kirby and Johanna Strong have provided excellent intellectual stimulation during my extended tour of duty in senior administration. Ian Hesketh, my former research associate at Queen's, and now at the University of Queensland in Brisbane, remains a close associate and fellow enthusiast for matters historiographical; apart from providing a few apposite references here and there (such as the passage from H. T. Buckle that opens Chapter 7), it is he who convinced me that in the present work I needed to pay more attention to 'Big History'. Attendance at a conference on historiography, philosophy and method at McMaster University in June 2018 organized by Sandra Lapointe occasioned some late rethinking of certain passages in Chapters 5 and 6, and I am grateful to attendees, especially Martin Kusch, Catarina Dutilh Novaes, Lydia Patton, Christopher Green and Michael Beaney for their papers and discussions.

My three adult children, Sarah, Samuel and David have always done a convincing job of feigning interest in historiography; in David's case, the interest must have been genuine since he spent a month providing a reading and extensive marking-up of *GHH* with a view to its abridgement. While I have not followed all his suggestions, this exercise proved invaluable in suggesting to me ways in which the original might be reduced and simplified without compromising its global reach. Both my late parents, Margaret and Cyril Woolf, took an interest in my work and this, regrettably, will be the first book I have produced that I shall not have the opportunity to share with them. Lastly, my wife, Julie Anne Gordon-Woolf, remains my greatest friend, life partner, supporter and affectionate critic.

On a final, and sad, note, two historiographers a generation my senior, who provided both role models and occasional criticism, have both died very recently. Hayden White, with whom I engaged at a few international conferences over the past fifteen years, did not especially like my approach to the history of history, which is far removed from his, but ours was a respectful disagreement. While we did not know each other well, his works have been a significant influence on my own over the years. The late Georg Iggers, a historiographer of a very different bent who attended most of the same conferences, was a friend and close ally for twenty-five years in my conviction that historiography needed to be globalized; he was a frequent commentator on and supportive critic of my work. I dedicate the book in appreciation of these two late giants of historiography.

Introduction

The historian, before he begins to write history, is the product of history.

E. H. Carr, *What is History?* (p. 34)

'History' is written and read today because humans have the biological and neurological capacity to remember things and to frame relationships of a causal or symbolic nature around those things that have been remembered. It exists also because we are social creatures whose survival has been more or less dependent upon connections with other members of our species. Knowledge of the past in some form is common to all humans, though specifically *historical* knowledge (which reaches beyond personal yesterdays and current memory) may not be. In a widely read book entitled *The Writing of History*, the late French psychologist and philosopher Michel de Certeau (1925–86) observed that societies supply themselves with a present time through historical writing, progressively separating past from present and providing modernity with knowledge of a temporal and sometimes geographical 'other'. And it allows that other, discarded in earlier periods as an irrelevant or 'repressed' fragment, to return anew – sometimes without being invited.

However, the capacity to remember, and the curiosity to inquire into a reality no longer extant except in human-made or natural artefacts, are not sufficient on their own to create the conditions for history to be made. Humans are the only species capable of *both* forming long-term memories (beyond the simple recollection of how to perform tasks or how to find a particular familiar location) *and* of communicating. It is this latter function that permits the transmission of those memories, and other knowledge, to humans both contemporary and future. Written communication has been a significant technological enhancement to the preservation and communication of information over long distances or across long spans of time, but it is a relatively recent development, dating back at most a few millennia to the earliest cuneiform tablets in Mesopotamia, to hieroglyphics in Egypt and to bone inscriptions in China. Before then, humans relied on spoken language to communicate, and we know that very ancient cultures used poetry and song to commemorate the deeds of the gods and heroes in their past. Today, history is undeniably and inescapably present in a vast number of forms, written, oral, visual and electronic. This is in part because the past itself is equally ubiquitous, looming over our daily lives even when we aren't thinking much about it – as the American novelist William Faulkner once wrote, 'the Past isn't dead; it isn't even past'. It is also because many centuries of human development have made an interest in that past, and a will to appropriate it into daily life (often unconsciously), a fixture of modernity. This is paradoxically true even in a culture such as that of the current moment, which seems on a daily basis to be ever more focused on a vision of the future oscillating between hope and dread.

'Historical culture' of course includes much more than written history, of which the governing, academic, 'professional' history of the last two centuries is a very recent development. As Peter Lambert and Björn Weiler have noted in their introduction to a recent essay collection, there are (and have been for centuries) many forms of engagement with the past that fall outside a narrow definition of historical writing, and modernity (much less Western modernity) did not invent these. ⌊What we now term 'history' (the written genre) must be understood within the broader historical culture – that wider set of forms of engagement with the past – that produced it.⌉

The English word 'history' (in the more restricted sense of the written narration of the past) goes by many different names in European languages alone: *histoire* in French, *Geschichte* in German, *storia* in Italian, *dzieje* in Polish. Many Asian cultures developed their own forms of recording and commemorating the past which have their own terms: *tamnan* and *phongsawadan* in Siam (now Thailand), *pangsavatar* and *thamaing* in Burma, *babad* in Java, *hikayat* in Sumatra, *itihasa-purana* in ancient India. History has often been conceived of in ways that we would now deem strange, even 'unhistorical'. Because this book is being written in English, I will use terms such as 'history', 'historical thought' and 'historical knowledge' frequently, but in doing so I embrace under these familiar phrases the world's collective names for ways of organizing and representing the past.

My choice of word usage in the present book requires a bit more elaboration. For the sake of clarity I have adopted the following practice. The word 'history', when used in English and not otherwise explained or clarified, should be taken as meaning, variously, the forms in which the past is recovered, thought of, spoken of and written down (but not the evidence used in its construction), among them a particular *type* of historical writing, composed in continuous prose (as distinct from other forms such as the annals or chronicles that were widely used in the European Middle Ages); or, especially in the last two chapters, the study or 'discipline' of history as it has developed since the mid-nineteenth century. There is a further commonplace usage, bequeathed us from the European Enlightenment (see below, Chapter 4), in which history is not the record or recitation of the past, but the actual events themselves, understood as a cumulative river of events, causes and effects leading to the present day. There will be occasion to refer to history in this sense too; in such cases, 'History' (the cumulative pattern of events to those who have believed that there has been such a pattern and that it is fathomable) will be capitalized to distinguish it from the more conventional uses, above. Virtually coterminous with this development there also matured another phenomenon, previously less common: thinking about both 'History' and 'history' as respectively an object of philosophical speculation and a mode of knowledge. This in turn occasioned other debates, from the late eighteenth century onward, as to the nature of the relationship between knowledge of the past and knowledge of God or of Nature.

Another word which will appear often, and which is known frequently to frighten students and discomfit some faculty, is 'historiography'. While this, too, has multiple senses, in the present book it will primarily denote what we might call the 'meta' level of historical practice: that is, the history of how history itself has been written, spoken or thought about over several millennia and in a wide variety of cultures. There have been different approaches taken to historiography-as-history-of-history, too, and different concepts of when exactly 'real' historical writing began – as Jonathan Gorman has argued, it's possible to compare histories of historiography and thereby go one level deeper still, in effect creating a historiography of historiography. The present book is thus concerned with historiography in the sense of 'the history of history' and *not* with particular debates such as 'the historiography of the French Revolution' or of 'American slavery'. Nor does it claim to outline, much less argue on behalf of, a set of 'historical methods' – except insofar as these are a recurring, and highly contested, element in discussions about how the past should be recovered and described. (An aside: I am not what the philosopher of historiography Aviezer Tucker would deem a 'historiographic esotericist' who believes one cannot teach proper methods and practices and that they must simply be acquired through experience. However, I will confess to finding works that self-describe as teaching historical methods – and in particular methods that exclude all other approaches – however comforting they may be to new students, naively mechanical. They also tend to be extraordinarily dry, rather like instruction books for fixing a particular car, or descriptions of a mining-smelting-refining operation.) The word 'historiography' has also been used, in some past cultures, as synonymous with history itself (the written genre). And we will have occasion to discuss not only historians (those who wrote works of history deemed significant because of the quality of their writing, the acuity of their perception, or sometimes simply their mastery of style and composition) but also historiographers, literary critics and, indeed, some philosophers of history, a few of whom wrote little or no actual history but had a deep impact on thinking either about the meaning of the past itself, or about the ways and means of representing it. This will be the case whether the writer or thinker in question originated in Europe, the Americas, Africa or Asia.

The previous sentence must be clearly understood at the outset. The 'West' neither invented nor enjoyed a monopoly on history. Nor has history been the closely guarded possession of history's high priesthood, academics working mainly in institutions of higher education. In fact, a multitude of different civilizations that have inhabited this planet have conceived of the past in different ways, formulated variable notions of its relationship to the present, and evolved distinctive terms – not always directly corresponding to those we use in English – to denote its representation. Past historical cultures must be taken on their own merits and judged by their own standards, not by the fairly narrow assumptions of modern professional historians. In short, we too should be wary of both a geographical and chronological parochialism. While many forms of history sprang up in isolation, they did not remain that way. Just as the history of the world is (in part) a story of encounters, conflicts and conquests among different peoples, so the history of history itself demonstrates that the different modes of knowing the

not historiography and not about scholarly ... (handwritten margin note)

past have often come into contact with and demonstrably influenced one another. These encounters were relatively limited until the early modern period (discussed in Chapter 3) and their full implications were not realized before the nineteenth century, at which point, with the advantage of hindsight, it can seem as if all the various streams of historical thinking that the world has seen were either dammed up or diverted into the rather large lake of professional history built on European and especially Germanic academic practice which has ruled the past ever since. But this result was by no means inevitable, nor was it necessarily an intellectual 'conquest', since Western practices were often quite willingly adopted, even zealously pursued, by social reformers in other countries seeking an alternative to long-standing and, to them, restrictive and progress-retarding indigenous conventions of describing their own pasts.

While there can be no question that Western history has come to be the hegemonic model (at this time), it has in turn been influenced by its encounters with other forms of historical knowledge, even if only sharpening definitions of what history should and should not be by comparing it with an exotic but 'lesser' 'other'. Spanish historical *academic* writing of the sixteenth century certainly had a huge impact on how the past of the newly discovered Americas was written, but the early *appropriation* modern missionaries who wrote those histories had to adapt their writings to the sources available in native oral and pictographic practices. I will argue further on that these contacts, and this growing awareness of alternative modes of 'historicity' (which in this sense means the capacity and will to preserve or recover and represent aspects of the past), obliged Europeans to make some decisions about what *they* deemed 'within-scope' for true history, and to prioritize the written record of the past over the oral or pictographic. This prepared the ground for a hardening of European attitudes in the seventeenth and eighteenth centuries, and the division of the world into those with history from those (apparently) without it. This in turn set the table for the achievement of Western dominance over history outlined below in Chapters 4 and 5. The book, in short, sketches the main world traditions of historical writing, and then the process whereby the European approach, which has generated its own self-policing 'discipline', achieved its hegemony, sometimes being adapted or altered better to mesh with very different cultures or competing ideologies (which themselves may be understood as differing beliefs about the moral, economic and political status of the present with respect to either a wistfully remembered past or a dreamed-of future).

That hegemony has not come without cost as some modern critics of the discipline have observed, a point we will revisit in later chapters. In particular, the enshrinement of historiographic authority within the academic community, while providing rigour and an almost factory-like system (our earlier mining-smelting-refining metaphor, now applied to people) for reproducing its scholarly progeny, can also be viewed as a constraint on creativity. It also introduces a buffer between author and reader unknown before the mid-nineteenth century. In *The Writing of History*, Certeau commented astutely on the chasm that has opened between historical authors and wider audiences, whereby the value of work is bestowed not by the reader at large (as it was in Europe's eighteenth century and much of the nineteenth) but by a peer-approval system whose criteria are often quite different from those of the lay person. The mere existence of this system (of which the present author is a product) both constrains historians from straying too far from the 'accrediting' rules of the discipline and inflicts *literal* discipline in the form of bad reviews, tenure denials and public embarrassment. At the same time, as professional historians and their students seek new angles, new approaches and something original to say about usually well-trodden ground (though almost always carefully within the academy's approved practices), the system guides them into a narrower and narrower field of view, often about subjects so minute, or too-often revisited, as to be of little interest beyond a minor subset of the profession.

[This raises a further issue. As 'world history' and latterly 'global' history have gradually won both academic and curricular acceptance in recent times, it has become clear that the noblest plans for inclusiveness often run aground on the shoals of Eurocentrism] As the Palestinian cultural critic Edward Said once observed, the alleged universalism of various disciplinary fields, among which he includes historiography, is 'Eurocentric in the extreme, as if other literatures and societies had either an inferior or a transcended value', a loaded view which Said traced (not entirely accurately) to Enlightenment thought. One can avoid this trap by taking an attitude that treats each historical culture as unique and of value. But, on the other hand, if we simply recount a number of parallel histories of history, West and East, we risk losing perspective; we will miss both the 'big picture', *and* a sense of the relative scale, significance and magnitude of different types of history. We will also jeopardize any hope of making meaningful generalizations and of finding similarities and connections. Here explicit comparison can help, together with attention to the ways in which historical cultures have been at least aware of one another for a very much longer time than they have interacted.

It is also worth remembering that although for the past two centuries historical traditions have been associated with particular nation-states, this was not always the case. In terms of political organization, the nation-state – which played a key part in the formation of 'modern' Western historical methods during the nineteenth century – is little more than a blip in the history of human society. Cities and empires (sometimes at the same time) were the dominant form of polity through most of human history; the latter were typically multi-ethnic and multi-lingual, leading to a degree of 'internal' interaction between cultures – the Mongol appropriation of both Chinese and Islamic forms of historical writing in the thirteenth and fourteenth centuries is but one example. Moreover, though founded on the basis of perceptions of shared pasts (and sometimes 'invented traditions'), nation-states themselves are scarcely more homogeneous than the empires from which they emerged, as a violent record of ethnic and racial persecution over the past hundred years illustrates. Given this, phrases such as 'French' historical writing (or English, Turkish, Chinese, etc) should not be understood in this book as always denoting the modern countries of these names, at least before the nineteenth century, and even then cannot be taken as monolithic essences.

The British historian J. H. Plumb (1911–2001) was certainly correct that ancient Chinese historicity was not that of the modern West (or, as we will see, even of post-nineteenth-century China), just as he was right to point to differences between the moral and didactic imperatives driving much 'Western' (a term used to denote Europe and its direct colonial offshoots) historiography from antiquity to 1800, and the less explicitly moralizing academic history that succeeded it. But does that mean that only modernity – and that in its European form – has produced 'real' history? This is among the issues which this book explores. Western historiography has repeatedly, and often defensively, fashioned itself, masking its internal insecurities and intellectual doubts, in response to other types of history that it encountered in the course of war, trade and other forms of contact. The great irony is that this occidental form of knowledge, having built itself into something unlike its 'oriental' and supposedly 'ahistorical' counterparts, was by the nineteenth century sufficiently refined, confident in its methods and clear in its goals (themselves closely associated with Western economic and technological superiority) that it could march with comparative ease – and sometimes by invitation – into those parts of the world that previously entertained different notions of what the past was and how and why it should be remembered. And there is a second irony: even with the assistance of the most willing local admirers, European historical practices could not be grafted wholesale on to foreign societies any more than American-style democracy can be imposed today on countries with no democratic tradition. In some instances (for example the transference of Marxism, a system built on Western perceptions of the process of historical change, to China, with its very different relation to its own past), European forms required considerable modification or domestication in order to achieve broad acceptance. The rough fit and the compromises have been elided from the story of history as the twentieth century wrote it, along with most of the indigenous historical practices that they supplanted.

In an influential book, Dipesh Chakrabarty has called for the 'provincializing of Europe', noting that Europe has traditionally provided the scale against which the rest of the world is measured. That being said, it is difficult to make European historiography simply one among several approaches. As most postcolonial scholars would concede, and as later chapters of this book will contend, the European-descended Western form of historiography, complete with its academic and professional institutions, *has* achieved dominance over other forms of writing or thinking about the past. It has by and large pushed out of consideration more traditional, oral forms of history that were commonplace in earlier ages, and in the West since about 1600 history has been associated overwhelmingly with writing rather than speech, a by-product of increased lay literacy over the previous two centuries and of perceptions of the fundamental unreliability of the record where a system of writing did not exist. The fact of the elimination of alternative forms of perceiving and representing the past, seen by Said and other postcolonial scholars as an imposition of a Western system of knowledge and language on the colonized, holds true, ironically, even in circumstances where Western historical methods have been seized and turned as a weapon on the very political or social structures that disseminated them (see below, Chapter 6). For the reader of this book, the more interesting questions are likely to be first, how 'modern' historiography achieved its apparent hegemony, and second, whether this occurred without the 'victor' being affected in some ways by contact with the 'vanquished' (or in some cases, the 'vanished'). The ways in which historiographical transferences have occurred are not merely intellectual – the result of author-to-author 'influences'. As Dominic Sachsenmaier has perceptively observed, the spread of academic historiography cannot be explained by a simple 'diffusion' model whereby ideas simply 'catch on' outside their country of origin; it must be understood as a consequence of a variety of social and political factors at work in Europe and throughout the world.

The landscape traversed in this book thus embraces a variety of different historiographic traditions, running along parallel tracks for much of the time, and on occasion (especially from the sixteenth century on) criss-crossing and intersecting. These traditions were embodied in different genres; they were transmitted in alternative forms of commemoration and communication (oral and pictorial as well as literate), and they emerged and evolved in widely varying social and political contexts. The balance of this book aims to describe these processes, and where, at present, they now stand.

Further Reading

Bentley, Michael (ed.), *A Companion to Historiography* (London and New York, 1997)

Breisach, Ernst, *Historiography: Ancient, Medieval, and Modern*, 3rd edn (Chicago, IL, 2007)

Brown, Donald E., *Hierarchy, History and Human Nature: The Social Origins of Historical Consciousness* (Tucson, CO, 1988)

Burrow, J. W., *A History of Histories: Epics, Chronicles, Romances and Inquiries from Herodotus and Thucydides to the Twentieth Century* (London, 2007)

Butterfield, Herbert, *Man on His Past: The Study of the History of Historical Scholarship* (Cambridge, 1955)

Carr, E. H., *What is History?* (1961; Basingstoke, 2001)

Certeau, Michel de, *The Writing of History*, trans. T. Conley (New York, 1988)

Chakrabarty, Dipesh, *Provincializing Europe: Postcolonial Thought and Historical Difference* (Princeton, NJ, 2000)

Cheng, Eileen Ka-May, *Historiography: An Introductory Guide* (London and New York, 2012)

Claus, Peter and John Marriott, *History: An Introduction to Theory, Method and Practice*, 2nd edn (Abingdon and New York, 2017)

Duara, Prasenjit, Viren Murthy and Andrew Sartori (eds), *A Companion to Global Historical Thought* (Chichester, 2014)

Fuchs, Eckhardt and Benedikt Stuchtey (eds), *Across Cultural Borders: Historiography in Global Perspective* (Lanham, MD, 2002)

Gorman, Jonathan, *Historical Judgement: The Limits of Historiographical Choice* (Stocksfield, UK, 2007)

Hama, B. and J. Ki-Zerbo, 'The Place of History in African Society', in J. Ki-Zerbo (ed.), *General History of Africa, Vol. 1: Methodology and African Prehistory* (Paris and London, 1981), 45–53

Iggers, Georg G., Q. Edward Wang with S. Mukherjee, *A Global History of Modern Historiography* (Harlow, UK and New York, 2008)

Jordanova, Ludmilla, *History in Practice*, 2nd edn (London and New York, 2006)

Kelley, Donald R., *Faces of History: Historical Inquiry from Herodotus to Herder* (New Haven, CT, 1998)

   Fortunes of History: Historical Inquiry from Herder to Huizinga (New Haven, CT, 2003)

   Frontiers of History: Historical Inquiry in the Twentieth Century (New Haven, CT, 2006)

Kemp, Anthony, *The Estrangement of the Past: A Study in the Origins of Modern Historical Consciousness* (Oxford, 1991)

Kramer, Lloyd and Sarah Maza (eds), *A Companion to Western Historical Thought* (Oxford, 2002)

Lambert, Peter and Björn Weiler (eds), *How the Past was Used: Historical Cultures c. 750–2000* (Oxford, 2017)

Lowenthal, David, *The Past is a Foreign Country – Revisited* (Cambridge, 2013)

MacMillan, Margaret, *The Uses and Abuses of History* (London, 2008)

Mali, Joseph, *Mythistory: The Making of a Modern Historiography* (Chicago, IL and London, 2003)

Maza, Sarah C., *Thinking About History* (Chicago, IL, 2017)

Paul, Herman, *Key Issues in Historical Theory*, trans. Anthony Runia (Abingdon and New York, 2015)

Plumb, J. H., *The Death of the Past*, rev. edn (1969; Houndmills, Basingstoke, UK, 2004)

Popkin, Jeremy, *From Herodotus to H-Net: The Story of Historiography* (Oxford, 2016)

Rublack, Ulinka, *A Concise Companion to History* (Oxford, 2011)

Rüsen, Jörn, *Western Historical Thinking: An Intercultural Debate* (New York and Oxford, 2002)

Sachsenmaier, Dominic, *Global Perspectives on Global History: Theories and Approaches in a Connected World* (Cambridge, 2011)

Said, Edward, *Orientalism* (London, 1978)

Schiffman, Zachary S., *The Birth of the Past* (Baltimore, MD, 2011)

Tosh, John, *The Pursuit of History: Aims, Methods and New Directions in the Study of Modern History*, 3rd edn (London and New York, 2002)

Tucker, Aviezer, *Our Knowledge of the Past: A Philosophy of Historiography* (Cambridge, 2004)

Wolf, Eric R., *Europe and the People without History* (Berkeley, CA, 1982)

Reference Books, Companions and Encyclopedias

Boia, Lucian (ed.), *Great Historians from Antiquity to 1800: An International Dictionary* (New York, 1989)

Great Historians of the Modern Age: An International Dictionary (New York, 1991)

Boyd, Kelly (ed.), *Encyclopedia of Historians and Historical Writing*, 2 vols (London, 1999)

Munslow, Alun, *The Routledge Companion to Historical Studies* (London and New York, 2000)

Tucker, Aviezer (ed.), *A Companion to the Philosophy of History and Historiography* (Malden, MA and Chichester, UK, 2009)

Woolf, Daniel R. (ed.), *A Global Encyclopedia of Historical Writing*, 2 vols (New York, 1998)

Some Anthologies of Historical Writing[1]

Budd, Adam (ed.), *The Modern Historiography Reader: Western Sources* (London, 2009)

Burns, Robert M. and Hugh Rayment-Pickard (eds), *Philosophies of History: From Enlightenment to Post-Modernity* (Oxford, 2000)

---

[1] This list includes only readings available in English given the target audience for the present book. It is also unavoidably Eurocentric, there being, as yet, no good collection of historiographical readings with a global range. Short extracts from some non-Western historiographic texts are included in the original book of which this is a revised abridgement, *A Global History of History* (Cambridge, 2011) but a full-scale anthology remains desirable.

Green, Anna and Kathleen Troup (eds), *The Houses of History: A Critical Reader in Twentieth-Century History and Theory* (New York and Manchester, 1999)

Hoefferle, Caroline (ed.), *The Essential Historiography Reader* (Saddle River, NJ, 2011)

Hughes-Warrington, Marnie (ed.), *Fifty Key Thinkers on History*, 3rd edn (Abingdon and New York, 2015)

Jenkins, Keith (ed.), *The Postmodern History Reader* (London and New York, 1997)

Kelley, Donald R. (ed.), *Versions of History from Antiquity to the Enlightenment* (New Haven, CT, 1991)

Mazlish, Bruce and Akira Iriye (eds), *The Global History Reader* (New York, 2005)

Roberts, Geoffrey (ed.), *The History and Narrative Reader* (London and New York, 2001)

Stern, Fritz (ed.), *The Varieties of History* (New York, 1956)

Stunkel, Kenneth R. (ed.), *Fifty Key Works of History and Historiography* (Abingdon and New York, 2011)

Tosh, John (ed.), *Historians on History*, 3rd edn (London and New York, 2018)

A Select List of English-language Journals Containing Historiographic Articles[2]

American Historical Review (1895)
Comparative Studies in Society and History (1958)
Gender and History (1989)
*History in Africa: A Journal of Method** (1974–)
*Historical Methods: A Journal of Quantitative and Interdisciplinary History** (1978; successor to *Historical Methods Newsletter*)
*Historiography East and West** (2003–06)
History and Memory (1989)
*History and Theory** (1960)
*History in Africa** (1974)
History of Humanities (2016)
History Workshop Journal (1976)
Journal of Contemporary History (1966)
Journal of Interdisciplinary History (1970)
Journal of the History of Ideas (1940)

---

[2] Titles followed by an asterisk focus on Historiography, Historical Methodology, History of Historical Writing or Philosophy of History.

Past and Present (1952)
Rethinking History * (1997)
Representations (1983)
Signs: Journal of Women in Culture and Society (1975)
Storia della storiografia/Histoire de l'Historiographie/History of Historiography/Geschichte der Geschichtsschreibung (multilingual)* (1982)

MILESTONES

25th cent. BC Likely date of the Palermo stone stele fragment (early Egyptian historical record)

c. 22nd cent. BC Sumerian King List

10th cent. to *c.* late 7th cent. BC *Tanakh* (the Hebrew Bible)

704–681 BC *Eponymous Chronicle*

7th–6th cent. BC Neo-Babylonian Chronicle series

c. 480 BC *Spring and Autumn Annals*

c. 440 BC Herodotus' *Histories*

c. 400 BC *Zuozhuan*; Thucydides' *History of the Peloponnesian War*

mid-2nd cent. BC Polybius' *Histories*

c. 90 BC Sima Qian's *Records of the Grand Historian*

mid-1st cent. BC Sallust authors his histories

after 27 BC Livy writes his history of Rome, *From the Foundation of the City*

c. AD 90 Josephus' *Antiquities of the Jews, Jewish War* and *Against Apion*

c. AD 105–117 Tacitus' *Annals* and *Histories*

c. AD 111 Ban Gu's and Ban Zhao's *Hanshu* establishes model for future single-dynasty 'Standard Histories'

c. AD 391 Ammianus Marcellinus' *Thirty-one Books of Deeds*

1 | *The Earliest Forms of Historical Writing*

The Ancient Near East

The Near East was a complex, multilingual region extending from Egypt and what became the land of the Israelites, through the Levant, embracing Mesopotamia proper and the land of the Hittites in Anatolia and northern Syria. Within this region dwelled a number of very long-lived civilizations, and they did not recall or preserve their pasts in the same ways or consistently in the same types of record. The evidence is literally fragmentary, deriving as it does from inscriptions on steles, stone tablets or rocks, and writings on papyrus; a majority of these objects have not survived entirely intact. One looks in vain for 'history' as a concept, much less for works devoted to it. Lexical equivalents for either 'history' or 'historiography' are scarce in any language of the region, though the Hebrew words *tôledôt* ('genealogies') and *divrê hāyyāmîm* ('words of those days') might be considered approximate equivalents. Terminology is important, especially when sorting out what peoples in the past thought, and so is the nomenclature of categories – the Greeks in particular would take the generic divisions of history seriously, as would Renaissance humanists two millennia later. But it would be unwise to leap from the dearth of linguistic terms, or the absence of a literary genre, to the conclusion that 'there was no history back then'.

Arguments can certainly be made for a sense of the past in ancient Egypt, and in particular an effort to memorialize the successive dynasties of the Old, Middle and New Kingdoms. Very few of the 'annals' recorded by the first pharaohs remain extant: an early specimen is the twenty-fifth-century 'Palermo stone', a fragmentary stele (so named for one of its portions, in Palermo, Sicily) inscribed with king lists from pre-dynastic times down to the mid-third millennium; and annals of the wars of a mid-second-millennium pharaoh, Thutmose III

(r. *c.* 1479–25), were eventually preserved on a temple wall. Historical inscriptions and texts are also attributable to the Hittites, perhaps the earliest people to have realized the didactic and especially political uses of history, either justifying a particular situation by appeal to the past or by using its episodes to advise and admonish. It is in Mesopotamia proper, however, that one first finds unmistakable evidence of a deliberate human intention to write about the past, especially among the Babylonians and Assyrians. The successive peoples that inhabited the land between the Tigris and Euphrates, who developed proto-alphabetic writing in cuneiform, also created elementary forms for the representation of the past (king lists and annals) and the institutions for preserving their own records, the library and the archive.

Many of the stories eventually captured in writing preceded its development and had previously been preserved orally. 'Epic', a genre that relates the martial deeds and adventures of Gilgamesh of Uruk, was the oldest form of historical narrative. That many of the episodes which epics recount are legendary and that their heroes were either exaggerated or may never have existed at all is not in itself evidence of a lack of history or historical thinking: the singers of and listeners to these stories almost certainly believed at some level either in their literal truth or at least in the moral principles that they embodied. Further afield, the great Greek epics, the *Iliad* and the *Odyssey*, ascribed to the bard Homer, portray what Greeks of the eighth to fifth centuries BC believed to be their own ancient past. The border between epic and something that looks to us more like history – the listing of undeniably 'real' figures – is often blurred.

Closer to a recognizably historical document are a class of text that can broadly be called 'chronographic' (ascribing particular events to a specific date within a sequence) and which include sub-genres such as 'king lists', 'annals' and 'chronicles'. Among the earliest of these is the Sumerian king list, probably initiated in the twenty-second century, which stretches back into mythical antiquity but goes beyond a mere list; it is a deliberate attempt to present the then-past in a particular light, necessitated by the circumstances of the author's own time. Various other forms of Sumero-Babylonian historical record exist, including building inscriptions, steles and other durable media. Chronicles, written in the third person, begin as early as a text now called the *Chronicle of the Single Monarchy* which may date from the Akkadian period (twenty-fourth to twenty-second century BC). Other genres, such as astronomical diaries, played a part in establishing a precise chronological grid against which to record events, and both the Babylonians of the second millennium and their Neo-Babylonian or Chaldaean successors of the mid-first millennium were keen astronomers and devoted list-makers. The neighbouring Assyrians also authored historiographic documents. An Assyrian king list that continues down to the late eighth century appears to have been compiled from other documents, thereby requiring what we would regard as 'research'. Assyrian royal inscriptions include annals, commencing in the early thirteenth century and composed in the first person; these recount the history of particular campaigns, and do not have a Babylonian or Sumerian counterpart. The Assyrians also produced third-person texts such as the *Eponymous Chronicle*, which relays the annual military campaigns of its kings down to Sennacherib (r. 704–681). The seventh and sixth centuries produced further works such as the Neo-Babylonian Chronicle series, running from 747 to the Persian capture of Babylon in 539, and the Late Babylonian Chronicle series that continued this down to the third century, by which time contact with the Greeks had broadened the outlook of the authors. The latest-known Babylonian work is that of the third-century BC writer, Berossus, who wrote in Greek. Nothing of his original work now survives though it was well known in Hellenistic and Roman times. It is among many ancient texts (the supposed near-contemporary *Aegyptiaca* of the Egyptian, Manetho, likely a product of a later period, is another) of which we possess indirect knowledge or fragmentary traces because later writers quoted from it. The Persians, successors to Babylonian power in the sixth century, would continue this historiographical activity; indeed, with the multilingual Behistun Inscription, Darius I (r. 521–486) became the first Persian king to whom authorship (at least indirectly) of a historical work – recalling events early in his reign – is ascribed.

There is evidence that, unlike straightforward king lists or chronicles that simply recorded events progressively as they happened, some of these authors sought to write about past occurrences, including those from before their own time. Since there is little evidence of a continuous tradition of record-keeping or chronicle-writing, wherein one author simply added to a work begun by his predecessors (such as would evolve in medieval Christendom), then many of the works must have been the result of what we would now call 'research' – the examination, selection from and collation of multiple earlier, non-narrative sources. Many went beyond simply relating former events, aspiring to provide advice, counsel or cautionary tales, a recurring theme through much of the global history of historical writing. A didactic purpose emerges from one of the best-known examples of early Mesopotamian historical writing, the Old Babylonian *Weidner Chronicle*, a propagandistic composition reaching back to the early third millennium but largely devoted to the Sargonic dynasty of Akkad in the twenty-fourth and twenty-third centuries. Surviving only in much later copies, this is one of the first historical works clearly designed to recover and preserve the past explicitly for the edification of present and future. Framed as a dialogue among divine beings, the *Weidner Chronicle* contrasts the godliness of Sargon of Akkad with the impiety of his grandson Naram-Sin to which the author attributes the fall of the Akkadian kingdom. The long-standing explanation of events through an alternating current of divine favour and punishment, a recurrent theme for many centuries, thus had an early start. It appears frequently throughout the travails of the children of Israel at the hands of foreign hosts depicted in the Hebrew Bible.

Jewish Historical Thought from the *Tanakh* to Josephus

Like most Near Eastern cultures, the ancient Israelites had a term for neither 'history' nor 'myth', and appear not to have held any strong belief about a distinction between the two. Somewhat exaggerated claims have been made for the uniqueness of the historical sense in the *Tanakh* (the Hebrew Bible), to the point of viewing the Hebrews as the inventors of history in its post-Enlightenment sense – that is, a cumulative flow of events towards a divinely ordained conclusion. All of this has been complicated by the modern and considerably more sophisticated understanding of the sequence and chronology of sections in the *Tanakh*, now known to have been the work of several authors writing from the tenth to the sixth centuries BC. It was also once virtually taken for granted that the monotheistic religion of the Hebrews, and their belief in a covenant with a single God, gave them a distinctive and unrivalled sense of past, present and future, and of a linear direction to time that differs sharply from the cyclical vision evident elsewhere. Apart from the fact that one finds both a linear and cyclical sense of time in Greek and Roman writers this view has been

discredited by the unmistakable evidence in Hebrew writings of historical cycles, the most obvious one being that of alternating divine
pleasure and displeasure with the chosen people, leading in this world
to the repeated experience of slavery and liberation, captivity and
freedom. It is also difficult to see how a distinctive Israelite/Jewish
sense of history could have emerged in isolation, given the early contacts between the Israelites and the other peoples of the region.

The most unarguably 'historical' section of the *Tanakh*, in that it
describes times, persons and events of whose existence we are reasonably
confident because there is evidence for them in external sources, and in
archaeological remains, was possibly the work of a single writer, the so-
called Deuteronomistic Historian, and stretches from Deuteronomy (the
last of the 'Five Books of Moses' or Torah) through 2 Kings, but even its
reliability has been challenged. Recent scholarship has challenged the
historicity of much of the *Tanakh* (that is, its basis in fact), without
necessarily jettisoning the idea that one can find *historiography* (a deliberate effort to represent the past) within it, albeit a historiography never
intended to capture literal truth, as opposed to a moral or religious truth
deemed more important. In the early genealogies of Genesis and in the
more chronological accounts of the Books of Samuel, Kings and
Chronicles, one finds both an effort to memorialize events accurately
as a written record and a strong sense of the divine destiny of the
Israelites as a chosen people, a linear progress through which runs
a recurrent cycle of triumph and misery as God alternately elevates or
punishes his children. This achievement is all the more striking given the
later dearth of Jewish secular historical writing during the centuries
between Flavius Josephus (*c.* AD 37 to *c.* 100) and the 1500s AD when
Jews, still scattered across Eurasia, began to rediscover the formal study
of the past.

Of all the Jews, it is Josephus who has given us the closest thing to
a history in the classical sense. Josephus, who became a Roman citizen,
had a foot in both the Jewish and the Roman-Hellenistic worlds,
making him an early example of a phenomenon we will see repeatedly,
a historian from one culture writing in the milieu and style of another.
The Romanized Jew wrote his surviving histories in Greek. Among
these, the *Antiquities of the Jews* has proved an invaluable source for
the social, legal and religious customs of the Jews; and the *Jewish War*
recounts conflicts between the Jews and their enemies, especially Rome,
from the Seleucid capture of Jerusalem in 164 BC to the defeat of the

Judaean revolt (in which he had been a participant) during Josephus' own time. Both works make a case for the antiquity of the Jews, and for their capacity to live peaceably within Roman rule, the rebellions having been in his eyes the work of successive generations of fanatics. Elsewhere, Josephus criticized his Greek predecessors by way of defending the greater antiquity of Jewish tradition, announcing a feature which recurs in later ages, arguments over the relative age of institutions, nations, religions and even families.

Early Greek Historiography

The Greeks have figured prominently in histories of history with good reason, even if this has often occurred to the neglect of achievements of greater antiquity further east. The very word 'history' itself is of Greek origin, first used in connection with the study of the past by Herodotus of Halicarnassus. And it is with the Greeks that Europe began routinely to associate histories with named authors. While there are some anonymous Greek writings, we by and large know the identities of the authors of most extant works, even the many that are fragmentary. Indeed, in some cases, *all* we have is the name and the knowledge that the person at some point wrote a history, once familiar to contemporary or subsequent writers but since lost. Finally, the Greeks were the first to experiment with different historical forms, and quickly managed to transcend the rather confining structure of annals and chronicles without abandoning chronological writing.

The origins of Greek historical thinking lay, as with Mesopotamia, in epic poetry, in particular Homer's *Iliad* and *Odyssey*, which portrayed the heroic Bronze Age deeds of the Achaeans in and following the Trojan War. They ascribed much of the action alternately to human emotion or to divine whim. With the earliest Greek prose historians, a few centuries further on, we have moved more fully into the realm of human actions, albeit punctuated by divine involvement and especially by the influence of an ineffable and unpredictable force that later ages have called 'fortune' but the Greeks referred to as *Tyche*. Greek contact with the Phoenicians, who in turn had had dealings with Mesopotamia and Egypt, probably resulted in the acquisition of alphabetic writing, and the Homeric epics, previously transmitted orally, were finally written down several centuries after they first were performed. The oldest prose historical writers are those that are known by the collective name of 'logographers', most of whom were from Ionia, which lay on the borderland with Persia in the eastern-most reaches of the Greek 'known world' or *oecumene*. Their works were often a combination of what we would now distinguish as the mythical and the historical, drawing on epic as well as the annals of particular cities about which they wrote.

Over a relatively short span of two or three centuries, the Greeks explored the past through several different genres of writing. These included, in the order in which they are now thought to have developed, genealogy or mythography; ethnography (the study of particular foreign lands and their people's customs); contemporary history/history 'proper' or a continuous narrative of sequential events with their causal connections; chronography (a system of time-reckoning, principally according to years of officials); and horography (the year-by-year history of a particular city). And we, for the first time, know some of the authors of those texts by name. These include the mythographer Hesiod (*fl. c.* 700), whose *Works and Days* had introduced the notion of a succession of declining ages, and Hellanicus of Lesbos (*c.* 490–405), the founder of Greek chronographic writing, notable for his attention to the problem of reconciling multiple chronologies (something that would much occupy European scholars two millennia later). The Ionian writer Hecataeus of Miletus (*fl. c.* 500) is important first because in his *Periodos Ges* ('Circuit of the Earth') he established the ethnographic genre built on personal travel and eyewitness reports, and second, because in his *Genealogia* he set a precedent for later writers by establishing a serious distinction between the fictional and the factual. But it is in fifth-century Athens that one first encounters both the word *history* and the two historians whose works have survived largely intact and who are also known to us by name.

Herodotus and Thucydides

While it is wrong to credit Herodotus (*c.* 484 to *c.* 420 BC), a wandering exile from his native Halicarnassus, with 'inventing' history, he was the first to use the word ἱστορια (*historia*) in connection with the past, though unintentionally. The Greek verb from which this derives means 'to investigate'; Herodotus derived the noun ἱστορια to denote something like 'inquiries' or perhaps 'discoveries', without specific reference to past or present. Herodotus was at least as interested in place as in time, his curiosity about the world owing much to Greek geographers and the genre of *periegesis*, geographic guide-books of the sixth century. It may legitimately be said, too, that Herodotus invented the historian as a distinctive personality that can be read out of his own prose. His Greek predecessors, though not anonymous, remain obscure figures, but with Herodotus we have the first real example of a historian self-identifying, sometimes giving personal details and at other times intruding with his thoughts or judgments on particular events. This trend would continue with Thucydides and the later Greek historians, and by the time we get to Dionysius of Halicarnassus in the late first century BC, it is virtually an obligation of the historian to declare up-front his preferences, methods and biases – even his position with respect to previous historians.

Like Hecataeus before him, Herodotus did not limit his scope to events themselves; he paid attention to ethnographic issues, recording the customs and traditions of the Persians and other, non-Greek peoples. If he is the 'father' of history, it is of history in its more inclusive sense, which in our own day has swung heavily back into vogue with the rise of interest in the social and cultural past. Herodotus began his *Histories* with perhaps the most succinct and naively unpretentious statement of purpose imaginable; he wished to inquire as to why, in the decades just prior to his birth, the Greeks and the 'Barbarians' (a Greek term for non-Greek-speaking peoples which had yet to acquire its modern derogatory association) fought each other; and, following the epics from which he drew inspiration, he wanted both to celebrate and to ensure the survival of their achievements. The barbarians in question were the Persians under Darius I and his successor Xerxes, and as it happens it is to Herodotus' story that we owe much of our knowledge of the rise of the Achaemenid dynasty, and of its failed attempts to exert hegemony over the Greeks. The Hellas of Herodotus' own time – dominated by an Athens increasingly resented by its own empire and feared by its rival Sparta – had been built on the outcome of the Persian conflict. But – importantly – to explain the early fifth-century struggles, Herodotus realized that he had to look back even further in time, and his account proper begins with the ascent of Persia in the mid-sixth century.

Although too young to have witnessed any of these earlier happenings, Herodotus travelled widely, spoke to many witnesses or those who had information from witnesses, and set down the truth as he believed it. This has exposed him over the centuries to accusations of credulity or even outright falsehood: the 'father of history' was often called the 'father of lies', his assertions not to be trusted. In perhaps the earliest European example of historiographical conflict, Ctesias, a Persophile with access to Achaemenid records, attacked Herodotus in a grumpy and intemperate tone worthy of some modern book reviewers. Later critics included the first-century AD biographer Plutarch, who would go to the trouble of cataloguing Herodotus' alleged crimes in a treatise 'On the Malice of Herodotus'. A more sympathetic modern reader, the great Italian historiographer Arnaldo Momigliano (1908–87) once noted that Herodotus' critics had stuck him between the rock of accusations that he plagiarized from his predecessors and the hard place of being charged with outright invention. He came out either thief or liar.

Herodotus' immediate successor, Thucydides (d. *c.* 401 BC), did not attack him by name but almost certainly had him in mind among the retailers of a history 'attractive at truth's expense' (*Pelop. War* 1.1.21). Thucydides may be the most widely revered past historian in the entire European tradition, and though he too was not without his critics, he was father to a very different sort of European history-writing than his predecessor had authored. Where Herodotus was a perennial traveller and cosmopolitan, Thucydides was an Athenian through and through, a politician and unsuccessful general who found himself out of favour at a critical juncture in the Peloponnesian War. That conflict between alliances led respectively by Athens and Sparta endured for three decades and ultimately proved the ruin of Athens. Although his history breaks off at 411 without the war resolved, it is a masterful account of the precipitous and unexpected defeat of the once-mighty *polis* that only decades before had led the humiliation of Persia.

Like Herodotus, Thucydides relied on the spoken much more than the written word, though in a very different way. Herodotus had built much of his *Histories* on the foundation of oral tradition rather than written authority. Thucydides similarly did not practise very often that most basic form of research to all modern historians, study of older documents and their criticism and comparison, something too often forgotten by those wishing to enthrone him as the visionary forefather of modern method. In fact, he relied on written sources only where he could not find a living witness. However, there the similarities end, and we observe Thucydides eschewing entirely several practices that were characteristic of Herodotus. For one thing, Thucydides was reluctant to look very far back for the causes of events. For another, he implied that only those who were 'insiders' to events such as himself could accurately recount those events: the long-practised assertion that the historian should be a 'man of affairs' (thereby excluding women and persons of low birth) was essentially born with his work. Privileged knowledge thus displaced an inferior form of hearsay: though Thucydides says rather little about his precise methods and sources, there would be no wandering interviews of possible eyewitnesses, and little reliance on oral evidence beyond the near-contemporary.

There is also scant reference in Thucydides to the marvellous and unusual, a feature that enlivens Herodotus and which has remained a commonplace of ethnographically focused history throughout the centuries as one culture has discovered others. And where Herodotus painstakingly intervened in his own narrative to ensure that readers understood the problem of conflicting versions and incomplete sources, Thucydides tended to present a picture of seamless confidence that obscures the ambiguities of evidence. There is apparent certitude in his assertion that the cause of the Peloponnesian conflict lay not in the public reasons or triggers (disputes over colonies of Athens and Sparta) but in the wider phenomenon of Athens' rise to power and Sparta's growing fear of that power. Finally, Thucydides is also perhaps the first historian in the West to state very clearly the target audience for his work. If Herodotus sought to explain to his contemporaries the events of the previous decades, Thucydides openly proclaimed that he wrote his work not for 'the applause of the moment, but as a possession for all time' (*Pelop. War* 1.1.23), asserting, too, that the human condition was such as to make the future sufficiently like the present, and thus make his history a benefit and not merely an amusement for subsequent ages.

Thucydides' reputation for strict accuracy and truthfulness has not passed unchallenged. As early as the first century BC, the Greek historian of Rome, Dionysius of Halicarnassus, who adhered to the general opinion that Thucydides 'has been most careful of the truth, the high-priestess of which we desire history to be', was nonetheless critical of the Athenian and rather laudatory of Herodotus, whose subject of the Persian Wars seemed more noble and less distasteful than Thucydides' tale of calamity, arrogance and folly. Moreover, many have preferred the more broad-based, inclusive accounts in Herodotus to the narrowly political account in Thucydides. The degree to which he has been praised as a 'scientific historian' who focused on 'causes' has been challenged, with Greek tragedy seen by some scholars as a powerful influence on his writing. In that vein, no feature of Thucydides' history has caused his defenders so much trouble as his practice of including supposedly genuine speeches at critical points in his narrative, a feature of historical writing that would have a long life over the next two millennia. In fact, Thucydides freely admits that he did not personally hear all of the speeches that he relates, and that his memory of those that he did hear is imperfect – he did not record them word for word; they are intended to represent the essence of what may have been said, not its literal words. The practice of including such speeches, possibly influenced by contemporary Greek tragedy, fulfilled an important role within a history, since words were deemed as significant and influential as deeds – in a sense, a famous and effective speech *was* a deed. The invented speech also provided an important narrative linkage between events, a device which the talented historian could use to enrich his account and transcend the boundaries of calendrical years. 'Speeches, so to speak, sum up events and hold the history together', the second-century historian Polybius would eventually comment; and the only ancient historian known to have avoided speeches entirely is Pompeius Trogus (*fl.* first century BC), so this seems a weak basis on which to criticize Thucydides.

Greek Historiography from the Fourth to the Second Centuries

With the declining autonomy and power of the independent Greek city-state, and the failure of Athenian democracy, the fourth and third centuries saw increasing numbers of prominent and colourful tyrants, mercenaries, warlords and monarchs, culminating in Alexander the Great. Historical writers reoriented their attention towards individuals and their achievements, and made more direct authorial commentary on their characters. The beginnings of another long tradition, the role of the historian as not only the reporter but also the 'judge' of past misdeeds, can be found in what remains of the highly oratorical work of Ephorus (*c.* 400 to *c.* 330 BC) and Theopompus (*c.* 380 to *c.* 315), both of whom were trained rhetoricians. The major fourth-century historian whose works survive largely intact, Xenophon (*c.* 431 to *c.* 352), described a particular event, the failed expedition in 401 of ten thousand Greek mercenaries (himself included) in service of a Persian princeling seeking to overthrow his elder brother King Artaxerxes II, including his own leadership of the retreat back to Greece. A one-time student of the Athenian philosopher Socrates, Xenophon also authored the *Cyropaedia*, an idealized biography of the Persian ruler Cyrus the Great, imbuing a historical ruler with traits derived from philosophy rather than from historical evidence. With him, the long connection between didactic exemplarity and rhetorical life-writing may be said to have originated.

Of the Greek historians after Thucydides, perhaps none has won as high praise as Polybius (*c.* 200–118 BC), though this admiration did not materialize until the Renaissance, which admired his sober tone, his keen attention to identifying the causes of events and his emphasis on the practical lessons of the past. Though he influenced the Roman historian Livy, a great Latin stylist, Polybius' own fame never rested on the literary quality of his writing, which is rather dull compared with his fifth-century precursors. He wrote, as he put it – coining a phrase later ages would borrow – a 'pragmatic history'. It is he who first framed the convention (more implicit than explicit in Thucydides) that the ideal historian would be a man of experience, a *topos* repeated periodically from his time to the nineteenth century. And, more than any other extant Greek historian, he also interrupted his account in places to provide the reader with explicit statements on methodology, discussing the need for historians to weigh different accounts, and criticizing his predecessors by name. He paid greater attention than Thucydides to what we would now call the 'primary' sources of history, especially archives and inscriptions.

Like the Jew Josephus two centuries later, Polybius was at first a wartime captive and eventually a guest of the ascendant Romans; he, too, adapted enthusiastically to a Roman world. Sheer good luck brought him into contact with the Aemilii, architects of the Romans' triumph over their long-time foe, Carthage. Polybius admired what he saw, and it led him to think carefully about how world powers rise and fall. He articulated in the sixth book of his *Histories* a theory of predictable constitutional cycles (generally referred to as the *anakuklosis politeion*) among three pure and three corresponding perverted forms of government previously delineated by the Athenian philosopher Aristotle, and he postulated the stability of 'mixed' regimes consisting of all three pure forms. This was to prove a powerful tool of historical analysis in later centuries: according to Polybius, Rome owed

its greatness to its balancing of monarchical, aristocratic and democratic elements, though even he evinced doubt that this balance could
be maintained in perpetuity, worried by the democratic reforms that
followed the final destruction of Carthage, the great external enemy, in
146 BC. Apart from Tacitus two centuries later, it is difficult to think of
an ancient historian who has had as profound an influence on the
course of later *political* thought – Polybius' ideas would be taken up
by the Florentine politician and historian Machiavelli in the sixteenth
century, by English republicans in the seventeenth and by Montesquieu
and the framers of the American constitution in the eighteenth century.

Polybius' *Histories* recounted a cumulative process throughout the
known world, leading to a particular destiny, the hegemony of the
Roman republic. Polybius' account was in part comparative, and –
most importantly – it was also interconnected. His term, *symploke*,
for the connections between different states, allowed him to resolve the
various threads of individual histories – not an easy task. Greek historians had traditionally dated events by years of civic officials; attention
to precise chronology was of little interest to the vast majority – even
Thucydides was normally content to describe an event as occurring
within a particular season. The problem of multiple calendars and
differing chronologies has from that day to this been among the things
that the international historian has had to sort out before ever putting
pen to paper. Polybius borrowed from earlier writers in organizing his
material around Olympiads (the series of four-year cycles, commencing
in 776, between Olympic games), in every book beginning with Italy
and then branching out to other regions such as Sicily, Greece, Africa
and even Asia and Egypt.

It is not simply the interconnectedness of his *Histories* that would give
Polybius weight; his stress on the process of history towards the single
goal or telos of Roman supremacy – driven there by a *Tyche* who
assumes a role much less like random fortune than like a kind of
deliberate fate – provided a model for much later Roman history.
Ultimately it would feature prominently in the combination of Greek,
Roman and Judaic views of the past that would characterize two millennia of Christian historical writing and, in its more secular variation, the
liberal progressivist strand within modern historiography that the late
Herbert Butterfield (1900–79) famously dubbed 'the Whig interpretation of history'. This is a formidable set of influences for a relatively
minor Greek political figure who spent much of his life in exile.

Roman Historical Writing from Republic to Empire

By Polybius' time, the centre of power around the Mediterranean had shifted westward to Rome, whose influence was rapidly expanding beyond Italy into the rest of Europe, Northern Africa, and the Near East. By the early first century, it was not very difficult to predict where all this was heading and to spin accounts of history in the same direction, as Polybius had already done.

The survival rate among known texts of Roman historians has been as bad as or worse than that of the Greeks. Scant fragments remain of Aulus Cremutius Cordus, famous for being forced to commit suicide in AD 25 during the reign of the Emperor Tiberius, perhaps for having treated Julius Caesar's assassins too even-handedly. Of others, such as Sallust, we have their relatively minor works but only fragments of their major ones; or, as with Livy and Tacitus, what we have is a body of work comprising much of what was written but missing significant sections.

Historiography started slowly in Rome: whereas in Greece it had followed epic, the greatest Latin epic, the *Aeneid*, was a late arrival, composed by Vergil in the first century BC, and thus at virtually the same time that Livy, the great historian of the republic, was writing his prose history. There were early verse efforts at a narrative of the city's early history, little of which remains. Apart from these, two major families or groups of history-writing survive from early Rome, both of which had Greek influences. The first, perhaps derived from Greek horography, consisted of records maintained by a civic and religious official, the *pontifex maximus*, and annually transferred to bronze inscriptions in the Forum. These *Annales maximi* were little more than records of the sequence of annually appointed major officials – consuls, praetors, etc. Apart from the pontifical records, funeral orations, public inscriptions, family records and accounts by other magistrates of their periods in office (*commentarii*) would also provide material for historians. The second major family includes Roman writers who may have written continuous prose and, at least at first, composed their works in Greek. This included Quintus Fabius Pictor (*fl.* 225 BC), little of whose history has, once again survived; Fabius is believed to have used a variety of sources ranging from earlier Greek writers to the *Annales maximi*, oral tradition, magistrate lists and chronicles kept by his own and other families.

The earliest-known prose history written in Latin, which has not survived, was the *Origines*, by the fiercely xenophobic politician and protector of Roman virtue, Cato the Censor (234–149 BC), whose very choice of Latin was a protest against the Greek influences that he saw as dangerously corrupting. Even he, however, followed the Greek model of continuous prose, and borrowed other aspects of Greek historiography such as the inclusion of what might be called 'remarkable facts'. Non-annalistic prose history remained for some time largely in the hands of Romanized Greeks. The first-century works of Diodorus Siculus (*c.* 90–30 BC) and Dionysius of Halicarnassus (*c.* 60 to after 7 BC) have survived rather more completely than most. Diodorus was a Sicilian Greek who, like Herodotus four centuries earlier, had travelled widely prior to writing his *Bibliotheca historica*, a universal history in the manner of Polybius, of which roughly a third survives. The title 'Historical Library' was a reference to the number of earlier sources from which Diodorus drew his materials, which has often been a reason for dismissing this author as an unoriginal hack, though he would have understood himself instead as the culmination of a long stream of predecessors. 'Tradition', a critical aspect of the historical enterprise, was beginning to weigh more heavily upon historians' choice of subjects and their arrangement of materials. Dionysius of Halicarnassus, in contrast, focused more exclusively on Rome, and the main point of his *Roman Antiquities* was to defend Roman influence over the Greek world. In it we see the triumph of the rhetorical and hortatory strain of history-writing first seen in the fourth century. It is Dionysius who coined the oft-repeated definition of history as 'philosophy teaching by example', and he continued the tradition of declaring, up-front, his own methods and preferences. Thus Dionysius would begin his *Roman Antiquities* with the following remarks:

Although it is much against my will to indulge in the explanatory statements usually given in the prefaces to histories, yet I am obliged to prefix to this work some remarks concerning myself. In doing this it is neither my intention to dwell too long on my own praise, which I know would be distasteful to the reader, nor have I the purpose of censuring other historians ... but I shall only show the reasons that induced me to undertake this work and give an accounting of the sources from which I gained the knowledge of the things I am going to relate. (*Roman Antiquities* 1.1, trans. E. Cary)

It should be clear by now that *historia* in its Latin or Graeco-Latin form had moved some distance from the senses in either Herodotus or Thucydides. Where Herodotus had intended the word to mean 'inquiry', and had not linked it specifically to the past, and Thucydides had defined it more narrowly as the recounting of recent or contemporary events, history had by the late second century BC become firmly associated with a *narrative of the past*, remote or recent, and increasingly with a focus on the political and military, despite the inclination of several authors to begin their works with geographic sections. Similarly, history was now quite definitively a branch of literature and specifically of rhetoric. Persuasion had taken primacy over research, with the praise of the virtuous and successful, and condemnation of the corrupt, wicked or weak, a key motivation for any historian. If 'renown' was a feature of Greek historical writing and epic, its Latin counterpart *fama* now became inextricably linked to history, not only because historians saw it as their duty to praise and blame, but because the very fact that they did so was believed to provide an inducement to current historical actors to do good.

The Romans were even less interested than the Greeks in acquiring knowledge of the past for its own sake and they thus produced very little of what a later age would call 'antiquarian' erudition since there was little hortatory value to be derived from it. A rare exception is the fragmentarily surviving *Antiquitates* by the prolific Marcus Terentius Varro (116–27 BC). And, in starker contrast to the Greeks, Roman authors spent very little time thinking about *how* to write about the past or in defining history's sub-genres. It is thus no accident whatever that the first really clear theorizing about history by a Roman was the product of a powerful politician and orator, Marcus Tullius Cicero (106–43 BC), whose discussion of history would be found principally in a dialogue entitled *De Oratore* ('On the Orator'). For Cicero (*De Orat.* 2.36), history was *testis temporum, lux veritatis, nuncia vetustatis* – the witness of times, the light of truth and herald of antiquity. He articulated certain principles that would become axiomatic in later times, such as the obligation of the historian to tell nothing but the truth, without partiality (*De Orat.* 2.62), and he emphasized its connection with rhetoric by promoting an ornate style. Cicero's definition was scarcely profound, but it had the benefit of conciseness, and the weight of his great reputation, especially fifteen centuries later, during the European Renaissance, when his posthumous star reached its apogee. The rhetorical emphasis would be maintained two centuries after Cicero's death in the earliest-known work devoted entirely to the proper composition of history (and to a merciless satire of those among his contemporaries who failed to meet the standard of Thucydides), Lucian of Samosata's (*c.* AD 129 to after 180) *How to Write History*. It is perhaps Lucian who also first articulated the notion, taken up in later centuries, that 'what historians have to relate is fact and will speak for itself for it has already happened'.

The major Roman innovation in historiography was a shaping of history into the cumulative story of world events. This was not, of course, strictly their invention – Polybius deserves much of the credit or blame for making Roman history move towards a goal. But the Romans had a stronger sense of the divine destiny of their city and its expanding empire, and this provided both a horizon and an occasion for their history-writing in the way that curiosity about the known world as a whole had done for the Greeks. The Romans, however, also injected a teleological and progressive element that was absent in Greek historians before Polybius. Where cycles of rise and fall and the random hand of *Tyche* (fortune) appear in many of the Greek historians, history becomes more purposeful and almost providential among the Romans. When linked eventually with the eschatological elements of Jewish thought (Josephus providing an important bridge between these two worlds), this would eventually provide a firm foundation for Christian historiography.

The first century BC produced two great Latin historians (or three if we include the general and dictator Julius Caesar) who composed rather different works. Easily the most influential was Titus Livius or Livy (59 BC to AD 17), who stands at the end of that line of republican annalists which began with Fabius Pictor. Most of Livy's long and ambitious work has been lost, but we have enough to know its shape and scope. (Of 142 books, 35 now survive and there are extant summaries of most of the lost ones.) Organized into a set of 'decades' and 'pentads' (units of ten or five books), and within these as annals, Livy's first book – a self-contained text that he published in order to test the market for a history by a provincial private citizen who held no major office or military command – begins with the Trojan arrival in Italy before moving to the establishment of Rome by Romulus (traditionally placed at 753 BC) and the period of the seven kings. Entitled *Ab Urbe Condita* ('From the Foundation of the City'), Livy's history was, for its

time, the definitive account of the Roman republic. Written in a Latin
that later ages regarded either as impeccably pure or overly florid, the
history combined the annalistic approach, with its recording of
the year's officers, and a continuous prose narrative. In a way, it turned
the genre of local history almost by accident into a variant of universal
history, since Rome, at its peak of international influence and on the
verge of becoming an empire in governance as well as influence, now
controlled most of the Mediterranean world.

The other, and perhaps more interesting, major first-century historian was the politician and soldier known to us as Sallust (Gaius
Sallustius Crispus, 86–34 BC). Following an undistinguished spell as
governor of the province of Africa Nova, Sallust returned to and
penned two histories of particular events, the conspiracy of the patri-
cian Catiline in the year 63 and an earlier war against the African king
Jugurtha. (A longer work, the *Histories*, survives only in fragments.)
A pessimistic critic of contemporary politics and values in the late
Roman republic, Sallust became widely respected in subsequent centuries, his works providing a template for writing the history of
a particular event. Sallust was (and declared himself to be) a disciple
of Thucydides. He articulated the enduring thesis that republican
decline could be traced directly to the destruction of Carthage, which
had left the Romans masters of their universe, but prey to the twin
corruptors avarice and ambition, their growing empire the playground
for internecine strife. Sallust also took Polybius' semi-rational *Tyche*
and turned it into the feminine, capricious *Fortuna*, thereby handing on
this all-purpose explanatory mechanism to late antiquity and beyond.

Imperial Rome, commencing with the rule of Augustus Caesar following the Battle of Actium in 31 BC, also had its historians, among
whom the most highly regarded was, and remains, Publius (or Gaius)
Cornelius Tacitus (*c.* AD 56 to *c.* 117). Where Livy had written in
a flowing rhetorical style, Tacitus seems closer to Sallust, whom he
admired, or, more remotely, Polybius. Where Livy's work had been
written with oral recitation in mind, Tacitus' was directed at the private
reader. Long rhetorical flourishes were replaced in his writing by
a terse, epigrammatic narrative, into which Tacitus intruded political
sententiae that readers in a later age would find irresistible. His very
name means 'silent', but Tacitus was in life a very skilful orator and
eventually author himself of a treatise on rhetoric. His fame, however,
has been built on a combination of apparently shrewd character

judgments and an ability to say much in few words: 'Tacitean' has even become an adjective to describe an entire style of writing.

Fortune has been kind to Tacitus, permitting the survival of most of his *Annals* and *Histories* through the Middle Ages (each in a single manuscript) during which time they were virtually unused, such was antipathy to a writer regarded as both pagan and hostile to Christianity. Like Sallust, Xenophon and Thucydides, Tacitus was a man of political and military experience, a senator who had advanced to very high office. In contrast to a much more prominent politician–historian, Caesar, he was able to effect an air of restrained neutrality, famously declaring that he wrote his works *sine ira et studio* (without anger, or, what we would now call an 'axe to grind'). And yet of Tacitus' political views there can be little doubt. For instance, his *Germania*, one of the most influential of all ancient texts, praised the rough, uncultured but unspoiled virtue of the German tribes, and later became a literary source and justification for German Protestants' revolt against Roman Catholicism in the sixteenth century, and eventually for German nationalism in the nineteenth and twentieth centuries.

The western Roman Empire lingered on three full centuries after the death of Tacitus before a combination of 'barbarism and religion' (to quote Edward Gibbon, the eighteenth-century historian of Roman decline) laid it low. So far as the evolution of Western historical writing is concerned, the most important developments of the late antique period were the advent of Christianity and, from the reign of Constantine in the early fourth century, its establishment as the official religion of the empire; the increasing instability, as Tacitus had predicted, of an empire whose leaders ruled only so long as they had the support of the army; and the splitting of the increasingly unwieldy empire in the late third century into a western half (based at Rome) and an eastern (based at Byzantium, later renamed Constantinople), whence sprang the Greek-speaking Byzantine Empire. Just as significant as any of these internal developments, however, was an external threat: the looming presence of a number of barbarian peoples in both east and west. These were the migratory tribes of Celts, Goths and Huns whose collective movements around Europe and Central Asia, known as the *Völkerwanderung*, would over the next several centuries encircle and infiltrate the empire. The Visigoths, one of these tribes, sacked Rome in AD 410 (precisely eight centuries after it had last been overrun, by the Gauls), and the last western Roman emperor was deposed by another Gothic general in 476. The Visigoths, Ostrogoths and other peoples such as the Franks, Saxons, Jutes and Lombards would eventually set up a series of independent monarchies in what remained of the former Roman dominions in Europe.

It is hard to dispute the suggestion that most of the late antique pagan historians, such as Cassius Dio (*c.* AD 155 to after 229), or Lucius Florus (*fl.* early second century AD), an epitomizer of Livy (including, usefully, many of Livy's lost sections), are less interesting than their illustrious predecessors. But it is also true that several centuries of historiographers have seen them as small fish struggling in a rising Christian tide. In many cases we know very little about these authors and have only traces of their original works. The most notable exception to this rule is a soldier from Antioch named Ammianus Marcellinus (*c.* AD 325 to after 391). The first thirteen books of Ammianus' thirty-one-book history, the *Res Gestae Libri XXXI* ('Thirty-one Books of Deeds'), have not survived, though we know from his own comments that he began it where Tacitus' *Histories* had left off in the last decade of the first century. Ammianus is widely held to be the last of the great ancient historians of Rome, and one of the last European historians for some centuries to compose his history in the grand rhetorical style, complete with speeches and a dearth of dates beyond those indicated by his annalistic framework. Though a native Greek-speaker, Ammianus wrote in Latin, the last in a series of citizens of the empire like Polybius and Josephus who had fallen in love with Rome. It is Ammianus who first gave us, or at least popularized, the familiar designation of Rome herself as *urbs aeterna* (the eternal city). Later historians have valued his eyewitness account of the decline of the once-mighty Rome and his attention to economic and social as well as political causes of these drawn-out death throes. Ammianus' history is full of interesting information on the various parts of the empire and its peoples, and he is rather less unsympathetic to most of them than Tacitus, for example, had been to the Jews. He even includes scientific topics such as earthquakes and eclipses. Ammianus' attention to such matters is all the more remarkable and perhaps even unintended since he himself proclaimed that history should concentrate on the important and prominent events and ignore the trivial or commonplace, which should warn us that the announced intentions of historians, and the theories or protocols to which they purportedly subscribe, are as often as not violated in practice. Thus the last great western ancient historian managed, after a fashion, to combine aspects of the approaches of both his fifth-century BC precursors, Herodotus and Thucydides.

Chinese Historiography from Earliest Times to the Han Dynasty

History in antiquity was never the sole possession, or even the creation, of the peoples of Europe and the Near East. No civilization in the world has consistently and continuously placed as high a priority on the recording and understanding of its past as the Chinese. Convention and their invention of the word 'history' has placed the Greeks earlier in the present narrative, but we could just as easily have begun much farther east. As in Mesopotamia, the earliest forms of what became historical writing started as record-keeping, but with a much clearer tie to the past. The 'oracle bones' (inscribed fragments of bone or shell first unearthed in the late nineteenth century) which are the earliest extant source for the ancient Shang dynasty (*c.* 1600 to *c.* 1046 BC), appear to have been created in direct response to the royal family's veneration of ancestors, and contain direct petitions to or communications with them; their closest analogue may be the omen-texts of the contemporary Assyrians.

Exact analogies between Chinese and classical European historiography should be drawn within an awareness of their fundamental differences. Though it changed its meaning after Herodotus' initial use, there is relatively little ambiguity about what the Greek word 'ιστορια denotes. In Chinese, the word *shi* is not unambiguously the word for defining either history or its author. One should also not underestimate the profound differences posed by the complexities of writing in a logographic system such as Chinese. Apart from their enormous reverence for tradition, one reason that scholars, from a very early stage, paid tireless attention to the verification of sources (and often deliberately eliminated inferior versions) is that the opportunities for a scribe to misunderstand what he was copying were considerably greater given the ambiguity of particular logograms.

Moreover, certain fundamental mental assumptions were quite different. Most European thought until relatively recent times has seen time as corrosive, and change as an inevitable but overwhelmingly bad thing. The earliest Chinese philosophers, for all their intense reverence of tradition, saw time, rather like the Polybian

Tyche, as an agent of change rather than a vessel in which change occurred, and they valued change as progressive and maturing rather than corrosive or regressive. The upheavals attending the transitions from one dynasty to the next were not so much the mark of failure as of the loss of the prime justification for rule, the 'Mandate of Heaven' (*tianming*). Chronology, to which Chinese historians paid careful attention, was also conceived of very differently, based on frequently changed era names (the practice used in many Asian countries until the twentieth century) rather than the single chronology *ab orbe condita* (from the creation of the world), *ab urbe condita* (from the founding of the city) or, especially since the seventeenth century, BC and AD – this accounts for the rather earlier development in China than in Europe of synchronous chronological tables. The Chinese also conceived of the various genres of history in ways we would find surprising: where 'annals' in the European tradition have usually been regarded as the most rudimentary form of historical record, traditional Chinese historiography regarded the annal as the highest form, the distillation of knowledge from other sources. One modern authority on ancient Chinese historical writing, Grant Hardy, has argued that the modern preference since the Renaissance (very much emulating Thucydides and Tacitus) for the single-voiced omniscient narrator and an internally self-consistent story fits ill with the multiple voices and often competing accounts of a single event included by the greatest of ancient Chinese historians, Sima Qian, in his *Shiji*.

Western historiography places a high value upon the independence of the historian from outside interference, though that arm's-length relationship has been ideal rather than fact in most circumstances. Official history, courtly history and other variants have traditionally not fared well in the estimation of modern Euro-American historiographers, for whom autonomy and freedom from influence is highly valued. In China, history was almost from the beginning connected with governance and eventually with the ruling dynasty of the day – yet Chinese historians saw no fundamental contradiction between this and their duty to record the truth, often at great personal risk. Indeed, it has been plausibly argued that the lack of a counterpart to the absolute truth of revealed religion in Christian Europe permitted the Chinese to invest the past itself with the equivalent quality of certainty. Finally, the historians of imperial China saw historical writing as a process of compilation from earlier sources, including verbatim inclusion of another historian's work. Confucius, the dominant philosopher through much of China's history, declared himself not a maker but a transmitter of wisdom, and the earliest historians similarly envisaged their work as primarily vehicles for the handing down of past knowledge. In practice they did much more, not uncommonly adding the value of moral judgments to bring out the normative aspects of the past and its clues to the meaning of the universe. Truth to an ancient Chinese historian was not the conformity of the history to *actual* reality, but its fidelity to its *sources*: the word *xin* does not mean truth in the modern sense but something more like 'trustworthiness' or reliability.

Chinese historians consolidated much earlier than their European counterparts a clear and consistent set of rules and practices for the representation of the past. They also acquired a progressively more 'official' status for the historian that has no counterpart in any other ancient culture. The word *shi* originally referred to a ritual official and subsequently came to denote the ruler's secretary or an official responsible for keeping records. Virtually never used by the Chinese, then or since, as a synonym for 'the past' (that is, the actual events that occurred in reality), history was, rather, the accumulated and arrayed *records* of that past (much later denoted as *li shi xue*). As such, it had become a major category of knowledge (along with philosophy, literature and the 'classics') as early as the fourth century BC. This was a status it never held elsewhere in antiquity and would not acquire in Europe before the late seventeenth century AD. History in China was also, far more than in Greece, the exemplar *par excellence* of an imperializing or 'hegemonic' practice (a concept we will have further reference to in later chapters), one which achieved influence far outside its nominal political domain and eventually governed the historiographical development of Mongolia, Japan, Korea and much of Southeast Asia.

Significant Chinese *thinking* about the past can be traced back to ancient canonical texts such as the *Yijing* (or *I Ching*, 'Book of Changes'), in the late second millennium BC. Taken as the authority of the past, history held equivalent status with philosophy and poetry. It was represented among China's original 'Five Classics' in two works, the *Shujing* ('Classic of History' or 'Classic of Documents'), one of the earliest collections of official documents, and in the *Chunqiu* ('Spring and Autumn Annals') once attributed to Confucius. The *Shujing* is a collection of decrees, declarations, public announcements and other texts by the kings of the Shang (mid- to late second millennium BC) and subsequent Zhou (1046–256 BC) dynasties. Deliberate writing *about* the past came later, and authorship in Chinese historiography prior to the Han dynasty is hard to establish, since with the exception of great sages such as Confucius, establishing the persona and identity of an author was a priority for neither writers nor readers. In some cases, the 'author' associated with a Chinese text is the politician or courtier who authorized its writing.

For all these differences in practice and context, the reasons for turning to the past, in China, were not remarkably different from those that drove such pursuits in ancient Europe, especially the urge to find in the past a source of stability in troubled times, and to identify in it models of correct behaviour. Earliest Chinese thought articulated the notion that there were discernible patterns in the flow of human affairs from which one could learn to govern oneself and navigate a world of continuous change. As this suggests, Chinese thought about the past was very quickly linked to philosophy and the search for the *Dao* (the 'path' or moral order). The first significant independent work of history, the *Chunqiu* (a chronicle of the state of Lu) recounts events from 722 to about 480 BC. It is generally associated with the influential philosopher Confucius or Master Kong (551–479), though what survives is probably a commentary on or revision by Confucius of an earlier work, now lost.

Later commentators drew on the *Chunqiu* and other early chronicles to present historical anecdotes and speeches in support of a Confucian outlook which tended to a cyclical view of time that dominated Chinese historical thought until the nineteenth century. The *Zuozhuan* (late fourth century BC) has been identified by one scholar as the first Chinese historical text to bring together two previously distinct Chinese preoccupations in a single narrative – namely the traditional concern for remembrance and the wish to find meaning in historical events. The notion of cycles is raised here to a level beyond that which a Greek like Polybius could embrace: specific events, not just general patterns, were so likely to recur that the properly prepared reader could divine their signs in earlier events through complete knowledge and attendance to ritual propriety. Given this conception of the orderly movement of events, Chinese historians acquired very early the understanding that history could provide a pool of examples with which to guide moral and especially political life. According to one account, Confucius believed that his own reputation would rest on his success as a historian. His reported declaration that his principles were better demonstrated by the examples of 'actual affairs' than in 'theoretical words' may be the first articulation of that superior exemplarity of history keenly advocated by European historians from Dionysius of Halicarnassus through the eighteenth century (and just as hotly denied by a number of philosophers and poets from Aristotle onward).

Other philosophical schools departed from the dominant Confucianism, and the range of opinions on the process of historical change is considerably more varied than anything in the West during antiquity or the Middle Ages. The Daoists, for instance, pursuing harmony with nature and retreat from a world of cyclical but unpredictable change, did not accept that history had any discernible pattern or didactic value. The Mohists (followers of Mozi) and the Legalists saw discernible patterns of progress, though the latter, adherents of a totalitarian philosophy adopted by the brutal Qin dynasty (221–206 BC), asserted that such progress, enforced by state control over naturally evil individuals, made the past largely irrelevant. After the Qin unification of various 'Warring States' into a single empire, their first emperor ordered an infamous book-burning and mass execution of scholars, virtually eliminating records of the subordinated kingdoms.

The succeeding Han dynasty took power for most of the next four centuries, in the course of which Confucianism became the dominant philosophical and educational system. The most important early figure in Chinese historical thought and writing emerged in this world of a consolidated *Zhongguo* (literally, the 'Middle Kingdom', the Chinese name for their own country). Sima Qian (145–86 BC) is the first Chinese historian about whom we know a considerable amount, both because he himself made no pretence at anonymity and included a detailed genealogy of his own family back to legendary times, and because a first-century AD historian, Ban Gu, wrote a biography of his famous predecessor. Sima Qian did not originally intend to take up scholarship but felt an obligation to continue a work already begun by his father, Sima Tan, who had himself occupied the apparently hereditary office of *taishi* (variously translated as grand astrologer, grand scribe, or sometimes grand historian) held by his family since the Zhou dynasty. By about 90 BC, having voluntarily suffered the humiliation of castration for causing offence to the emperor (rather than committing suicide, which would have prevented him completing his history), Sima Qian had composed the *Shiji* ('Records of the Grand Historian').

The *Shiji* was divided into five major sections, each of which became a foundational model for future genres of Chinese historical writing. The first section of twelve chapters, 'Basic Annals' (*benji*), provides an account of the major dynasties in series, from rise to fall; the second is a set of ten chapters of chronological tables (*biao*); the third holds eight chapters of 'treatises' (*shu*) on branches of knowledge from astronomy and the calendar through agriculture, literature and music; the fourth includes thirty chapters on the great 'hereditary houses' (*shijia*) along with biographies of famed sages like Confucius; and finally, the fifth section contains seventy biographical 'arrayed traditions' or 'transmissions' (*liezhuan*) on statesmen, scholars and other categories, often paired (as the Greek biographer Plutarch would later do) to illustrate a character type. At the end of most of his chapters, rather like the author of the fourth-century *Zuozhuan*, Sima offers up a comment upon the history just recounted. This, too, is not unlike classical European practice with the exception that the Chinese, as noted above, signal their authorial interventions much more clearly: Sima Qian's little digressions are prefaced 'The Grand Historian says ... ', but as with most Chinese historians and the Greeks he makes free use of invented speeches, some of them admittedly copied from earlier works. The chronological tables, where some of Sima's most original writing occurs, were a particularly brilliant innovation, presenting a great deal of disparate data in grid format, and with synchronous dating – no mean feat given the earlier Qin destruction of the chronicles of rival kingdoms – and signifying a recognition that there could, indeed, be a universal set of dates shared between different realms and transcending particular dynasties.

This unusual and original organization had advantages and disadvantages. On the one hand, Sima Qian did not need to interrupt the narrative of an event in one section to explain who a particular person was, since they were probably discussed elsewhere in one of the other principal sections – there are no lengthy Herodotean digressions to provide needed background or to explicate an event's longer-term significance. He could also escape strict chronology in the fifth, biographical section, allowing him to give precedence to the character types and patterns which he believed were played out in individual lives at various times. On the other hand, there being no index, the reader would be faced with looking for materials on a particular topic in several different places. And in some places the accounts may mutually contradict one another, though it has been argued that this was either a deliberate pluralism of interpretation on Sima's part, or that, like Herodotus, he felt compelled to repeat even conflicting sources verbatim. Here the differences with classical Greek historiography become even more apparent: the goal of the *Shiji* was not to impart a particular account of the past as unchallengeable or definitive – this is no Thucydidean 'last word' – but to remain faithful to the sources while promoting the wisdom that will allow the intelligent reader to judge well. Sima is rather like the modern professor who tells his students that he is not interested in their ultimate recollection of the facts that have been imparted, but in their development of critical thinking skills.

Sima Qian did far more in the *Shiji*, a work four times the length of Thucydides' *History of the Peloponnesian War*, than write a comprehensive account of Chinese history: he provided a history of what for the Chinese was the known world. The *Shiji* was also a literary collection, and an encyclopedia of chronology and biography, replete with collected wisdom for the use of his own and future rulers. According to a letter included in a later history, Sima intended as clearly as Thucydides that later generations should profit from his work. He evinced a clear sense of the historian's purpose: to record major and minor occurrences accurately in order to counsel the present and to bestow fame on the good and shame on the wicked. The *Shiji* offered a model for the compilation of facts about the past with its clearly worked-out format, a combination of year-by-year annals and individual biographical treatments; it would influence the next two millennia of Chinese historical writing, though ultimately it did not provide an exact template for it – later authors would not emulate precisely its complex combination of formats and its comprehensive coverage. Nonetheless, it would be difficult to over-state the degree of Sima Qian's impact, which in the world of history-writing would come to exceed even that of Confucius and the post-Confucian commentaries. No ancient European historian, not Polybius or Tacitus, not even Herodotus or Thucydides, can claim that kind of influence, nor does European historical writing display the continuity of a systematic and eventually (under the Tang dynasty) bureaucratized study of the past that is exemplified by China. Sima consistently details his sources, presents alternative opinions and generally lets the reader know why he has written an account of an event or person in a particular way. Consequently, the *Shiji* is also the first work of Chinese historiography to raise that question which has gnawed at us from antiquity to yesterday afternoon's senior undergraduate seminar: *how is the past knowable?* Again, a comparison with the Greeks is salutary: Sima Qian begins his story with the legendary, pre-dynastic Five Emperors, and he nowhere crisply dismisses myth in the manner of a Hecataeus or even firmly separates it from history. In fact, he completely lacked, because it did not exist in Chinese, an equivalent term to the Greek *muthos* meaning fiction.

Reference to the lessons that the past can provide occur frequently, and speakers in Sima Qian's narrative routinely appeal to history to provide advice for rulers. Sima adopts a common metaphor for history – one which we will see turn up periodically throughout the globe – that of the mirror, wherein we can see ourselves reflected, but he does so cautiously, and with a marked preference for recent rather than ancient examples. A ruler would be unwise to adopt the successful actions and wisdom of the more remote past without allowing for the alteration in current circumstances. This sceptical recognition, that the past can trick us with its superficial resemblances, has been repeated periodically over the centuries, for instance by the Renaissance Florentine historian Francesco Guicciardini (see below, p. 92). The further point, that examples from recent history are not necessarily inferior to those from antiquity, would also recur in subsequent writers such as the eighteenth-century English statesman Lord Bolingbroke (see below, p. 134).

Although the *Shiji* would eventually be counted as the first in a long series of twenty-four 'Standard Histories' (*Zhengshi*), the official history of a dynasty written under its successor dynasty, no subsequent work emulated its scale and scope for over a millennium. Most did not use all five of Sima's sections, though they invariably contained at least the annals and biographies. Unlike the *Shiji*, which covered both the Han and their predecessors, subsequent Standard Histories typically covered only one dynasty and were written after its fall, their conclusion providing the justification for the succession of the new dynasty. The historians of the Former or Western Han dynasty (which ended in AD 9), Ban Gu (*fl.* AD 32–92) and his sister Ban Zhao (AD 48–*c.* 116) typified this model. The Bans' *Hanshu* ('History of the Former or Western Han'), intended as a continuation of *Shiji*, took on a more explicitly moralizing tone than their predecessor, for example in condemning the usurpation of Wang Mang (AD 9–23) that preceded the return of the Han (as the Eastern Han dynasty). *Hanshu* even includes an enormous table listing two thousand personalities from antiquity to the Han, arranged into categories such as 'sage' and 'fool'. Both in style and in scope it, rather than the more expansive *Shiji*, would set the pattern for subsequent histories to cover only a single dynasty. When we next pick up the story of Chinese historiography, we will see, too, that the connection between historians and governance that began with Confucius would become much closer, as later emperors moved to institutionalize the writing of history.

Conclusion

Our brief survey of the foundations of history across three millennia has revealed a number of themes that will recur throughout most of this book: the relation (or lack thereof) of history to actual events in the past; the duty of the historian to be truthful (though truth itself is a slippery target); the educative role of the historian; the belief that the past was, more or less, an exemplary mirror from which the present could learn; the relative value, for some, of written sources versus oral information; and the emerging ties between control over the writing of the past and the exercise of political power. A further, significant point is the impact of contact with an 'other', with alien races, on the perception of representation of the past, either through providing a perspective on a past previously seen as special or unique or through outright adoption of a ruling power's forms of historical representation and endorsement of its hegemony. It is striking how, in different ways, most of these features can be found in both ancient Europe and in pre- and early imperial China. The next several centuries would see many of these threads further developed, refined and spread outside their homelands.

QUESTIONS FOR DISCUSSION

1. Why did ancient cultures begin to record and study the past?
2. At what point did historians begin to use the past as a source of moral authority and wisdom?
3. The eighteenth-century British historian David Hume commented that 'real history' begins with the first page of Thucydides. Is this a fair judgment?
4. How did different cultures approach the categorization of different types of writing about the past? Why was this important?
5. In what ways did early Chinese historical writing and thought differ from European? In what ways was it similar?
6. How did religion influence the writing of history in ancient cultures?

Further Reading

General

Butterfield, Herbert, *The Origins of History*, ed. A. Watson (London, 1981)
Feldherr, Andrew and Grant Hardy (eds), *The Oxford History of Historical Writing*, Vol. 1:*Beginnings to AD 600* (Oxford, 2011)
Lloyd, G. E. R., *The Ambitions of Curiosity: Understanding the World in Ancient Greece and China* (Cambridge, 2002)
Marincola, John (ed.), *A Companion to Greek and Roman Historiography* (Malden, MA and Oxford, 2007)
Momigliano, Arnaldo, *Studies in Historiography* (New York and Evanston, IL, 1966)
Pocock, J. G. A., 'The Origins of Study of the Past: A Comparative Approach', *Comparative Studies in Society and History* 4.2 (1962): 209–46

Raaflaub, Kurt A. (ed.), *Thinking, Recording, and Writing History in the Ancient World* (Malden, MA and Oxford, 2014)

The Ancient Near East

Grayson, A. K., *Assyrian and Babylonian Chronicles* (Locust Valley, NY, 1975)
Liverani, Mario, *Myth and Politics in Ancient Near Eastern Historiography* (London, 2004)
Van Seters, John, *In Search of History: Historiography in the Ancient World and the Origins of Biblical History* (New Haven, CT and London, 1983)

Jewish Historical Thought from the Tanakh *to Josephus*

Brettler, Marc Zvi, *The Creation of History in Ancient Israel* (London and New York, 1995)
Holladay, Carl R. (ed.), *Fragments from Hellenistic Jewish Authors, Vol. 1: Historians* (Chico, CA, 1983)
Ishida, Tomoo, *History and Historical Writing in Ancient Israel* (Leiden, 1999)
Rajak, Tessa, *Josephus: The Historian and His Society*, 2nd edn (London, 2002)

Early Greek Historiography

Fornara, Charles W., *The Nature of History in Ancient Greece and Rome* (Berkeley, CA, 1983)
Hornblower, Simon (ed.), *Greek Historiography* (Oxford, 1994)
Marincola, John, *Greek Historians* (Oxford, 2001)
Scanlon, Thomas F., *Greek Historiography* (Chichester, 2015)
Sorek, Susan, *Ancient Historians: A Student Handbook* (London and New York, 2012)
Woodman, A. J., *Rhetoric in Classical Historiography* (London, 1988)

Herodotus and Thucydides

Balot, Ryan K., Sara Forsdyke and Edith Foster (eds), *The Oxford Handbook of Thucydides* (Oxford and New York, 2017)
Dewald, Carolyn and John Marincola (eds), *The Cambridge Companion to Herodotus* (Cambridge and New York, 2006)

Foster, Edith and Donald Lateiner (eds), *Thucydides and Herodotus* (Oxford, 2012)

Hartog, François. *The Mirror of Herodotus: The Representation of the Other in the Writing of History*, trans. Janet Lloyd (Berkeley, CA, 1988)

Hau, Lisa, *Moral History from Herodotus to Diodorus Siculus* (Edinburgh, 2016)

Roberts, Jennifer T., *Herodotus: A Very Short Introduction* (Oxford, 2011)

Greek Historiography from the Fourth to the Second Centuries

Flower, Michael (ed.), *The Cambridge Companion to Xenophon* (Cambridge, 2017)

McGing, B. C., *Polybius' Histories* (Oxford, 2010)

Parmeggiani, Giovanni (ed.), *Between Thucydides and Polybius: The Golden Age of Greek Historiography* (Cambridge, MA, 2014)

Sacks, Kenneth S., *Polybius on the Writing of History* (Berkeley, CA, 1981)

Walbank, F. W., *Polybius* (Berkeley, CA, 1972)

Roman Historical Writing from Republic to Empire

Clarke, Graeme et al. (eds), *Reading the Past in Late Antiquity* (Rushcutters Bay, NSW, Australia, 1990)

Cornell, T. J. (ed.), *The Fragments of the Roman Historians*, 3 vols (Oxford, 2013)

Feldherr, Andrew (ed.), *The Cambridge Companion to the Roman Historians* (Cambridge and New York, 2009)

Mellor, Ronald, *The Roman Historians* (London, 1999)

Rohrbacher, David, *The Historians of Late Antiquity* (London and New York, 2002)

Syme, Ronald, *Tacitus*, 2 vols (1958; Oxford, 1989)

Chinese Historiography from Earliest Times to the Han Dynasty

Durrant, Stephen W., *The Cloudy Mirror: Tension and Conflict in the Writings of Sima Qian* (Albany, NY, 1995)

Hardy, Grant, *Worlds of Bronze and Bamboo: Sima Qian's Conquest of History* (New York, 1999)

Li, Wai-yee, *The Readability of the Past in Early Chinese Historiography* (Cambridge, MA, 2007)

Martin, Thomas R., *Herodotus and Sima Qian: The First Great Historians of Greece and China, A Brief History with Documents* (Boston and New York, 2010)

Ng, On-Cho *and* Q. Edward Wang, *Mirroring the Past: The Writing and Use of History in Imperial China* (Honolulu, 2005)

Schaberg, David, *A Patterned Past: Form and Thought in Early Chinese Historiography* (Cambridge, MA, 2001)

MILESTONES

c. AD 330 Eusebius' *Chronicle* and *Church History*

4th cent. AD Sri Lankan *vamsas* commence

c. 417 Orosius' *Seven Books of History against the Pagans*

c. 551 Procopius of Caesarea's *Secret History*

early 6th cent. AD Gildas' *On the Ruin of Britain*

629 New Bureau for the Writing of History is created in China

mid-7th cent. AD Beginnings of Islamic historical writing

708–21 Liu Zhiji's *Comprehensive Perspectives on Historiography*

712 *Kojiki* (Japan)

720 *Chronicles of Japan*

c. 731 Bede's *Ecclesiastical History of the English People*

9th cent. to *c.* 1154 AD *Anglo-Saxon Chronicle*

10th cent. Abu'l Hasan al-Mas'udi's *The Meadows of Gold and Mines of Gems*

early 11th cent. Career and travels of al-Biruni

c. 1084 Completion of Sima Guang's *Comprehensive Mirror in Aid of Government*

c. 1120 to *c.* 1143 William of Malmesbury's various historical works

early 12th cent. Anna Komnene (Lat.: Comnena) authors *Alexiad*; earliest known European woman to write a work of prose history

c. 1136 Geoffrey of Monmouth's *History of the Kings of Britain*

c. 1148–9 Kalhana's *River of Kings*

c. 1220 Jien's *Jottings of a Fool*

1274–1461 *Great Chronicles of France*

c. 1305 to *c.* 1309 Jean de Joinville's *Chronicle of the Crusade of St Louis*

1337? to after 1405 Jean Froissart's *Chronicles of France, England and Nearby Countries*

1339 Kitabatake Chikafusa's *Record of the Legitimate Succession of Divine Sovereigns*

1375–8 Ibn Khaldun's *Introduction to History*

1498 Philippe de Commynes completes his *Memoirs*

2 | History in Eurasia to the Mid-Fifteenth Century

Historical Writing in Christian and Barbarian Europe

Christianity established itself in part by writing its own history and in part by recasting the history of the known world into a form that rendered the ancient past a prologue to the incarnation, ministry and resurrection of Christ, and saw in subsequent history a modern cosmic drama to be ended in human time by Christ's return. The roots of the Christian historical outlook, like the religion itself, lay in both Judaism and Greco-Roman culture, with Hellenized Jews such as Josephus providing a bridge between the two through their accounts of Jewish antiquity. Christianity adapted a vision of the past marked by the direct and frequent intervention of God, the punishment of the wicked and earthly triumph of the righteous, and, often, a messianic conviction that the world had been created at a particular date and would ultimately expire.

The influence of Greek and Roman historiography is less obvious but equally important. Chronography, which the Greeks had developed, was a crucial element in the Christian search for a usable past. Some of this had an expressly millenarian or apocalyptic purpose, as it attempted to calculate time not only backward to Creation but forward to the end of days, borrowing dates from pagan writers and prophesies from the Bible. Roman historical writing proved useful in a different way: once the empire itself turned Christian, it became the secular arm of God's will and a major force in the spread of Christianity throughout Europe. The Roman past, and with it the collected pasts of all the great empires of more remote antiquity, from the Babylonians through the Persians and the Macedonians, formed another river of successions and events, parallel with Jewish history, and leading to a Christianized world – the world then being taken to include Europe, the Near East and northern Africa.

Among early attempts at a Christian chronology, the most influential by far was that of the Greek-speaking Eusebius of Caesarea (*c.* 260 or

275 to *c*. 339), who lived during the transition from an era of persecution to the toleration of the religion under Constantine. Eusebius' writings included a world chronicle. This included a series of *Chronological Canons*, or tables, beginning with the birth of Abraham, which he placed at a year corresponding with 2016 BC. A typical entry for a year would list several corresponding dates and usually include information on persons or events. Translated into Latin and continued by St Jerome half a century later, Eusebius' *Chronicle* proved a foundational text to European efforts to establish firm dates for the various events recorded in different ancient calendars. Moreover, Eusebius' chronological entries borrowed extensively from Roman civic history and often included mentions of interesting phenomena such as comets or eclipses. In a later work, his *Church History*, Eusebius more or less invented 'ecclesiastical history' as a sub-genre of historical writing and, indeed, a major category in European literature up to the twentieth century. The separation of ecclesiastical from secular history, though far from absolute, proved fundamental to medieval and early modern historical writing and to later Renaissance divisions among historical genres.

In contrast to their secular counterparts and the entire classical tradition on which they rested, and despite their frequent appeal to oral sources, the authors of ecclesiastical history, though they often quoted dialogue, were generally averse to the practice of extended fictional speeches. Eusebius seems to have recognized at the outset that documents would serve his purpose better than rhetorical set-pieces, and his successors followed suit. They chose to buttress their arguments in a different way, by inserting original documents and letters, either verbatim or summarized, which had not been a characteristic of most classical histories, in part because it made for tedious reading and interrupted the textual flow. Sozomen (*c*. 400 to *c*. 450) boasted of his careful attention to eyewitness testimony, which the Greek historians had taught him, but he was equally proud of his widespread travels to gather firewood-like armloads of documents, 'some of which are preserved to this day in the archives of the imperial palace and in churches, while others are kept scattered about in the files of learned men'. Some he would summarize while others, following Eusebius' example, were presented in full. This documentary practice would continue through early modern times.

In the fourth century, following the foundation of the eastern Roman Empire at Constantinople (the former Byzantium) and the establishment of Christianity as the official religion of the empire, western and eastern European historical writing evolved in rather different directions, and the break with classical forms, so noticeable in the annal-writing Latin West, is much less obvious in the Greek-speaking East. The most notable secular historian of this period, and the most obvious imitator of Thucydides' focus on military affairs, was Procopius of Caesarea (*c.* 500 to *c.* 554) whose religious views have long been a matter of controversy. Procopius chronicled the campaigns of the Emperor Justinian (r. 527–65), for whose reign his *Wars* is the principal authority. It is a narrative after the fashion of Thucydides and has generally enjoyed a positive reputation. Perhaps unfortunately, Procopius has become more famous for a minor work, rediscovered in the Renaissance, initially called the *Anekdota* (literally 'unpublished work') but more popularly known as the *Secret History*, completed *c.* 551, in which the author sought to emulate Suetonius' *Lives of the Caesars*. Unrelentingly hostile to 'the demon in human flesh', Justinian, and his promiscuous empress, Procopius unwittingly spawned a new genre that eventually embraced a number of seventeenth- and eighteenth-century exposés offering lascivious details about the private lives of royalty and other worthies, and their modern journalistic descendants the 'tell-all' memoir and celebrity tabloid.

In Latin Christendom, religion provided the closest thing to a unifying force in the development of a common vocabulary and a shared set of standard themes for history-writing. Eusebius had been translated into Latin and beginning with St Augustine of Hippo, mainstream Christian thought embraced a Neoplatonic juxtaposition of two 'cities', a heavenly and an earthly, according to which events that unfolded in the human and natural world were inferior shadows or reflections of a higher reality in the divine sphere. These spheres were interlocking rather than separate. The divine will, under the rubric of 'Providence', lay behind major cataclysms such as the sack of Rome (AD 410), and it inscrutably micromanaged the punishment of wrongdoing down to the level of the individual, though Augustine explicitly avoided discerning any overarching pattern to a rather wild sea of historical events. 'In general, the bad come to bad ends and the good enjoy eventual success', Augustine observed, though he had to concede that some times Bad Things happened to Good People, something China's Sima Qian, five centuries earlier, had pointed out in analysing the seemingly unmerited fates of the worthy and the wicked. Borrowing from Genesis and the Gospels, Augustine also articulated a comprehensive periodization of the past, lacking in Eusebius, that divided the world's eras into a 'Great Week' analogous to the Six Days of Creation. Augustine's disciple Orosius (*fl.* 414–18) gave his mentor's vision more concrete definition in the polemically titled *Seven Books of History against the Pagans*, the first universal history to narrate the unfolding of the divine will through all recorded time. It proved highly influential beyond Christendom, too: translated into Arabic in the tenth century, the *Seven Books* would eventually become a significant conduit for the transfer of Christian historical thought into the work of much later Muslim historians such as Ibn Khaldun. Orosius also heightened the apocalyptic element in universal history by substituting for Augustine's 'Six Ages' the biblical notion of 'Four Monarchies' or world empires, lifted from the Book of Daniel, thereby investing human time with a deeper meaning than Augustine had contemplated.

Augustine's 'two cities' concept would also be reshaped and revisited many times, most explicitly in the twelfth century by Otto, bishop of Freising (*c.* 1111–58), who used it as the title of his major historical work entitled *The Chronicle of the Two Cities*. Otto expanded the Heavenly City to include the Roman Empire itself, drawing a distinction between the rather depressing circularity of earthly events and the *progressus* of the sacred sphere (the origin of our modern word 'progress', though Otto simply meant a course of providential events toward a redemptive end). It was Otto who would provide the classic formulation of a historical continuity argument in a concept historiographers refer to as the *translatio imperii*, the thesis that the Roman Empire, Christianity's secular arm, had not in fact fallen, but merely been 'translated' (transferred) from Rome to the Franks and eventually to their emperor Charlemagne, the latest step in a process whereby each world empire of antiquity had been succeeded by another; on this view, the Carolingian was not a new empire but rather a continuation of that of Rome. The ultimate heirs of this process were the German Hohenstaufen emperors of Otto's own day, such as the bishop's own nephew Frederick I, called Barbarossa (r. 1156–90). The conceit of 'translation' of imperial authority, rather than its creation *de novo*, became almost infinitely adaptable in the hands of medieval and early modern monarchs and their propagandists: the fifteenth-century Ottoman conquerors of Constantinople would appropriate the *translatio* to justify their own claims to be the true heirs of Rome, while the Spaniard Hernán Cortés would eventually use a comparable argument to justify the transfer of authority from the Aztec ruler of Mexico to the Emperor Charles V.

Historical writing in Latin Christendom during the so-called 'Dark Ages' from the fifth to the ninth centuries is a much more heterogeneous affair than in the Greek east. The collapse of the western Roman Empire and its displacement by various barbarian kingdoms obscured, but did not wholly break, the continuity with ancient models: a writer like the Briton Gildas (*fl.* early sixth century), whose *De Excidio Britanniae* ('On the Ruin of Britain') recounts the last days of pre-Saxon invasion Britain, sounds like an Old Testament prophet or a latter-day Tacitus in his moralizing criticism of the British and their kings. Yet the period was more shadowy than dark, for historians wrote significant accounts about the various Germanic tribes. The challenge facing their authors was to integrate peoples of obscure origin, who had until recently fallen outside the 'universal' empire, into the emerging Christian meta-story. Throughout the world, contact with alien societies would provide in later centuries a critical agent of historiographical change as well as a problem for historians faced with finding a place in their narrative for previously unknown or obscure peoples.

There now began what would become a core activity of historians until the era of nineteenth-century nationalism: the tracing of ethnic, linguistic and even familial history back to its origins. This generally involved identifying an ancient people mentioned in classical sources, and often a suppositious individual founder – in several cases an immigrant who conquered an indigenous race of humans or giants. The most important variant of the early medieval quest for exalted ancient forebears, and the one that did the most damage – intellectual and physical – in the long run, is that known by the Latin term *origo gentis* (pl. *origines gentium*, literally 'the origins of peoples'): Nazi Aryan purity theory and modern 'ethnic cleansing' are among its most violent recent products. The game of finding illustrious antecedents was especially prominent during and immediately after the barbarian migrations (or *Völkerwanderung*), but it continued through the early modern period, when upwardly mobile families similarly sought or invented lengthy and famous descents. In a different form, it acquired a new lease of life in the early nineteenth century when, however, attention would shift away from remote ancestors and towards the identification of national character, cultural continuity and 'racial' attributes. Those who stuck to biblical lineage could trace all peoples, Christian and pagan, back to one of the three sons of Noah, who had repopulated the earth after the Flood. Historians in search of a more recent descent could turn to various ancient peoples such as Greeks, Egyptians and 'Scythians' (an actual Central Asian tribe mentioned by Herodotus that now became an ill-defined conglomeration of several distinct peoples). By far the most popular and flexible ancestral people, the Trojans, were already deployed in Vergil's *Aeneid* to explain the origins of Roman civilization in Italy and, by the end of the Middle Ages, they were held to have colonized and named other parts of the globe, such as Britain (for 'Brutus') and France ('Francion'). This incidentally made the Trojans especially useful to those challenging Roman secular authority, since their own existence (and by implication, independence) could thereby be argued to have *preceded* Rome's foundation by several centuries.

A by-product of early medieval sacred history was the saint's life (usually known as 'hagiography', a term that does not really do it justice), which in the early church had commemorated the piety and deeds, including miracles, of Christian martyrs, monks and hermits, and soon spread to cover scholars and secular clergy such as bishops. The success of monarchs such as Charlemagne had inspired, earlier in the Middle Ages, a number of individual royal biographies such as Einhard's and Notker Balbulus' of the Frankish emperor (the latter of which liberally embellished the facts and thereby inaugurated Charlemagne's transformation from historical figure to chivalric folk hero). The relation between these lives and the more common form of annals is complex and variable. Einhard (*c*. 770–840) seems deliberately to have avoided an annalistic approach to his life of Charlemagne, and chose to imitate ancient biography in the manner of Plutarch or Suetonius. Three generations later, Einhard's own English reader Asser (d. 908/9) would include in his *Life of Alfred* extensive passages drawn from a work known to us as the *Anglo-Saxon Chronicle*, the name given to a series of manuscripts, mainly written in Old English, that began towards the end of Alfred the Great's rule (r. 871–99) and which was continued until the mid-twelfth century by successive anonymous annalists. It is virtually unique in the West at this juncture as an ongoing national history composed in a vernacular language. Latin remained, for the moment, the language of learned discourse, and the literate order, the clergy, continued to use that language to write histories, reflecting the larger Latin Christendom that was both the context for their activity and the extended audience for their works.

The most important quartet among the 'barbarian' historians of the sixth through tenth centuries produced remarkable works. Written in Latin, still the international language of western Europe, they included histories of the Goths (Jordanes' [d. 554] *Getica*, in part summarizing a lost history by the sixth-century writer Cassiodorus), the Franks (Gregory of Tours [538–93/4], whose work might more accurately be described as a history of his own times, though it is framed as a Eusebian-style universal history), the Lombards (Paul the Deacon [d. 799?]) and the Anglo-Saxons (Bede [d. 753]). One example will suffice. The 'Venerable' Bede authored several historical and bibliographical works including his *Ecclesiastical History of the English People*, a wonderful blend of sacred and secular, recounting the story of Britain from pre-Roman times to the year 731.

Bede was no more dispassionate and neutral a commentator than any other historian of his time: his Christianity is both fervent and clear, as is his adherence to the Roman rite on which the English had settled. The *Ecclesiastical History* was also replete with the miraculous events and saintly lives that enlivened monastic historiography throughout the Middle Ages. To see in Bede a proto-modern, hard-edged archival scholar and to ignore the literary and rhetorical aspects of his work would be seriously misguided. Nevertheless, his is a history of discrimination among sources, intelligent balancing of the oral and the written, shrewd interpolation of biographical and hagiographical anecdotes on particular individuals at various points, and a well thought-out, thematic vision of the whole. It is a creative and a critical work, not simply a transmitter of tradition. In it we see most of the essential characteristics of medieval historical writing, practised at a high level: a firm belief in the 'praise-and-blame' aspect of history; its role as an educator of the powerful; the reliance on spoken as well as written sources and a relative indifference to the distinction between them (a more meaningful differentiation being that between trustworthy and untrustworthy informants); and the design of the book not just for private reading but for performance, through oral recitation, in a society only marginally literate. Bede was also diligent in telling his readers not just where and from whom he got his information, but often how his informants in turn acquired theirs, establishing a chain of information back to proximity with events.

In this last aspect he shared something with the historians produced by the new religion that had recently emerged in the Middle East, Islam.

Islamic Historiography from Muhammad to Ibn Khaldun

The Islamic is the youngest of the great world historiographical traditions, and (unlike the Chinese) its authors had access relatively early to both classical and Judeo-Christian works. Islamic historiography thus lies at a somewhat lesser degree of 'independence' from classical/Judeo-Christian historiography than do the Chinese or South Asian (see below) traditions, which helps to explain its somewhat closer resemblance to the former than the latter. Like the religion it was developed expressly to support, Islamic historical writing had a very quick birth and a rather short formative period of two to three centuries before it settled into a clear pattern with distinctive genres and rules of practice, taken up by Muslims composing initially in Arabic but eventually in Persian and other languages as the faith spread beyond its Arab homeland. Islamic historiography expressed a sense of temporal progress from Creation through the prophets (culminating with Muhammad) and leading eventually to the world's end. Both Muhammad and subsequent Muslim historians took Judeo-Christian biblical history as a point of departure, a back-story, rather than as a false account to be discredited. To a Muslim, as much as to a Jew or Christian, the world was finite and had been created at a particular point; Adam and Eve were the first humans, and Muhammad was not the only prophet in history, but rather the last and greatest of a line stretching back, via Jesus, to Abraham. The determination of Muslim scholars to provide justification for their statements by establishing chains of authority reaching back to the Prophet makes them seem in some ways very modern.

Though Islamic historiography was very new, it thrived in a region with a pre-existing interest in the past. There are indigenous examples of historiography, genealogy, semi-legendary stories and oral traditions among both Arabs and Persians, such as popular stories about battles (*Ayyam*), or about the history of particular regions such as Yemen. Islamic historiography proper began in the mid-seventh century, its first subject being the life and deeds or expeditions (*maghazi*) of Muhammad himself, whose *Hijra* to Medina in AD 622 provided a firm date on which to anchor an Islamic chronology. Both an attentiveness to dating and an interest in narrating the past developed within a generation or so of the death of Muhammad. From virtually the beginning, a zealous effort to record only true statements about or by the Prophet, derived ultimately from the testimony of eyewitnesses (themselves evaluated for trustworthiness), led to careful attention to the chain of transmission (*isnad*) whereby one successive authority passed information, often orally, down to the next: a *hadith* or report of the words of the Prophet generally consisted of an *isnad* followed by a *matn* (the actual text). By the ninth century a virtual 'science of traditions' had evolved with rules for evaluating particular texts or testimonies and the capacity to expunge false or corrupt *hadith*s. This did not stand in the way of literary creativity – Muslim authors shared with their Byzantine, Chinese and classical counterparts a fondness for using the fictitious speech to convey a message or lesson, and they loved to include lists of various sorts – but it does signal a rather different predisposition than applied elsewhere in Eurasia. The degree to which the standards of *hadith* were successfully exported to historical writing as a whole is a matter of debate for specialists. The salient point is that whereas with most historians up to this point we are left to guess as to the basis of their statements, the chain of authority here is detailed and explicit.

The principal disadvantage of a historiography built on the *isnad* is that little room is left for the testimony of non-believers. What was one to do with the evidence provided by a Christian or Jew? Conversely, how did one judge the truth of evidence about foreign lands where no *isnad* equivalent existed? An early writer such as Ibn Ishaq (*fl.* mid-eighth century), active before the rules for the system had really settled, had no difficulty conferring with non-Muslims on pre-Islamic history. The problem would become more severe for later historians such as al-Tabari (*c.* 839–923), who regularly had to qualify his assertions, as his universal history approached his own times, with phrases such as 'I have heard' or 'it was said'. But the willingness of historians to depart from the stricter observance of *isnad* practised by *hadith* scholars ultimately provided some distance between history and *hadith*, as historians increasingly adopted the practice of *adab*, what we might call philology or 'belles-lettres'. Histories written under the influence of *adab* provide more information as to the author's intentions in writing them. One remarkable work, the tenth-century *Muruj adh-dhahab wa ma'adin al-jawahir* ('The Meadows of Gold and Mines of Gems') exemplifies this broadening of perspective: a geographically and temporally wide-ranging work, it begins with the descent of man from Adam and includes discussion of the contributions of various nations both ancient and modern to the arts and sciences. Its author, the Iraqi historian Abu'l Hasan al-Mas'udi, reflects these humanistic tendencies and his book is notable both for its critical apparatus (he was among the tiny minority of Muslim historians who departed from strict adherence to the *isnad*s and, indeed, distrusted tradition in general) and for his assertion that 'for any science to exist it must be derived from history ... The superiority of history over all other sciences is obvious.' For al-Mas'udi, history was both entertainment and science (in its older and broader sense of 'knowledge'); it should be accessible to both the learned and the ignorant, and its practice transcended the differences between Arab and non-Arab. There is here an unambiguous link back to the Greeks, with whose works al-Mas'udi and other Arabic writers were familiar (and shared credit with Byzantine scholars for preserving), in the conception of history as a form of 'discovery' and as the register of all known experience – a source for understanding the natural world as well as the past.

By the advent of the Baghdad-based Abbasid dynasty in the mid-eighth century, terminology to express the idea of an account of the past had also developed. The modern Arabic term for history, variants of which are in use in most Muslim countries, is *ta'rikh*, which first appeared about 644. Another word, *khabar*, denoted a report of the past (sometimes no longer than a paragraph) composed for historical interest rather than to shed light on Islamic law, and often devoted to the relation of a single event. Unlike some Western historians since Thucydides, however, it is also clear that many of them did not see an obligation to provide a definitive verdict on the past where sources disagreed, but rather to provide multiple accounts from which the reader could choose: this puts them closer, in a sense, to the approach of Han China's great historian, Sima Qian, than to the classical sources with which the Muslim authors were much more familiar. A further peculiarity of early Islamic historiography is its orientation towards remote rather than more recent times. Whereas a Herodotus asked questions about the past of a generation or so before his time, and Thucydides virtually repudiated any past that was not contemporary, the first few generations of Muslim historians had a seeming aversion to contemporary or recent history. To put it another way, if the early

Greek historians privileged modernity in their accounts, Islamic historians, working within a scholarly tradition that valued not the past in general but that slice of the past which was foundational to Islam, gave priority to the time of the Prophet and then of the civil wars, reserving little attention for their own day.

The 'classical' period of Islamic historiography would produce a great deal of writing by Persians, particularly under the Ghaznavid dynasty of the eleventh and twelfth centuries. Persian Muslim historiography would also continue the departure from strict attention to *hadith* and the adoption by many historians of a rather more liberal intellectual outlook characterized by *adab*. The Persian approach to history as a branch of the tree of scholarship, rather than as handmaiden to theology, is embodied by the much-travelled polymath Abu'l Rayhan Muhammad ibn Ahmad al-Biruni (973–1048), much of whose life was spent in India. Al-Biruni, who wrote in both Arabic and Persian, employed his mathematical and philological knowledge to the resolution of calendrical and chronological conflicts between the world's nations; he also exemplifies a sceptical turn of mind with respect to remote and legendary history, and in particular to mendacious genealogies of the sort that arise in times of social ferment, when familial and dynastic shifts require the construction or invention of a noble past.

The defining conflict for late medieval Islam was not that with Christian Europe (though Europeans understandably thought otherwise), but rather with the Mongols to the east. One branch of this nomadic people, the Golden Horde, sacked Baghdad in 1258 and executed the last Abbasid ruler and his family, killing with them the ideal of a universal Muslim caliphate. A warlike non-Muslim people who came into contact with Persia to the west and China to the east in the course of the thirteenth century, the Mongols had their own sense of universalism; a divine entitlement to world rule given to Genghis (or Chinggis) Khan and his successors provided the theme of much of their early historical writing. Aside from the dominant Yuan branch that ruled China, the Mongol expansion had established a number of subordinate khanates in western and Central Asia, regimes which adopted the Islamic rather than Chinese style of historiography. The Timurid dynasty, which sprang from the late fourteenth-century warlord Timur or Tamerlane (d. 1405), ruled much of the region during the fifteenth century and had, it seems,

an especially strong interest in history, frequently listening to the
reading of chronicles and accounts of great men. On one occasion,
Timur found himself being interviewed by a Tunisian Muslim
whose name is among the most famous in the history of historical
thought. Ibn Khaldun (1332–1406) is deservedly praised, though he
was less unique a figure than admiring Westerners, unfamiliar with
Islamic historiography of the previous seven centuries, attest. He is
more correctly seen as a culmination of the philosophical tendencies
previously observed in al-Mas'udi. His fame has traditionally rested
not on the history itself but rather on its prolegomenon or
Muqaddimah ('Introduction to History'), an ambitious attempt to
work out the many factors underlying historical change including
customs, manners, climate and economics.

Ibn Khaldun's idea that individuals and groups that come to power
are animated by a group spirit or *'asabiyya* (which in itself often
works against the maintenance of that power and must be suppressed) has counterparts in much later European writers such as
J. G. Herder (see Chapter 4, pp. 148–50), while his belief that
regimes once consolidated will almost inevitably become divided or
corrupted and fall echoes the cyclical politics of the Greek Polybius.
His analysis of power also anticipates a historical generalist of the
sixteenth century, Florence's Niccolò Machiavelli. But the
Muqaddimah is not only about the macro-questions of historical
processes and influences. Since the ninth and tenth centuries, when
theologians had challenged both the utility and reliability of history, its
practitioners had fought back, typically articulating in their prefaces
the basis of their methods and assumptions. Ibn Khaldun, though his
remarks are much more extensive, fits into a pre-existing tradition of
thinking about what history as a branch of study should involve,
and where its weaknesses lie. At the very opening of his book, Ibn
Khaldun ponders the limits of historical truth – or rather, of untruth.
Historical knowledge is afflicted by several kinds of falsehood, of
which the first is 'prejudice and partisanship', by which he really
meant unthinking allegiance to a particular sect or opinion within
Islam. Further kinds of falsehood are occasioned by a range of
human weaknesses – reliance upon transmitters of testimony without
proper examination of the transmitters themselves, ignorance of the
purpose of an event, baseless reliance on the truth of an event, the
inclination of historians to embellish accounts in order to flatter

the powerful and, above all, 'ignorance of the various conditions arising in civilization'. All of these are themes that would be explored at a theoretical and philosophical level by later Europeans.

Forms of History in Southern Asia

The values and style of both Chinese and Islamic historiography were not those of its Christian European counterparts, but their products are nonetheless clearly recognizable as histories, and they share common concerns with matters such as chronology, a normative function, a declared allegiance, at least in theory, to representing 'the truth' and a commitment to the memorialization of particular facts about the past. For this reason, even the respect accorded to Chinese historical traditions in most Western histories of history (when mentioned at all) has usually been withheld entirely from other modes of apprehending the past that seem much more distant. Early South Asian historical writing is among these. Its very capacity – especially in its Hindu-inspired forms – to generate thought and writing about the past has often been rejected – the Muslim al-Biruni commented on the Hindu lack of interest in 'the historical order of things' as early as the 1020s; Gibbon commented on a general 'Asiatic' lack of history in the eighteenth century; and the indictment was echoed by James Mill and by Georg Wilhelm Friedrich Hegel early in the nineteenth.

The multiplicity of ethnic groups and languages, and the complexities within and between religions, did not permit anything like Western historiography to develop, if by that we mean a canonical set of historians in the style of Thucydides. Nor was there the central government apparatus that had stimulated and would soon bureaucratize post-Qin Chinese historiography. However, thought about the past, and both oral tradition and writing derived therefrom, did exist in ancient India, and in several traditions. The most notable is that known as *itihasa-purana*, which by the mid-first millennium AD had become an authoritative source for the ruling Brahman caste. *Itihasa* translates as 'thus it was' and has come in more recent times to mean 'history', though it had no such association in ancient times. *Purana* (in Sanskrit) refers to 'that which pertains to ancient times' or 'old lore', either heard or remembered. The *Visnu Purana*, from the mid-first millennium AD, contains a 'succession' chapter which illustrates both its outlook and the emergence of history from myth. It begins in remote mythical antiquity and continues generationally through a great flood and a major war which marks the end of a heroic age.

Pre-Islamic India also developed other traditions of writing about the past distinct from *itihasa-purana*, frequently centred in religious institutions. The other major religion in the region, Buddhism, also showed an early commitment both to written history and to chronology. Buddhist historical writing, also found in Tibet and Sri Lanka, diverged from the Brahmanic in at least one important respect, its conventional dating of events from a single point, the death of the Buddha *c.* 483 BC (a controverted date also used by some, but not all, Buddhist-influenced countries). The Pali-language chronicles from Sri Lanka, for instance, focus on the history of a particular Buddhist order or monastery but also stray into secular history and the history of earlier times. The most prominent of these are the *vamsas*, a genre that continued from the fourth century AD for many hundreds of years, preserving a cumulative history of nearly two millennia. The durability of the *vamsas* is remarkable: for sheer longevity, the only comparable examples are the Chinese *Zhengshi* or 'Twenty-Four Standard Histories'. To put it in perspective, consider what European historiography might look like if the kinds of chronicles written in Europe's Middle Ages had remained the main stream of historical writing until the time of Napoleon.

The most unusual of Hindu histories – unusual in its provision of a clear chronology – is a twelfth-century Sanskrit text called the *Rajatarangini* ('River of Kings', comp. *c.* 1148–9) ascribed to Kalhana (*fl.* mid-twelfth century). This verse composition covered the history of Kashmir from remote antiquity to the author's own time and was derived from legends, oral traditions, written records and inscriptions; it refers to other histories from which its author drew, suggesting that it was not, in its time, *sui generis*. Kalhana's poem shows a much greater sense of chronology than most Indian historical writing to this time, and it covers issues familiar to us from other regions: the errors of illustrious predecessors; the need to consult various sources; the importance of style; and the educative function of the historian.

In northern India, both Buddhism and Hinduism were confronted by a radically different religion, Islam, which introduced to the subcontinent its own variant of historical writing. There had been a minor Muslim presence in India for some time, including visitors like al-Biruni, but Islamic India really dates from the establishment of Muslim regimes, such as the Delhi Sultanate (1206–1526) and the later Deccan sultanates (1490–1596), of South Central India. The Muslim chroniclers attached to these courts introduced a very different historical thought, and a tradition of Islamic history-writing already several hundred years old. Among these Indo-Muslims no historian has enjoyed as high a reputation as Ziya al-Din Barani (*fl.* 1284 to after 1357), both for the thoroughness in recording contemporary information which makes him a useful source, and also for his philosophic outlook. Barani completed his *History of Shah Firuz* in 1357, when he was in his seventies, having reflected seriously on the purposes of history, the 'queen of the sciences' and highest form of learning other than those dealing with the *Qur'an* or the laws. He outlines seven different reasons for studying history: it bestows familiarity with sacred texts and with a stock of examples; it is the twin brother of *hadith* and helps confirm its testimony; it strengthens reason and judgment by forcing us to confront the experience of others; it comforts the powerful in times of stress because it shows that there are tried solutions to most problems; knowledge of it will induce patience and resignation in good Muslims; it clearly delineates the contrasting characters of the virtuous and pious and the evil, displaying the consequences of good and bad behaviour and thereby induces rulers to behave themselves; and finally, as a foundation of truth, it will present ordinary readers with valuable examples and encourage them to take a righteous path. The duty of the historian is itself a moral one, to inculcate history's lessons. In his corollary statement that 'history is a science that requires no proofs so long as the historian is a trustworthy person', trustworthy really means 'of respectable birth': Barani anticipated much later European attitudes to scientific and historical truth which located epistemological authority in the social standing of its speakers.

Historiography in East Asia from the Tang to the Yuan

The turmoil and disorder of the centuries around the collapse of the western Roman Empire have a close Chinese counterpart in the disunity that followed the end of the Eastern Han dynasty in 220, as a series of short-lived and sometimes coeval dynasties ruled pieces of the defunct Han Empire. A significant quantity of history was written by private scholars in both the northern and southern parts of the empire, including a number of contemporary histories of the mid-third-century 'Three Kingdoms' of Wei, Shu and Wu. Such was the proliferation of history-writing that by the end of the period the very word *shi*, which till then had meant the *writer* of a history, began increasingly to be used to denote the textual product itself. The successor states to the Han Empire each produced during the next four centuries a significant stock of histories (increasingly composed on the newer medium of paper in lieu of bamboo or silk). In all, as many as 140 dynastic histories may have appeared between the end of the Han and the return of stability under the Tang; whereas Ban Gu had been able to list only a dozen historical works in the first century AD, by 656 the authors of the *Suishu*, the dynastic history of the Sui (r. 581–618) counted nearly 900. By the mid-sixth century, in an effort to weed out unauthoritative histories, the Emperor Yuan of Liang (r. 552–5) declared some to be *Zhengshi* ('Standard Histories'), thereby giving birth to that term (the numbering of them into Twenty-Four canonical texts would come much later, in the eighteenth century).

The advent of the Tang dynasty (618–907) produced a significant change in both the status and practice of historiography. In addition to creating the system of civil service exams (AD 622) that would endure for centuries, the Tang wove history-making into the operations of government and inaugurated a systematic 'bureaucratization' of history, building on the imperial sponsorship of histories under previous dynasties. In 629, a new Bureau for the Writing of History (*shiguan*) was created, attached initially to the Chancellery and a little over a century later moved to the Secretariat; the Bureau also had a branch office in the eastern capital of Luoyang.

The Tang historiographic enterprise was conceived with the intent of creating a reliable set of records, or national history (*Guoshi*) of recent times, which would eventually be used for the future construction of a dynastic history. The Bureau also produced new histories of several post-Han dynasties, taking the orthodox Confucian Ban Gu's *Hanshu* rather than the rather more eclectic *Shiji* as its model. As institutionalized in the Bureau, the process thus clearly distinguished between the *recording* of historical events as they occurred and the *writing* of histories which subsequently commemorated them in the form of a narrative. We will find no such clear conceptualization of this distinction elsewhere in the world at this time, or anything remotely approaching this assembly-line approach to production, with its ascending stages of composition from the daily event to the dynastic summary. The process began with the court diaries kept during the reign of an incumbent emperor, a memento of his sayings and actions to which the emperor himself was theoretically not supposed to have access – one emperor was even denied a look at what his own diarists were recording. From these and other materials a set of 'Veritable Records' (*shilu*) would be developed at the end of each reign and, sometimes, a 'national history' of the reign itself usually emulating the annals–biography format of the Standard Histories. An innovation of the Tang for which there is no earlier precedent, the *shilu* formed an essential part of all later dynasties' official historiography; after the final eclipse of a dynasty and ascension of its successor, they would provide the basis of the Standard History of that dynasty, a work which invariably included the two essential elements of basic annals and biographies of individual notables and sometimes foreign peoples.

Not all history that was written was dynastic history, nor was it all controlled by the Bureau. There were also spin-offs, including institutional histories, historical encyclopedias and privately authored histories, some of which were the work of Bureau members writing on their own initiative. Many private writers eschewed the complexities of the annals–biography format for a straightforward year-by-year chronicle. Towards the end of the Tang dynasty, private histories began to proliferate as the Bureau lost some of its control; unofficial histories written in the chronicle format appeared as a few scholars sought to rewrite or condense the often-lengthy dynastic histories. While the Tang historiographical apparatus could be stifling and resistant to innovation, it is noteworthy that it generated its own critics. Among these was Liu Zhiji (661–721), a near-contemporary of England's Bede, whose *Shitong* ('Comprehensive Perspectives on Historiography') is an especially perceptive commentary on history-writing. Bred to history from an early age, Liu's own career as an official historian was short. He grew deeply disillusioned with the Bureau, a 'refuge for idlers' and 'den for time-servers' from which he resigned. He despised the comfortable and easily corruptible lifestyle of its members and the vulnerability of the compilation process to political interference, whether by the emperor or by overly controlling chief ministers. Liu was also sceptical about the literary merits of collectively composed histories. Liu identified talent, knowledge and insight as the essential ingredients of the good historian, with truth and factuality being the highest goals to which that historian should aspire in writing; he also categorized historical genres more formally and organized all previous histories according to six 'schools'.

The historiographic contribution of the Song dynasty (960–1269) was just as formidable. Song historians have been praised for their work on the tools of 'modern' historical thinking. Song historians compiled the mandatory Veritable Records of each emperor, and they further developed the writing of gazetteers or *fangzhi* for individual administrative regions, including bibliographical, geographical, genealogical, biographical, historical and social information. They also produced no less than six comprehensive *Guoshi* ('national' histories in the limited sense that they comprised both ruling regimes and their territories), complete with annals, monographs and biographies. The dynasty produced perhaps the greatest Chinese historian since Sima Qian, another member of the Sima family, Sima Guang (1019–86). A politician and official of high standing until rivals drove him into retirement, Sima produced works on a variety of subjects, but his major legacy was the vast text, nearly two decades in the making, that goes by the name of *Zizhi Tongjian*. This title, bestowed on the work by Sima's own admiring and financially supportive emperor after the historian had recited some early sections of it at court, is usually translated as 'Comprehensive Mirror in Aid of Government'. Sima Guang had inherited some of Liu Zhiji's Tang-era dissatisfaction with the limits and quality of the Standard Histories, among which was surely their inability to capture a wider span of history than a single dynasty (a problem that would perplex late nineteenth-century Chinese scholars who would, as we will see further on, seek solutions from entirely outside their own country). He aspired to write a comprehensive (*tong*) general history of China back to the pre-Qin Warring States era; when finished, it covered the years 403 BC to AD 959. Where Sima Qian had solved the problem of organization by cutting his material multiple ways into annals, chronologies, biographies and so on, Sima Guang chose a simpler route which eliminated redundancy of coverage in order to bring into prominence the lessons of the past: a straightforward chronological account. He pressed the need to examine original evidence where possible rather than later works – an early articulation of the distinction between primary and secondary sources – and he evinced a severe scepticism towards the invocation of the supernatural as a causal agent. Sima Qian's work became a centrepiece of the Song historiographical legacy, which emphasized the practical lessons of history and the distillation of erudition into a usable past via topically arranged books such as encyclopedias. Knowledge of history became a critical part of the Chinese educational system all the way up to the imperial court. A system of imperial lectures or seminars on the lessons of history, and regular recitations of Sima Guang's and other works, would endure till the empire's end in 1911.

History developed much later in Japan (a recognizable 'nation' from the fifth century AD) than in China, and then not in the same forms, despite the adoption of Chinese script, the mass importation of Chinese learning, the influences of both Confucianism and Buddhism, and the frequent use of Chinese as the language of composition. The differences are important. It has sometimes been observed that while Confucian principles and Chinese historiographical models were adopted by the Japanese, none of the critical attitude to sources and to unverified traditions accompanied this importation and that to the contrary, most Japanese historians regarded it virtually as a duty to accept ancient traditions: the eighteenth-century historian and nationalist, Motoori Norinaga, who disliked the Chinese influences on his country and explicitly rejected Confucian source criticism, would advise his readers not to approach old books with a sceptical 'Chinese heart' (*karagokoro*). Moreover, where official history took some time to evolve in China, the Japanese connected history-writing with the imperial household right out of the starting gate, as a means of buttressing the relatively young Yamato dynasty. Private historical writing emerged much later, when the early tradition of official histories came to an abrupt halt in the early tenth century, rather than, as in China, in parallel with them.

The earliest extant historical texts date from the beginning of the Nara period (710–94): the *Kojiki* ('Record of Ancient Matters', completed AD 712) and *Nihon Shoki* ('Chronicles of Japan', otherwise known as *Nihongi*, comp. 720). The *Kojiki* was commissioned in 711, ostensibly by the Empress Gemmei, while the *Nihon Shoki* may have been the result (or a later version of that result) of the work that her father-in-law, the Emperor Temmu, had ordered. Both texts relayed a powerful mythology of the creation of the world and the subsequent foundation of the empire by the first human monarch, Jimmu, a direct descendant of the sun goddess. A more or less consistent theme of Japanese perceptions of the past, belief in the *Tenno* or emperor's divine ancestry would continue to be taught in twentieth-century Japanese schools. Both the *Kojiki* and *Nihon Shoki* begin their accounts from the creation of the world, drawing on legend, myth and oral tradition as well as on earlier documents that they purport to correct.

There are important differences between these two early works. The *Kojiki*, which has no clear chronology, ends about 628 while the *Nihon Shoki* (in contrast, almost relentlessly chronological) concludes in 697. The *Nihon Shoki* was intended to establish Japan on a world, or at least regional stage, on the wings of which loomed the Chinese juggernaut. It was composed in Chinese in a more explicit attempt to imitate Chinese historiography, including the tendency we noted earlier in Sima Qian to include multiple versions of the same event, introduced by phrases such as 'another work says' or 'in another place it says'. Its authors clearly used Chinese *Zhengshi* as both models and sources: the work borrows sections from Chinese works and converts them into speeches by Japanese rulers. By 901 the *Nihon Shoki* had been augmented by the five other Chinese-language works, again modelled on *Guoshi* and *Zhengshi*, that with it form the 'Six National Histories' or *Rikkokushi*.

By the late tenth century, the rather mechanical replication of Chinese dynastic histories in Japan was beginning to wear thin. The office in charge of producing a planned continuation of the *Rikkokushi* was abolished in 969. There are several reasons for this, but the most important is that in fundamental ways the Chinese system of historical writing, and in particular the use of the dynasty as the basic unit of the Standard History, was ill-suited to Japan. From the Japanese point of view, all emperors belonged to the same dynasty, being directly descended from Jimmu: both the *Kojiki*'s collected tales and the more chronologically organized *Nihon Shoki* presume the continuity of the imperial line rather than the cycle of dynastic rise and decay that characterizes the Chinese Standard Histories. Notwithstanding a number of minor rebellions, there was relatively little instability before the twelfth century. Changes in lineage within the dynasty were duly noted, and even the cycle of 'good first emperor/bad last emperor' was transplanted from China to Japan; but these changes did not constitute for Japanese writers a major shift in the 'Mandate of Heaven'. This linealism, and a degree of resistance to Chinese cultural dominance in spite of the influence of Confucianism, ensured that while its language was initially borrowed, the edifice of Chinese historical writing was never reconstructed wholesale in Japan. In this respect, there is a marked contrast here with neighbouring Korea, which recognized distinct dynasties and much more easily adapted Chinese historical writing, down to specific genres such as *sillok* (= *shilu*) and *chongsa* (= *Zhengshi*).

Beginning in the eleventh century, about midway through the Heian period (794–1185), a different type of history, written in Japanese, began to appear in the form of *monogatari*, stories composed in prose or verse. Some of these are closer to fiction than to history, providing another instance of the resistance of many earlier historical cultures to the imposition of rigid boundaries between the two. The *Rekishi monogatari* ('Historical Tales') consists of six works written by independent scholars and courtiers, sometimes following the chronicle form but departing considerably from the National Histories in scope and tone, and sometimes featuring a first-person narrator. A number, such as the group known as *Gunki monogatari* ('War Tales'), dealt with violent conflicts, and were often recited orally (not unlike the Homeric epics or the medieval French *chansons de geste*, which they resemble for their heroic values) before being committed to writing in prose form and often also painted. Five of these works remain extant, mainly dating from the twelfth century. The last in the series, and the longest, was *Taiheiki* ('Chronicle of Great Peace'), written somewhat later, in the mid-fourteenth century.

Among the most widely read among medieval Japanese historical writings were the *Gukansho* ('Jottings of a Fool', *c.* 1220) by the Buddhist monk Jien, and another Buddhist-influenced work, in the *Rekishi monogatari* genre, the early twelfth-century *Okagami* ('Great Mirror'). Jien (1155–1225) wrote in a time of great instability amid challenges to imperial authority by a rising warrior class; this drove him to search the past for underlying patterns, and it is his reflections on 'Reason' as an underlying cause of events in the Japanese past that are of greatest interest. It is difficult not to see some of the same concerns that arose in late Roman historiography and which would recur in subsequent times – how to reconcile a theoretically divine imperial power with the reality of a military determined to have direct influence on governance. The past itself was an ongoing process not of accidents and contingencies, but of the working out of something like 'Reason'. This was not, it must be stressed, the same sort of 'Reason' that European thinkers of the eighteenth and nineteenth centuries had in mind, but rather an impersonal law of the cyclical rise and fall of things (including states) within an overarching phase of decline; it had more in common with Polybius than with Hegel. The *Okagami* is similar in tone: framed as a conversation between two very old men, its author shared Jien's notion of decline, and the conviction that the world was well along in *mappo*, the last of the Buddhist Three Ages, a 10,000-year era of decay. Although it is the first Japanese-language historical work to imitate the annals–biography form of Chinese Standard Histories, *Okagami* was an anonymously written private work, not an official history like the *Rikkokushi*. Also unlike the National Histories (but like Jien's *Gukansho*), *Okagami* and its successor works (all with similar *kagami* or 'mirror' terms in their titles) were written in Japanese, and by individuals rather than committees.

In a later work, *Jinno Shotoki* ('Record of the Legitimate Succession of Divine Sovereigns', completed 1339), however, we have almost come full circle back to the original Japanese use of history in the eighth century to legitimize the imperial regime, and the work was much cited over the next several centuries as a call for loyalty to the emperor. Its author, Kitabatake Chikafusa (1293–1354), is one of the few medieval Japanese historians, apart from Jien, about whom we know more than his name. Chikafusa (he is usually referred to by his given name) was a former imperial advisor, warrior and nobleman who seems to have undertaken the task of writing his work while under siege in his home province and with access to only one work, 'an abridged imperial genealogy', though he was able to revise it a few years later. *Jinno Shotoki* is a review of the entire history of the imperial line, emperor by emperor, ending with the death of Emperor Go-Daigo (r. 1318–39) in the year the work was composed. Chikafusa's history was an unashamedly partisan attempt to promote support for the emperor over the powerful samurai (warrior) class. Chikafusa knew his Chinese history from works such as the *Shiji* and *Hanshu*, and he contrasted the kind of dynastic change that China had experienced and the resulting 'unspeakable' disorder with the stability of Japan's imperial line. Japan would always return to the same ruling house – even diversions into separate lineages were merely tributary streams which would eventually return to the main river. This notion of Japan's special status is worth highlighting here for two reasons: first, because we will see the theme recur in later Japanese historical thought; and second, because it resembles 'exceptionalist' arguments made in other parts of the world at different times, from the Israelite notion of a covenanted Chosen People, through Bede's comparable view of the Anglo-Saxons, down through early modern Protestant providentialism, and eventually modern German nationalism with its notion of a *Sonderweg* ('separate path') and nineteenth-century American convictions of Manifest Destiny.

The Age of the Chronicle: Historical Writing in Later Medieval Christendom

The long-standing disparagement of medieval historical writing for various sins of style, composition, alleged deficiency of a critical attitude to sources and outright reliability, was an attitude first taken by Renaissance humanists and echoed well into the twentieth century. It betrays a serious and unfair tendency to judge all historical writing by the standards of later times. Yet even while rejecting value-laden conclusions, one must concede that much medieval historiography does look odd to a modern reader. In a group of European historians that includes Thucydides or Tacitus at one end and Leopold von Ranke or Karl Marx at the other, virtually any historian writing between the late fifth and the mid-fifteenth centuries will seem, to differing degrees, rather alien. Various explanations have been adduced for the oddities of medieval histories, often focusing on chroniclers' tendency to paratactic composition, wherein multiple events, seemingly unrelated, follow one another, even in works that verge on continuous narrative.

The settling of kingdoms in western Europe during the eighth and ninth centuries more or less brought an end to the period of migrations, the establishment of territorial if not yet genuinely national boundaries, and the establishment of aristocratic and royal houses. By the year 1000 it is possible to speak of countries called 'England', 'Scotland' and 'France', all of which had kings, even if hereditary succession had not quite eradicated the older Germanic practices of elective monarchy. Other geographic regions would remain divided for many centuries to come. By the early tenth century, what passed for imperial power in central Europe rested with the Ottonians, a German Saxon line, while the French, as the northwestern Franks were now called, were ruled by the Capetians. An England unified in the tenth century by the kings of Wessex would spend two centuries defending itself against incursions from the Norsemen and Danes. The Iberian Peninsula, previously united under the Visigothic monarchy of Toledo, had meanwhile disintegrated into several competing kingdoms and now included a powerful Muslim presence in Andalusia.

Historiographically, it becomes possible at this point to highlight some major developments. The first and most important is a significant increase in the number of distinguishable genres, beyond the older distinctions between universal history and ecclesiastical history, but without anything like the classical Greek or Chinese strict attention to form and classification. The Middle Ages had available, especially in Latin Europe, a partial and disrupted classical heritage. On the one hand, they knew of and practised the teaching of classical rhetoric and were aware of distinctions in genre. The Anglo-Norman historian Orderic Vitalis would protest that his history was neither fictitious tragedy nor 'wordy comedy' but simply a record of different sorts of events for attentive readers. On the other hand, awareness of genre distinctions seems rarely to have been translated into historiographic practice. The very word *historia* now applied indiscriminately to secular history, religious history and to the historical books in the Bible. The term would soon include romance and other fictional works, and it is far from clear that medieval audiences made a distinction between the two or that they were bothered by the overlap.

The further from antiquity they found themselves, the greater the difficulty writers of history had with fitting accounts of newly emerged monarchies into the box of classical models. One trouble lay in the modest supply of such models. It is certainly not true that medieval historians were ignorant of ancient historiography, its practices and values, or that classical works were uniformly 'lost' till the Renaissance. To the contrary, there is a visible line – albeit sometimes a dotted and jagged one – from the ancients to the humanists, via the 'classicizing' late antique historians, down through most of the Middle Ages, including twelfth-century *romans d'antiquité* and thirteenth-century adaptations or translations of Lucan, Sallust, Suetonius and Caesar. Classical rhetoric and its devices, even including the invented speech, were routinely pressed into service, often with didactic intent. The early ninth-century court historian Nithard (d. 844), author of an account of events during the final years of the Carolingian state, had read Sallust, and similarly sought to preserve these recent occurrences for the benefit of both contemporary readers and posterity.

However, the supply of ancient authors was quite limited, often fragmentary, and frequently distorted through several centuries worth of scholarship and commentary. Few ancient historians apart from Sallust were known in whole to Latin Europeans, and the fragments and paraphrases contained in early medieval successors such as Bede or Gregory of Tours, or quoted by Byzantine scholars, were informative on a factual level but not much of a help to writing. For many authors, the simplest solution was to fall back on that tried and true unit of historical organization, the annal. As has been pointed out already, this was not the invention of unimaginative monks incapable of writing a continuous and connected narrative ('lives' aside) in the classical style, and from whom history had to be rescued with the rediscovery of classical Latin models in the Renaissance. Annals were an ancient form of historical writing, known through early Christian historians such as Eusebius and used in chronological and calendrical works such as the Easter Tables developed by Bede. The use of annals, when expanded and combined into the longer form of chronicles, seemed to resolve several problems at once. Chronology was straightforward, major dates and calendrical issues having been established by the string of chronographers from Eusebius to Bede. And annals freed the writer from having to do a number of things that we might see as important for a historian: to discriminate between the important and the ephemeral, and to tell the story of an event or a chain of events that lasted, as most do, beyond the bounds of a single year. Annals tended to have similar contents, ranging from reportage of omens and comets or severe storms, to the travels and wars of individual kings (and details on where they spent particular parts of the year such as Christmas); other matters, including comments on the lessons to be drawn from a particular event, or comparisons across time, were very much dependent on the skill and creativity of the historian and his ability to think outside of this almost literal 'box'. Alternative forms of historical writing, including hagiography and *gesta* or 'deeds' of great men, continued, but annals soon became the favoured mode for both recording current events and narrating past ones.

At the distance of a millennium, the most important cultural change to occur during the later Middle Ages lay in communications, specifically the transition away from the predominantly oral culture of earlier centuries towards one in which written texts and documents carried considerably more weight, and in which their preservation, transmission or even, when necessary, fabrication became necessary. This shift had profound implications for historiography. Most obviously, literacy gradually expanded beyond the upper clergy and monasteries. Systematic record-keeping increased in the eleventh and twelfth centuries, as the quantity of surviving documents demonstrates: commitments once solemnized by ritual or verbal promise were now also preserved on paper or parchment. This produced a wealth of material for historians living in later periods, though it should not be regarded as complete in any sense. Just as archivists and librarians today have to be selective in what they retain, their early second millennium forebears often jettisoned materials that no longer seemed relevant, thereby eradicating the memory of them permanently. Furthermore, oral means of communication remained in vigorous use in the transmission of historical narratives, especially in song and poetry, and for the next several centuries history would float between oral/aural modes of transmission and cognition on the one hand and written/visual ones on the other, with traffic between them in both directions as written history fed into oral tradition and thence back into writing. A simple manifestation of Europeans' enduring oral mindset is the tendency of many historians to think of the words that they wrote as matter to be listened to, not seen. 'I am going to tell you a great tale,' begins one fourteenth-century chronicle of lost Frankish glory, 'and if you will listen to me, I hope that it will please you.'

A further consequence of this complex communicative situation, and of the increased importance of written records, was a broadening of the older search for a 'usable' past – one from which lessons, or even proofs of ownership and territorial or dynastic legitimacy, could be drawn. Certain groups increasingly felt pressed to preserve, find or even produce from scratch historical documents in support of particular claims or assertions they wished to make about their present status and its roots in a remote or even immemorial antiquity – some documents were indeed taken not as foundational in their own right but rather as later codifications of traditional or customary rights and privileges granted at some unspecified earlier time. This documentary turn had benefits, of course, in the generation of new kinds of historical writing, but it also had pernicious side effects, since it generated a good deal of textual forgery, a practice that began its life in antiquity, but now flourished with few checks. If a supporting document was now useful, if not yet quite *de rigueur*, in this newly textual culture, then one often needed to be produced for inspection. Where it could not be found, or had never existed at all but 'ought to have', and even where its meaning was simply not clear enough, there were talented calligraphers and scholars willing to invent a document outright or creatively emend it, whether a cartulary containing records of monastic land transactions, the genealogy of an aristocratic family or, in the most famous case of all, the Donation of Constantine, an eighth- or ninth-century forgery that purported to be the genuine fourth-century gift of authority over

Latin Europe from the Emperor Constantine to Pope Sylvester I – and thus of great utility to the defence of papal supremacy over troublesome secular rulers. One should bear in mind first, that most forgeries, the Donation among them, were probably not created maliciously or with intent to deceive but with a desire to provide documentation in support of claims fervently held to be true; and second, that for the medieval European, there was no easy test by which falsity and truth could be assessed, whether it came from a written text, a picture or the word of witnesses.

Between 1095 and 1291 the epicentre of military activity, and consequently of historical writing, would shift eastward, its dominant engine being a new round of engagements with the Muslim world. Islam had made contact with Christian Europe early, its forces at one point advancing well into France. While this unquestionably produced useful cultural cross-fertilization in both directions, it also generated conflict between two expansionist religions, though a good deal of the warfare involved less spiritual motivations than territorial ambitions and aristocratic martial impulses thinly garbed in the cloak of holiness. The flashpoints included the Iberian Peninsula, into which North African Muslims or 'Moors' had expanded by the early eighth century, and the borders of the Byzantine Empire, which would finally fall in 1453 to the dominant Islamic power of the fifteenth through nineteenth centuries, the Ottoman Turks. But nowhere was such conflict more productive of historical writing than in that recurrent battleground, the Holy Land, during the period of the 'Crusades' from the late eleventh to the late thirteenth centuries.

To modern eyes a rather unsavoury early chapter in the history of troubled relations between Christianity and Islam, the Crusades were nonetheless productive of an enormous wealth of historical writing on both sides of the conflict. William of Tyre (*c*. 1130–90) set the bar high for subsequent Crusade chroniclers. William was a native of Jerusalem, an archbishop and a seasoned author who had previously written several historical works, mostly now lost. It is on his *History of Deeds Done Beyond the Sea* that his reputation rests. William's intent was both to praise the champions of the first two Crusades and to encourage readers in his present to renewed commitment to the cause. This was a long book, filled with vivid geographical descriptions and frequent allusions to and quotations from classical and Christian authors. These references were largely decorative – as William admitted, he was in uncharted territory, with 'no written source, either in Greek or Arabic' and thus had to depend for his information 'upon tradition alone'. The work would influence many later accounts of the Crusades, which incorporated his account of the First Crusade into their own. The two most famous lay-authored histories to emerge from the Crusades were both by men of high birth. The first of these was Geoffroi de Villehardouin (*c.* 1150 to *c.* 1213), who dictated in 1207 his own eyewitness account of the seizure of Constantinople three years earlier. It is one of the oldest extant texts in Old French, its style originating as much in the *chansons de geste* of an earlier age as in the chronicle. A century later the second of these men, Jean de Joinville (1224–1317), wrote an admiring if critical account of the heroic and pious French King Louis IX (r. 1226–70), whose close companion he had been during the Seventh Crusade.

Throughout the later Middle Ages, wars, both international and domestic, provided the single most potent stimulus for the writing of history, especially aristocratic chronicles ('aristocratic' implies audi-ence and subject rather than, necessarily, author), increasingly pre-sented in vernacular tongues. The Catalan Ramón Muntaner (*c.* 1270–1336) wrote a detailed account of his life as a soldier. The Castilian chancellor Pedro López de Ayala (1332–1407) turned in retirement to history, producing a translation of parts of Livy, a family genealogy and the collection of chronicles known as the *History of the Kings of Castile*. History composed in this key appealed to both rulers and their fighting nobility, alike members of a single social 'order' or 'estate'; it celebrated wealth, plunder and bloodshed, and commented matter-of-factly about military victories without much sensitivity to the human cost or to the morality of conqueror or victim. But at the same time, it perceived a wider significance to human actions. Perhaps the most widely read aristocratic works both at that time and since have been the narrative by Jean Froissart (1337? to after 1405) of the first phases of the Anglo-French Hundred Years' War (1337–1453) and the various vernacular Scots' accounts, in verse and prose, of the Scottish wars of independence against the English. Drawn in large measure on the oral testimony of participants and witnesses, Froissart's *Chronicles of France, England and Nearby Countries* remains a classic of European historiography, extraordinarily readable and entertaining. While Froissart himself was a priest, he had spent a good deal of his life in royal and noble households, and had absorbed the values of their inhabitants. It is not surprising that his *Chronicles* are much closer in both subject and language to Villehardouin and the thirteenth-century romances than to the works of monastic or secular clerical chroniclers.

As the Crusades wound down in the thirteenth century, and with them their historians' almost instinctual perception of warfare as a localized version of sacred conflict, the focus of much historical writing becomes decisively narrower. 'Christendom' began to cede centrality as an organizing concept to individual kingdoms or principalities, and a chivalric hero such as St Louis or even Charlemagne becomes less a devout soldier of the Church than a champion of his people, an upholder of courtly values and a bestower of wealth and favour on the military aristocracy. If there were no 'nations' in the modern, post-nineteenth-century sense of the word, there were at least national or patriotic sentiments. There is an observable trend, beginning no later than the mid-twelfth century, towards the refocusing of historical interests away from the Christian world as a whole and on to specific kingdoms' pasts, and to intra-Christian, rather than Islamo-Christian, conflicts. There were exceptions, and universal history, having peaked in the twelfth century, by no means disappeared. It was read at late medieval courts, and provided an obvious channel through which clerical authors could offer secular princes advice; new examples appear right through the period. But even its authors narrowed their focus down to imperial or national history as they approached their own times: their 'universality' tended to be temporal and theological rather than spatial. Conversely, chroniclers of the twelfth to fourteenth centuries, such as the Danish cleric Saxo Grammaticus (*c.* 1150–1220), not all of whom were comforted by the growth of hereditary monarchical authority (which occurred just as often at the expense of the Church as of feudal magnates), continued to situate nationally based accounts within a Eusebian framework of *historia mundi*.

There are similarly great examples of ecclesiastical history, such as the enormous *Historia ecclesiastica* by the Benedictine monk Orderic Vitalis (1075–1142), which range widely, continuing to use the Church as the common link between multiple political realms, and envisioning mundane events as signposts along an eschatological highway; but universal history in the Eusebian mould was in decline. By the mid-fourteenth century, the English monk Ranulf Higden (*c.* 1280–1364), in writing his *Policronicon* was providing a summation of world history rather than a new contribution to it. The huge subsequent

popularity of that work, soon translated into English, suggests a ready
market for a 'quick summary' of the universal story rather than the
continued vitality of the genre. The expansion of readership into the
laity was beginning to feed back into the writing of history, as readers'
interests guided authors' choice of subject, a trend that would be
significantly enhanced by the arrival of printing.

Simply put, the varieties of historical literature were beginning to
proliferate, as were both the forms it took (verse and prose) and the
languages in which it was written. Among the regional variants that do
not have obvious counterparts elsewhere, the twenty-three Norse
(Norwegian and Icelandic) sagas of the twelfth to fourteenth centuries
(initially an oral record but committed to writing after about 1150)
present an especially interesting departure from the prose chronicle and
form a link between the world of the annalist and that of the heroic
poet; they are the major source for modern Norway's medieval past,
though allowances have to be made for the propagandistic role they
were designed to serve. Culminating in Snorri Sturluson's (1179–1241)
compendious *Heimskringla* ('History of the Kings of Norway'), itself
a reference point for Norwegian national consciousness in later centuries, the sagas existed alongside Latin prose works such as Saxo
Grammaticus' *Gesta Danorum* ('Deeds of the Danes').

Outside of Crusader literature, the preponderance of histories written during the twelfth, thirteenth and early fourteenth centuries almost
invariably concern a particular nationality/ethnicity or region.
The Latin-language historians of England may serve as an example.
William of Malmesbury (*c.* 1095 to *c.* 1143), widely regarded as one of
the more perceptive and critical of medieval monastic chroniclers,
wrote a number of historical works over a career mainly spent as
a librarian, which gave him privileged access to materials. All of his
works are devoted to the history of England, the past of which is taken
as naturally involving *both* ecclesiastical and secular matters. The same
applied to the long line of Benedictine monks at St Alban's Abbey, from
Roger of Wendover (d. 1236) and Matthew Paris (*c.* 1200–59) in the
thirteenth century down to Thomas Walsingham (d. *c.* 1422) in the
early fifteenth century: all were relentlessly Anglocentric, however
variable the quality of their judgment and use of sources or originality
of their writing. A textual description such as this does little justice to
the experience of a reader, for whom the vivid and lush illustrations in
many of the extant manuscripts of these later medieval chronicles

would have been as striking and powerful as the prose they were intended to illuminate.

Late medieval monarchs increasingly saw the utility in history, beyond its moral, panegyrical and entertainment value, as they solidified control and pushed back against a resistant Church and unruly aristocrats. Some literally took the matter of providing histories into their own hands, including a number of Iberian kings (Castilian, Aragonese and Catalan) virtually from Visigothic times up to the arrival of the Habsburgs in the sixteenth century. Others sponsored new histories. Among the most celebrated are those compiled under the direction of Alfonso X 'The Learned' of Castile and León (r. 1252–84), including a vast six-book universal history called *General Estoria* and the *Estoria de España*. Alfonso's 'history workshop' – the arena for several competitive and argumentative minds rather than a table for simple 'scissors-and-paste' assemblage – generated a number of other works over the ensuing decades, all of which constitute what is known as the Alphonsine Chronicles. In France the achievement is even more remarkable, albeit lacking any royal author. The roughly counterpart series to England's St Alban's chronicles or to the various Spanish royal histories was a very different product created at the abbey of Saint-Denis. The abbey had a distinguished historiographic record and an inclination to royalism. Its twelfth-century abbot, Suger (*c.* 1081–1151), was himself a remarkable historian, intimate advisor of the forceful King Louis VI ('the Fat', r. 1081–1137), and biographer of that king and his son. During Suger's abbacy (1122–51) the monks compiled from earlier sources a complete history of France from which sprang a continuous set of chronicles concerning the Capetian kings. In contrast with East Asian historiography, this sort of 'official history' had hitherto been a rarity in Europe, certain Spanish exceptions aside.

The Latin originals produced at Saint-Denis were rearranged and translated in the late thirteenth century by a monk known only as Primat into a lavishly illuminated vernacular series called the *Grandes Chroniques de France* ('Great Chronicles of France'), with additional materials added from other vernacular histories. The *Grandes Chroniques* appeared in instalments beginning in 1274 and ending in 1461. Their dissemination was restricted by the monarchy, the translation being for the benefit of courtiers untrained in Latin, rather than a wider readership, and the printing of the *Grandes Chroniques* for the first time at Paris in 1477 brought the tradition to an end at a time when the newer humanist form of historical writing was beginning to make its presence known in France. In both the *Grandes Chroniques* and their Latin originals we have something not dissimilar to Chinese Standard Histories or the early Japanese Six National Histories: a carefully woven, national view of the past framed as an uninterrupted sequence of rulers since the election of the mythical king Pharamond.

A consequence, and perhaps also a cause, of this historiographic nationalism, was the resurgence of semi-fictional histories in Latin providing elaborate accounts of the foundation of kingdoms and even some early theories of racial descent. The most notorious work of this sort, arising from the growing rivalry between England and France, was the *History of the Kings of Britain* composed about 1136 by Geoffrey of Monmouth (*c.* 1100–54). This was the source of much of the whole late medieval (and modern) Arthurian legend as well as a line of entirely fictitious British monarchs leading up to the Saxon invasions. Building on an early ninth-century text known as the *Historia Brittonum*, Geoffrey cited as his main authority a 'certain very ancient book written in the British language [i.e. Welsh]', of which there has been no trace since. Geoffrey filled in gaps in the history, providing very few actual dates but, perhaps in imitation of Bede, inserting into his narrative synchronisms between events in Britain and those elsewhere, all of which made the scholarship look rather impressive. Thus a description of the reign of Ebraucus 'who was very tall and a man of remarkable strength' and to whom the foundation of the city of York (Latin: *Eboracum*) would be ascribed, is followed by the information that 'At that time King David was reigning in Judea and Silvius Latinus was King in Italy. In Israel, Gad, Nathan and Asaph were the prophets.'

Geoffrey's book has become almost infamous, but it was neither unique nor, despite its massive popularity, was it accepted without challenge by contemporaries. Indeed, before the twelfth century was out Geoffrey's veracity was attacked by a younger contemporary, William of Newburgh (1136 to *c.* 1201), who made the discrediting of Geoffrey's history – in large measure because it departed from the revered account in Bede – the subject of a prologue to his own *History of English Affairs*. Geoffrey's work exemplified a tradition of history-writing the main object of which was to provide a glorious past for a particular kingdom or people. His Latin prose history proved astonishingly fecund, eventually spinning off a whole series of vernacular 'Brut' tales (so-called for Brutus the Trojan) in verse and prose over the next three centuries. That doubts were raised about his reliability, and that Geoffrey himself felt obliged to tie his statements to a notional ancient source, is a proof, were such needed, that the medieval mind was quite capable of discerning *fabula* from *historia*.

Similar examples come from central and eastern Europe, areas that had shown scant historiographic activity independent of Rome or Constantinople during the first millennium. The Bohemian priest Cosmas of Prague (1056–1125) laid the grounds for later generations of Czech nationalism by summarizing several centuries of legends and saints' stories in the *Chronica Bohemorum*, tracing his people's origins back to one 'Bohemus'. The beginnings of Russian historical writing can be traced to a twelfth-century Kievan work usually called the *Russian Primary Chronicle*, whence sprang much Russian historical literature for the next several centuries. To the southeast, Byzantine historical writing entered on a second phase of intense activity beginning in the eleventh century. A disproportionate number of the newer writers were persons of very high or even royal status. The Emperor John VI Kantakouzenos (or Cantacuzenus, r. 1347–54), who retired to a monastery, wrote an extensive history, but he was neither the first nor the most distinguished member of an imperial family to do so. Among these, the princess Anna Komnene (or Comnena, 1083–1153), who was married to another Byzantine historian and continued her husband's work following his death, merits particular attention. She is among the very few women in Europe to write, under her own name, a history of substantial length before the eighteenth century – and one still readily available in modern editions. The *Alexiad* is an account both of her own early life and the reign of her father, Emperor Alexios I Komnenos.

Urban readers had an interest in their communities' pasts, and what often began as records of civic officials evolved in the fourteenth and fifteenth centuries into urban chronicles, most of which were written in tongues other than Latin. The urban chronicle first sprouted in Italy in the eleventh and twelfth centuries, flourished during the era of autonomous Italian city-states in the thirteenth and fourteenth centuries, and fully blossomed elsewhere in Europe during the fifteenth and early sixteenth centuries. Often developing from lists of civic officials or simple annals, and mainly written by laymen, these chronicles recorded local events in varying degrees of detail and were an important counterpart, for the emerging middling sort of merchants and townsmen, to the more learned chronicles of the monastic and secular clergy, or to aristocratic works. Of particular note is the Florentine merchant and sometime soldier Giovanni Villani (c. 1275–1348) who set out to write a chronicle that, unlike previous Florentine chronicles, had an overarching theme, which was the greatness of Florence and its place as rightful successor to the stature of a now-decaying Rome. With its identification of causes in human actions and motives rather than only providence, and its ruminations on the significance of fortune in the rise and fall of men and states, Villani's *Istoria* edges us closer to the humanist historiography of the next two centuries.

Nowhere did the urban chronicle proliferate more than in German-speaking territories, the output of which is extant in many volumes of the *Monumenta Germaniae Historica*. A great many of the authors were not native to the places about which they wrote and they were also occupationally diverse. Many towns even had an official chronicle, kept up over multiple generations: the successive fifteenth-century authors of the Council Chronicle (*Ratschronik*) of Lübeck, all of them clergy, built on a pre-existing work by a local Franciscan. The fifteenth-century urban chronicles, in contrast to earlier examples, were mainly a category of works written (or later printed) in a town, rather than a type of history *about* a particular town. The physician Hartmann Schedel's *Nuremberg Chronicle* (1493), among the earliest historical works to roll off a printing press, is so-called not because it was about Nuremberg (it was actually a universal history, printed in both Latin and German editions) but because it was published there. The urban chronicles often tell us less about the towns themselves than they do about the awakening public interest in history, which was now spreading unmistakably beyond its traditional audience of royal and aristocratic courts and monastic scriptoria. The growing interest in history can be illustrated in the success of a Carthusian monk named Werner Rolewinck, whose *Fasciculus Temporum* (literally 'Small Bundles of Time') – its text made more accessible by a presentation that looks something like a modern 'infographic' – went through over forty editions in its author's lifetime alone.

Another sector of the laity, the aristocratic houses of the great feudal kingdoms, continued to develop an interest in both history and – especially as new families rose in rank and prosperity – genealogy, that would be sustained for two or three centuries. The same level of creativity that had spun tales of Brutus and Francion and chronicles of the Crusades would be deployed to provide noble families with genealogical rolls and sometimes full-scale histories reaching back to Noah or Adam, or to Brutus and thence the Trojans. The dukes of Burgundy, the spectacularly wealthy rulers of much of northern France and the Low Countries during the fourteenth and fifteenth centuries, developed a remarkable collection of historical materials, with the history of France given pride of place. Duke Philip the Good's (r. 1419–67) court in particular regularly hosted historians seeking to present their work to him, and the duke sponsored a host of chroniclers. The pay for their labours was often not especially good: Enguerrand de Monstrelet (*c.* 1400–53) received only a modest sum for his lengthy continuation of Froissart.

But courtly historical writing was not all about flattery and display. By the mid-fifteenth century, in the context of the struggles of the French crown with English power and with Burgundian independence, one begins to discern a sharper political analysis in certain historians such as Philippe de Commynes (1447–1511), who anticipate the flavour of Renaissance humanist historiography. Commynes signifies both a new kind of historical narrative, and a return to the larger international canvas of previous centuries. Like the most accomplished Italian historian of the next half-century, Francesco Guicciardini, and harking back to Polybian *symploke*, Commynes saw the interplay of individual nations as part of a larger whole, namely Europe, though he did so from the perspective of a firm adherent to Louis XI and his successor Charles VIII (r. 1483–98). Writing after Louis' death, and frequently intruding his own persona into the narrative, Commynes crafted his subject as a balance of virtues and flaws; Louis comes off looking shrewd and politic rather than merely crafty and deceitful. In comparing this with the rather negative judgment of political duplicity that one finds in chroniclers only a couple of centuries or so previously (one recalls William of Tyre) it is clear that we are no longer in the world of devout piety and chivalry. European historiography had arrived in the world of Machiavelli.

Conclusion

Some key themes are worth highlighting here before we move on to the early modern era (and a significant expansion of geographic scope). The first point is that historical writing from late antiquity to the mid-second millennium AD flourished alike in circumstances of political and social instability, or in times of good order. The second is that religion and secular interests cut across each other rather than dwelling in entirely separate spheres, an interplay manifest in historiography from most of the regions examined. The third is that the cumulative achievements of Western historical writing to this point, while better known, seem much less impressive when set against those of China and Islam than when examined on their own. While there were capable chroniclers, lay and clerical, in significant numbers, historiography remained confined to a relatively limited number of forms. In contrast, the variety of different genres developed by the Chinese in particular – including encyclopedias, biographies and historical novels, and the Song historians' sophisticated linking of history and philosophy – command our respect. And there is similarly little in Christian Europe to compare with the intellectual range, perceptive observations and capacity to generalize that Islam produced in Ibn Khaldun, China in Liu Zhiji or Sima Guang, or Japan in Jien.

Mention of such comparison brings us to the fourth, and most important point: that many historians were already aware of, and a few were substantially influenced by, other cultures, whether one thinks of Christian–Muslim contacts, Muslim–Mongol, Sino–Mongol or Indo–Muslim. The extent of this contact would increase considerably in the ensuring three centuries. During this next period, the reality of two large, unexplored continents in the Americas, combined with more sustained ventures to the Far East, forced Europeans and Asians alike to rethink their picture of the world's history. It also made at least a few of them realize that their own modes of historicity were neither entirely unique nor universally shared.

QUESTIONS FOR DISCUSSION

1. What aspects of ancient historical practice were taken up by medieval authors? Which ones were abandoned?
2. How did rulers and social elites throughout the regions surveyed use history to buttress their authority? How did others use it as a means of resistance?
3. To what degree do you think medieval readers believed legends of ancient founders such as the Trojans?
4. What features do Christian, Muslim and East Asian (China, Japan, Korea) historical thought and writing share? In what ways do they differ?
5. Did the historical cultures depicted in this chapter make a firm distinction between history and literature?
6. How important was history in different parts of the world compared to other forms of writing such as religious works?
7. To what degree did differing concepts of chronology and time affect the writing of history during these centuries?

Further Reading

General

Deliyannis, Deborah Mauskopf (ed.), *Historiography in the Middle Ages* (Leiden and Boston, 2012)

Dunphy, R. G. (ed.), *The Encyclopedia of the Medieval Chronicle*, 2 vols (Leiden and Boston, 2010)

Foot, Sarah and Chase Robinson (eds), *The Oxford History of Historical Writing*, Vol. 2: *400–1400* (Oxford, 2012)

Neville, Leonora, *Guide to Byzantine Historical Writing* (Cambridge, 2018)

Smalley, Beryl, *Historians in the Middle Ages* (London, 1974)

Historical Writing in Christian and Barbarian Europe

Chesnut, Glenn F., *The First Christian Histories: Eusebius, Socrates, Sozomen, Theodoret, and Evagrius*, 2nd edn (Macon, GA, 1986)

Cox, Patricia L., *Biography in Late Antiquity: A Quest for the Holy Man* (Berkeley, CA, 1983)

Goffart, Walter A., *The Narrators of Barbarian History (AD 550–800): Jordanes, Gregory of Tours, Bede, and Paul the Deacon* (Princeton, NJ, 1988)

Hen, Yitzhak and Matthew Innes (eds), *The Uses of the Past in the Early Middle Ages* (Cambridge, 2000)

Kempshall, Matthew, *Rhetoric and the Writing of History, 400–1500* (Manchester and New York, 2011)

McKitterick, Rosamond, *History and Memory in the Carolingian World* (Cambridge, 2004)

Murray, Alexander Callander (ed.), *After Rome's Fall: Narrators and Sources of Early Medieval History* (Toronto, 1998)

Treadgold, Warren, *The Early Byzantine Historians* (Basingstoke, 2007)

Islamic Historiography from Muhammad to Ibn Khaldun

Khalidi, Tarif, *Arab Historical Thought in the Classical Period* (Cambridge, 1994)

Lewis, Bernard and P. M. Holt (eds), *Historians of the Middle East* (London, 1962)

Mahdi, Muhsin, *Ibn Khaldun's Philosophy of History* (1957; Chicago, IL, 1964)

Meisami, Julie Scott, *Persian Historiography to the End of the Twelfth Century* (Edinburgh, 1999)

Robinson, Chase F., *Islamic Historiography* (Cambridge, 2003)

Rosenthal, Franz, *A History of Muslim Historiography*, 2nd edn (Leiden, 1968)

Simon, Heinrich, *Ibn Khaldun's Science of Human Culture*, trans. F. Baali (Lahore, 1978)

Forms of History in Southern Asia

Ganguly, D. K., *History and Historians in Ancient India* (New Delhi, 1984)
Hardy, Peter, *Historians of Medieval India: Studies in Indo-Muslim Historical Writing*, 2nd edn (New Delhi, 1997)
Hazra, Kanai Lal, *The Buddhist Annals and Chronicles of South-East Asia* (New Delhi, 1986)
Perrett, Roy W., 'History, Time, and Knowledge in Ancient India', *History and Theory* 38.3 (1999): 307–21
Rocher, Ludo, *A History of Indian Literature*, Vol. 2, fasc. 3: *The Puranas*, ed. Jan Gonda (Wiesbaden, 1986)
Singh, G. P., *Ancient Indian Historiography: Sources and Interpretations* (New Delhi, 2003)
Thapar, Romila, 'Some Reflections on Early Indian Historical Thinking', in Jörn Rüsen (ed.), *Western Historical Thinking: An Intercultural Debate* (New York and Oxford, 2002), 178–86
   The Past Before Us: Historical Traditions of Early North India (Cambridge, MA, 2013)

Historiography in East Asia from the Tang to the Yuan

Bentley, John R., *Historiographical Trends in Early Japan* (Lewiston, NY, 2002)
Brownlee, John S., *Political Thought in Japanese Historical Writing: From Kojiki (712) to Tokushi Yoron (1712)* (Waterloo, Ontario, 1991)
Ch'oe Yŏng-ho, 'An Outline History of Korean Historiography', *Korean Studies* 4 (1980): 1–27
Ji Xiao-bin, *Politics and Conservatism in Northern Song China: The Career and Thought of Sima Guang (A.D. 1019–1086)* (Hong Kong, 2005)
Lee, Thomas H. C. (ed.), *The New and the Multiple: Sung Senses of the Past* (Hong Kong, 2004)
Ng, On-cho and Q. Edward Wang, *Mirroring the Past: The Writing and Use of History in Imperial China* (Honolulu, 2005)
Pulleyblank, E. G., 'Chinese Historical Criticism: Liu Chih-chi and Ssu-ma Kuang', in W. G. Beasley and E. G. Pulleyblank (eds), *Historians of China and Japan* (London, 1961), 135–66
Robinson G. W., 'Early Japanese Chronicles: The Six National Histories', in Beasley and Pulleyblank (eds), *Historians of China and Japan*, 213–28

Taro Sakamoto, *The Six National Histories of Japan*, trans. J. S. Brownlee (Vancouver and Tokyo, 1991)
Twitchett, Denis Crispin, *The Writing of Official History under the T'ang* (Cambridge, 1993)

The Age of the Chronicle: Historical Writing in Later Medieval Christendom

Ainsworth, Peter F., *Jean Froissart and the Fabric of History: Truth, Myth, and Fiction in the Chroniques* (Oxford, 1990)
Albu, Emily, *The Normans in their Histories* (Woodbridge, 2001)
Archambault, Paul, *Seven French Chroniclers: Witnesses to History* (Syracuse, NY, 1974)
Ashe, Laura, *Fiction and History in England, 1066–1200* (Cambridge, 2007)
Aurell, Jaume, *Authoring the Past: History, Autobiography, and Politics in Medieval Catalonia* (Chicago, IL, 2012)
Blacker, Jean, *The Faces of Time: Portrayal of the Past in Old French and Latin Historical Narrative of the Anglo-Norman Regnum* (Austin, TX, 1994)
Given-Wilson, Chris, *Chronicles: The Writing of History in Medieval England* (London, 2004)
Glenn, Jason, *Politics and History in the Tenth Century: The Work and World of Richer of Rheims* (Cambridge, 2005)
Gransden, Antonia, *Historical Writing in England*, 2 vols (Ithaca, NY, 1974–82)
Linehan, Peter, *History and the Historians of Medieval Spain* (Oxford, 1993)
Neville, Leonora, *Anna Komnene: The Life and Work of a Medieval Historian* (Oxford, 2016)
Partner, Nancy, *Serious Entertainments: The Writing of History in Twelfth-Century England* (Chicago, IL, 1977)
Shopkow, Leah, *History and Community: Norman Historical Writing in the Eleventh and Twelfth Centuries* (Washington, DC, 1997)
Southern, R. W., collectively entitled, 'Aspects of the European Tradition of Historical Writing', reprinted in *History and Historians: Selected Papers of R. W. Southern*, ed. R. J. Bartlett (Oxford, 2004), 11–85
Spiegel, Gabrielle, *The Past as Text: The Theory and Practice of Medieval Historiography* (Baltimore, MD, 1997)
Treadgold, Warren, *The Middle Byzantine Historians* (Basingstoke, 2013)
Wood, Ian and G. A. Loud (eds), *Church and Chronicle in the Middle Ages* (London, 1991)

MILESTONES

1439 Leonardo Bruni's *Twelve Books on the History of the Florentine People* completed, establishing a new classical model for narrative history

1440 Lorenzo Valla discredits the Donation of Constantine

early 16th cent. Niccolò Machiavelli and Francesco Guicciardini's major works

1535 Gonzalo Fernández de Oviedo y Valdes' *General History of the Indies*

1552 Bartolomé de Las Casas' *Brief Account of the Destruction of the Indies*

1559–74 *Magdeburg Centuries* is published

1566 Jean Bodin's *Method* is published

1586 Juan González de Mendoza's *History of the Great and Mighty Kingdom of China* is published

1588 Cardinal Cesare Baronio's *Ecclesiastical Annals* is published

1590 José de Acosta's *Natural and Moral History of the Indies* is published

1598 Abu'l Fazl 'Allami's *Book of Akbar* is completed

1615 Felipe Guaman Poma de Ayala finishes *First New Chronicle and Good Government*

1617 El Inca Garcilaso's *General History of Peru*

1629 Iskandar Beg's history of the reign of Shah 'Abbas

1681 Jacques-Bénigne Bossuet's *Discourse on Universal History*; Jean Mabillon's *Six Books on Diplomatic*

1697 First edition of Pierre Bayle's *Historical and Critical Dictionary* is published

1698–9 Mustafa Na'îmâ is commissioned to write the *The History by Naîmâ*

1702 Cotton Mather's *Magnalia Christi Americana; or the Ecclesiastical History of New England* is published

1702–4 Earl of Clarendon's *History of the Rebellion* is published posthumously

1724 Jean-François Lafitau's *Customs of the American Savage, Compared with the Customs of Earliest Times* is published

3 | The Sense of the Past, 1450–1700

Renaissance and Seventeenth-Century Europe

European historians from the fifteenth to the seventeenth century believed that the primary purpose of history was didactic. While medieval writers considered history to have an educative function, its place in their hierarchy of learned culture was middling at best. The Renaissance promoted history several rungs up the intellectual ladder and made it in equal parts a stern enforcer of the status quo and a powerful weapon to brandish in pursuit of radical and often violent alterations to the accepted order of things. Knowledge of the past both exalted tradition and at the same time promoted change, not as today in the pursuit of 'progress' or 'innovation' but generally the opposite – recovering aspects of an idealized prior period.

Renaissance humanists enthusiastically appropriated Greek and especially Roman authors as their models of style, genre and suitable content. This was true across many areas of intellectual activity, but the rediscovery of classical texts and categories would have wide-ranging effects on historical thought and writing, not least because from the mid-fifteenth century, the advent of printing permitted the easier replication of texts in larger numbers. Over the course of two centuries this would also create something new: a public appetite for history well beyond the princely courts and noble households. Yet history still remained overwhelmingly the property of only one sex, a historic imbalance now deepened by emerging notions of gender and reinforced by humanist works which parroted the ancient notion that the historian must be a *man* of affairs living in the public arenas of politics, battlefields and commerce, not the private spheres of children, religious devotion and domesticity.

The Renaissance signalled a shift in thinking about the past in relation to the present. A sense of remoteness from classical times and an urge to reconnect with them bestowed in humanist writers a temporal perspective absent in much medieval historiography. By the early seventeenth century a 'sense of anachronism' is routinely if inconsistently discernible in various media, for instance in art and in drama, though it was still possible in the late sixteenth century for a Spaniard, Pedro Mexía, to write a popular history of the Roman emperors from Augustus to Charles V as if these were all members of a single dynasty. A more acute visual sense of the past was slower to develop, though archaeological discoveries, especially the ruins of Rome and of former Roman encampments across Europe, soon stimulated this too. The art of the time displays an ambivalence to this new perspective with respect to antiquity, often simultaneously recognizing the distance and eliding it by placing obviously non-contemporaneous figures together – but now in a conscious artifice. Much more quickly, however, there developed a sense of *linguistic* change. The humanists of the fifteenth century acknowledged, and often despaired of, a *medium aevum* standing between them and antiquity. Above all, they were devoted in the first instance to the restoration of Latin to its classical purity, though the notion that a language could be transplanted in an archaic and frozen form into a different era actually negated 1,500 years of gradual change and introduced a different sort of anachronism.

One of the early consequences of this new study of language was the realization that all was not well with the textual and documentary heritage of the previous millennium. Documentary forgeries such as the Donation of Constantine, discredited by the greatest philologist of the mid-fifteenth century, Lorenzo Valla (*c.* 1407–57), were exposed through analysis of their language and, eventually, through study of their physical aspects including handwriting. More recent late-medieval spurious texts began to fall by the wayside, including the relatively recent contributions of an infamous textual mischief-maker named Giovanni Nanni (*c.* 1432–1502), better known as 'Annius of Viterbo', whose *Antiquities* purported to include the lost ancient writings of the Babylonian Berossus (see above, p. 17). These exposures were not entirely comforting, as they provided a stark reminder to contemporaries of how little they knew, or could ever know, about the remote past.

The rediscovery of particular ancient historians, and the ebbs and flows in popularity among them, restored the writing of history as continuous narrative, in neoclassical Latin and vernacular languages.

With it came an increasing hostility towards medieval historical writers for a range of sins including bad Latin, inability to judge the causes of actions, a failure to discern the important from the trivial and a credulous acceptance of hearsay and fiction. This distancing posture was an exaggeration, accepted far too easily by subsequent ages, but it was highly effective. Although the term 'chronicle' remained in common usage in several languages, by the late seventeenth century the annalistically organized texts that had dominated historical writing for nearly a thousand years had become in many parts of Europe a relic of a past age, its specimens evolved from a living genre into a source.

The most obvious models for humanist history-writing were to be found in antiquity. One by one, reformed Latin editions of Roman historians appeared, with the Greeks close behind as émigré Byzantine scholars trained attentive Italian pupils; thus the Florentine humanist Poggio Bracciolini would translate Xenophon and parts of the *Bibliotheca historica* of Diodorus Siculus, in addition to composing his own Latin history of Florence. By 1700, over two thousand editions of twenty Greek and Roman historians were in print. Both the quantity of classical work and its quality made Renaissance writers reluctant to reinvent the ancient wheel of historiography – what vain fool thought he could improve, at some centuries' distance, on Tacitus and Livy? So instead, they turned to narrating the post-classical past, and to non-narrative, 'antiquarian' types of scholarship (see below, pp. 93–95).

The beginnings of humanist historical narrative, in Latin, and modelled on the ancients, are by consensus located in the early fifteenth century. Leonardo Bruni of Arezzo (*c.* 1369–1444) is justly singled out both for the quality of his historical writing and for the originality of its form. Chancellor of the Florentine Republic from 1427 till his death, Bruni presented his *Historiae Florentini populi libri xii* ('Twelve Books on the History of the Florentine People') to Florence's ruling council in 1439. Its author's self-conscious realization that he was doing something fundamentally different from the historians of the immediately previous centuries signalled a break with the medieval chronicle. Bruni followed Polybius, Thucydides and Sallust, and eschewed the model of late medieval chroniclers such as Giovanni Villani. He soon found imitators in Venice, Milan, Ferrara, Mantua, Rome and other cities from the mid-fifteenth to the late sixteenth centuries, and bit by bit, often through itinerant Italians employed in foreign courts, the fashion spread to other parts of Europe.

The political crises and religious wars that afflicted Europe for nearly three centuries provided a profound stimulus to historical writing in general. They also occasioned something else: a subtle and gradual shift in thinking – barely noticeable at first – about the relation of past to present, and a new emphasis on their aetiological or *linear* connection. To put it another way, historians, and eventually their readers, gradually began to comprehend the past as a road that brings us from then to now, in contrast to the more traditional emphasis on using the past (even when its events were presented in a chronological series) as a source of examples and models of behavior; from that more traditional perspective, the distinctive temporal context of events and persons had been of less moment than similarities and moral values which transcended time and place. The contrast between these two ways of looking at the past is nowhere better illustrated than by comparing two near-contemporary Florentine historians caught up in political crises, specifically their city's transition from republic to monarchy and the disorders of war and invasion. Francesco Guicciardini (1483–1540) and his more famous older contemporary, Niccolò Machiavelli (1469–1527) each wrote histories of Florence, and in Guicciardini's case, a lengthier history of Italy. Both men authored works of political wisdom, Machiavelli memorably yoking together examples from the recent and remote past in *The Prince* and *Discourses*. Guicciardini, Machiavelli's more pessimistic junior, had as a young man written a history of Florence; but he grew less interested than Machiavelli in pursuing the history of his city back to barbarian times than in narrating the unfolding of its and all Italy's current troubles (the invasions by French and Spanish armies and the erosion and collapse of republican independence). Perhaps as a consequence of this Thucydidean focus on the very recent past, he was more attentive to detail and, unusually for his day, more sceptical about the capacity of past examples to serve the present, owing to variations of circumstance between superficially similar historical situations. 'How wrong it is to cite the Romans at every turn', he commented in his *Ricordi*, a set of maxims and thoughts. 'For any comparison to be valid, it would be necessary to have a city with conditions like theirs, and then to govern it according to their example. In the case of a city with different qualities, the comparison is as much out of order as it would be to expect a jackass to race like a horse.'

Repeatedly in early modern Europe, in the face of often abrupt political change, historians would narrate the recent or remote past to explain the origins of the world in which they lived, or the causes of recent events, as opposed to merely recounting an entertaining and exemplary story. In early sixteenth-century Italy, several decades worth of grand humanist narratives *après* Livy had already been produced; historians had almost run out of things to write about when the French and Spanish invasions forced a refocusing of their attention on recent events, in the manner of Guicciardini. A century later, another Italian, Enrico Caterino Davila (1576–1631), provided a similar account of the French religious wars of the late sixteenth century in which he had participated. The Frenchman Jacques-Auguste de Thou (1553–1617) was among many participants in events to pen a *History of his Own Time*, while a few decades later, England's earl of Clarendon (1609–74) wrote a history of England's mid-century civil wars, setting a new standard for the elegant narration of a recent event in Thucydidean style.

None of this, of course, meant that the use of history to provide examples and guidance was dead. Far from it: this remained the primary reason adduced for writing or reading it. However, the way in which examples were treated was subtly altered. The isolated historical case, removed from its narrative, proved very popular to sixteenth-century readers who would arrange extracts and examples from a wide variety of sources into 'commonplace books'. By 1700, however, readers were more reluctant to rely on characters and incidents removed from the contexts in which their actions had occurred, and much life-writing (or biography as we now call it – the term did not yet exist) begins to situate its subjects within a historical narrative. A further change is noticeable: historical 'characters' in the sixteenth and seventeenth centuries are increasingly judged not according to a set of criteria derived from medieval standards, themselves underwritten by Christianity, such as piety, charity and honour, but according to newer, pragmatic ones such as judgment, 'prudence' and even financial prosperity.

Some of those interested in the past went beyond even the library and the archive. The discovery of material sources including physical ruins, statuary, coins and buildings in Italy and elsewhere nurtured an ancillary branch of historical study often referred to by the generic title 'antiquarianism'. Its origins lay in philology, but also in sensory perception of the remnants of lost times, both linguistic and tangible, and the rupture with the past, especially (at first) the classical past that they signified. Antiquarianism took various forms in different countries, but beginning with Flavio Biondo's (1392–1463) mapping of the topography and antiquities of Roman-era Italy, its practitioners engaged principally in inquiries into what might be called the non-narrative past. Characteristically, they exploited material and non-textual types of evidence such as coins, tombs and steles as a supplement to chronicles and written records. From studying these human-made artefacts it was a relatively short step to pondering the origins of prehistoric monuments such as England's Stonehenge as well as features of the landscape, many of which of course had featured in medieval writers, often attributed to a particular event or legendary figure.

By the end of the seventeenth century, antiquarianism had, rather like its more prosperous sister, history, become an umbrella concept for a variety of different activities, including the study of ancient monuments, the examination of records to establish genealogies and pedigrees (an important activity during an era of considerable social mobility in many parts of Europe), the deciphering of tombstones, coins and medals, and ultimately the cataloguing of natural rarities, including fossils. Scholars such as England's William Camden (1551–1623) contributed studies of individual towns or regions and their antiquities, while his younger friend Sir Robert Cotton assembled a vast repository of historical manuscripts, much of which still survives in the British Library. The packrat tendencies of late Renaissance 'virtuoso' collectors, while beginning as cabinets and chambers of 'curiosities', began to merge with the kinds of scientific inquiries practised by European academicians of the later seventeenth century, including the beginnings of systematic archaeology. Antiquarianism had also evolved on another front, so that it pressed up against and often overlapped with another new discourse, 'natural history', and by the early eighteenth century it had acquired the classificatory and empirical inclinations we associate with contemporary naturalists such as Linnaeus. Finally, legal scholarship proved an especially fecund branch of antiquarianism, attracting some of the subtlest historical minds of the day, for whom the changes in and, in some countries, multiple systems of law provided a proxy for wider economic, social and political changes. Three generations of sixteenth-century French legal scholars adumbrated a distinctive approach to sources that initially stressed textual editing, fixing the historical meaning of words and documents, and understanding laws as time-bound creations of a specific period. It eventually broadened its scope to include the comparison of different legal systems, for instance Roman civil law and local customary law. By the late sixteenth century, in an early example of what we now call 'knowledge mobilization', a relatively detached study of esoteric points of Roman law had become more useful in the 'real world', as France ripped itself apart in religious wars, and a new generation of humanist legal scholars such as François Hotman (1524–90) put their erudition to work in ideological debates about such matters as the extent of, and limits on, royal authority. Seventeenth-century English jurists would use (or ignore) these techniques to argue whether the Norman Conquest of 1066 had been a 'real' conquest, whether institutions such as parliament preceded it and whether the common law of the land dated from time immemorial, all of which had real implications for contemporary political debates.

One of the consequences of the assemblage of evidence in the fifteenth and sixteenth centuries was the shaking of belief in time-worn origin tales – by 1600, few reputable historians were prepared to accept the Trojans and their offspring without question. Popular culture remained a different matter, and the various chapbooks, ballads and broadsheets that circulated through Europe well into the eighteenth century peddled a mixture of romance, legend and history that fed into and sprang back out of oral culture. And court-sponsored historians were often reluctant to challenge time-honoured myths. Moreover, a persistent problem lay in the establishment of precise timelines for the events of history, especially ancient history, and the reconciliation or 'synchronism' of events in different parts of the world and their calendars. Indeed, one by-product of humanist philology and linguistic proficiency was a wave of highly complex chronological scholarship by polyglots such as Joseph Justus Scaliger (1540–1609), and eventually the great mathematician Isaac Newton (1643–1727). There were many quirky attempts to fix with certitude the exact date of the Creation, famously assigned by the Irish archbishop James Ussher (1581–1656) to twilight on 23 October 4004 BC.

There was a further dimension to all of this, an epistemological one, in the buoyant optimism of some thinkers that the past could indeed be recovered and represented accurately. One of these, the legal theorist Jean Bodin (1530–96), contributed a widely read *Methodus* ('Method') for the reading and understanding of history. Perhaps the most widely influential among a whole genre of writing known collectively as the *ars historica* ('art of history') which continued well into the eighteenth century, the *Methodus* was intended to guide the reader through the thorny thickets of past historians, even providing a chronological bibliography of histories, but Bodin went well beyond this. He was concerned to identify rules for the 'correct evaluation' of histories and (like Polybius) the types of government, 'since history for the most part deals with the state and with the changes taking place within it'. He also wished to dispel certain timeworn schemes such as the 'Four Monarchies', inherited from the Middle Ages and now appropriated by writers of apocalyptic literature and Protestant propagandists. This was fatally flawed in Bodin's opinion by its conflating of some empires and the ignoring of several others; it had no room, for instance, for 'the monarchy of the Arabs, who forced almost the whole of Africa and a great part of Asia' to adopt their language and religion, or for the Tartars (that is, the Mongols). A European had thus recognized the inherent Eurocentrism of historiography as practised up to his own time.

With the Protestant Reformation in Europe, and a century of religious warfare erupting soon after, the inherently polemical capacity of historical writing reached new levels. It was no longer used to promote mere conflicting perspectives or scholarly differences, however vicious, over particular points of fact, but something qualitatively different. The public display of opposed interpretations – what we would now call 'ideology' – began for the first time to splinter historical writers into recognizably conflicting camps, now able to conduct their campaigns in print. Early Protestant reformers, needing to discredit the papacy and the medieval church generally as one long decline from apostolic purity, provided works such as Johannes Sleidanus' (1506–56) account of the first stages of the Reformation, and the multi-authored *Magdeburg Centuries* (1559–74), so-called after the city in which it was printed and its organization into hundred-year periods. Catholic Europe responded in kind, for instance in the *Ecclesiastical Annals* by Cardinal Cesare Baronio, a riposte reprinted, abridged and continued in dozens of editions up to the nineteenth century.

As Bodin and certain other authors of *artes historicae* had correctly discerned in the later sixteenth century, a consequence of successive authors attacking the integrity of their opponents as well as the reliability of their sources was a shaking of faith in the knowability of the past. The response to this lay, in the main, not in philosophical defences of knowledge but, once again, in the execution of increasingly exacting levels of scholarship. The Bollandists – Belgian Jesuits – commenced the *Acta Sanctorum* ('Acts of the Saints'), organized as a month-by-month calendar of feast days, in order to set the lives and deeds of the historical saints on a sounder scholarly footing, examining every possible piece of evidence connected with individual holy figures to sort myth from historical reality. Their project continued well into modern times and significantly improved the level of source criticism then practised. The Maurists – French Benedictine monks – set out to defend the reliability of history by producing editions of the Christian Church Fathers based on original sources, but more importantly they began to formalize rules and conventions connected with the emerging 'ancillary disciplines'. These were the technical skills needed for dealing with late antique and medieval documents, in particular systematic palaeography (interpretation of historical scripts and hands) and diplomatic (knowledge of the structure, layout and conventional formulae of documents). The Maurist Jean Mabillon's (1632–1707) *Six Books on Diplomatic*, which focused on the authenticity of medieval charters, illustrates a broader shift in historical theory (if such it can be called) away from ruminations about the proper literary composition of history towards nuts-and-bolts 'coal-face' work on its sources, though concerns with style were to remain a feature of the late seventeenth and eighteenth centuries.

A recurring controversy in these centuries was the so-called *querelle* (quarrel) between the 'ancients' and the 'moderns'. This began in the sixteenth century with a revolt against the early humanists' rather slavish devotion to imitation of the classics, and continued to develop against a backdrop of significant social and economic change, which some writers refused to accept as inexorably negative. At its core a narrower argument about the relative literary merits of modern writers compared with their ancient predecessors, the *querelle* had expanded by the end of the seventeenth century into a wider debate about 'progress' in human learning. It soon took account of the emerging natural sciences, where technology had clearly invented tools (the compass, gunpowder and printing were the examples most often cited) that antiquity had lacked. The growth of scepticism towards received knowledge, and the belief that reason and experience must take precedence over, or at least be adduced to clarify, the revealed truth of scripture, was related to the *querelle*. As applied to history, the sceptical tone of the late seventeenth century is perhaps most famously represented in Pierre Bayle's *Dictionnaire historique et critique* ('Historical and Critical Dictionary'), a celebrated book that appeared in the middle of an especially intense period of intellectual speculation and rampant doubt. Bayle (1647–1706) was among the many French controversialist-historians driven abroad for reasons of religion. His *Dictionnaire* appeared in several editions beginning in 1697, and was enormously influential in subsequent decades, though its approach to historical truth – a relentless series of demolition exercises and controversial statements about a wide variety of topics and persons – would ultimately be rejected, since it seemed powerless to erect anything in place of the truths that it challenged. Bayle's views were not unique, and others began to doubt the biblical account of the Creation and the Flood. In reaction to such tendencies, the French bishop Jacques-Bénigne Bossuet (1627–1704) authored a widely read *Discourse on Universal History* reasserting the literal reliability of the biblical account of history, but he was fighting a growing tide of scepticism which would only increase as eighteenth-century *philosophes* built on the critical scholarship of their predecessors.

Chinese Historical Writing under the Ming and Early Qing Dynasties

In 1580, an Augustinian priest arrived in Ming-dynasty China on a mission from Philip II of Spain. Juan González de Mendoza (1545–1618) would spend three years in China before moving on to Mexico and finally back to Spain. A former soldier, Mendoza was one of many Catholic missionaries to sojourn in China, and in 1586 he became the first European to publish in print a history of the land known to the West for centuries as Cathay. Translated the same year into Italian and soon after into English, the *History of the Great and Mighty Kingdom of China* would become the principal introduction for many readers to the history of the giant in the Far East. This is the period during which the Chinese, who had experienced intermittent encounters with European traders for centuries, now came into more intense contact with its culture, especially through missionaries such as Mendoza and the Jesuit Matteo Ricci (1552–1610). By the end of the seventeenth century, Western knowledge of China had considerably increased, extending to some familiarity with its historical writing.

The Ming dynasty (1368–1644) was already in decline by Ricci's time. Under it a philosophical approach to the study of the past had flourished, and literacy had increased, as it was doing in late medieval and early modern Europe. Books were much more widely available, leading to a growth in personal libraries and the circulation of historical works, including some of the Standard Histories, outside the courtly circle of literati to which they had been previously confined. Whereas historical study in previous eras focused largely on past dynasties, Ming historians took a considerably greater interest in the recent past. As in Europe, genres continued to proliferate, and when the Standard History of the dynasty was eventually written, a bibliography of Ming works named ten varieties of historical writings, organized around 1,378 categories. Students in sixteenth-century civil service examinations were asked to reflect on the relative merits of chronologically organized histories as compared with more topically arranged works such as Sima Guang's *Comprehensive Mirror* (see above, pp. 66–67) recalling the tensions between erudite research and narrative historical writing in the West at about the same time.

The Ming ensured the survival of the Veritable Records of individual reigns through an orchestrated process of copying, ceremonial presentation of the master copy to the emperor according to rules laid down in 1403, and taking greater care in their storage. The most serious criticism of Ming official history was that it was prone to the spectre of political interference to an extent that had not (or so it was supposed) been true under previous dynasties. Cases occurred of previously sealed records being opened and rewritten, for example the Veritable Records of the dynasty's founding Hongwu Emperor. Other records are known to have been destroyed. And the old tendency to glorify the achievements of successful emperors and to vilify the morally deficient, the usurper and the tyrant, remained very much in play.

Paradoxically, the very weaknesses of Ming official historiography promoted creativity in other scholarly spheres. Greater access to documents was afforded to non-official historians, and private historiography, hitherto a relatively minor proportion of the Chinese historical output, increased substantially, sometimes authored by the very same individuals who also contributed to official writings. The imperial functionary Qiu Jun (1421–95) contributed to several officially sponsored works including Veritable Records of two reigns, but he was able independently to write a much more original and insightful work,

The Correct Bonds in Universal History, offering philosophical reflections on the course of Chinese events since the Qin. More important
than the proliferation of private historical writing in itself was the
spread of a much more critical attitude to historical writing in general.
Liu Zhiji's (see above, pp. 65–66) withering criticism of the Tang
Bureau for the Writing of History nearly a millennium earlier was
echoed in the late Ming historian Tan Qian's (1594–1658) denunciation of the works previously written on the Ming, and in his widespread
travels across China in search of reliable sources for what became his
own massive history of the dynasty, which Tan completed under the
ensuing Qing dynasty (1644–1912). The difference between criticism
during the Tang and that under the Ming is largely one of degree rather
than kind. Liu had focused on the weaknesses of the history Bureau in
particular; Ming critics attacked the entire collaborative history enterprise, along with much else, in works like Wang Shizhen's *Critical
Treatise on the Errors in Historical Works*. The period also witnessed,
in tandem with the spread of historical readership and increase in the
availability of texts, a proliferation of public debate about the past that
resembles the pattern we have seen in contemporary Europe.

   Something like French historical scepticism (often referred to as
'Pyrrhonism') and relativism also emerged in China at this time, mirrored
in the plaintive cry of Zhang Xuan (*fl.* 1582) that 'Writing a truthful
history is difficult!' Jean Bodin and Pierre Bayle each have counterparts
of sorts during the Ming, though it is rather unlikely that the Chinese
authors, despite Western contact, knew of their French opposite numbers or vice versa. Qu Jingchun (1507–69), a contemporary counterpart
to France's Bodin, offered in his *On the Merits and Deficiencies of
Historical Learning from Past to Present* a systematic and at times
harsh criticism of past historians. Qu outlined 'four responsibilities' of
a historian that read like the mantra of the modern professional association: focusing on the task at hand against other distractions; being patient
and deliberate rather than hasty; having a sense of professional devotion
to his craft; and collecting sources assiduously such that all publicly
available ones are consulted. Pierre Bayle, had he read Chinese, would
have found his match in two much earlier Ming authors. Zhu Yunming's
(1461–1527) *Records of Wrongful Knowledge*, completed in 1522, is
a bold attack on historiographic orthodoxy and deflater of great names;
Li Zhi (1527–1602) went even further down this sceptical path, so much
so that he was thrown into prison, where he committed suicide, for

'daring to propagate a disorderly way, deceiving the world and defrauding the masses'. Apart from his judgments on individuals and their motives, which often run diametrically against received opinion, Li promoted an impatience with what we would now call 'essentialism', noting that what is meritorious to one age may not be to the next, and repudiating the attribution of virtue to past figures on the basis of timeless values. His ability to think beyond the individual indeed makes him the superior of a contrarian such as Bayle and puts him in the ranks of those, like Bodin and Ibn Khaldun, who have thought more widely and systematically about the past and how we perceive it in subsequent ages.

Early Modern Historiography in Islamic Asia and Africa

In 1501, Persia (now Iran) came under the rule of the Safavids (1501–1736). Like other new dynasties, the Safavid Shahs had an interest in promoting favourable accounts of their origins, and they had inherited a long-standing Islamic practice of using genealogy as a legitimizing authority, a habit shared with European noble and royal houses. Historical writing prospered under the Safavids as a succession of rulers commissioned what amounted to official histories of which perhaps the best known example, *The World-Adorning History of 'Abbas*, was the work of a chancery scribe called Iskandar Beg (*c.* 1560–1632). Like Leonardo Bruni and so many other Renaissance Italian officials-turned-historians, Iskandar Beg put his public experience and his privileged access to official records to good use. Completed in 1629, his text is perhaps the most important source for Safavid history, its introduction reaching back to the dynasty's origin. Most of the work focuses on Shah 'Abbas (r. 1588–1629) himself, its subjects ranging from battles, rebellions and court politics to the inclusion of short biographies. The long familiarity of Muslims with Judeo-Christian culture ensured that their vision of history prior to Muhammad (which features the Fall, Noah and the Flood and other Old Testament episodes) and that of European chroniclers were not remarkably different. There was considerable overlap between Christians and Muslims in the writing of universal or world history, marked by the sharing of certain major figures from antiquity, especially Alexander the Great who, we recall, had enjoyed an afterlife in the Middle Ages as a chivalric hero.

In nearby India, by the late fifteenth century, Islamic historiography had begun to proliferate in the subcontinent. Early in the sixteenth century, a Timurid leader named Babur invaded and conquered much of India, absorbing the remnants of the Delhi Sultanate. Babur, who claimed descent both from Timur and Genghis Khan, thereby founded the Mughal (a Persian word derived from 'Mongol') dynasty which would rule much of northern and central India until the advent of British colonial rule in the late eighteenth century. It is no accident that several of the conventions of Safavid writing, including formulaic prefaces and declarations by the historian of the 'inspiration' that led him to write, are repeated by the Mughal historians, since Persian was their preferred tongue for both literature and administration. At virtually the same time that their Christian counterparts elsewhere in India were wrestling with indigenous South Asian sources and finding them wanting, so too were Muslims like the Persian Ferishta (*c.* 1579 to after 1623) who used Hindu sources such as the *Mahabharata* (in Persian translation) to write accounts of India before and since the advent of Islam, but expressed irritation at that ancient epic's thirteen different accounts of the creation of the world, none of which appeared to merit acceptance above the others.

Southern Asia remained a complex, multilingual region, with a wide variety of traditions and genres of history-writing that both preceded and survived the Mughals, whose domain did not encompass the entire subcontinent. These genres were sufficiently fluid and open-ended that they could permit the trading and sharing of particular stories: just as in Europe the same tale could feature in local oral tradition, vernacular urban chronicle and Latin humanist history, so episodes and figures from one region or language group were portable and could surface elsewhere, in other tongues and entirely different formats. The polyglot village literati or *karanam*s of southern India, taking advantage of increasing literacy and the transition of information from inscriptions to paper, palm leaves and other portable media, composed a distinctive prose historiography in vernacular languages like Marathi, Telugu and Rajasthani, as well as 'official' tongues such as Persian. The Maratha of western India, who established an empire of their own in the late seventeenth century, kept chronicles to assert their property claims in which are included dates and notes of important events. The information could then be used to write a *karina* or history of the family's business affairs and land acquisitions – a process not unlike that followed by the Italian worthies who kept household *ricordanze*, or the family chroniclers of early modern Germany.

By the later sixteenth century, Perso-Islamic cultural influences on historiography had spread with the Mughal domain. Emperor Babur himself composed or dictated a detailed autobiographical history of his times, the *Baburnama*, inaugurating a string of 'namas' (a nama being literally a 'book', though the word can be understood as 'history' or 'chronicle'). Among these was the *Humayun-Nama*, unusually the work of a woman, Babur's daughter, Gul-Badan, concerning her father's reign and that of her brother, the second Mughal emperor, Humayun. Gul-Badan is thus a Muslim successor to that earlier, Byzantine princess-historian, Anna Komnene. Perhaps the greatest of the genre was the *Akbarnama* ('Book of Akbar', the third Mughal ruler), the work of Abu'l Fazl 'Allami (1551–1602), a colourful figure eventually assassinated at the behest of the future emperor Jahangir. Abu'l Fazl brought together a variety of sources in the *Akbarnama*, a work also notable for its many interesting reflections on the nature of history, which he conceived of as both a philosophical, rational genre and as a source of solace for grief in the present. At precisely the same period that court-sponsored histories were in vogue in early modern Europe, the same feature can be observed in Mughal India, and the appointment of Abu'l Fazl by Akbar inaugurated the policy, which endured to the early eighteenth century, of having an official historiographer write the history of the empire.

By the time of the Mughal entry into India, Islam already had a new western standard-bearer in the Ottoman Turks, who by 1453 had brought down the beleaguered Byzantine Empire and captured Constantinople. Despite intermittent periods of weakness they became the favoured eastern bogeyman for Europeans through the late seventeenth century, filling the role that the Mongols had played for central Eurasia in an earlier age. By virtue of their situation on the borders of Europe and the East, virtually no other Asian power received as much attention from European writers, including a whole sub-genre of 'Histories of the Turks' and speculations about Ottoman origins.

The efforts of the early fifteenth-century sultans retroactively to justify their infamous habit of eliminating rivals, exemplified by 'Abdu'l-vasi Çelebi's (*fl.* 1414) account of the accession of Mehmed I, bear comparison with the slightly later histories written in some of the Italian city-states ruled by family dynasties, and in early Tudor England. This chronicle tradition continued with works by Aşikpaşazade or Aşiki (1400 to after 1484) and the obscure Mevlana Neşri (d. *c.* 1520), who synthesized many of the sources up to his own time. Sixteenth-century Turkish literati, rather like their humanist counterparts to the west, objected to both the language and the content of the chronicles and to their simple style, suffused with nostalgia for an earlier era of free-ranging warfare, as incompatible with a centralized bureaucratic regime. Sultan Bayezid II (r. 1481–1512) initiated a change in historical styles when he commissioned the first histories devoted specifically to the Ottomans, by Idrîs-I Bidlîsî (d. 1520), in both Persian and Turkish. After a dry spell for several decades, further commissions followed with Suleyman the Magnificent's (r. 1520–66) creation in the 1550s of the position of *sehnāmeci* or court-writer to write a new dynastic history in Persian (eventually superseded by Turkish). While this early venture into court-sponsored history was not terribly successful, the Ottomans finally established 'official' history in the stricter sense of an office of state historiographer (*vak'a-nüvis*) in the late seventeenth century. By the 1700s, the products of these historians had evolved into vehicles for the promotion of a now-solidified Ottoman state, rather than courtly writings tied to the sultans, who had by this time lost a good deal of their personal power. There had also been a movement during the seventeenth century away from explorations of the origins of dynasties and towards the coverage of more recent history – also a phenomenon we have seen in contemporary western Europe.

There are obvious parallels to be drawn both with China's mandarin-dominated historical writing (and its evolution under the Tang from receiving informal sponsorship to becoming an explicit arm of government) and, more remotely, with the less bureaucratically organized civic and princely historiography of many European states. The Chinese practice of maintaining court diaries as the source for imperial Veritable Records has a counterpart in the day-books of court activity or registers that would subsequently be transformed into histories. The major Turkish histories of the sixteenth and seventeenth centuries, even when written unofficially, were often the labour of ministers or bureaucrats such as Mustafa Na'îmâ (1655–1716), who wrote an important history of the empire in the first half of the seventeenth century, the *Tarih-i Na'îmâ* (literally, 'The History by Na'îmâ'). Generally regarded as the first of the new official chronicles, it remains one of the most cited sources for that period; its author's views on the reasons for writing history and the ways in which it should be done look remarkably similar to any European *ars historica* of the day.

Like its Mughal and Safavid contemporaries, the Ottoman Empire was a multilingual and multi-ethnic state. Accordingly, Ottoman historiography embraced writings in languages other than Turkish by ethnic minorities including Kurds, Armenians and Arabs, as well as Greeks in the conquered Byzantine territories. It is worth noting, too, that the interest of western historians in Turkish matters was reciprocated by their Ottoman counterparts, who sometimes wrote about the non-Ottoman world. The bibliographer and geographer Kâtip Çelebi (1609–57) was a frequent observer of and commentator on European affairs who collaborated with a former Christian priest; one Ibrahim Mülhemi devoted a chapter to French history in his *Murâd-nâme* ('The Book of Murad [IV]'), which despite its title was designed as a universal history. In 1572 two chancery officials had compiled a chronicle of the kings of France from several French sources, covering the period from the legendary Frankish king, Pharamond, to their own day. And an unknown Ottoman writer, around 1580, possibly with the help of a Spanish co-author, even cast his gaze overseas to the Americas in a history of the West Indies.

By 1500, Islam had also been present in the northern parts of the African continent for several centuries – Ibn Khaldun, one recalls, was a Tunisian – and had gradually extended its cultural reach south of the Sahara. Many indigenous African tongues were represented with Arabic script (a practice known as *adjami*), for instance those of the Hausa of Sudan and the nomadic Fulani who would conquer much Hausa territory in the nineteenth century. By the early eighteenth century, a West African coastal kingdom, Gonja, was transferring its oral traditions into Arabic-language annals. Elsewhere in East Africa, the history of the town of Kilwa in modern Tanzania was recounted in an anonymous early sixteenth-century work commissioned by Sultan Muhammad b. al-Husayn and later used by the Portuguese historian João de Barros. Ethiopia has perhaps the richest and most long-standing tradition of historical writing in sub-Saharan Africa, though this sprang predominantly from Christian rather than Muslim influence. Royal chronicles written by court scribes, in an alphabet derived from the archaic Ethiopian Ge'ez tongue, first appear in the thirteenth century and would continue in both Ge'ez and Amharic (the country's modern language of government) down to the twentieth century.

A good deal of our knowledge of pre-colonial African history now derives not from written sources but from oral traditions and oral literatures, many of which have only been transcribed within the past half-century. One example is an account of the fifteenth-century Songhay ruler Askia Mohammed (r. 1493–1528); previously referred to in sixteenth-century Muslim histories, it was recorded as recently as the early 1980s from the mouth of a griot – a West African bard or poet – in Niger. There are many variants of these by different names, such as the Wolof *woy jallore* or *cosaan* (a song of great exploits or of genealogy), or the *deeda* (the Songhay term for a long narrative about the past with genealogical detail). Some of these words have clear ties to others denoting written historical genres: the *tariko* of the Gambia and the *tariku* of Upper Guinea appear to derive from the Arabic *ta'rikh*. We will have more to say about Africa in subsequent chapters: the key point here is that it was not, as was once believed, a continent bereft of historical writing, and much less of historical thought.

New World Encounters 1: Europeans in Asia and the Americas

Geography, the study of place and space, has nearly always been related to history, the study of past times. That connection has never been more influential than between about 1450 and 1700. Ultimately, the uncertainties noted above regarding the past in general, chronology, and even the proper forms in which history should be cast, would be magnified by two centuries of European overseas exploration and colonization. The discovery of other peoples, especially primitive indigenous cultures – both completely 'savage' tribes such as the Brazilian Tupinamba and more advanced 'barbarian' societies such as the Incas and Aztecs – would complicate inherited schemes for the periodization of history and even the creation story contained in Genesis. What was outwardly new was at first slotted into categories quite old, and contextualized within the boundaries of learned and popular tradition. Legendary figures, monsters, the Garden of Eden, fountains of youth, King Solomon's mines, cannibals and Amazon women all seemed to be borne out by discoveries in the Americas, Africa and the East Indies, and some truly wild speculations, stimulated by late medieval frauds like Annius of Viterbo's pseudo-Berossus, would eventually explain the native inhabitants as lost citizens of Atlantis, or exiled Israelites, or some subsidiary branch of the sons of Noah. The theoretical justification of imperial and ecclesiastical power overseas rested on the assumption that the Americas and other hitherto unknown terrains were in fact part of the Old World, had been alluded to in ancient legends and romances (as well as in scripture and in classical geography), were subject to the same authority as European lands and were occupied by populations sharing universal human values, though much more primitive in behaviour.

Apart from earlier Viking expeditions depicted in medieval sagas, the first systematic explorers of the Atlantic world were the Portuguese, whose ventures were bent more towards commerce than conquest. Unlike the Castilians, Aragonese and Catalans, the Portuguese had produced relatively little historical writing prior to the early fifteenth century. The earliest Iberian account of Portuguese expansion came from Gomes Eanes de Zurara (*c.* 1410–74), who in 1448 authored a chronicle of the conquest of Guinea in West Africa. As the Spanish would later do in New Spain and Peru, so the Portuguese encountered indigenous knowledge of the past in Africa and the Indies that was difficult to reconcile with either their Christian notions of world history or their hardening sense of the boundary between myth and 'fact', but which they were often obliged to use in the absence of alternative sources. A Portuguese chronicler who visited the Moluccas (now the Maluku islands) in the Malay Archipelago, recorded its inhabitants' belief that their founding rulers had been hatched from four serpents' eggs. 'This is said to be the origin of all the kings of these islands ... One may believe it if he wants to, as also that story of the serpent; they insist that it is true, as they do with all their poetic fables, which are very much in vogue with them.' João de Barros, famed as the 'Portuguese Livy' (*c.* 1498–1570), ventured to both East Africa and southern India during his career, sometimes using indigenous histories. Barros was simultaneously the author of both romance and history, and well aware of the difference between the two. He raised the classic distinction between *verum* and *fabula* in order to dismiss the historical writings that he encountered in Malabar as 'fables like those of the Greeks and the Latins'.

Asia and Africa had been known, if often unfamiliar, territory to Europeans for centuries. With the Americas, explorers and writers alike were on a thoroughly alien terrain, one that justified the term 'New World' once it became clear that it was not, in fact, the eastern Indies but something quite different. Historical literature on the Americas was the work of both clergy and laymen, including many Spanish administrators and jurists who wrote briefs and reports (*relaciones*) that included a good deal of historical information about their territories and indigenous inhabitants. Some came from a humble background, among them a number of *soldados cronistas* who would, at home, have been unlikely to engage in a humanist historiography increasingly the preserve of the middling and upper classes. This group included Pedro Cieza de León (1518 to *c.* 1554 or 1560), a soldier who travelled extensively through Peru; his *First Part of the Chronicle of Peru* ranges more widely than its title indicates, and is full of oral information from Andean informants about their own culture and history. It was widely published in several languages and more than any other book cultivated the idea of the Incas as sophisticated rulers who had imposed a level of civility on the much more primitive peoples whom they had subjugated a century earlier.

Scholarly writing about the New World began very early, overlapping with the experiential narratives, with a man who never saw the Americas in person, Pedro Mártir de Anglería or Peter Martyr d'Anghiera (1457–1526), a Lombard émigré commissioned by the Holy Roman Emperor Charles V (who was also king of Spain) to write a history of the discoveries. Although his work was in most respects textbook humanist historiography, its Livian inspiration indicated by its organization into decades, Mártir included the geography and the natural features of the Americas, thereby blurring the boundaries between natural history and historical narrative, a genre-mixing that would prove useful to subsequent historians of the Americas. The first books of Mártir's *Decades on the New World* were published in Latin in 1516, and expanded in subsequent editions. It was probably the earliest attempt to domesticate the 'wild' past of the new territories by integrating it into European history. The natives could not, in a biblical interpretation of world history, be seen as utterly alien; it was easier to turn their culture into the remnants of a lost 'golden age'.

Mártir proved only the first of several historians willing to write about the discoveries without ever venturing in person to the New World. Others include Antonio de Herrera y Tordesillas (*c.* 1549–1625), a prolific author of histories of France, England and Scotland. Herrera was appointed Chronicler of the Indies by Philip II in 1586, one of a long line of such official historians stretching into the eighteenth century. As *Cronista*, Herrera enjoyed privileged access to state documents, which he exploited in his encyclopedic *General History of the Deeds of the Castilians on the Islands and Mainland of the Ocean Sea Known as the West Indies* (1601–15). Herrera's relentless devotion to telling his story in strict chronological order brought out a tension created when a set of historical genres in the process of being fine-tuned to contain European experiences had to be pressed into service to represent completely foreign territory, and where the conveyance of practical information rather than the provision of heroic or moral models was often the principal goal.

This was not necessarily a weakness. Much of the Conquest historiography was read by its target audience – kings, ministers, senior clergy – neither for entertainment nor exemplarity, but for more practical, informational purposes. For many, the standard humanist practice of providing a brief treatment of geography prefatory to a main chronological narrative was no longer sufficient, and their histories integrated sections on customs, geography, beliefs and commerce into the divisions of the book as a whole. The inclusion of geography and history together in ways rather different than conventional humanist narratives proved trend-setting, and many of the most important histories of the New World are thus much more than chronological accounts. The discoveries, quite apart from their impact on the understanding of human history, thereby mitigated some of the rigidity in the genre boundaries of this classicizing age.

Gonzalo Fernández de Oviedo y Valdés (1478–1557), the first historian who actually spent time in the western Indies (as the Americas were to be called by Europeans for some time), was also the earliest to write about it in Spanish, and he, too, decided to integrate chronological history with the description of geography and nature. Oviedo went to the New World in 1512 and apart from visits back to Spain, remained there as a crown representative and eventually 'Chief Chronicler of the Indies'. His magnum opus, the *General History of the Indies*, which emphasized events only since the discovery, exemplifies the half-classical, half-medieval roots underlying historical accounts of the discoveries, even when they were trumpeted as an achievement that had outdone the ancients. A former writer of romance, Oviedo saw the conquistador Cortés as a latter-day Julius Caesar (in his medieval, knightly incarnation), and sought evidence for an earlier, pre-Columbian Spanish conquest in so dubious a source as Annius of Viterbo.

Peering back into the pre-Spanish past was harder, and required some understanding of native tongues, in particular Nahuatl, the dominant language family in Mesoamerica. Although the humanist Francisco López de Gómara (1511–64) never set foot in Mexico, he eventually served as Cortés' chaplain and used his employer's information as the major source for his account of the Conquest, the *Historia de la Conquista de México* (1552). This work was almost immediately joined to another he published in the same year, *Historia general de las Indias*, which now included Peru, concerning which he had considerably less reliable information. Peru had been colonized slightly later and in a much less orderly fashion, its government never quite achieving the stability of New Spain. Conquest there quickly turned into civil war between rival groups of conquistadors. Official or semi-official histories nonetheless began to appear from mid-century, starting with Agustín de Zárate's (*c.* 1492 to *c.* 1560) *History of the Discovery and Conquest of Peru*. From the beginning, would-be historians in both New Spain and Peru were heavily dependent on native informants for pre-contact history. Linguistic gaps could be overcome – Toribio de Benavente (*c.* 1500–69), who adopted the Nahuatl name 'Motolinía', meaning 'poor one', and his fellow Franciscan Bernardino de Sahagún (*c.* 1499–1590) made extensive use of interpreters and informants. But deciding what to do with such information put them on the horns of a dilemma. On the one hand, they needed to dismiss the religious and ritualistic aspects of native history as both false and morally repugnant. On the other, they could not throw out all native information since it was virtually their sole source. The quandary is illustrated by Pedro Sarmiento de Gamboa, who was sceptical of the veracity of Peruvian oral tradition but nonetheless felt compelled by the earnestness of natives' apparent belief in it to 'write down what they say and not what we think about it'. Consequently, his history, unpublished till the early twentieth century, can now be taken as a reasonably accurate record of Andean attitudes to the past in the mid-sixteenth century.

The richness of this New World historiography provided another episode in that ancient, recurring struggle between the impulse to write particular histories of anything or any place, and the need to generalize effectively and construct a comprehensive universal history embracing all regions and all peoples. The same problem that late antique European and early Chinese imperial historians had faced in integrating barbarian tribes into their own past (taken as providing the core of a universal history) now reappeared on a vaster, transoceanic scale. Some authors tried to synthesize the disparate histories of the Indies,

East and West, into a general history, one that in turn could be plugged easily into the even larger inherited Christian master-narrative. The goal was less eradication of indigenous history than its wholesale transplantation into a globalized version of the medieval Christian-biblical view of the past. Diego Durán (*c.* 1537–88), the Dominican author of one of the earliest histories of the Aztecs, exemplifies this mindset, convinced that 'these natives are part of the ten tribes of Israel that Shalmaneser, king of the Assyrians, captured and took to Assyria in the time of Hoshea, king of Israel, and in the time of Ezekias, king of Jerusalem'. This would prove to be only the first step in a process of European historiographic colonization that would achieve maturity in the nineteenth and twentieth centuries.

Commerce as much as curiosity drove the production of historical texts: there was a market for summary, synthetic works as much as for the accounts of particular events or regions, fuelled by print and by a growing literate public that thirsted for easily accessible information. The Catholic church, for its part, was heavily invested in situating heathen natives within a biblical account of the world as it was simultaneously bringing them to the Christian faith. Early missionary-historians such as Andrés de Olmos (*c.* 1480–1570) and Motolinía envisaged the discoveries as falling into a broader Franciscan apocalyptic narrative; according to this, the conversion of the Indians would provide the prelude to a more general reform and the achievement of a Christian utopia on both sides of the Atlantic. With the Counter-Reformation came a further imperative: the insurance of religious orthodoxy and often rivalries among different religious orders. Thus the Franciscan Juan de Torquemada's (d. 1664) *The Indian Monarchy* (1615) covered both religious and secular history, turning the story of the pre-Conquest natives into the equivalent of the Israelite captivity in Egypt, with Cortés fashioned into a deliverer ordained by God to destroy the Aztec Empire because of its idolatry, and the Franciscans as creators of a new Eden – now sadly turned, through the colonists' abuse and decadence, into a new Babylon.

Among the clerical authors of general histories, two merit special mention: Bartolomé de Las Casas (1474–1566), and José de Acosta (1540–1600) respectively a Dominican and a Jesuit. Las Casas has appealed to later generations because of his early criticism of Spanish mistreatment of the natives (including forced conversion to Christianity), which led this erstwhile adventurer to become a friar and commit his life to their protection. Las Casas wrote a number of works, including an unfinished *General History of the Indies*. Much of his fame, however, rests on his *Brief Account of the Destruction of the Indies* (1552), a passionate defence of native rights which had the unintended consequence of reinforcing Protestant countries' anti-Catholic propaganda. Las Casas aroused antagonism at the time, running counter to the anti-Indian sentiments of lay historians such as Gómara and to the efforts of fellow clergy engaged in the business of conversion. Modernity has learned to take his statements with a healthy degree of scepticism, even when sympathizing with the motives behind them.

José de Acosta was of a later generation, and a member of the Jesuits, the new religious order associated closely with the Counter-Reformation. Acosta's much-translated *Historia natural y moral de las Indias* ('Natural and Moral History of the Indies') appeared in Spanish in 1590 and was the result of both his philosophical training and time spent in both Peru and Mexico. As the title suggests, it continued in the tradition of combining natural history with narrative. Acosta is credited, among other things, with articulating the notion of a land bridge between Asia and America whence came natives who had deteriorated into degrees of primitivism, thus bringing him into rough accord with the modern theory of transcontinental migration (even though Acosta derived this conclusion from entirely fallacious assumptions built on biblical and Noachian theories of descent). From our point of view, the most interesting features of his book are its moderately adulatory history of pre-contact native cultures, especially Aztec and Inca, and Acosta's reminder to his readers that the kind of bloodthirsty barbarity that these appeared to exhibit, including human sacrifice, had also featured in the European past (a point that Las Casas, too, had made).

Acosta divided 'barbarians' – that is, non-Christians – into three distinct groups: the civilized (including Chinese, Japanese and certain peoples of India) who had laws, government, writing and records of the past; the semi-civilized (including Aztecs and Incas) who had government, religion and some recollection of the past but neither books nor script; and finally, the completely savage, devoid of government, religion, law and writing. While these sorts of divisions and even a notion of progress from one stage to the next were not entirely new, the wide purview of Acosta's comparison, which includes Asian peoples, is of interest – a product of his order's global evangelizing ambitions. It is also notable for its insistence on the supremacy of observed experience over tradition in explaining or describing the new territories, their peoples and their natural history. Despite his ruthlessly strict adherence to the necessity of the Church to human salvation, Acosta points both backward to Aristotelian visions of the plenitude of nature and ahead to the comparativist eighteenth-century *histoire des moeurs* (see below, Chapter 4) – even though this thoroughgoing providentialist, completely convinced of Spain's destiny to bring Christian monarchy across the seas, would have found the values of a Voltaire completely repugnant.

New World Encounters 2: Indigenous Histories from the Americas

The collaborations of Spaniards such as Sahagún with native interpreters and informants remind us that there were two sides to the Conquests, and leads into the question of how the indigenous peoples saw their own past, both before and after they were introduced to gunpowder, Christianity and devastating Old World diseases. The degree to which the introduction of Western historiography eradicated or distorted native historical thinking and its representations is fiercely contested. Some modern commentators, writing from a 'postcolonial' perspective (see below, pp. 268–71), have criticized the attempted appropriation of indigenous writings, the imposition of Renaissance literacy and the extirpation of both oral and pictorial forms of historical representation; the anthropologist Claude Lévi-Strauss went so far as to assert the primary function of all writing to be enslavement. Even the imposition of the alphabet has been seen as an attempt to replace native historicity with European, and in a form that only the Europeans could understand. This understates the capacity of the natives themselves to adapt their historical thinking to literacy. It also assumes that influence was unidirectional whereas in fact the histories that travelled back to Europe were far from unaffected by the 'conquered' culture.

The natives colonized by the Europeans had, contrary to the belief of many of their conquerors, a well-developed sense of their past and various means, graphic and oral, to represent it. Starting about 500 BC, the Maya, Mixtec, Zapotec, Aztec and other Mesoamerican peoples had developed non-alphabetic writing in a combination of pictographic, logographic, ideographic and phonetic elements, carved on monuments or written on various portable media – animal skins, bark and cloth. Archaeologists have uncovered remnants of Mesoamerican commemorative paintings and carvings from as far back as a millennium before the Conquest, some of which mark dates in the native calendar. The degree to which natives made use of this is a matter of judgment, but regardless of the intensity of interest in the past, knowledge of it was undoubtedly undercut or modified by the purging of old rituals and the renaming of towns for Christian saints, or the intermixing of native and European cultural practices. Pre-Conquest Mayan glyphs recount a dynastic history for the centuries from 250 to 900, and recorded dates can be found from early in the first century AD. Paper from bark was developed perhaps as early as the fifth century, and with it the possibility of making 'books', typically in gatefold format, such as the Dresden Codex, one of the handful of these pre-Conquest documents surviving to the present. Most of the several hundred historiographic codices produced in New Spain, and still extant, were the product of post-Conquest hands, even if they derived from earlier tradition and, perhaps, lost predecessors. The Boturini Codex, painted in the 1530s, tells the story of the mythical Aztec journey to the valley of Mexico. The Codex Chimalpopoca, which survives in a later copy of a lost original, contains two anonymous works, the *Annals of Cuauhtitlan* (or Quauhtitlan, a town north of Mexico City) and the *Legends of the Sun*, both of which stretch back into remote antiquity and derive from now-lost pictographic sources and oral accounts.

Acosta would compare European, American and Asian recording systems in his *Natural and Moral History*, but he waxed sceptical on the pictorially represented Amerindian sense of the past when he saw a Mexican chronicle in 1586–7. 'In the first place, what certainty or authority does this relation or history possess?' he asked. 'In the second place, since the Indians did not have writing, how could they preserve such a quantity and variety of matters for so long a time?' Acosta was only half right. Extant central Mexican codices cannot, of course, be read as if they were chronological histories, since they contain myth and legend mixed in with events that may actually have occurred; but one must remember, again, that Europeans were themselves struggling to determine the boundaries between history and fiction at this very time. When the Spanish lawyer Alfonso de Zorita visited the

Guatemalan highlands in the 1550s, he was able to discover details of the natives' ancient governance 'with the aid of paintings which they had which recorded their history for more than eight hundred years back, and which were interpreted for me by very ancient Indians'. Sahagún refers to the 'old men, in whose possession were the paintings and recollections of ancient things', on whose information he rested his assertion that the Mesoamericans were not indigenous but rather earlier migrants from the north.

From Diego Durán's perspective, the natives' own ideas of their origins were 'clearly fabulous' and demonstrated that they were ignorant of their beginnings. But on the other side of this determination to find a biblical origin for them lay Durán's more open-minded attitude to native accounts of recent times. He reveals a genuine determination to use both painted histories and conversation with informants, conducted in Nahuatl, to enrich his account. Despite the interest of early observers, much of the pictorial heritage of Mesoamerica met with a bad end. Although they survived longer than the ancient religious books, which were almost immediately consigned to the flames, and though new specimens were being created throughout the sixteenth century, indigenous pictorial history suffered from neglect or concerted destruction. This phenomenon was in itself not alien to the peoples affected; while the depredations of the Conquest should be neither ignored nor underestimated, much historiographical purging and distortion had occurred among the natives long before a single Spaniard had set foot on their shores. Around 1430, for instance, the rulers of the newly hegemonic Aztec city of Tenochtitlan decided to burn old pictographic histories because they contained 'falsehoods' and did not accord with the Aztec vision of the past. Interference with pre-existing records was also practised, as was outright fabrication. Mixtec rulers, who organized their codices by event rather than by year, are known to have had some of these repainted in order to insert themselves retroactively into genealogies to which they did not belong. The Maya and Zapotec would deface or destroy stone monuments whose messages no longer supported current political reality. In this respect, the Mesoamerican natives were not so very different from their European counterparts of about the same period.

The Spanish, with different motives, would step up the pace of destruction. But the suppression of native historical memory was never fully complete. Traces of pre-Conquest and early post-

Conquest historical thinking have survived into modernity, to be recovered from the distant descendants of pre-Conquest Amerindians, frequently by ethnohistorians, archaeologists, art historians and linguists
rather than historians. The Conquest failed to eliminate indigenous
historical memory for a number of reasons, one being the ambivalent
approach of numerous missionaries, many of whom quickly realized
that in order to convert the natives they needed to understand not just
their language but also their world view, including its sense of the past,
and that they would have to explain European concepts, and
Christianity, in terms that resonated for the indigenous population.
Occasional interventions from Spain reinforced efforts to study extant
codices and interview the natives, such as the 1553 decree of the
Council of the Indies which authorized the questioning of 'old and
experienced Indians' who should be made to produce 'any pictures or
lists or any other account' of past times. The Spaniards for their part
tried to make sense of the oral and written genres that they discovered
among the natives by translating them into approximate European
equivalents. Thus Alonso de Molina (1514–79), author of the first
Nahuatl–Spanish dictionary, rendered the pictographic equivalents of
the Spanish *cronista* variously as *altepetlacuilo* ('community-painter'),
xiuhtlacuilo ('year-painter') and *tenemilizicuiloani* ('life-painter', that
is, biographer), while also distinguishing a further '*contador de historia*', the *tenemilizpoa*, which appears to refer to reciters of oral
tradition.

It was not only the sympathetic approach of some of the missionaries that helped to secure the indigenous heritage in the face of
destruction worthy of the Qin book-burning, but native adaptability
to the tools of the conquerors. Writing provided a medium for presenting their own history to the Europeans, and it even offered the
ethnic groups suppressed by the Aztecs an outlet for distinguishing
themselves in Spanish eyes. It also gave indigenous writers a venue in
which they could defend native practices by identifying similarities
with Christianity. Just as European writers had since antiquity tried to
integrate myth and history through 'euhemerism' (the explanatory
reduction of pagan gods and demigods into historical figures), so
Mesoamerican natives practised the reverse, turning ancestors into
deities, the records of this being adduced by later generations as proof
of how things had been. From this it was a very short step to find
linkages or equivalences between their gods and Christian saints,

a process in which some of the Spanish collaborated. What many of the indigenous writers who used older native sources appear to have done is to embellish their works with Christian additions (especially chronology) and Spanish words, transmitting an elastic version of the originals, most of which have been lost. Thus the *Crónica Mexicáyotl*, written at the end of the sixteenth century by the Mexica historian Fernando Alvarado Tezozómoc, appears to have been a transcription of older annals. The annals composed by one writer of Nahuatl, the Franciscan-educated nobleman known usually as Chimalpahín (Hispanicized as Don Domingo de San Antón Muñón Chimalpahín Quauhtlehuanitzin, 1579–1660), provide years both Anno Domini and imputed according to the *xiuhpohualli* (the pre-Conquest 'year count' or cyclical calendar): thus '9 Flint Year, 1592' is followed by '10 House Year, 1593', '11 Rabbit Year, 1594', and so on. Chimalpahín's annals for post-Conquest times follow a pattern familiar to any reader of medieval chronicles. The rather spare entries for more remote years during which the adult author, a child at the time of the events recorded, was dependent on others for information, gradually broadened as he began to write annals year by year, as events occurred – or sometimes even day by day. It is also remarkable, though not unique, for its wide purview, since Chimalpahín's vision of history embraced the whole world. The events he recorded occurred in virtually every quarter of the globe, and include even a recent European tragedy, the 1610 assassination of King Henri IV of France.

To the south, in the Andes, writing was not introduced at all before 1532, and no complete narrative history of the ruling Incas pre-dates the arrival of the Spanish, though echoes of earlier oral histories have been found in later works, and a set of paintings of Inca monarchs, commissioned by the ninth Inca, Pachacuti Inca Yupanqui (r. 1438–71), awaited the Europeans. But even if they lacked the Mesoamericans' sense of chronicity, the Andeans were not a people without history. The ruling Incas in particular had a strong interest in the past and had developed the means to preserve its memory. They had used the quipu, or coloured, knotted cords, whose meaning was retained and interpreted by *quipucamayocs* (quipu-keepers), to record numerical data for administrative purposes, and also as cues to those charged with memorizing and performing oral traditions, which were maintained through periodic performances called *cantares* (the Spanish term for their songs). Pedro Sarmiento de Gamboa, no admirer of the Inca rulers, nonetheless believed that this was a historically minded people, and that Pachacuti Inca Yupanqui had instituted the collection of annals by sending out a summons to 'all the old historians in all the provinces he had subjugated'.

From the Europeans' perspective, these forms of record-keeping were inferior to alphabetic writing, just as oral tradition was deemed less trustworthy than history, but they initially refrained from dismissing them outright. By the mid-seventeenth century, however, a more general hostility to non-traditional media was emerging in Europe, including non-alphabetic writing and oral traditions arising from the 'vulgar'. Contemporaries were fully prepared to draw comparisons between exotic native barbarism and the home-grown forms that they had themselves escaped (soon to be a major theme of eighteenth-century analyses of the progress of civil society). The seventeenth-century English bishop Edward Stillingfleet (1635–99), who doubted the worth of both oral tradition and non-alphabetic writing for either record-keeping or the determination of chronology, lumped native histories together with those of Eurasian heathen nations as altogether false, riddled with 'monstrous confusion [and] ambiguity'. While the attitude of many subsequent Enlightenment thinkers was often sympathetic to oral culture (seen as a natural form of early communication) and even critical of European dependence on writing, most would continue to assert the impossibility of deriving history from non-textual sources.

We can close this section with two indigenous historians who represent, in different ways, the impact of one civilization's historiographical conventions on another's, and the potential of the two to mix. The first of these was an aristocratic mestizo, Gómez Suárez de Figueroa, better known as Garcilaso de la Vega, who adopted the title 'El Inca'. Garcilaso (1539–1616) had left Peru as a young man in 1560, and spent the rest of his life in Europe; he was thoroughly Hispanicized, and he wrote his works in polished Castilian prose. But he was also a native of Cuzco, 'formerly the Rome of that empire', and immensely proud of his Inca heritage. He could read Italian and had absorbed the historical style of the Renaissance via Guicciardini and Bodin; he repudiated the reading of romances in favour of history after studying Pedro Mexía's *History of the Caesars*. However, Garcilaso was also keenly affected by the stories he had heard as a child from relatives. His interests extended to the more northerly Spanish ventures in America. An early

work about Hernando de Soto's failed expedition to the American southeast in the 1540s, recounted with the enthusiasm of a Xenophon, and
usually referred to as *The Florida of the Inca* (1605), is among the first
histories of ventures into what is now Florida and the Gulf coast; its
depiction of native resistance to the Spanish hearkens back to Tacitus'
Germania. By the time he completed his most celebrated works, *Royal
Commentaries of the Incas* (1609) and especially its posthumously published companion volume, *The General History of Peru* (1617),
Garcilaso had entirely assumed the garb of a humanist historian, enliven-
ing his story with invented speeches, attempting to reconcile the conflicting accounts in his sources and appealing, not without some scepticism,
to the authority of earlier historians such Cieza de León. That a mixed-
blood Peruvian, living in Spain, would now rest his case not on native
tradition but on the words of sixteenth-century Spaniards, taken as
authoritative because of their personal experience in the lands about
which they wrote, says a good deal about the nature of literary traffic
by the beginning of the seventeenth century, and about the cultural
hybridity of history and historians.

Despite Garcilaso's ancestry and his attentiveness to oral tradition,
his work lies much closer to the European culture he had adopted than
the Andean one he had abandoned: he stretched the normal genre
boundaries of narrative history by venturing extensively into philology and linguistics, but in the end these are all part of the broader
humanist discourse. Our second author, Felipe Guaman Poma de
Ayala (*c.* 1535–after 1616) is a very different case. Although he too
saw natives and Spanish as compatible – he wrote the Andeans into
world history by repeatedly asserting that they were directly descended from Adam – there is a sharper edge to his history, and an anti-
Incan perspective. Guaman Poma was of humble background, though
he called himself a nobleman. Patrilineally descended from an Andean
ethnic group previously subjugated by the 'usurping' Incas, he chose
to stress this heritage rather than his Inca maternity. Consequently,
Europeans are not the sole villains of his piece: the Incas get as harsh
a treatment as the Spanish who succeeded them. Indeed, it was the
Incas, subjugators of neighbouring populations, who had displaced
a proto-Christian monotheism in the region with paganism.

Guaman Poma wrote his *First New Chronicle and Good Government*
in both Quechua and Castilian, and he included numerous pen and ink
drawings, even a depiction of his imagined presentation of his work to

King Philip III. Guaman Poma was well versed in the works of earlier Spanish historians including Las Casas and Acosta, and he freely exploited and paraphrased other histories, even those of which he was critical. Yet his 'chronicle', while wearing the cloak of Western historiography, and outwardly adopting its forms, is unlike any European history of the day. Not written sequentially, its chapters mix narrative and non-narrative sections, and show throughout traces of its author's indigenous culture: its table of contents is divided according to the Andean decimal system, and the book employs narrative to explain the pictures rather than using the pictures to illustrate the narrative, thereby undercutting the primacy of alphabetic literacy. It is not necessary to assume that Guaman Poma failed to grasp the conventions of European historiography – he may simply have chosen to adapt them to his own ends. He wrote, he said, both to set the record straight on the story of the Spanish Conquest and to preserve rapidly disappearing oral narratives by translating them into written form. However, his work is just as much a polemic on a number of issues that enraged him, from flaws in the governance of the kingdom of Peru, to the evils of the clergy, the sins of both Europeans and miscegenated natives, and the need for a Christian ruler to preside over the whole region under the Spanish king's authority (a post to which Guaman Poma helpfully nominated his own son). His is an early instance of a phenomenon that would occur more extensively in the twentieth century; the adoption by the colonized of Western historicity and European historical methods as tools of resistance against the colonizing powers.

Historiographically, the New World had offered historians and geographers the equivalent of modern particle physics' dark matter: after initially failing in their valiant efforts to accommodate it within the rules of the classical–scriptural universe, they were ultimately forced to revise their theories under the weight of empirical evidence. This would prove to be a slow process, and the full impact of the discoveries on European thought about world history would really not be felt till the eighteenth century as writers, despite hyperbolic assertions about the significance of the New World, continued to treat it as marginal to world history. Similarly, in the sphere of natural history, the idea of the simultaneous creation of all species at a single point in time a few thousand years earlier would not be thoroughly displaced before the nineteenth century. But, as noted above, it was becoming clear to some that there were fundamental problems with inherited, biblically supported chronology.

Without highly elaborate mental gymnastics, it could not explain archaeological, fossil and botanical discoveries, nor account very convincingly for the existence of previously undetected peoples. The long-standing foundations for Europe's understanding of both past and present were beginning to crack.

New World Encounters 3: History in Early Colonial North America

A convenient passage from the Renaissance to the Enlightenment is provided by the historical thought and writing of British and French colonial writers in North America, where, too, Europeans discovered indigenous residents. Here, the writings of the Spaniards, especially Acosta, were influential in the formulation of North American colonial ideas about the natives they encountered. They promoted the belief that despite their record-keeping capacity, savages can have no 'civil history' in the form of a narrative of events, and must therefore be studied as a branch of natural history, or as 'philosophic' or 'conjectural' history, as the eighteenth-century Scot William Robertson would do in his *History of America*. To the examples provided by sixteenth-century Spaniards there could be added the observations of more recent travellers such as the French Jesuit Joseph-François Lafitau (1681–1746), whose 1724 opus *Customs of the American Savage, Compared with the Customs of Earliest Times* provided an explicit comparison between the North American natives and the tribal societies documented by Caesar, Tacitus and other classical historians. The direct linkage between the barbarians of antiquity and modern savages is illustrated in Lafitau's declaration that he found ancient text and modern observation to be mutually reinforcing, the practices and dress of contemporary natives providing insights into the textual descriptions by Greeks and Romans of the primitive peoples of long ago. This would be a theme much taken up in the eighteenth century.

Seventeenth-century English-speaking colonists were aware that they shared the continent not only with the French to the north and the Spanish to the south, but also with a native population. Their coexistence was uneasy from the beginning. An important difference from the Spanish American experience, however, affected the shape of writing about colonial-native history. In North America, unlike Peru or Mexico, there was no datable 'Conquest' to relate but rather a slower process of settlement, pacification and the occasional massacre. The colonial period was marked by a series of wars between the new-comers, often allied with some tribes against other tribes, who in turn were usually aligned with European rivals. The culminating episode in this phase of conflict with the indigenous population was the 'French and Indian War', the North American theatre of the Seven Years' War between alliances led respectively by Britain and France (1756–63). The accounts of these struggles furnish us with a loose counterpart to Spanish sixteenth-century Conquest narratives in the sense that they provided a military subject to authors for whom war ran a close second to religion as the natural matter of history.

Like the Spanish, the earliest historians in the future United States looked to Europe for their historiographic models as well as for the conceptual glasses through which they viewed their world. Older forms such as the chronicle and providential themes lingered across the Atlantic rather longer than at home. Towards the end of the period, the great Enlightenment historians of Europe would be read, influencing revolutionary ideology. History played an enormous role in the creation and consolidation of the colonies' sense of identity, and then in the establishment and growth of the new republic. As with other modern nations that originated as settler offshoots of European powers, histor-ical writing in the North American colonies had begun as a variant of travel literature, designed less to narrate the past than to describe for readers in the mother country the flora and fauna of the new territories and to provide some sense of the customs of their peoples; this drew on the model then emerging in England, often referred to as 'chorography', a term derived from ancient geography and applied to the description of towns or counties. The first writer to compose a 'history' in the sense of a more or less true story about the recent past, in narrative form, was the explorer John Smith (1579–1631), in his *A True Relation* (1608) and later in his *General History of Virginia, New England, and the Summer Isles* (1624), a work modelled on contemporary English accounts of Near Eastern peoples such as the Turks.

In Puritan New England, history rapidly developed a providential strain, characteristic of early modern Protestant societies, that has never entirely disappeared from America's account of its own past. If missionary zeal in Latin America attempted to impose the doctrinal uniformity of the Counter-Reformation, much of the English/British colonial venture sprang from its Protestant antithesis. In New England, early historians were influenced by a number of relatively recent English histories. Most prominent among these was John Foxe's *Acts and Monuments* (or 'Book of Martyrs', as it was popularly known), a complete ecclesiastical history that included graphic examples of the Catholic persecution of Protestants; first published in 1563, it was expanded subsequently, and reprinted many times during the next century; nearly as influential was the Elizabethan courtier Sir Walter Ralegh's *History of the World* (1614), a tome with Reformation-era apocalyptic overtones that appealed to the militant Protestantism of the settlers. Colonists composed histories recounting the settlement of these rugged territories, interpreting the near-miraculous deliverance of the *Mayflower* migrants from hunger and cold as proof that God had willed a godly community to be established and to thrive. The separation of the wicked from the worthy and the redemption of sin, mirroring the transformation of the untamed wilderness into a fruitful land of milk and honey, runs through most of this material, sometimes linked with millennial expectations of Christ's imminent return. And as in Old Testament times, antinomians and apostates are cast out into the wilderness.

Easily the most influential colonial history of the early eighteenth century, and a fitting place to close this chapter, was the work of Cotton Mather (1663–1728). The *Magnalia Christi Americana; or the Ecclesiastical History of New England*, which Mather began to write in 1693, was published in 1702. Its seven books have a composite structure that is strangely reminiscent of the annals-and-biography format of Chinese historiography (of which Mather himself was un-likely to have known). Beginning with an account of the establishment of New England's colonies in Book I, Mather then provides two books' worth of biographical accounts of important public figures, clerical and secular, and, in Book IV, a narrative of the history of Harvard College, of which his father, Increase Mather, had been president. These appealed to the growing public appetite for exemplary biography, offering accounts of the godly lives of Puritan colonists. The last three books turn to ecclesiastical history proper, with Book V – clearly influenced by Foxe – entitled 'Acts and Monuments of the Faith and Order in the Churches of New England'; the final two books chronicle instances of God's providence and 'the Wars of the Lord' respectively. While Mather was very much the product of seventeenth-century reli-giosity who actively supported witch trials, aspects of his book point ahead to the Enlightenment and Revolutionary eras: in particular its sense of the mission of the colonial 'saints' to establish a new society separate from the corruption of old Europe.

Conclusion

As the eighteenth century opened, global historical culture had been significantly transformed from its appearance less than three hundred years before, especially within Europe. A sense of the past as distinctive and different from the present had emerged, one quite different from that which characterized ancient and medieval times. We can summarize the reasons for and evidence of the change: generation after generation of philologists, the emergence of antiquarian 'erudition', a keener sense of the differences between epochs, the alternately stimulating and limiting influences of ideology and religion, and the willingness to look seriously at the foundations of historical knowledge – all of this magnified through the mechanical marvel of print, the arrival of history as a vendible commercial genre, the decline of the chronicle as the dominant literary form of history-writing, and a considerably higher literacy rate in many parts of the continent. While some of these changes are less obvious in the great Asian empires, in some respects these (and China in particular) maintained the most systematic state-sponsored apparatus for writing about the past. But Europe was fast catching up as the flourishing of courtly historiography throughout the period demonstrates.

The next century would give rise to a capacity to generalize and theorize about the overall course of human events with an eye on the future as much as the past. Meanwhile, the map of the world had been both enlarged and redrawn, and Europe's expansion both eastward and westward had initiated what would eventually become its dominant influence over the historical thought and writing of all the inhabited continents.

QUESTIONS FOR DISCUSSION

1. In what ways did Renaissance humanists depart from the conventions of medieval historical writing and thought? What aspects of their heritage were they unable to escape?
2. Identify three common features shared by European, Islamic and Chinese historical writing during the period from 1450 to 1700.

3. Was the process of expanding European ideas of history and conventions of writing a one-way imposition on conquered peoples? How did encounters with 'barbarians' and 'savages' affect the Europeans?
4. What were the major factors encouraging greater circulation and production of historical writing through much of the world?
5. Was a sense of calendrical time and of chronology a necesssary condition of history-writing? On its own, was it sufficient?
6. Why did Europeans, more than other cultures, develop a sense of historical change and distance from antiquity?

Further Reading

General

Anderson, Benjamin and Felipe Rojas (eds), *Antiquarianisms: Contact, Conflict, Comparison* (Oxford and Philadelphia, 2017)
Burke, Peter, *The Renaissance Sense of the Past* (London, 1969)
Rabasa, José, Masayuki Sato, Edoardo Tortarolo and Daniel Woolf (eds), *The Oxford History of Historical Writing*, Vol. 3: *1400–1800* (Oxford, 2011)
Schnapp, Alain et al. (eds), *World Antiquarianism: Comparative Perspectives* (Los Angeles, 2013)

Renaissance and Seventeenth-Century Europe

Cochrane, Eric, *Historians and Historiography in the Italian Renaissance* (Chicago, IL, 1981)
Grafton, Anthony, *What was History? The Art of History in Early Modern Europe* (Cambridge, 2007)
Huppert, George, *The Idea of Perfect History: Historical Erudition and Historical Philosophy in Renaissance France* (Urbana, IL, 1970)
Ianziti, Gary, *Writing History in Renaissance Italy: Leonardo Bruni and the Uses of the Past* (Cambridge, MA, 2012)
Kagan, Richard L., *Clio and the Crown: The Politics of History in Medieval and Early Modern Spain* (Baltimore, MD, 2009)
Kelley, Donald R., *Foundations of Modern Historical Scholarship: Language, Law, and History in the French Renaissance* (New York, 1970)
Kelley Donald R. (ed.), *History and the Disciplines: The Reclassification of Knowledge in Early Modern Europe* (Rochester, NY, 1997)
Knowles, David, *Great Historical Enterprises: Problems in Monastic History* (London and New York, 1963)

Ranum, Orest, *Artisans of Glory: Writers and Historical Thought in Seventeenth-Century France* (Chapel Hill, NC, 1980)

Skovgaard-Petersen, Karen, *Historiography at the Court of Christian IV (1588– 1648)* (Copenhagen, 2002)

Woolf, Daniel, *The Social Circulation of the Past: English Historical Culture, 1500–1730* (Oxford, 2003)

Chinese Historical Writing under the Ming and Early Qing Dynasties

Brook, Timothy, *Geographical Sources of Ming–Qing History* (Ann Arbor, MI, 2002)

Franke, Wolfgang, 'Historical Writing during the Ming', in F. W. Mote and D. C. Twitchett (eds), *The Cambridge History of China*, Vol. 7: *The Ming Dynasty, 1368–1644*, Part I (Cambridge, 1988), 726–82

Ng, On-cho and Q. Edward Wang, *Mirroring the Past: The Writing and Use of History in Imperial China* (Honolulu, 2005)

Struve, Lynn A. (ed.), *Time, Temporality, and Imperial Transition: East Asia from Ming to Qing* (Honolulu, 2005), 73–112

Early Modern Historiography in Islamic Asia and Africa

Fleischer, Cornell H., *Bureaucrat and Intellectual in the Ottoman Empire: The Historian Mustafa Ali (1541–1600)* (Princeton, NJ, 1986)

Hardy, Peter, *Historians of Medieval India: Studies in Indo-Muslim Historical Writing*, 2nd edn (New Delhi, 1997)

Meserve, Margaret, *Empires of Islam in Renaissance Historical Thought* (Cambridge, MA, 2008)

Mukhia, Harbans, *Historians and Historiography During the Reign of Akbar* (New Delhi, 1976)

Narayana Rao, Velcheru, David Shulman and Sanjay Subrahmanyam, *Textures of Time: Writing History in South India, 1600–1800* (New York, 2003)

Philips, C. H. (ed.), *Historians of India, Pakistan, and Ceylon* (London, 1961)

Piterberg, Gabriel, *An Ottoman Tragedy: History and Historiography at Play* (Berkeley, CA, 2003)

Quinn, Sholeh A., *Historical Writing during the Reign of Shah 'Abbas: Ideology, Imitation and Legitimacy in Safavid Chronicles* (Salt Lake City, UT, 2000)

Tezcan, Baki, 'The Politics of Early Modern Ottoman Historiography', in V. H. Aksan and D. Goffman (eds), *The Early Modern Ottomans: Remapping the Empire* (Cambridge, 2007), 167–98

New World Encounters 1: Europeans in Asia and the Americas

Brading, D. A., *The First America: The Spanish Monarchy, Creole Patriots, and the Liberal State, 1492–1867* (Cambridge, 1991)

Burke, Peter, 'America and the Rewriting of World History', in K. O. Kupperman (ed.), *America in European Consciousness, 1493–1750* (Chapel Hill, NC, 1995), 33–51

Delgado-Gómez, Angel, *Spanish Historical Writing about the New World, 1493–1700* (Providence, RI, 1994)

Pagden, Anthony, *European Encounters with the New World: From Renaissance to Romanticism* (New Haven, CT, 1993)

Rubiés, Joan-Pau, *Travel and Ethnology in the Renaissance: South India through European Eyes, 1250–1625* (Cambridge, 2000)

New World Encounters 2: Indigenous Histories from the Americas

Adorno, Rolena, *Guaman Poma: Writing and Resistance in Colonial Peru* (Austin, TX, 2000)

Baudot, Georges, *Utopia and History in Mexico: The First Chroniclers of Mexican Civilization (1520–1569)*, trans. Bernard R. Ortiz (Niwot, CO, 1995)

Boone, Elizabeth Hill, *Stories in Red and Black: Pictorial Histories of the Aztecs and Mixtecs* (Austin, TX, 2000)

Florescano, Enrique, *Memory, Myth, and Time in Mexico: From the Aztecs to Independence*, trans. Albert G. Bork and Kathryn R. Bork (Austin, TX, 1994)

Julien, Catherine, *Reading Inca History* (Iowa City, 2000)

Lockhart, James (ed. and trans.), *We People Here: Nahuatl Accounts of the Conquest of Mexico* (Eugene, OR, 1993)

Mignolo, Walter D., *The Darker Side of the Renaissance: Literacy, Territoriality, and Colonization*, 2nd edn (1995; Ann Arbor, MI, 2003)

New World Encounters 3: History in Early Colonial North America

Arch, Stephen Carl, *Authorizing the Past: The Rhetoric of History in Seventeenth-Century New England* (De Kalb, IL, 1994)

Gay, Peter, *A Loss of Mastery: Puritan Historians in Colonial America* (Berkeley, CA, 1966)

Read, David, *New World, Known World: Shaping Knowledge in Early Anglo-American Writing* (Columbia, MO and London, 2005)

1712 Arai Hakuseki's *Reflections on History* is published

1723 Pietro Giannone's *Civil History of the Kingdom of Naples* is published

1725 Giambattista Vico's *New Science* is published (revised in 1735 and 1744)

1751 Voltaire's *The Age of Louis XIV* is published

1752 Henry St John, Viscount Bolingbroke's *Letters on the Study and Use of History* is published posthumously

1770–87 Guillaume Thomas Raynal's *Philosophical and Political History of the Two Indies* is published in over thirty editions

mid- to late 18th cent. Scottish Enlightenment historical thought and writing achieves prominence; 'stadial' view of historical change advanced

1772–1800 Zhang Xuecheng writes *General Principles of Literature and History*

1774 Johann Gottfried Herder's *Also a Philosophy of History*; Lord Kames' *Sketches of the History of Man*

1776–89 Edward Gibbon's *Decline and Fall of the Roman Empire* is published

1783 Catharine Macaulay completes her history of seventeenth-century England, a major work by a female historian, noted for its political radicalism

1784–91 Johann Gottfried Herder's *Reflections on the Philosophy of the History of Mankind* is published

1795 Marie-Jean-Antoine-Nicolas Caritat, marquis de Condorcet's *Sketch for a Historical Picture of the Progress of the Human Mind* is published posthumously

1798 Motoori Norinaga's *Commentary on Kojiki* is completed

early 19th cent. Era of Romanticism and heroic historiography often linked to national liberation movements; renewed interest in medieval past in Europe, and in folk tradition

1805 Mercy Otis Warren's *History of the Rise, Progress, and Termination of the American Revolution* is published

4 | Enlightenment, Revolution and Reaction, c. 1700–1830

Eighteenth-Century European Historical Culture

Understanding the eighteenth century historiographically, at least within Europe and its colonial offshoots, is complicated by what appears on the surface to be countervailing forces running both for and against the study of the past. On the one hand, this was the 'Age of Enlightenment', concerned with natural and philosophical universals – the period of post-Newtonian science, of the classifying activities of physical scientists such as Buffon and Linnaeus, and of philosophical arguments on abstract concepts of natural rights and liberty. On the other hand, Britain's David Hume (a philosopher best known in his day as author of the most widely admired history of his country to be published in the eighteenth century) was not boasting idly when he declared his the 'historical age' (and his native Scotland the 'historical nation'). The stream of published history produced in the previous two centuries swelled even further, its very commonplaceness now posing a problem for readers and critics, as publishers used innovative marketing methods such as subscription (a kind of early 'crowd-funding') and serial publication (releasing very large books unbound and in instalments to appeal to those on a budget) to sell their wares more widely. Popular print spread history geographically and socially, and the growth of public and circulating libraries increased the readership of even the most expensive books. Meanwhile, major research libraries such as the French Bibliothèque du Roi continued to expand their collections of manuscripts, now extending to material from the Americas, the Arabic world and East Asia, making possible a more detailed universal or world history. Large publishing projects by collaborative teams produced several such projects in the course of the century, beginning with the *Universal History* (1747–68). A wide-ranging work which included Asia in its scope, it was quite unlike medieval and early modern universal histories, or even Bossuet's late seventeenth-century *Discourse*. More impressive still was the multi-volume *Philosophical and Political History of the Two Indies* published in Amsterdam in 1770 by the Abbé Guillaume Thomas Raynal (1713–96). This multi-authored work, perhaps more philosophy than history, was a virtually global account of the non-European world (the 'two Indies' of its title, East and West, covered a great deal of territory), and in particular of the growth of commerce, the consummate engine of social progress and a favoured subject of the philosophic historian. The *Two Indies* was astonishingly successful, with over thirty editions appearing from 1770 to 1787; Napoleon Bonaparte would eventually take it with him to Egypt.

As we saw in an earlier chapter, the authors of European historical writing had become aware both of its own competing genres and, gradually, of the relationship of these to other modes of capturing the past including myth and fiction. Historians who evaluated the record-keeping and tradition-telling of the Americas and India recognized that these practices were unlike those of the West to a greater degree than the historiographic traditions of that nearest of non-Christian neighbours, the Islamic world. The development of comparative linguistics by scholars such as the philologist William Jones (1746–94), whose exposure to Persian literature had already influenced his sense of the relations between language families, opened up consideration of India's Hindu epics as history. The capacity to grasp the essential differences between European genres of history-writing and, say, an Inca quipu remained limited, and alien forms of recollection and representation alike were slotted into Western categories, even Western literary genres, that were often a poor fit. But that a deeper awareness of the distinctiveness of European historiography (and eventually European History) was developing, and in ways it could not have during either antiquity or the Christian Middle Ages when it had little to be compared with, there can be no doubt.

This consciousness of the 'other' extended as far east as China, thanks to the writings of earlier missionaries and of sinophiles like the late seventeenth-century historian, mathematician and philosopher, Gottfried Wilhelm Leibniz (1646–1716). Various aspects of Chinese history and culture proved popular, including the study of Confucianism. Chinese historiography, it was conceded, was not to be placed in the same category as those native societies without alphabetic writings. (Some such as the early eighteenth-century cleric

William Warburton believed Chinese characters to be a kind of transitional stage between Egyptian hieroglyphics and true alphabetic writing.) But neither was it simply a parallel tradition. By the mid-eighteenth century, when comparison between cultures was especially in vogue, it was possible to generalize about the differences between Europe's historiography and that of other peoples, beyond the type of internal audits that Bodin and subsequent authors of *artes historicae* had conducted. Voltaire, notably, was provocatively enthusiastic about Chinese historiography. 'If any annals carry with them the stamp of certainty', he wrote (the 'if' is important: he was never certain that any actually *did*), 'they are those of China', which had escaped the tyranny of allegories, myths and absurd descent legends. 'Here is a people who, for upwards of four thousand years, daily write their annals.' Edward Gibbon (see below, pp. 141–42) attributed modern knowledge of ancient and medieval Tartar history to that illiterate people's interactions with various European nations, but also to the Chinese historians, several of whom he cites in translation. He was acquainted with many of them, and with 'Sematsien' (Sima Qian) in particular, through the earlier writings of the eminent French historian and academician, Nicolas Fréret (who had studied Chinese), and in the work of Gibbon's French, and Chinese-fluent, contemporary, Joseph de Guignes. The latter's *General History of the Huns, Turks, Mongols and Other Western Tartar Peoples* (1756–8) was an ambitious attempt to compare the civilized cultures of Europe (including their historical writings) with the nomadic societies of central Eurasia.

History was a conversational subject in the salons and coffee houses, while gentlemen's clubs, secretive orders such as the Freemasons – with whom both the German philosopher of history J. G. Herder and the Russian historian Nikolay Karamzin (1766–1826) were affiliated – and more formal societies of *savants* on the model of the Académie française (est. 1635) and Académie royale des Inscriptions et Médailles (est. 1663; renamed the Académie des Inscriptions et Belles-Lettres in 1716) continued to spring up in Europe's capitals and even its provincial towns. The age of historians' dependence upon private patronage and of the prominence of court-sponsored or 'official' history was drawing to a close, despite the persistence of such offices in several European monarchies and the Ottoman Empire. Historians had become public figures, widely recognizable in polite society, their own portraits painted and often engraved within books. The success of their works depended upon public tastes and patterns of consumption. While expensive, lavishly bound folios and quartos graced the libraries of the wealthy and the powerful, they did not suit the habits of an increasing number of readers of middling status. Carl Christoffer Gjörwell, a Swedish publisher, championed the greater saleability of small-format books, pointing to bestsellers such as the Frenchman Charles Rollin's (1661–1741) thirteen-volume *Ancient History* (1734–9). The quality of much of this output was naturally mixed, and critics such as England's Lord Bolingbroke publicly lamented the absence of historians of the elegance and credibility of Thucydides.

University appointments dedicated to history, rare thitherto, drew the major teaching institutions of Europe more closely into the historical enterprise, laying foundations for the academic dominance of historical writing in subsequent times. Oxford and Cambridge both acquired 'Regius' (that is, royally nominated) professors of modern history in 1724, Edinburgh its professorship in 'Universal History and Greek and Roman Antiquities' five years earlier. The new university of Göttingen (est. 1734) would become the intellectual centre of the German Enlightenment and a locus of special significance for historical education. The periodical became for the first time a significant medium for public discussions of history. *Fin-de-siècle* literary journals such as Bayle's *Nouvelles de la République des Lettres* (1684–7) were succeeded in the early eighteenth century by many other such titles like Britain's *History of the Works of the Learned* (1699–1712) and *Gentleman's Magazine* (1731–1907), which responded to the already noted welter of historical books by offering their readers reviews of new works and advertising their publication.

Women were among the beneficiaries of this publishing explosion. Female readership of history had increased considerably during the sixteenth and seventeenth centuries and a modest number of histories and biographies had been authored by women. The eighteenth century continued both of these trends, as England's Catharine Macaulay (1731–91), author of a politically radical history of seventeenth-century England, and the United States' Mercy Otis Warren (1728–1814) and Hannah Adams (1755–1831) wrote historical works of lasting value. History assumed a privileged place in female libraries, its virtues praised by a host of educational writers of both sexes, including alike conservative women such as Hester Chapone (1727–1801) and the feminist Mary Wollstonecraft (1759–97). The personal collection of Russia's Tsarina Elizabeth (r. 1741–61), principally in French, was dominated by history books from the ancients through Rollin's *Ancient History* while Catherine the Great (r. 1762–96) found the time to publish her own 'Notes' on Russian history. The Swedish noblewoman Charlotta Frölich (1698–1770) anonymously published a history book in 1759 for poor people and peasants, while Madame Roland (1754–93), guillotined during the Terror, wished in her last days that she might have lived to have become the Catharine Macaulay of the French Revolution. Apart from religious tracts and courtesy manuals, history's only credible rivals for educated women's literary attention proved to be the French romance and its cross-Channel cousin, the English novel.

In an effort to ensure that their accounts appealed to both women and men (male readers, too, being increasingly drawn to sentimental matters), historians leavened their normal fare of battles and political events with human interest, personality and emotion. This was not opportunistic artifice: the historian was obliged not simply to *depict* virtuous behaviour in a moral history but to go one step beyond and actively arouse in the reader sympathetic reactions to its characters. The Scottish philosopher and jurist Lord Kames, expressing the wish that his own *Sketches of the History of Man* (1774) become a popular work 'chiefly with the female sex', took pains to translate any foreign or classical quotations. Voltaire formulated his own thoughts on the proper writing of history partly in response to his sometime lover Emilie du Châtelet's complaints about untidy assemblages of facts, disconnected details and 'a thousand accounts of battles which have decided nothing', a comment echoed by one of Jane Austen's fictitious characters, Catherine Morland. It is not exaggerating to say that the eighteenth-century prototype of the modern 'cultural turn' away from political and military history was hastened by historians' wish to seem more relevant to female readers.

Mary Wollstonecraft had asserted that women were fully capable of understanding political history, and a number of women embraced it. Mercy Otis Warren, among the first historians of the new American republic, serves as a good example. A correspondent of England's 'republican virago' Catharine Macaulay, Warren's sympathies were thoroughly revolutionary and democratic. In a curious twist of fate, she would write her *History of the Rise, Progress, and Termination of the American Revolution* (unpublished until 1805) in the former home of Thomas Hutchinson (1711–80), himself a historian of Massachusetts and its last civilian governor before the Revolution. Encouraged to write by another prominent woman, Abigail Adams (whose husband, the second American president, had insisted that history was 'not the province of the ladies'), Warren's ability to combine eyewitness recollections from major political figures along with material derived from documents into a narrative forcefully told has made her history the best known of the Revolutionary era.

Enlightenment historiography leaned heavily on many of the accomplishments of the previous two centuries and in particular on the enormous corpus of 'erudite' knowledge in the form of printed documents and texts, engravings of archaeological and architectural remains, and extensive studies of different legal systems. Two centuries of overseas travel also encouraged many of the historians of the late seventeenth and eighteenth centuries to undertake a comparative approach to the study of the past. Comparison of persons or episodes had been a part of historical writing since antiquity, but now they were being made synchronously across space as well as backwards in time, and between collective entities – societies, peoples, customs and manners. At the same time, there was emerging a healthy degree of scepticism towards Plutarchan analogies between individuals and events divorced from their contexts. Linear thinking about the present's relation to what came before it was elbowing into the literary margins – advice-books, religious texts and morality literature – the more traditional time-indifferent search for exempla and lessons wherever they could be found. The English politician and commentator on history, Henry St John, Viscount Bolingbroke (1678–1751), appeared to endorse the ancient idea of history as 'philosophy teaching by example', but he echoed Guicciardini's views of two centuries earlier in giving priority to recent history over the ancient and medieval past on the grounds that more remote periods were sufficiently different (and their records less reliable) as to undermine their applicability to the present day.

From scepticism as to the utility of the isolated example wrenched from a remote and different historical context, it was but a short step to more general theorizing about the process of human change and development, already anticipated by the legal scholars of the later

Renaissance. By 1800, a similar grasp of collective human develop-ment, and of the need to trace the step-by-step birth, growth and development of institutions, had turned the past into a cumulative process – that is, into 'History' with a capital 'H'. This is the period during which it became common for Europeans to begin to conceive of history as both an unfolding accumulation of events *and* the writings that recorded this – an intermixing of meanings that, readers will recall from Chapter 1, would never be replicated in Chinese culture before modern times. (And consequently, the reader will notice from this point on, a diminishing focus in the present volume on the literary achieve-ments of individual historians, soon numbering in the thousands, and an increased attention to what had hitherto, exceptions like Jean Bodin aside, been relatively rare – theorizing about history as a process and thinking systematically about how best to write it.) *Res gestae* and *historia rerum gestarum* were beginning to merge, things done with the account of those things, an observation borne out by the early nineteenth-century German philosopher G. W. F. Hegel's declaration of the dual meaning of the German word *Geschichte*:

> In our language, the word 'history' combines both objective and subjective meanings, for it denotes the *historia rerum gestarum* as well as the *res gestae* themselves, the historical narrative and the actual happenings, deeds, and events – which in the strictest sense, are quite distinct from one another. (*Lectures on the Philosophy of World History*, trans. H. B. Nisbet, 1975, p. 135)

For Hegel (see below, pp. 185–87), this would be no coincidence: the writing of history and History itself, subjective and objective, had appeared contemporaneously because they were both products of a transcendent order, and each was instrumentally created by the state, which is simultaneously the fundamental subject of history (the narrative) as well as the maker and self-aware recorder of History (the pattern of events).

Philosophic History, Conjecture and Stadialism

The story of eighteenth-century Europe's search for a meaning in the past – derived elsewhere than from religion, and without the primary purpose being entertainment or the provision of utilitarian

examples – might be said to have begun in the 'philosophic' histories of two Italians largely ignored in their own time. The younger
of this pair, Pietro Giannone (1676–1748), was a Neapolitan jurist
who authored a *Civil History of the Kingdom of Naples* (1723).
This blended detailed knowledge of documents (albeit often derived
at secondhand from the erudite works of earlier generations) with
a focus on social history and a reform-minded and specifically anti-
ecclesiastical outlook that would characterize much later
Enlightenment thinking. In Giannone's eyes, he had created in
'civil history' a new model of historical writing, though for a time
it had few imitators. Giannone's older contemporary Giambattista
Vico (1668–1744), Professor of Latin Eloquence at Naples, was
largely ignored for a century. His masterpiece, the *Scienza Nuova*
('New Science') was first published in 1725 and substantially
revised in later editions of 1735 and 1744. Critical of conventional
historiography, Vico perceived that humans in different ages did
not, contrary to common assumption, perceive, think about or
represent the world in the same way through all times, a profound
insight that had the effect of imposing an even greater distance
between modernity and antiquity than that realized by his fifteenth-
century Italian predecessors. And in his notion of the important role
of imagination in the task of understanding the past, Cecilia Miller
notes, Vico anticipated the ideas of later writers, such as
R. G. Collingwood, that from our perspective in the present we
must try to enter into the minds of past actors and their times.

Hard to read, allusive and ambiguous, Vico did not much appeal to
eighteenth-century audiences, and even today his impact has been
selective rather than overwhelming. It is not easy to say what the
New Science is 'about' since it veers between history, philology and
what we would now call sociology, from recommendations for proper
history-writing to speculations about the nature of early society, to
discussions of the Homeric poems and Vico's theory (taken up by later
scholarship) that they were the work of many different hands.
Moreover, the content of the *New Science* would not have resonated
with most eighteenth-century readers. Repudiating the well-worn practice (so popular in the early modern era) of periodizing history according to dynastically centred chronologies inherited from pagan and late
antique writers, Vico sought to demonstrate the progress of cultures

over time. This 'progressive' vision of history came, however, with an important limiting condition: it occurred within a larger, recurring cycle of *corsi e ricorsi*. Although he conceded 'progress' from one age to another, Vico saw no cumulative and absolute progress in the affairs of humanity. In one way, this is a reworking (and extension of scope from the political to the mental and social spheres) of the Polybian *anakuklosis politeion* (see above, Chapter 1, pp. 26–27). Vico erected this edifice on a postulated series of cycles of progress and decline, dividing the past into a series of recurring ages: of gods, of heroes and of men (the historical age) – there had been two such cycles up to his own time. Each age, which occurred at variable times and over variable durations in different parts of the world, was characterized by distinctive modes of speech, thought, law and government, and all unfolded against the imagined horizon of an 'ideal eternal history', a sort of template against which the history of all nations unfolded. Vico's insight allowed him to explain the transition from one era to another, and the emergence of civility from that pre-social state of nature postulated by seventeenth-century philosophers such as Hobbes and Locke.

While there was certainly progress between and within Vico's cyclical eras, he was no believer in absolute human progress. In this important respect, Vico was an outlier among the philosophic historians of the eighteenth century many of whom, to the contrary, took as an article of faith the notion of progress and the development of civilizations from primitive to more advanced states. Among these, no group contributed more to the recasting of history as the story of human progress, to its global scope, and to the analysis of its non-narrative forms than a number of Scots intellectuals. Adam Ferguson (1723–1816), John Millar (1735–1801), Adam Smith (1723–90) and Henry Home, Lord Kames (1696–1782), among others, wrote variants of what eventually became known as 'conjectural' history, a label that has stuck. This involved using reasoned speculation or 'conjecture' to fill in the blanks left by the historical record, especially as applied to the most remote periods of time, and to arrive at informed generalizations with respect to the history of humanity. It was comparative, it was generally erudite (albeit often eschewing the details of antiquarian research) and it focused not on politics and war but on culture, society, government and law – quite a different notion of 'universal history' than that practised by ancient and medieval historians or so recent a writer as Bishop Bossuet. It remained, however, confined by the same chronological boundaries – a world no older than six millennia – that had circumscribed all previous attempts to describe the process of long-term civilizational change. The conjectural historians thus notably avoided assigning dates to their different stages of society.

The sources of this spectacular burst of intellectual energy from a relatively obscure and underpopulated corner of Europe were diverse. They included both seventeenth-century legal scholarship and prior rationalist and sceptical discussions about how history, for all its manifest flaws and imperfections, could nonetheless be retained as a meaningful form of knowledge and literature. Instinctively cosmopolitan, the eighteenth-century Scots, living in the newly constituted United Kingdom (1707) of Great Britain, went out of their way to efface the nationalist tendencies of their medieval and early modern predecessors and repudiate their country's rough and uncivilized past. 'Nations, as well as men', remarked Scotland's Historiographer Royal, William Robertson, 'arrive at maturity by degrees, and the events, which happened during their infancy or early youth . . . deserve not to be remembered.'

Like Robertson (whose *History of America* would have considerable influence on nineteenth-century Latin American historians), the Scottish economic and social theorists knew their French historians. But they also learned a great deal from a subtler-minded Frenchman who wrote no narrative history, Charles-Louis de Secondat, baron de Montesquieu (1689–1755), whose focus on civil society and analysis of manners and culture in *The Spirit of the Laws* (1748) and elsewhere are all on display in the work of the Scots. Ferguson in particular saw his *Essay on the History of Civil Society* as a working out of Montesquieu's ideas. Ferguson's attitude to progress was ambivalent: the very peace and security that he prized had a cost, in the production of a second-rate society and consumer culture dominated by mediocre men. This historicization of the ancient theory whereby luxury leads to indolence, corruption and the loss of liberty would be quoted approvingly by Karl Marx in the next century, and it is not hard to see in it an anticipation of later cultural critics such as Nietzsche, Huizinga or Spengler. One finds also in Ferguson a sympathetic understanding of past societies which differs markedly from most contemporary French scholars and anticipates the early 'historicism' of Germans such as Herder (see below). 'Every age hath its consolations, as well as its sufferings', he observed, and those living in modern comfort will tend to exaggerate the misery of 'barbarous times'. Like Vico, Ferguson thought of fable and myth as characteristic of primitive thought about the past, and thus paradoxically a better kind of evidence than the earliest forms of historical writing. Stylistically a neoclassicist, he was particularly critical of medieval historiography, flogging anew that dead horse, the 'monkish chronicler', and his alleged incapacity to listen past the buzz of disconnected serial events.

Much of the vocabulary of the Scottish writers was inherited from the ancients through Renaissance thinkers such as Machiavelli, while their interest in customs and manners is traceable as far back as Herodotus and was to be found more recently in Conquest-era works such as Acosta's 'natural and moral' history. That said, the eighteenth-century Scots knew that they lived in neither antiquity nor the Renaissance. They had to factor a variety of evidence into their picture of the cumulative past, including 250 years of encounters with other worlds both 'savage' (the most primitive tribes of the Americas and parts of Africa) and 'barbaric' (semi-civilized peoples like the Incas, northern Laplanders and the nomads of central Eurasia), along with the observable conversion of empires to the advancement of commerce rather than simple aristocratic or dynastic aggrandizement. Adding these ingredients into the mix allowed them to jettison some time-worn explanatory paraphernalia: euhemerist inventors, miracles and even the reliable old crutch of the supposititious 'lawgiver' such as Sparta's Lycurgus, Athens' Solon or even Moses himself, men who could single-handedly invent and impose complex legal codes. Vico had doubted whether such figures ever really existed; several of the Scottish thinkers, while regarding them as historical, denied the lawgivers their authoritative role, seeing the kinds of institutions once ascribed to their genius as merely the natural outcome of a particular stage of development; these followed one another not in great leaps but 'by degrees'. States, said Ferguson, 'proceed from one form of government to another, by easy transitions, and frequently under old names adopt a new constitution', human nature containing the seeds that spring forth and ripen at particular times.

The eighteenth century thereby converted the old medieval discourse of *origo gentis* into reasoned discussion of the transitions from one stage of civilization to another, and of the impact of conflict between peoples at those different stages. While the Trojans and their litter of fictitious kings were now by and large written off, the Scythians, Goths, Israelites and even Noah's children could not be dispensed with entirely. They still offered, along with the biblical confusion of tongues at Babel (Genesis 11:1–9), the readiest explanation of both the population of the world and the forgetting of much ancient knowledge by the far-travelled descendants (Acosta's migratory native Americans among them) of once-wise founders. And while they had inherited the Hobbesian concept of a pre-social 'state of nature', they displaced this abstract and rather atemporal notion with a more concrete set of theories, empirically derived from natural history and travel literature; these described human development out of primitive states set in real periods in the past, though not always at the *same* times in different countries.

The most sophisticated formulations of this evolutionary scheme of social progress are now collectively called 'stadialism', and were not without precedent. Greeks and Romans had speculated on the progress of mankind from one type of society to the next, and there are hints of a developmental or 'civilizing' theory in the twelfth-century chronicler William of Malmesbury, while several Renaissance thinkers and historians had painted a picture of cultural or legal change as a slow and gradual process. In the late seventeenth century, the legal scholar and historian Samuel Pufendorf (1632–94) had insisted that the 'state of nature' beloved of philosophers and jurists needed to be considered as a real historical phenomenon, part of a temporal process, rather than as a Hobbesian theoretical abstraction, while asserting that commercial sociability lay at the end of historical progress. Building on Acosta's sixteenth-century view that 'savages' can have no narrative history and must therefore be studied as a branch of natural history, the Jesuit Joseph-François Lafitau (see above, p. 121) provided an explicit comparison between the North American natives and the tribal societies documented by Caesar, Tacitus and other classical historians. The direct linkage between the barbarians of antiquity and more recent writings about modern preliterate peoples is expressed in the oft-quoted remark by John Locke that 'In the beginning all the world was America.'

The unique contribution of the eighteenth century was to systematize much of this thought, along the way integrating the impact of the New World discoveries – much more fully than had most of their sixteenth- and seventeenth-century predecessors – into accounts of the development of human society and civilization. Stadialism, a special case of this thinking, is generally associated with the Scottish exponents of this perspective on the past. It postulated (usually) four stages of human development, defined principally as modes of subsistence ranging from a savage hunter-gatherer stage, through pastoral/nomadic and then agrarian stages, ending in a modernity characterized by advanced political institutions, cities and, above all, the practice of commerce. The culminating mode of subsistence featuring money, trade and inter- course between peoples would eventually provide the subject of Adam Smith's magnum opus, *An Inquiry into the Nature and Causes of the Wealth of Nations* (1776); its economic invisible hand quietly dis- placed an older Providence, much as in the natural realm Newton's *Principia* had turned God into an arm's-length creator operating through mathematically discernible laws.

An important difference between eighteenth-century stadial theory and later ideas of human development (such as nineteenth-century posi- tivism or the theories of Karl Marx) should here be stressed: the stadi- alists assumed no inevitability to progress. The failure of certain peoples to advance beyond a particular stage demonstrated this. Moreover, the stages could overlap, even within geographic proximity of one another. Human achievement occurred as a consequence of combined environ- mental and social factors, not simply as the direct consequence of either climate, as Ibn Khaldun, Bodin and Montesquieu had asserted, or providence – though both could be allowed a place. And 'progress' was not yet the only possible metanarrative, for histories still testified to many examples of social and political decline, as Ferguson observed in his account of the death of the Roman republic. Rome, indeed, remained the great case study of imperial collapse, and it would be left to an Englishman, Edward Gibbon, rather than a Scot, to describe the lengthy and gradual steps in its demise – not merely from the follies of bad emperors or even the traditional explanation of corrupting luxury, but through a complexity of forces – above all, 'barbarism and religion' – which wrought their influence over several centuries. Gibbon's magnum opus, the *Decline and Fall of the Roman Empire* (1776–89), is a work still read with enjoyment today. Generations of readers have admired its author's synthesis of elegance, sceptical treatment of sources, and an ability to generalize, the heaviness of the erudition lightened by Gibbon's ironic wit, his occasional contrarian judgments on individuals – perhaps most notoriously, the fourth-century Emperor Julian the Apostate – and his deliberatively provocative (to the ire of contemporary churchmen) views on early Christianity. Gibbon is held by many modern scholars to have most effectively managed a delicate balance among three competing streams of European historical writing; the erudite, the philosophical and the narrative.

Historical Thought in the French Enlightenment: Voltaire, Condorcet and Rousseau

Gibbon was especially indebted to the work of seventeenth- and eighteenth-century French scholarship, including the publications of the famous Académie des Inscriptions. Such gallic erudition was not, however, the most influential strain of French writing about the past. In fact, the eighteenth-century Frenchman who, at least in the short term, exerted the greatest influence on historical thought and writing outside his homeland, Voltaire, was more journalist and essayist than either scholar or *philosophe*, his ideas generally derived second-hand. But Voltaire (born François-Marie Arouet, 1694–1778) merits our attention both for his reputation and for the ambitious global scope of some of his works. His *Essay on the Manners and Spirit of Nations* was an overview and critique of institutions and customs as they had developed over several centuries. Voltaire included non-Western civilizations such as the Chinese, though his references outside European culture were often superficial and offered more as a contrarian antidote to the idea of Judeo-Christian superiority. Over the course of a lengthy career, Voltaire consistently praised features in other civilizations while still concluding that Western culture represented the apogee of human reason, though its beneficial influences were undercut by superstition and religious fanaticism. Disparaging of ancient barbarism, Voltaire could nonetheless be sympathetic to contemporary North American aboriginal 'savagery', an even more primitive state. He contributed to public knowledge of alien societies, often employing contemporary travel accounts as sources, and scoffed at the kinds of etymological and genealogical tricks still used on occasion to fabricate false ancestries.

Voltaire arrived only gradually at this cosmopolitan perspective on the past, and its emphasis on culture and civilization. Indeed, his very commitment to history is in some ways surprising, as he had inherited a good deal of the scepticism of the late seventeenth century, to the point of eventually writing his own essay *Le Pyrrhonisme de l'histoire* (1769). His initial offering as a historian was the dramatic and entertaining but thoroughly conventional *History of Charles XII* (1731), focusing on the great achievements (and ultimate failure) of that Swedish king (r. 1697–1718), juxtaposed with his modernizing foil, Russia's Tsar Peter the Great. In a Thucydidean flourish, Voltaire boasted that in *Charles XII* he had 'not set down a single fact on which we have not consulted eye-witnesses of unimpeachable veracity'. Notwithstanding this bold assertion, Voltaire's temperament was ill-disposed to the pursuit of details; he preferred the mantle of the authentic *historien* whom he distinguished from the mere *historiographe*, an assembler of facts, documents and dates from whose materials true historians can draw. Details were important only to the degree that one might learn from them something of real significance, otherwise they ought not clutter the historian's page. Documents themselves are only believable if they were written during an enlightened time. In this he had something in common with David Hume, who deplored the 'dark industry' of the archive-dwelling researcher.

The shifts in Voltaire's interests are in themselves a sign of the eighteenth-century movement from the history of *men* towards a history of *man*. Twenty years after *Charles XII*, Voltaire would publish a very different type of history in *Le siècle de Louis XIV* ('The Age of Louis XIV', 1751). Though it praised that king, the book is not in any sense *about* Louis – despite its many entertaining courtly anecdotes – or even about France, but rather about the climax of civility and reason under a generally wise monarch. While more of it is concerned with battles and political life than its author might have liked to admit, Voltaire nonetheless included much on culture, science and the arts, finding in the first part of Louis' reign one of only four truly great eras in human history, comparable with Greece, Augustan Rome and the Renaissance. The reign provided Voltaire with a benchmark for reforms urgently needed in his own time. Voltaire's optimism had limits, and never turned him into a living version of his own fictional Professor Pangloss canting that all is for the best in the best of possible worlds, especially late in life when the horrors of the Lisbon earthquake of 1755 shook confidence in a benevolent universe. Voltaire the believer in overarching progress was consistently challenged by Voltaire the contemporary social critic.

Perhaps the century's most optimistic views on human progress were espoused by Voltaire's French Revolutionary-era successor (and literary executor), Marie-Jean-Antoine-Nicolas Caritat, marquis de Condorcet (1743–94). This aristocratic *philosophe* ended his life in a Revolutionary prison, but he had completed a few months previously his *Esquisse* or 'Sketch for a Historical Picture of the Progress of the Human Mind' (intended as the introduction to a larger *Tableau historique* that he never wrote). The *Esquisse* adumbrated a nine-stage history of humanity's development, with a climactic tenth stage of reason and achievement projected to follow the Revolution, the French republic marking a culmination in the joint progress of Virtue and Enlightenment. Published in a somewhat altered form in 1795, after the Terror had subsided, the *Esquisse* became a manifesto of progress and would influence a number of important nineteenth-century thinkers from the radical Henri de Saint-Simon to the positivist Auguste Comte.

Condorcet epitomizes some of the Enlightenment tendencies against which scholars of later eras have reacted, such as its supposed hostility to all things medieval, and its historical thinkers' willingness to hypothesize with boldly assertive generalizations based on an abstract homogenization of the histories of different periods and countries. Given the lack of information about remote, preliterate times, Condorcet adopted the conjectural method of projecting the observed life of modern tribal societies on to an imputed prehistory. At the point where the historical record begins, generalization requires further hypothesis. 'Here the picture begins to depend in large part on a succession of facts transmitted to us in history', he wrote, 'but it is necessary to select them from the history of different peoples, to compare them and combine them in order to extract the hypothetical history of a single people and to compose the picture of its progress' (*Sketch for a Historical Picture of the Human Mind*, trans. Barraclough, 1953, pp. 8–9).

Condorcet's explanation of progress allowed for both individual achievement and collective advances. Change could occur either in a sudden burst or more quietly over time; it was affected by climatological factors (echoes here of both Bodin and Montesquieu, as well as Ibn Khaldun, who was known to French readers by the end of the seventeenth century) and by custom, both of which can accelerate, retard or altogether halt progress, leaving some peoples permanently stranded in the tribal and pastoral stages. Condorcet's general optimism and his faith in the capacity of the 'common man' admits the presence of countervailing, regressive aspects within any period: his eighth stage thus saw the shackles of priest-craft loosened by print but also witnessed the horrendous atrocities of the Conquests and the wars of religion. But of the general forward movement of both consciousness and man's estate, Condorcet had no doubt. He is in that sense a key transitional figure between the stadialism of the eighteenth century and the positivism of the nineteenth.

No consideration of the French Enlightenment and its views on history would be complete without reference to one of the century's most enigmatic figures, the radical Swiss thinker Jean-Jacques Rousseau (1712–78). While, like Montesquieu, he wrote no narrative history, Rousseau nevertheless gave much thought to the course of civilization and its modern discontents. Arguing for the innocence and nobility of pre-social man, he repudiated the Hobbesian notion that a violent state of nature had necessitated human society, and Locke's variant that held property and commerce, not merely safety, as among the benefits bestowed by civil society. Indeed, early civilization was the source of the economic and social inequalities that had become enshrined in his own time. Taken up by French revolutionaries after his death, Rousseau's radical political views aroused the ire of conservatives during and following the Revolution; but his views on property and class would endure and ultimately influence Karl Marx, while his admiration of the so-called 'noble savage' and of the natural state would have a potent impact on early nineteenth-century Romanticism.

The German *Aufklärung*

The Enlightenment unfolded somewhat differently in the German-speaking world, and some of the contrasts visible between historical thought elsewhere in Europe before and after the French Revolution are much more nuanced among the Germans. In part this was because Enlightenment (or *Aufklärung* as it became known) came slightly later to Germany and thus could draw eclectically on strands of thinking developed elsewhere, and even define itself in opposition to some of these; in part it was also because despite an antipathy to dogmatism (inherited from the late seventeenth-century Saxon theologian and historian of the church Gottfried Arnold [1666–1714]), the Protestant German states remained a Lutheran and Pietist stronghold fundamentally unreceptive to Voltaire and his anti-clericalism. Influenced, too, by Leibniz and his view of the universe as a series of 'monads' within which any aspect is a self-contained reflection of the whole, German thinkers also managed to accommodate Christian views of the past more easily within their belief systems. This included the framework of universal history and chronology to which the Germans had an especially strong scholarly commitment. Aesthetically, where many across Europe still saw Rome as the zenith of antiquity's achievements, the German taste ran preferentially to Greece and especially fifth-century Athens. As in the Renaissance, philology provided the master-tool for understanding a past age, and Friedrich August Wolf (1759–1824) would lay the groundwork for an interdisciplinary approach to the study of antiquity in his *Prolegomena to Homer*. Wolf's blunt declaration that 'The Homer that we hold in our hands now is not the one who flourished in the mouths of the Greeks of his own day, but one variously altered, interpolated, corrected, and emended' was built on a thorough grasp of centuries of scholarship and commentary on the *Iliad* and *Odyssey*; his reconstruction of how the epics had been composed and subsequently migrated from orality to writing would also help set the stage for a revival of interest in oral culture early in the next century. Wolf's younger, Danish-born contemporary B. G. Niebuhr (1776–1831), a diplomat turned scholar, pioneered a holistic, source-driven and integrated study of antiquity in all its aspects, a kind of problem-based scholarship which would utilize the techniques of the philologist, the historian, the epigrapher and the literary critic in a unified study of antiquity, or *Altertumswissenschaft*. Niebuhr's *Roman History*, its volumes published at intervals beginning in 1812, would become the dominant text on its subject through much of the nineteenth century.

All of this had implications for German historical thought. Where a conservative like Johann Christoph Gatterer (1727–99) clung to a literal reading of the Old Testament and a conventional Christian chronology, others kept their faith while jettisoning strict adherence to biblical time. Sceptical of scripturally derived chronology, they read the Old Testament as sacred poetry, a prophetic and moral rather than historical text, written by different authors at different times and not to be understood as a literal record of events, but with its very contradictions providing evidence of its historicity, that is, its sequential authorship over a long duration. Church history remained a major subgenre, and in the hands of some such as Johann Lorenz von Mosheim (1693–1755), chancellor of the University of Göttingen, its scope was expanded to include both secular politics and the history of learning and philosophy. The long tradition of biblical hermeneutics – the theory of interpretation as applied to the scriptures – would evolve in German hands into a potent tool for the criticism of all sorts of texts. It is the Aufklärers who developed a philosophy of the movement of human History towards perfectability, while retaining the belief that each individual period was a valuable part of the whole, both hallmarks of nineteenth-century German historical thought. The classic antithesis, once beloved of intellectual historians, that opposes a profoundly historical nineteenth century to a rationalist and naively ahistorical eighteenth, seems nowhere less convincing than among German historians, theologians and philosophers.

Among the other Enlightenments, Britain had more influence on German thinkers than France (Montesquieu being a notable exception), and within Britain, the Scots more than the English. Hume and Robertson were quickly translated into German, and Ferguson's histories seem to have enjoyed exceptional popularity, earning him the rare honour of election to the Royal Prussian Academy of Sciences and Arts. Influenced by Adam Smith, a number of Germans ventured into economic thought, trade, technological change and the study of statistics. Comparison strongly attracted them, complete with the use of parallels between societies at different stages of development: August Ludwig von Schlözer (1735–1809), the Göttingen-based student of Russian history, opened a published letter on historical methods with an explicit comparison of various ancient, medieval and modern peoples, and called for a global approach to the study of the past. The Aufklärers also attributed influence, apart from environmental factors favoured by Montesquieu, to more ineffable notions such as 'national character' and what has come to be called *Zeitgeist* (the spirit of the age), impersonal forces that could – though this was certainly not their intention – ultimately displace providence altogether as suprahuman causal agents.

Already frequent contributors to the *ars historica* literature since the late sixteenth century, Germans had now become authors of numerous companions, introductions and handbooks. But many went beyond this to think more deeply about the past, about the mechanics of change and human agency in it, and about the 'science' (*Wissenschaft*) of history. Gatterer, a formidable thinker, was critical of history arranged as serial national accounts which missed the connection of part to whole. In its place he championed a revival of biblically rooted universal history, which was a major strand of early *Aufklärung* thought. His *Handbook of Universal History* (1761) and *Introduction to Synchronistic Universal History* (1771), early entries in his prolific output of historical handbooks, exploited the observations of natural history to explain problems in the biblical account of early history, such as the great longevity of prediluvian man. He would eventually overlay his conventional Christian periodization of history with a quadripartite division of time according to degrees of social organization, forms of knowledge, including history, and major events in the Christian and non-Christian worlds.

The discontent of the German Enlightenment with a rationalist universalism that would ultimately be unable adequately to explain the uncontrollable revolutionary furor that exploded in Paris in 1789, is well displayed in the fecund mind of Johann Gottfried Herder (or von Herder, 1744–1803). A schoolmaster and clerical official, Herder was a rolling stone in both career and intellect, a man who would change his mind abruptly on issues and people, often falling out with former friends. Like Rousseau a transitional figure between the Enlightenment and the post-Revolutionary, Romantic era, Herder provides an appropriate point to bring this section to a close. A sardonic critic of abstract speculation in his polemical *Also a Philosophy of History* (1774) Herder proved just as capable of making philosophic generalizations. This work is sometimes seen as the earliest articulation, Vico aside, of a core principle of nineteenth-century historicism (for which see below, pp. 157–60), that every age must be judged on its own terms and according to its own values.

Widely translated, Herder helped set the ideological table for the nationalism of the next century, together with its repudiation of the particular variant of the generalizing universalism it associated with the Enlightenment. In Herder's view, all nations were not the same, nor did they follow a common developmental path; he was fond of organic metaphors which allowed him to see change and variety in biological terms. Each nation was part of nature, but germinated from different seeds; each would grow according to its own proclivities, the shape of the future being immanent in the past. Rejecting the French version of progress seen as the forward movement of the human mind, Herder drew attention to the role of irrational elements, including chance: he is among the very first modern authors to speculate using historical counterfactuals (see below, pp. 304–5), the 'what-if?' game which ponders how things might have turned out if, for instance, Rome 'had been founded on a different spot' or 'how Caesar would have ruled in the place of Augustus', a variant of Pascal's question about the length of Cleopatra's nose and its impact on the final years of the Roman republic. Herder also renewed attention to oral sources, his published collections of folk songs anticipating the later works of folklorists such as the Brothers Grimm.

Herder suggests that, although successive civilizations pass the torch of global leadership from one to the next, none can ever truly die since it will be contained in the final story of *Humanität*, the essence of humanity progressing towards the fulfilment of universally shared goals. Culture underlies events, rather than the other way around, and the bearer of culture and thus the vessel of *Humanität*'s history is the *Volk*, or people. This was a product of its language (itself variable and historically conditioned), social customs, manners, climate and experience, and the commonality of these transcended both political borders and the periods of political history. States might come and go, or be subdued by external conquerors, 'but the nation remains'. *Völker* were not strictly comparable with one another, and they developed at different rates, not on the single accelerating scale measured out by Condorcet. Where Condorcet was ambivalent towards the humanity of savages, Herder is clear that they are contributors to the larger human story and not to be judged inferior: they all own shares in *Humanität* while maintaining a distinct identity. Yet the march of progress is obvious, and the mere flow of time ensures that humanity moves forward, learning from the past but also outdoing it. Herder directed attention away from political and military history towards the 'inner life' of humans discernible from art, music and literature, an approach that would ultimately evolve into the nineteenth-century idea of *Kulturgeschichte*. Like Voltaire but with less condescension, he included alien peoples such as the Chinese, Africans, Eskimos and

American Indians in his sampling of *Humanität* while remaining fundamentally a Eurocentrist.

Voltaire's simplistic universalism was odious to Herder, and he similarly rejected its subtler formulations which had admitted regional variation. Instead, Herder looked to Rousseau for an authorizing myth that could displace cosmopolitanism, substituting for the latter's praise of Sparta and the Roman republic an older, Tacitean idealization of the simplicity and independence, unspoiled by modern luxury, of early German tribes. Yet we should still place Herder closer to the tradition of Enlightenment cosmopolitanism than to the Prussian and Germanic nationalism of the ensuing century. Inconsistent and changeable in his opinions, Herder's more mature work, *Reflections on the Philosophy of the History of Mankind* (1784–91) is both a synthesis of the previous century's discussions as well as a retreat from some of his earlier views, since it offers a kind of universal vision of history that the younger Herder would have found more problematic. (It would draw the criticism of Herder's one-time teacher and supporter, the distinguished philosopher Immanuel Kant [1724–1804], whose own *Idea for a Universal History from a Cosmopolitan Point of View* also appeared in 1784.) The late Herder still stands apart from the more common Enlightenment rationalist view of an unchanging nature common to all humans at all times, but he had settled on a middle ground not unlike that taken by Giambattista Vico, with whom he shared both a sense of empathy with former ages and a vision of the whole as contained within the particular.

East Asian Enlightenments

By the later eighteenth century, the Qing Empire, as complex and multi-ethnic an enterprise in the East as that of the Ottomans, French or British further west, had absorbed not only China but adjoining regions like Tibet and Mongolia. Allowing for its very different circumstances, China under the Qing, a non-native Chinese dynasty originating in Manchuria, experienced many of the same historiographical developments as the West. This included a homogenizing tendency over minority historiographies: thus a late medieval tradition of Mongol historiography, revived in the seventeenth century, had by the late eighteenth century been expunged and rewritten from a Manchu point of view. A Qing version of history, supported by official history-writing, cartography and physical monuments, over-whelmed competing versions of the past in most of the conquered territories. Qing China also shares the eighteenth-century West's inclination to universalism, though in this instance a Sinocentric rather than Eurocentric version. And, something of the classificatory tendency in contemporary European thought can be observed in the late Ming–Qing principle of *jingshi* or 'ordering the world' within which history occupied a central role.

Yet if there are similar historiographical developments in East and West, they did not unfold in the same order. This is most striking in the early Qing period when there was a flight from the philosophical abstraction of the Ming era back to close textual study. It has been characterized by the sinologist Benjamin Elman as a transition 'from philosophy to philology', as scholars placed new emphasis on evidentiary research. At the same time, the 'classics' lost something of their immutable quality as critics began to treat them like any other historical text. This trend culminated in the philosopher and literary historian Zhang Xuecheng's declaration that 'the Six Classics are History' – meaning that they were the creation of the bureaucratic institutions of the ancient sage-kings, created for specific governmental purposes, rather than the wisdom of those sages deliberately committed to writing as timeless wisdom; a more thorough 'desacralization' awaited the late nineteenth century and the influence of German historicism. The process is visible in civil service examinations, always a good litmus test of the standing of historical knowledge in China: by 1800 they required students to reflect on the development of the ancient classics as historically created documents.

Some of these phenomena are visible elsewhere in East Asia. Korea had been a largely faithful satellite or tributary of China since as far back as the Tang, and the Yi family that ruled the peninsular kingdom for five centuries were especially loyal to the Ming, who had helped expel Japanese invaders in the 1590s. The Korean monarchy also depended heavily on its mandarin class, especially the *yangban*, a hereditary caste of Confucian bureaucrats, and something analogous to the Chinese style of official history-writing had matured by the end of the sixteenth century. These ties began to loosen even as learning followed a similar trajectory, and moves to 'de-centre' China's place in the geographical and historical universe occurred, a foretaste of nineteenth-century nationalism. Yi Ik (1681–1763), an advocate of *sirhak* or 'practical learning' was a former politician-turned-historical thinker, who called for the study of Korean history in its own right. Yi's pupil, An Chŏng-Bok (1712–91) authored the first general history of Korea, *Tongsa Kangmok* ('An Outline History of the East', 1778), and similarly advocated using the lessons of the past as a reformist tool. Such concern for utility did not make truth, in a strict sense, the highest goal: morals would invariably trump evidence.

In a sense, the very shift taking place in eighteenth-century Europe from narrowly focused humanist philological erudition to rationalist and conjectural speculation about the past was, in both China and Korea, unfolding precisely in reverse. The focus of much of this learning was, as in Europe, the solution to social and political problems; and, also as in Europe, many of the most original thinkers counted themselves primarily as scholars in other areas than history. The pursuit of truth by Qing evidentiary (or *Kaozheng*) scholars would ultimately clear the way, towards the end of the Qing era, for more explicitly Western-influenced calls for a 'new historiography'. The Chinese stress on erudition continued to develop to the end of the eighteenth century, and the mounting attention given to collection and analysis of inscriptions on bronze and stone (the discovery of bones, urns and bamboo as epigraphical sources had yet to occur) as supplements of or correctives to venerable texts, neatly parallels the activities of the French Académie des Inscriptions. The *Kaozheng* opinion that learning was best done as a collective endeavour, with the findings of one scholar followed up by others, led its practitioners to consider their own and older works not merely as stand-alone texts but as research tools. The effort to make the Standard Histories more usable in this regard through the addition of visual aids such as tables of major events replicates the use of tables and charts in seventeenth- and eighteenth-century European works, part of the wider shift to a graphic and visual culture that followed the introduction of printing.

Amid all this historical criticism, the business of maintaining the formal genres of Chinese historiography continued. The Qing ordered the compilation of a Ming History within a year of their accession, but in contrast to the precipitate speed at which the early Ming historians had produced an inferior *Yuanshi*, the Qing historians took their time about it. An interim draft *History of the Ming* was completed early in the eighteenth century, and the long-lived Kangxi Emperor (r. 1661–1722), who saw himself as a scholar, undertook revisions to the work as it was produced. His insistence on commenting on every successive draft held up the writing and poisoned the atmosphere in the History Bureau, appointment to which was in any case fast deteriorating into a sinecure. The pattern of interference continued under Kangxi's successors. The much-trumpeted autonomy of the Chinese official historian since antiquity, already challenged under the Ming, became under their Manchu successors a relic of the past.

In spite of this creeping imperial micromanagement, history prospered. A number of earlier histories were revised in the light of two centuries of bibliographical and philological research: thus Shao Jinhan (1743–96) collected materials with which he could purge the Song Standard History of mistakes. Moreover, a number of other important genres of historical writing appeared during the period. Histories of institutions, previously annexed to the Standard Histories and other works, were now presented as independent reference books. The *fangzhi*, a pre-existing local 'gazetteer' dating back to the Song dynasty, continued to proliferate. Nearly one thousand Ming and five thousand Qing-era *fangzhi* survive; although they have no exact counterpart in other countries, their local focus and emphasis on multiple sources bear comparison with the natural histories and county 'surveys' of seventeenth-century and early eighteenth-century Europe.

With Zhang Xuecheng (1738–1801) we find some close parallels to contemporary European thought. Zhang wrote a great deal on many different topics, including the proper way to do local history, on family history, on the need for readable style and brevity in historical writing, on the topic of 'Virtue in the Historian', and on the very meaning of the word 'historian'. To the Tang-era critic Liu Zhiji's (see above, p. 65) trio of qualities that the historian must possess, literary skill, erudition, and insight, Zhang would add a fourth, moral integrity. Several of his projects were stillborn, such as a proposed revision of the Song Standard History, and a good deal of what he wrote has been lost. What survives, however – including Zhang's *Wenshi tongyi* ('General Principles of Literature and History') – contains some of the most interesting historical thought produced during the dynasty. Zhang called for a *Critique of Historical Writings*, a taxonomical bibliography that would embrace more than works narrowly considered historiographic. Most bibliographical work made the mistake of assuming that history could be confined to one category or another, and such fixation on formal nomenclature was arid and unproductive. Zhang's investigations of the history of history firmly distinguish it from record-keeping, the one having the virtue of the 'circle', the other of the 'square'. Only a man of genius and perception, oriented to the future, can be a true historian; the record-keeper is a workmanlike memorial-ist, a useful preserver of facts, oriented to the past. We hear in this something like Voltaire's distinction between *historien* and *historio-graphe*. In Zhang's theories of the origins of ancient writing and the transition from orality, and of the movement of man from an age of sages and poetic rites to one of philosophers and more prosaic expres-sion, we can see obvious similarities with the thought of Vico, an earlier figure similarly academic, poor and largely neglected till long after his death. Looking ahead, in Zhang's systematic philosophizing about human wisdom evolving as the *Dao* taking form through the agency of successive sages and wise rulers – Zhang's equivalent of 'world historical individuals' – there are shadows of a slightly later Westerner, Hegel, and of the march of History towards Reason's awareness of itself.

In contemporary Japan, the course of historical writing ran some-what differently. From the seventeenth to mid-nineteenth century, a shogunal junta or 'bakufu' effectively ruled the country on behalf of a figurehead emperor through regional *daimyo* or warlords, a system sometimes classed as 'feudal' using a Western model for medieval military governance. Since the shogunate acknowledged that all authority ultimately derived from the emperor, it was possible at least in theory to support the bakufu and cling to imperial loyalism. During much of this era, Japan was secluded from outside influences, and Christian missionaries were either persecuted or driven out. In the early Tokugawa, neo-Confucianism dominated Japanese intellectual life, protected and promoted in Japan by the bakufu. The use of Chinese for historical writing resumed after Japan's medieval experi-ments with vernacular works such as the *Rekishi monogatari*. The *Dai Nihon Shi* was based on Sima Qian's *Shiji*, leading off with annals of the emperors, and allotting the shoguns a special section of biogra-phies. The Chinese historiographic practice of writing critical assess-ments of emperors, and recording the fall of dynasties as the unfolding Mandate of Heaven, continued to be a poor fit with a foreign culture that could not conceive of a breach in dynastic succession; even making assessments of the emperors seemed inappropriate and they would be purged from the *Dai Nihon Shi* during the eighteenth century.

Furthermore, a nationalistic sentiment that rejected a notion of Chinese superiority, a thread picked up in the next century, is already detectable in some of this work. Yet the Chinese evidentiary approach, or *Kaozheng xue*, proved profoundly influential: it had a Japanese equivalent in *koshogaku*.

Hayashi Razan (1583–1657), a former Buddhist monk with the ear of the shogun, was a leading figure in scholarship who established the bakufu's official academy. Though his interests were not at first historical, history was a core element of neo-Confucianism, and the shogunate saw the value of both. Razan was especially impressed by the *Spring and Autumn Annals* (still then believed to be the work of Confucius himself) and by the twelfth-century commentary on Sima Guang's *Comprehensive Mirror* by the influential Song-era exponent of neo-Confucianism, Zhu Xi (1130–1200). In 1644 Razan began to write a new history of Japan, in classical Chinese, at the request of the shogun. Razan's high opinion of the original Six National Histories and their Chinese models carried over into his own work, which repeats the old accounts and renders Japanese texts into Chinese. But he also took the trouble to compare the Six National Histories with some of their Chinese sources and endeavoured to reconcile anachronisms or errors he found in both.

In the early eighteenth century, historical thinking achieved higher intellectual prominence to the extent that Ogyu Sorai (1666–1728) could confidently proclaim history the highest form of scholarly knowledge. Among his contemporaries, Arai Hakuseki (1657–1725) stands out for his *Tokushi Yoron* ('Reflections on History' [1712]), a set of lectures on the past intended as exemplary instruction for the shogun which made use of a wide variety of sources. Hakuseki was a child prodigy who mastered the Chinese classics while very young and embarked on a scholarly career which saw him progress from employer to employer, rising to the post of tutor to a future shogun Ienobu (r. 1709–12). When Ienobu finally succeeded to the shogunate, Hakuseki was able to apply his knowledge of history to practical statecraft. His *Reflections* drew inspiration from a Song-dynasty Chinese work, Sima Guang's *Comprehensive Mirror*. Considered a textbook in 'benevolent despotism', it compares in that regard with the many European histories written for the benefit of enlightened absolutists. An orthodox neo-Confucian, Hakuseki was deeply suspicious of errors in the early history of Japan. He resolved the issue of the monarchy's divine origins by sidestepping it – he began his history in the ninth century AD. Where he did have to refer to more ancient times, he employed euhemerism, a tactic by now losing fashion in the West, according to which the supposed acts of the gods could be interpreted not as myth but as the real deeds of living men who had been understood in later times as gods largely owing to spelling errors and misunderstandings of ancient sources.

Differing attitudes to the veracity of tradition were of course possible. Motoori Norinaga (1730–1801), in contrast to Hakuseki, subscribed to a literal interpretation of the age of the gods, and believed that *Kojiki* was the product of an uninterrupted and accurate oral tradition. Norinaga was an exponent of the emerging 'National Learning' (*kokugaku*) school. This rejected Chinese-influenced accounts of the past in favour of the earlier record of *Kojiki*, which thanks to Norinaga's masterpiece, *Kojiki-den* ('Commentary on *Kojiki*'), completed in 1798, now regained a status it had not enjoyed for a millennium. He also rejected the neo-Confucianism of scholars such as Arai Hakuseki and their allegorical readings of early myths. 'It is a great misconception for one to believe that, if something does not exist in the present, then it did not exist in the past', he wrote about 1757. A trained physician and formidable scholar, his views were not easily dismissed and he was right in one essential logical point: absence of evidence is not, in and of itself, evidence of absence.

Norinaga's thought also mirrored European efforts to sentimentalize the study of the past, a movement that would reach fruition in the Romantic historiography of the early nineteenth century. Early in his career Norinaga developed a concept to explain one phenomenon of human emotion. *Mono no aware* translates rather crudely as 'the sadness of things', but it is more accurate to say that it is a theory of empathy, combining regret at the impermanence of things with an aesthetic appreciation for even short-lived beauty or joy. This interestingly developed at almost the same time that Europeans were attempting to understand this side of human psychology, and to infuse it into their writing (Hume had explicitly sought to arouse emotion in his audience, especially his female readers). Artistically, *mono no aware* provided Norinaga, an older contemporary of Germany's Schiller, Herder and Goethe with a tool for understanding the appeal of medieval works like the *Genji monogatari* – the emphasis on love in these works appealed to the strongest human sentiments, the heart being essentially feminine in men and women, even when superficially covered by manly virtues. He used the example of a loyal samurai, prepared to defend his lord to the death: however faithful such a servant, would not the same man, when dying, regret in his final hour the loss of his wife and children, or sorrow at never seeing his parents again? By the end of his life, when a series of economic and social problems had intruded on Japan (as well as a volcanic explosion comparable in its impact to the Lisbon earthquake), Norinaga's thinking had evolved into the view that ancient Japanese culture represented his country's peak, from which it had declined under Chinese influence. This conservative nationalism would continue to grow in the next century and a half, and survive the reintroduction of Western culture in the later nineteenth century, principally from the region of Europe that by that time led the historiographical world, Germany.

Revolution, Romanticism and Historicism

Within Europe, History had now truly arrived in that 'capital-H' form which the great speculators of the next century could develop further. Eighteenth-century theorists such as the stadialists had empowered History to move forward but admitted it could also stop cold. The nineteenth century would be less willing to give History much choice in the matter, bestowing on it at times an almost mechanical and unstoppable momentum (positivism) or prepared to give it a push, using force and education to restart progress in recalcitrantly 'backward' corners of the globe. At the same time, 'small-h' history, a literary genre soon to become a professional discipline, was changing too. These two sets of changes, and their interrelationship to one another, are the concern of the balance of this chapter and much of the next.

In 1815, the western hemisphere set upon its recovery from the unsettling experiences of the French Revolution and Napoleonic wars. The almost inevitable consequence in the first decades of the century, though one that would not last, was a cultural revolt against the political and intellectual rationalism of the late Enlightenment, and a challenge to the eighteenth century's dominant neoclassical aesthetic. The Jacobin-era critiques of radicalism associated with Edmund Burke were taken up with enthusiasm during the Napoleonic and post-Napoleonic period by conservatives fondly recalling the *ancien régime*, including Joseph de Maistre (1753–1821) and François-René, vicomte de Chateaubriand (1768–1848). Part and parcel of this new perspective was the emergence of what we now call medievalism, a positive reappraisal of the centuries between the fall of Rome and the Renaissance, and a conscious appropriation of its values and its aesthetics into art and literature. For the Romantic writer Chateaubriand, rethinking the Middle Ages was intimately tied up with the recovery of its spirituality. He described the experience of entering a Gothic church with the phrase: 'ancient France seemed to revive altogether'. Novelists such as Sir Walter Scott (1771–1832) mixed history and fiction in their tales of heroism and martial struggle to great public acclaim, frequently selecting medieval settings and glorifying chivalric values. Artists turned historical episodes into paintings, reimagining famous scenes from the past, with medieval subjects proving especially popular. The Venetian Francesco Hayez's painting *Pietro Rossi*, which virtually launched Italian romanticism, was inspired by the artist's reading of older chronicles and recent histories, in particular the Swiss historian Jean Charles Léonard de Sismondi's (1773–1842) *History of the Italian Republics in the Middle Ages* (1807–18).

Nor was medievalism exclusively the property of conservatives. Thomas Carlyle (1795–1881), also author of a highly emotive history of the French Revolution, and not yet the reactionary he would become in later life, made a rewriting of Jocelyn of Brakelond's (d. 1211) *Chronicle* the centrepiece of his influential social commentary entitled *Past and Present* (1843). The failed moderate politician Prosper de Barante wrote a highly successful history of the Dukes of Burgundy (1824–6) stylistically modelled on Froissart, while the liberal Augustin Thierry, an enthusiastic antiquarian and champion of 'new scholarship', introduced his history of the Norman Conquest of England by declaring that his retention of the original spelling of eleventh-century names was a matter of historical truth. England's historians throughout the century, keen to stress a surviving Germanic heritage, paid renewed attention to their Anglo-Saxon past, and revived seventeenth-century attempts to find continuity in English institutions across the divide of the Norman Conquest.

An essential concept in the understanding of European (and by extension, global) historiography over the period from the late eighteenth to the mid-twentieth century is 'historicism'. An Anglicization of a German term, *Historismus*, it has acquired nearly as many meanings as 'history' itself; perhaps most famously (and unhelpfully), the modern philosopher Karl Popper (1902–94) linked it to theories of totalitarianism and historical inevitability that few of its mainstream exponents would have recognized. The early twentieth-century German historian Friedrich Meinecke (1862–1954) did not coin the term, but it acquired currency through his book, *Die Entstehung des Historismus* (1936), better known in the English-speaking world as *Historism*. Meinecke denoted in 'historism' (the different spelling is not consequential for this discussion) a particularly Germanic historical outlook, though he paid attention to the non-German precursors of that *Weltanschauung* and, like many of his generation, tended to view the German approach as universally applicable in modern Western scholarship. For our purposes, historicism is best understood as an outlook on the past that builds on certain aspects of Enlightenment thought while rejecting others. Meinecke singled out the jurist Justus Möser's (1720–94) *History of Osnabrück*, for instance, for its sensitivity to the uniqueness of the local community and emphasis on social and cultural aspects. Herder's understanding of the cultural differences among various peoples and the integrity of the *Volk* similarly anticipated a number of coming trends in European historical thought. In fact, though it is customary to draw a sharp line between the Enlightenment and its Romantic antiphony, there are strong continuities between the two, especially in Germany, where the entire century from 1750 to 1850 has been dubbed a *Sattelzeit* or bridging period. As a thorough recent study by Frederick C. Beiser demonstrates, historicism evolved – appropriately enough – in stages through the works of writers from Möser to Max Weber in the early twentieth century.

Historicism embraced a concept of the past that both differentiated among cultures and peoples and saw each of these as valuable in their own right. Favouring an organic explanation of change and growth (and much influenced by the natural sciences of the age), it eventually supplied the nationalism of the nineteenth century with a new theoretical underpinning to replace the old discredited legends of the past. Historical arguments about national origins depended rather less upon Trojans, Scythians and mythical or pseudo-biblical heroes such as Spain's Tubal, grandson of Noah, even as figures of exemplary virtue, since the entire course of a nation's past could be conceived as an organic process, as natural and predictable as the blooming of a plant. From the spirit and character of a people, opined the Czech historian and politician František Palacký, 'a nation's history is born, as a flower from a seed and a fruit from a flower'. Historicism also facilitated the appropriation of indisputably historical figures around whom could be woven a whole new set of myths. Certain venerable tropes – the Tacitean image of the free and virtuous Germanic warrior and his various national counterparts, Czech, Slovak, Dane and so on – remained very much in play.

History in the Service of Nations

At the same time, the past *in toto* was shaping new, national states and citizenries whose primary loyalty was to their nation. This is the period at which recent historians have suggested 'modern' nationalism emerged, complete with public celebrations of past heroism, the construction of statuary and other *lieux de mémoire* ('sites of memory') and even the outright 'invention of tradition'. In its most zealous form, it can be seen in the writings of nationalists such as Britain's Edward Augustus Freeman (1823–92), or the Berlin professor Heinrich von Treitschke (1834–96), the 'herald of the Reich' whose multivolume history of early nineteenth-century Germany (1879–94) provided both an adulatory narrative of the making of the Bismarckian state and a script, of sorts, for *fin-de-siècle* German imperial ambitions.

There is a noticeable change of intellectual tone throughout most of Europe in the aftermath of the Napoleonic wars, and amid the Romantic reaction to Enlightenment rationalism. Crucial exceptions such as Hegel, Comte, Marx and Britain's Henry Thomas Buckle (for each of whom see the next chapter) aside, the general direction of historical thought in the first decades of the nineteenth century was away from grand theories and speculative world histories, and towards the narration of the heroic individual and the nation – something of the same narrowing of scope we saw towards the end of the Middle Ages. National champions of either recent or remote vintage (Switzerland's William Tell, France's Charlemagne, England's King Alfred, and Romania's Michael the Brave) were popular historical subjects. This was entirely reconcilable with a conception of history that also emphasized the collective agency of the nation as a whole, since heroes were now valued not merely for their achievements but because they embodied national characteristics and virtues to be celebrated and inculcated into the nation's youth.

Mid-nineteenth-century French historians such as François Guizot (1787–1874) and Adolphe Thiers (1797–1877) postulated a unified past for their country, while their more radical contemporary, Jules Michelet (1798–1874) directed readers to the history of *Le peuple* ('the common people') in a ground-breaking work by that title published in 1846. Michelet was a multifaceted man of letters and a part-time naturalist. A brilliant literary stylist, he maintained a safe distance from fiction, and often used scientific vocabulary, describing historical study as a kind of chemical process working upon the historian's consciousness. His historical masterpieces included a mammoth history of France completed in 1867 after thirty years of toil, and a seven-volume history of the French Revolution. A national icon in his time, his reputation declined in the latter part of the century in the face of the cult of objectivity and the dominance of political history, only to be revived in the twentieth when the pendulum swung back toward the study of culture and society. Among the liberal romantics of his day Michelet had a far-reaching influence, but rather like Vico (whom he introduced to nineteenth-century audiences) his greatest impact was long in coming. Modernity has profound debts to him: Marc Bloch, a founder of the Annales School (see below, pp. 229–33) embodied many of Michelet's values as a historian, while Bloch's colleague Lucien Febvre openly acknowledged a debt to their long-dead predecessor. A great many historiographical trends of the second half of the twentieth century can also trace at least part of their lineage from him. For example, Michelet reaffirmed the value of oral sources, thereby becoming a father of modern oral history, his respect for it in no way seeming to conflict with his affection for old documents.

However, Romanticism had outcomes more immediate than Michelet's legacy to the twentieth century. Initially a culturally elitist or even reactionary movement that privileged nature over reason and revalued neglected periods such as the Middle Ages, it proved adaptable in subsequent decades into a creed for a later generation of liberal revolutionaries, and for those promoting nationalist causes. Nationalist sentiments had been stirring for some time, and paradigmatic wars of independence such as the sixteenth-century Dutch revolt against Spain were celebrated even by the likes of Friedrich von Schiller, no admirer of fanaticism or extremism, in a history published in 1788. The American Revolution provided a more recent model of emancipation. It was thus possible for subject peoples to look for inspirations to struggle elsewhere than a French Revolution which had veered off course first into Terror and then into a centralizing, anti-nationalist empire. Herder's articulation of the *Volk* and of the critical role of language provided an intellectual basis for further rearrangement of the borders of Europe along ethno-linguistic lines over the next century and a half. New national states would emerge from the western European and Ottoman empires, such as 'Romania' (the former Dacia), a polity whose very name reflected remote ties to the Roman Empire, created to encompass a region inhabited by people of perceived common ethnic origin and language yet embracing linguistic minorities.

There had certainly been eminent historians in newly established kingdoms such as Belgium prior to their political birth. Nonetheless, autonomy provided an urgent need to establish both the shape of a national past and the capacity to articulate it in written or monumental form: recent struggles for independence were grafted on to a longer master-narrative that included much earlier, medieval conflicts with external oppressors. Even those regions such as Bohemia that did not achieve political autonomy during the period still celebrated their separate identity within the umbrella of the Habsburg domains and marked out a distinctive past. The siren of nationalism was hard to resist even among those such as Palacký (1798–1876) who believed that history could not simultaneously be both a servant and a whore. The pattern is similar elsewhere, including nations with complex multilingual and polyethnic populations such as Belgium and, among older states, Switzerland, whose historians stressed the continuity of their republic back to the age of legendary medieval hero William Tell.

Not infrequently, people's own sense of their historical identity was fashioned in response or reaction to the perceptions of outsiders. The Greek attempt to reject the more immediate Ottoman and Byzantine pasts and position their new state in direct kinship with the classical Hellenes was manifested in the substitution of classical Greek names for children in lieu of traditional Christian baptismal names. Greek writers marshalled their new historical consciousness to beat off a challenge to their historical continuity from the German ethnographer and historian Jakob Philipp Fallmerayer (1790–1861), who held that the modern Greek population had been predominantly Slavic since the early Middle Ages. The first national history written in reply to this by Spirídon Zambélios (1815–81) in 1852 began as a 600-page introduction to a collection of folksongs; it would soon be followed by a work that would become the foundation of modern Greek historiography, Konstantinos Papparigopoulos' (1815–91) *History of the Greek Nation from the Most Ancient Times until the Present.*

Nationalism was not necessarily a good thing for history under all circumstances. Although patriotically minded historians like Palacký saw no contradiction between their promotion of a political agenda and their duty to the emergent 'profession', there were inevitably points of conflict – signalled in Palacký's own warning against making Clio a whore – between strict devotion to the evidence and the impulse to tell a coherent narrative that affirmed a continuous national identity. The case of Hungary is apposite, and illustrates the tensions between nation-building and accurate history-writing, which were most acute in the first half of the century when historians such as István Horvát (1784–1846) created a popular if highly fictionalized remote past for the Hungarian people. Nationalist history could be extraordinarily blinkered in gaze and (for all its gestures in the direction of folklore and inherited tradition) aristocratic in voice – were not the great heroes of the past overwhelmingly nobles and monarchs rather than the common man? Some of the nationalist-inspired histories still clung to the even older racial myths and fictitious founders of an earlier age. Folklorists like the Norwegian Peter Andreas Munch (1810–63) used their countries' ancient pasts to construct heroic national histories where none had previously existed. Swedish Historiographer Royal Eric Gustave Geijer (1783–1847), a Romantic nationalist who became a professor at Uppsala in 1817, penned *Svenska folkets historia* ('A History of the Swedes') which praised the country's preservation of liberty and independence during its medieval period. Historical consciousness was stimulated in Finland by authors such as the journalist, educator and novelist Zacharias Topelius (1818–98), a Finnish counterpart to Sir Walter Scott.

Among nationalism's more lasting historiographical legacies were some of the institutions that we associate with the modern discipline. This was often, though not always, centred in national academies and especially in the universities, whose academic historiography would gradually marginalize the kind of history-writing associated both with gentlemen of leisure, and with increasingly suspect foundational myth and undocumentable falsehood. Romania, which achieved independence in 1877, established a national academy shortly thereafter, and history was introduced at its newly founded universities. Polish aspirations for independence and political reform are likewise reflected as much in the great quantity of sources published in the early nineteenth century, such as the multivolume history of Poland by Joachim Lelewel (1786–1861), a fierce nationalist who spent the last three decades of his life in exile in France or Belgium.

This was still an age of multinational empires, not merely of nation-states, and the latter should not be assumed to have been more pluralistic and less oppressive than the former; indeed, ethnic and linguistic minorities often enjoyed far greater protections and liberties within the wide expanse of (some) empires than in the narrower domain of a new nation struggling towards an aspirational homogeneity in the present, built on a dubious rewriting of the past. There were exceptions in both cases. Unsurprisingly, ethnic minorities could be either written out of the national past in accounts written by Russian, Polish and German historians, or simply shoehorned into the national narratives of the larger states, as were many of Russia's subordinated populations, most notably Ukrainians. In the next chapter we will take up more explicitly the relations of empires to peripheries, and of dominant to subordinate histories, but it is important to note here that the same dynamic which can be observed *between* the West and the rest of the world had already emerged in the major European states' treatments of their minority subjects.

The redrawing of maps often led to divergent paths in the interpretation of the past. In British North America, the colonies separated historiographically as well as politically following the American Revolution. The northern colonies – what eventually became Canada – remained firmly within the British imperial orbit (despite the existence of a distinctive Francophone Catholic majority within the future province of Quebec). To the south, a prototype for a nationalist historiography had already been established in colonial-era writings that acknowledged the colonies' place in the empire but also celebrated aspects of their New World distinctiveness. A nationalist American historiography had emerged quite quickly following independence from Britain, as early-republic historians such as Mercy Otis Warren and David Ramsay (1749–1815) narrated the United States' emergence as a free nation built on democratic values. Washington Irving (1783–1859) and other biographers of major figures such as George Washington helped establish a pantheon of national heroes analogous to those being created or resuscitated in Europe. Historical novelists like James Fenimore Cooper (1789–1851) imitated Sir Walter Scott in creating a highly romanticized, heroic vision of the past. Both American and world history were enormously popular among readers during the first half of the nineteenth century, but their writing remained the domain of gentlemen of leisure (and the occasional woman like Warren) or of journalists. Famous examples, both severely sight-impaired through most of their careers, include William Hickling Prescott (1796–1859), narrator of the Spanish conquests, and Francis Parkman (1823–93), historian of the western frontier. Both were members of a northeastern intellectual elite (the centres of which were Boston and New York) that also included the Göttingen-trained John Lothrop Motley (1814–77), historian of the Dutch Republic and US minister to Austria, and literary figures such as Cooper and Irving. Internationally, the most widely recognized American historian was yet another 'Boston Brahmin', George Bancroft (1800–91), a former Harvard professor-turned-diplomat and one of the first of his country to earn a PhD from a German university, a trend that would increase in the second half of the century.

Perhaps nowhere was the efficacy of history in establishing new states clearer than in the southern Americas, most continental parts of which were emancipated from direct European rule by mid-century amid numerous wars of independence and subsequent internecine conflicts. Enlightenment-era histories such as William Robertson's played a part in promoting progressive values – Raynal's *History of the Two Indies*, an early critique of slavery, was notably influential in Haiti's successful rebellion against France. But if older histories could furnish rebels with ideology, they were an insufficient foundation for the building of brand new nations. Throughout Latin America, the liberal values of the late Enlightenment informed the writing of new histories during the nineteenth century, first in the work of constitutionalist historians who focused on the European-inherited legal institutions underlying independence, and later in a more autonomous and Romantic kind of writing that, following Herder and Michelet, emphasized instead the importance of the spirit of the people in establishing well-functioning new societies in a postcolonial era. A mid-century Chilean Literary Society held regular meetings in which selections from Herder and other eighteenth-century historians were read. European historians were heavily utilized in the highly politicized task of writing books for schoolchildren. The liberal and anti-clerical Chilean historian Diego Barros Arana (1830–1907), deliberating on textbook choices in the 1850s, criticized one because it had plagiarized whole paragraphs from Robertson. The committee of which Barros Arana was a member eventually settled on the safe choice of a French work, Victor Duruy's (1811–94) *Course of Universal History*, to supply the role of a general textbook, supplemented by Barros Arana's own two-volume *Compendium of American History* (1865).

Conclusion

The period from 1700 to the mid-nineteenth century marks a further significant transition in the modern history of history, the watershed at which a number of the streams of thought we have been tracing over several centuries begin to merge. Out of their confluence, fully realized by the early twentieth century, would spring most of the subjects that, in different ways, continue to preoccupy historians today. Apart from definitively establishing history as the queen of the humanities, the Enlightenment had developed the notions that history as a whole had both pattern and meaning, that society, custom and economic conditions were legitimate subjects for historical description, and that comparisons between peoples and systems of thought could generate universal truths. The Romantic aftermath, reactive in many ways to eighteenth-century rationalism, contributed a revived attention to the historical agency of the individual and a willingness to reappraise once-neglected eras such as the Middle Ages; but the scepticism of the Enlightenment to older conventions such as eponymous founders and mythic descents made Romantic re-imaginings of them seem more obviously fictive and rhetorical. Such scepticism was not limited to Europe as the writings of some of the Japanese and Chinese figures mentioned above indicates, and the period also witnessed an increased familiarity between Asian and European cultures. It thereby set the stage for perhaps the most critical development of the next hundred years, the spread of Western historicity to most of the rest of the world, sometimes by force, but often by invitation.

QUESTIONS FOR DISCUSSION

1. What were the major characteristics of Enlightenment era historiography? How did these differ from one part of Europe to another?
2. Why did eighteenth-century thinkers focus to so great an extent on notions of human progress? How did they use history to support their arguments? What role did the New World discoveries discussed in the previous chapter contribute to their overall conceptualization of the course of history?
3. Did the French Revolution and subsequent reaction mark a break with Enlightenment ideas about history?
4. In what ways did eighteenth- and early nineteenth-century East Asian historical thought and writing resemble that of Europe and its colonies? In what ways did they differ?
5. What were the principal hallmarks of Romanticism? Of historicism? Are the two different?
6. In what ways did history prove useful in the creation of new nations and in the creation of what the late scholar Benedict Anderson has called 'Imagined Communities'? Did this differ between Europe and the Americas?

Further Reading

General

Burns, Robert M. and Hugh Rayment-Pickard (eds), *Philosophies of History: From Enlightenment to Post-Modernity* (Oxford, 2000)

Miller, Peter N. and François Louis (eds), *Antiquarianism and Intellectual Life in Europe and China, 1500–1800* (Ann Arbor, MI, 2012)

Phillips, Mark Salber, *On Historical Distance* (New Haven, CT, 2013)

Rabasa, Jose, Masayuki Sato, Edoardo Tortarolo and Daniel Woolf (eds), *The Oxford History of Historical Writing*, Vol. 3: *1400–1800* (Oxford, 2011)

Trevor-Roper, Hugh, *History and the Enlightenment* (New Haven, CT and London, 2010)

Eighteenth-Century European Historical Culture

Cañizares-Esguerra, Jorge, *How to Write the History of the New World: Histories, Epistemologies and Identities in the Eighteenth-Century Atlantic World* (Stanford, CA, 2001)

Davies, Kate, *Catharine Macaulay and Mercy Otis Warren: The Revolutionary Atlantic and the Politics of Gender* (Oxford, 2005)

Davis, Natalie Zemon, 'Gender and Genre: Women as Historical Writers, 1400–1820', in Patricia H. Labalme (ed.), *Beyond their Sex: Learned Women of the European Past* (New York, 1980), 153–82

Looser, Devoney, *British Women Writers and the Writing of History, 1670–1820* (Baltimore, MD, 2000)

Pocock, J. G. A., *Barbarism and Religion*, 6 vols (Cambridge, 1999–2015)

Wolloch, Nathaniel, *History and Nature in the Enlightenment: Praise of the Mastery of Nature in Eighteenth-Century Historical Literature* (Farnham, UK and Burlington, VT, 2011)

Philosophic History, Conjecture and Stadialism

Kidd, Colin, *Subverting Scotland's Past: Scottish Whig Historians and the Creation of an Anglo-British Identity, c. 1689–1830* (Cambridge, 1993)

Miller, Cecilia, *Giambattista Vico: Imagination and Historical Knowledge* (Basingstoke and New York, 1993)

Phillips, Mark Salber, *Society and Sentiment: Genres of Historical Writing in Britain, 1740–1820* (Princeton, NJ, 2000)

Phillipson, Nicholas, *David Hume: The Philosopher as Historian* (New Haven, CT, 2012)

Pittock, Murray, 'Historiography', in Alexander Broadie (ed.), *The Cambridge Companion to the Scottish Enlightenment* (Cambridge, 2003), 258–79

Pompa, Leon, *Vico: A Study of the 'New Science'*, 2nd edn (Cambridge, 1990)

Smitten, Jeffrey R., *The Life of William Robertson: Minister, Historian and Principal* (Edinburgh, 2017)

Verene, Donald Phillip, *Vico's Science of Imagination* (Ithaca, NY, 1981)

Womersley, David, *The Transformation of 'The Decline and Fall of the Roman Empire'* (Cambridge, 1988)

Historical Thought in the French Enlightenment: Voltaire, Condorcet and Rousseau

Gearhart, Suzanne, *The Open Boundary of History and Fiction: A Critical Approach to the French Enlightenment* (Princeton, NJ, 1984)
Manuel, Frank E., *The Prophets of Paris: Turgot, Condorcet, Saint-Simon, Fourier, and Comte* (New York, 1965)
O'Brien, Karen, *Narratives of Enlightenment: Cosmopolitan History from Voltaire to Gibbon* (Cambridge, 1997)
Pierse, Siofra, *Voltaire Historiographer: Narrative Paradigms* (Oxford, 2008)

The German Aufklärung

Beiser, Frederick C., *The German Historicist Tradition* (Oxford, 2011)
Berlin, Isaiah, *Three Critics of the Enlightenment: Vico, Hamann, Herder*, ed. H. Hardy, 2nd edn (Princeton, NJ, 2013)
Iggers, Georg G., *The German Conception of History: The National Tradition of Historical Thought from Herder to the Present*, rev. edn (Middletown, CT, 1983)
Mah, Harold, 'German Historical Thought in the Age of Herder, Kant, and Hegel', in Lloyd Kramer and Sarah Maza (eds), *A Companion to Western Historical Thought* (Oxford, 2002), 143–65
Reill, Peter Hanns, *The German Enlightenment and the Rise of Historicism* (Berkeley, CA, 1975)

East Asian Enlightenments

Brownlee, John S., *Japanese Historians and the National Myths, 1600–1945: The Age of the Gods and Emperor Jinmu* (Vancouver and Tokyo, 1997)
Crossley, Pamela Kyle, *A Translucent Mirror: History and Identity in Qing Imperial Ideology* (Berkeley, CA, 1999)
Elman, Benjamin A., *From Philosophy to Philology: Intellectual and Social Aspects of Change in Late Imperial China* (Cambridge, MA, 1984)
Matsumoto, Shigeru, *Motoori Norinaga, 1730–1801* (Cambridge, 1970)
Nakai, Kate Wildman, *Shogunal Politics: Arai Hakuseki and the Premises of Tokugawa Rule* (Cambridge, 1988)

Nivison, David S., *The Life and Thought of Chang Hsüeh-ch'eng (1738–1801)* (Stanford, CA, 1966)

Revolution, Romanticism and Historicism

Armenteros, Carolina, *The French Idea of History: Joseph de Maistre and His Heirs, 1794–1854* (Ithaca, NY, 2011)
Bann, Stephen, *Romanticism and the Rise of History* (New York, 1995)
Crossley, Ceri, *French Historians and Romanticism: Thierry, Guizot, the Saint-Simonians, Quinet, Michelet* (London and New York, 1993)
Flitter, Derek, *Spanish Romanticism and the Uses of History: Ideology and the Historical Imagination* (London, 2006)
Heffernan, James A. W. (ed.), *Representing the French Revolution: Literature, Historiography, and Art* (Hanover, NH, 1992)
Iggers, Georg G., 'Historicism: The History and Meaning of the Term', *Journal of the History of Ideas* 56.1 (1995): 129–52
Meinecke, Friedrich, *Historism: The Rise of a New Historical Outlook*, trans. J. E. Anderson, 2nd edn (trans. rev. H. D. Schmidt) (London, 1972)
Mitzman, Arthur, *Michelet, Historian: Rebirth and Romanticism in Nineteenth-Century France* (New Haven, CT and London, 1990)
Rearick, Charles, *Beyond the Enlightenment: Historians and Folklore in Nineteenth-Century France* (Bloomington, IN and London, 1974)
Rigney, Ann, *Imperfect Histories: The Elusive Past and the Legacy of Romantic Historicism* (Ithaca, NY and London, 2003)

History in the Service of Nations

Berger, Stefan with Christoph Conrad, *The Past as History: National Identity and Historical Consciousness in Modern Europe* (Basingstoke and New York, 2015)
Berger, Stefan, Mark Donovan and Kevin Passmore (eds), *Writing National Histories: Western Europe Since 1800* (London, 1999)
Berger, Stefan and Chris Lorenz (eds), *Nationalizing the Past: Historians as Nation Builders in Modern Europe* (Basingstoke and New York, 2010)
Brading, D. A., *The First America: The Spanish Monarchy, Creole Patriots and the Liberal State, 1492–1867* (Cambridge, 1991)
Cheng, Eileen Ka-May, *The Plain and Noble Garb of Truth: Nationalism and Impartiality in American Historical Writing, 1784–1860* (Athens, GA, 2008)
Crane, Susan A., *Collecting and Historical Consciousness in Early Nineteenth-Century Germany* (Ithaca, NY, 2000)

Furtado, Peter (ed.), *Histories of Nations: How their Identities were Forged* (London, 2012)

Tollebeek, Jo, 'Historical Representation and the Nation-State in Romantic Belgium (1830–1850)', *Journal of the History of Ideas* 59.2 (1998): 329–53

Zimmer, Oliver, *A Contested Nation: History, Memory and Nationalism in Switzerland, 1761–1891* (Cambridge, 2003)

1801	'Abd al-Rahman al-Jabarti completes his *The Demonstration of Piety in the Destruction of the French State*
1811–12	First two volumes of Barthold Georg Niebuhr's *Roman History* is published (third volume published posthumously in 1832)
1817	James Mill's *The History of British India* is published
1824	Leopold von Ranke's *The History of the Latin and Teutonic Nations from 1494 to 1514* is published
1830–42	August Comte's *Course in Positive Philosophy* is published
1837	G. W. F. Hegel's *Lectures on the Philosophy of World History* is published posthumously
1852	Karl Marx's *18th Brumaire of Louis Napoleon* is published
1858	Johann Gustav Droysen's *Outline of the Principles of History* is published
1859	*Historische Zeitschrift* is founded
1860	Jacob Burckhardt's *The Civilization of the Renaissance in Italy* is published
1874	Friedrich Nietzsche writes *On the Uses and Disadvantages of History for Life*
1875	Fukuzawa Yukichi's *Outline of a Theory of Civilization* makes extensive use of western European writings
1883	Wilhelm Dilthey's *Introduction to the Human Sciences* is published
1890s	Karl Lamprecht, advocating an interdisciplinary approach to history or *Kulturgeschichte*, sparks the *Methodenstreit* among German historians
1892	Kume affair, first of several episodes involving historical researchers questioning Japanese national traditions
1897	Samuel Johnson composes *History of the Yorubas from the Earliest Times to the Beginning of the British Protectorate*; Charles Langlois and Charles Seignobos' *Introduction to Historical Studies* is published in French
1902	Liang Qichao's *New Historiography* is published in Chinese
1917	Benedetto Croce's *Theory and History of Historiography* is published
1919	India establishes the Historical Records Commission
1928	He Bingsong publishes a Chinese translation of Langlois and Seignobos
1932–5	Carl Becker and Charles A. Beard advance historical 'relativism' in the *American Historical Review*
1942	Jawaharlal Nehru's *Glimpses of World History* is published
1943	Nellie Neilson elected president of the American Historical Association, first and only female president between 1884 and 1987
1946	R. G. Collingwood's *The Idea of History* is published

5

Disciplining the Past:
Professionalization, Imperialism
and Science, 1830–1945

An Introductory Overview

If the first half of the West's nineteenth century is characterized by literary historical writing in a Romantic and nationalist vein, the second half may be noted for a rapid growth in what may be loosely called 'professionalization'. Although this, too, had nationalist aspects, it is associated not just with the 'nation' in an ethnic or linguistic sense but also with the emergence of the modern 'nation-state' and its political–bureaucratic apparatus. In France, for instance, the nascent Third Republic (1870–1940) promoted its version of French nationhood through semi-official historians like Ernest Lavisse (1842–1922), author of an influential school textbook. Italy provides an example of the evolving relationship (and not infrequent tension) between nationalism and professionalization. The new regime encouraged historical writing and promoted pedagogy, just as popular historians had themselves, earlier in the century, prepared the way for the Risorgimento. Prior to this, history had enjoyed at best a peripheral role in Italian universities, with chairs of history existing only at a select few such as Pavia and Turin. This changed in the 1860s as professorial posts were created and their occupants appointed directly by the Minister of Public Education. But for many of the most influential historians of the latter part of the century, the militant patriotism of the previous decades now needed to take a back seat to a more methodologically 'scientific' approach, embodied in important scholars like Pasquale Villari (1827–1917). They stressed the importance of research into the facts of the Italian past; for them, the primary purpose of historiography was no longer the explicit promotion of a nationalist agenda, though political history remained the overwhelmingly dominant subject of inquiry.

During the middle and later decades of the century, in the wake of a further wave of revolutions in 1848 and a second Napoleonic empire, the Romantic liberalism of national independence and unification movements refashioned itself in much of Europe back into an institutional conservatism dedicated once more to preservation, consolidation and social stability. Changes were signalled by a number of developments (many of them external to the emerging academic 'discipline' of history) such as a significant growth in the professional classes which created a market for history, a cadre of professors and schoolteachers to teach it, a ready supply of textbooks for them to use – routinely enlivened by heroic pictures – and civil servants to apply both its lessons and the critical skills that its study offered. Technological changes such as mechanized printing made books much more affordable to a mass audience previously dependent on serialization or on public libraries. Among the most significant changes specifically affecting the emergent historical profession one should note in particular these: state support for historical activity, including particular publication programmes; the expansion of university systems and the turning of many of them by the century's end to formal training in historical scholarship; the introduction of earned doctorates with a research component; the systematization of public record systems; the advent of new professional associations, frequently accompanied by a new style of learned, peer-reviewed periodical or journal; a continuation of the publication of archival documents, now often under government sponsorship (as in the case of Prussian support for the scholar Georg Pertz and his vast publication of medieval documents and texts, the *Monumenta Germaniae Historica*) and with increasingly rigorous standards of accuracy; and, finally, the systematic convergence of the erudite skills that had matured over the previous three centuries (palaeography, diplomatic, numismatics and epigraphy) within an overarching historical science (*Geschichtswissenschaft*).

The link between history and science was no accident. Following a further revolution, an industrial and economic one experienced most acutely in Britain and America, the century would see huge strides in science and technology and enormous optimism in civilized humanity's ability to improve the world. Industrialization and mechanization had critics across the ideological spectrum, both conservatives who disliked the dissolution of long-standing community and agrarian values, and radical social theorists such as Marx, who espoused a materialist view of History both to explain the rise and internal contradictions of capitalism and to prophesy its ultimate downfall. For the religious, the post-1815 return to the values of Christianity soon faced new challenges such as David Friedrich Strauss's (1808–74) controversial *Life of Jesus* (1835), which demystified Christ and challenged his divinity. Anti-clericalism remained attractive to some historians – Michelet and his sometime collaborator Edgar Quinet (1803–75) joined with liberal critics of the Church in the 1830s and 1840s, targeting the Jesuits as an especially malign influence. Marx famously derided religion as the opiate of the masses, a crutch clung to by the downtrodden in the face of overpowering social inequities. To make matters worse for the faithful, the biblical scheme of chronology, including the Creation story, under severe stress for at least two centuries, was soon irreversibly shaken by Charles Lyell's *Principles of Geology* (1830–3) and, a generation later, Charles Darwin's *Origin of Species* (1859).

Yet this was no age of unbelief. While many historians espoused anti-clerical views so far as the influence of the church on secular affairs was concerned, they continued to take their personal faiths very seriously. Several of Victorian England's most celebrated historians, Sir John Seeley (1834–95), James Anthony Froude (1818–94) and Samuel Rawson Gardiner (1829–1902), were similarly religiously minded, while the social historian John Richard Green (1837–83) was an ordained cleric. So were Mandell Creighton (1843–1901) and William Stubbs (1825–1901), both of whom abandoned professorial chairs in Cambridge and Oxford respectively to take up bishoprics. The French historian Ernest Renan (1823–92) survived a youthful crisis of faith to become a historian of both race and religion and, like David Strauss, author of a life of Jesus (1863). The French clerical tradition of advanced erudition, interrupted by the Revolution's abolition of the orders and the royal academies, was revived as early as 1795–6, when the old academies were recreated as the Institut de France. A strong tradition of Catholic narrative historiography (by both clerics and lay authors) continued to flourish throughout the nineteenth century both in majority Catholic countries such as Italy and France, and in officially Protestant ones such as England, where by the century's end the Catholic essayist and one-time controversialist Lord Acton (1834–1902) would plan the *Cambridge Modern History* (1902–12) from his position as Cambridge's Regius Professor.

The Great Transformer: Ranke and His Influence

Leopold von Ranke (1795–1886), too, was no atheist. A devout Protestant who believed that his documentary research into the past could provide insight into the divine plan for humanity, Ranke counted Martin Luther among his most important intellectual inspirations. Initially a student of ancient history and philology, he at first had little time for modern history, deeming it an inferior form of writing to the classics. This beginning as a classicist was anything but a false start, and to understand Ranke we must first appreciate the influence of two more senior scholars of antiquity, Barthold Georg Niebuhr and Friedrich Carl von Savigny. They were all at one time at the newly founded (1811) University of Berlin (now the Humboldt University of Berlin), which would occupy for German scholarship the same dominant space held in the previous century by the older university of Göttingen. The philologist Niebuhr's (see above, p. 146) identification of an entire period as an object to be studied through a methodology with a distinctive set of rules and standards would be complemented and reinforced by a student of Roman law, Savigny (1779–1861), heir to several centuries of Roman law jurisprudence going back to the French Renaissance. Savigny advocated studying law as the product of particular times and circumstances – a historically changing set of rules and customs – rather than an absolute unchanging reflection of an idealized 'right'. If laws characterized civilization at a particular period, then it followed that the periods themselves were both distinctive and not strictly comparable, and that they needed to be studied independently, as organic entities.

In some ways, Ranke's eventual achievement would be to merge the cutting-edge philological methods of Niebuhr with Savigny's sense of historical development and apply them to the study of post-1500 political history. In part because of an awakening interest in contemporary issues, he abandoned the ancient for the modern history of the world, beginning with *The History of the Latin and Teutonic Nations fom 1494 to 1514* (1824), a book roughly covering the same period tackled three centuries earlier in Francesco Guicciardini's *History of Italy*. Ranke appended to his work one of his earliest theoretical pronouncements, *A Critique of Modern Historians*, republished separately in the same year; a bold step from a historian still very young. In this essay Ranke took to task a number of his predecessors in the writing of early modern history, but none so fiercely as Guicciardini, whose vaunted use of original documents had in Ranke's eyes been grossly overestimated. Ranke's own research methods, built on such sources as the reports of Venetian ambassadors to Europe's various courts in the sixteenth century, soon featured in his history of *The Ottoman and the Spanish Empires in the Sixteenth and Seventeenth Centuries* (1827) and the subsequent *History of the Popes* (based on private Roman archives, access to the Vatican Library having been denied him as a Protestant), which found a place on the Index of Prohibited Books.

It was during the same decade that Ranke began to put together the views on universal history that would guide the remainder of his career. By the end of the 1830s the first part of one of his greatest books, *The History of the Reformation in Germany*, had appeared, in which he finally found a connecting theme in the struggle between universal religion and particular nationality. Ranke's subsequent works traced the emergence of the European state system that this good German public servant much admired as the source of modern civilization and individual freedom. His career closed with an unfinished multivolume *Weltgeschichte* ('World History') which, despite its title, was largely focused on Europe – even though a younger Ranke had conceded the importance of other cultures, and had once believed languages such as Arabic as important as Latin.

Though he vehemently disagreed with the philosophical speculations of his sometime Berlin colleague, G. W. F. Hegel (see below, pp. 185–87), Ranke himself saw no contradiction between his attendance to the particularity of history, displayed through the most meticulous and painstaking attention to a single document, and the interrelations between men and nations, among nations themselves, and between all of the above and God. The state, the fundamental political unit of his narratives (encompassing more than simply the government), was preeminently worthy of study – not on its own but as the channel through which one accessed the past of the wider 'nation'. Nations in turn are the windows through which one sees the cumulative History of humanity. The close studies by modern historiographers such as the late Georg Iggers (1926–2017) have revealed that there are, in fact, tensions in Ranke's thought. The historian famous for valuing the God-given individuality (*Eigentümlichkeit*) and particularity of each era still believed in something like progress, and he also affirmed that there are timeless, transcendent ideas, especially in ethics. What he did not accept was the union of these two things in the way a philosopher like Hegel had put them together. Individual actions, not reified ideas, drove the movement of the human race through time, under the all-seeing eye of Providence.

Above all, Ranke is associated with the idea that the historian's duty is first and foremost to relate the past *wie es eigentlich gewesen* – as it actually happened, without judgment or embroidery. This famous phrase is often the only thing many students know about Ranke. Uttered early in his career as little more than an aside, it was neither a lightning bolt of methodological insight nor even entirely original to him: Thucydides had made a similar observation in antiquity, as had Tacitus; the founder of the University of Berlin, Wilhelm von Humboldt (1767–1835), himself an important figure in the development of German historicism, had declared in 1821 that 'The historian's task is to present what actually happened.' Ranke's particular formulation of this idea appears in the introduction to the *Latin and Germanic Peoples*, in the specific context of the author's extensive use of the Venetian archives, rather than as a philosophic generalization. It carries with it – though this was probably a secondary issue for Ranke – an abdication of the historian's long-standing judicial–didactic role. 'History has had assigned to it the office of judging the past and of instructing the present for the benefit of the future ages. To such high offices the present work does not presume: it seeks only to show what actually happened.' This may not in fact be the most accurate translation of *wie es eigentlich gewesen*, which is rendered more accurately as 'the past as it *essentially* was'. For our purposes what Ranke meant is of less consequence than how it came to be interpreted by some later admirers elsewhere in the world. Many of them wrongly believed that the master had intended the complete avoidance of anything not based on a specific fact and the repudiation of conjecture or interpretation, thereby ignoring the moral and philosophical side of Ranke's writings, which is so obvious in later works as to make nonsense of his purported early utterances against didacticism.

The Institutions of History and the Beginnings of the 'Profession' in Europe and North America

Thanks to Ranke, his immediate disciples such as Georg Waitz (1813–86) and Heinrich von Sybel (1817–95) and the celebrated university seminar environment, German scholarship loomed large over

European intellectual life in the second half of the nineteenth century and beyond. The Sorbonne historian Ernest Lavisse was initially so taken with Ranke's successes that he introduced the historical seminar into French higher education. There is no doubt that German scholarship also captured the imagination of many of Britain's leading historians, such as Stubbs and Edward Augustus Freeman (1823–92), for whom it was not easily separable from their enthusiasm for ancient Germanic freedoms. F. W. Maitland (1850–1906) modelled his legal scholarship on Savigny, one of whose works he translated. Acton had trained with the German Catholic scholar Johann Joseph Ignaz von Döllinger (1799–1890). Stubbs emulated Rankean source criticism, and his own pupils or disciples would in turn 'modernize' the British historical profession in the decades leading up to the First World War. Its over-arching goal remained education rather than research for its own sake, however. Indeed, by the end of the century, history at the British universities had arguably become the ultimate indoctrination programme for young men in undertaking the duties of empire together with the privileges and entitlements of class.

The post-Rankean German influence was arguably stronger outside western Europe than within. To the east, for instance, several generations of early twentieth-century Romanian historians derived inspiration from Germany, including the archaeologist Vasile Pârvan (1882–1927) and the methodologist Alexandru Xenopol (1847–1920). To the north, the Dane Kristian Erslev (1852–1930) and the Norwegian Gustav Storm (1845–1903) both spent extended periods in German seminars. A particularly apposite illustration of the eastward spread of western European tendencies is provided by Russian historical writing. This continued to be influenced by other national histories (in particular French and German) in the late eighteenth and nineteenth centuries as it had in the time of Schlözer and Karamzin. As elsewhere, considerable activity was devoted in the post-Napoleonic era to the collection and publication of source materials, especially government documents, under the leadership of the Chancellor Nikolai P. Rumiantsev (1754–1826). An 'Archeographic Commission' undertook a nationwide survey of archives and repositories analogous to Victorian Britain's later Historical Manuscripts Commission (est. 1869). By the turn of the century, the link between history and science had been made in Russia, too, as Pavel Nikolaevich Miliukov (1859–1943), who taught courses in historiography at Moscow University, proclaimed in 1892 that the proper subject of scientific history was the process of a people's develop-ment. Thus western European methodology became the key to establish-ing, on evidentiary grounds, the genius of the Russian people.

Across the Atlantic, American students flocked most frequently to Germany, returning home to teach history at colleges and universities in the United States, including new, research-oriented schools such as Johns Hopkins. Of those historians working at American universities in the 1880s and 1890s, roughly half had spent some time studying in Germany, though frequently of too short a duration to permit them really to absorb German historical method – much less its complex philosophical underpinnings – quite thoroughly. The 'objectivity' man-tra chanted in American historiography for many decades is often ascribed to the importation of a naive version of Rankeanism which upheld Ranke himself as an idol while misunderstanding or neglecting the subtler aspects of his thought (though the degree to which this was the case has been challenged by more recent American historiogra-phers). Indeed, the myth of Ranke was far more powerful in America than his methods. Nor did every American student enjoy their time in Germany. The prominent African-American historian and educator, W. E. B. Du Bois (1868–1963), a founder of what would become Black History in the twentieth century, suffered through a racist rant by the arch-nationalist and colonialist Berlin historian Heinrich von Treitschke (1834–96) in 1890. Some American scholars, such as Henry Adams, who introduced a seminar at Harvard, even held the entire German university system in low esteem. However, it was the aura of 'professionalism' radiating from the ambition of objective, value-free scholarship that was most appealing, and Germany appeared to provide the most advanced model of both. Professional standards which outlined a creed of 'scientific history' were upheld by the newly founded American Historical Association (1884) and policed by influential academics like the Johns Hopkins-trained J. Franklin Jameson (1859–1937), the first editor of the *American Historical Review* (*AHR*).

The *AHR* was North America's premier example of another major development of the nineteenth century, also emanating from Germany: the professional historical journal. History had appeared prominently in periodicals before this time, in literary reviews and the publications of learned academies. Local history societies, principally with an anti-quarian focus, had sprung up in the late eighteenth and early nineteenth centuries. But the free-standing, edited academic journal to which new historical research could be submitted for peer review and publication was a creation of mid-nineteenth-century Germany. Ranke's pupil Sybel, a professor at Munich and eminent historian of the French Revolution, became in 1859 the founding editor of *Historische Zeitschrift* (*HZ*). By its survival and longevity, its devotion exclusively to history, and its insistence on a common standard of scholarship, the flagship German journal lit the path for imitators elsewhere. The German-trained reformer of French historical scholarship, Gabriel Monod (1844–1912) created his own version of *HZ* in the *Revue historique* (*RH*, 1876). The *Rivista Storica Italiana* (1884) and *English Historical Review* (*EHR*, 1886) followed; and in 1895 the *AHR* was created as the official publication of the American Historical Association. Interestingly, in several cases the journals were started by relative outsiders seeking to alter the practice of historical scholarship in their country. The innovators would soon evolve into insiders, conservative guardians of historiographic orthodoxy, 'objectivity' and 'sound' methods; new rebels would then spawn breakaway or rival venues to publish work on previously excluded topics. Many of today's best periodicals such as *Annales* and *Past and Present* were created decades ago specifically to fill gaps in then mainstream scholarship; that pattern of disciplinary fission and re-fission continues today.

If new journals represented the vanguard of historical research (with a heavy focus on national pasts, one's own or others'), historical pedagogy, bringing up the rear, was assisted by handbooks. Some, such as the much-published epitomes of Carl Ploetz (1819–81), kept to the older format inherited from the eighteenth century (and the earlier *ars historica*) summarizing world historical events. Others, however, outlined the elements of historical research. The methodological discussions and disciplinary refinements of the nineteenth century were digested and disseminated to students through a series of these manuals, beginning with Johann Gustav Droysen (1808–84) and continuing with Ottokar Lorenz (1832–1904) and Ernst Bernheim (1850–1942). Bernheim's massive *Lehrbuch der historischen methode* ('Textbook on Historical Method', 1889), which by its 1908 edition had swollen to over 800 pages, proved influential as far afield as Japan. Bernheim confidently avowed that many facts of history could be known with certainty, though he conceived that others could only be surmised as 'probable'.

This trend towards a rather narrow preoccupation with method – in essence, the nascent discipline's ring-fencing establishment of rules and conventions that differentiated it from other types of humanistic study (and eventually from the natural sciences, though this was not the original intent) – was also observable in *fin-de-siècle* France. The apparatus of modern French historiography was established with the founding of the famous graduate research centre, the École pratique des hautes études, in 1868 and of the *Revue historique*. Perhaps the most innocent expression of the evidentiary confidence at the root of scientific history – a belief in the rock-solid documentary foundation and continuous advancement through source criticism of historical knowledge, without reducing all human knowledge to the natural sciences – can be found in a more concise French counterpart to Bernheim's *Lehrbuch*. A hugely successful manual on method, based on a set of Sorbonne lectures, the *Introduction to Historical Studies* (1897) by the medievalist and palaeographer Charles-Victor Langlois (1863–1929; later Director of the Archives Nationales) and the historian of nineteenth-century politics Charles Seignobos (1854–1942), was soon translated or adapted into several other languages.

Langlois and Seignobos were both serious scholars in their respective fields, so it is somewhat unfortunate that they are now known principally for a book that has become the symbol *par excellence* of the naive confidence of late nineteenth-century European scholarship, with its step-by-step delineation of the preparatory, analytical and 'synthetic' operations required in the writing of history. This came with some riskily bold assertions of what was (and was not) proper method, and a ringing declaration of the dependence of history on writing. The act of assembling the disparate facts from multiple documents into a coherent history, say Langlois and Seignobos, is akin to the scientific construction of a building. One has to choose one's materials carefully, since the wrong ones will prevent any design from being executed. It would be, said the learned authors, like proposing to construct an Eiffel Tower out of stone.

History, Science and Determinism

 [One of the many paradoxes of the nineteenth century is that it is the great age of history as literary masterpiece and simultaneously of the argument advanced by many that when properly done it was also a 'science'.]The contradiction is more apparent to us than it was to contemporaries, since science then was a broader term that still retained something of its Renaissance meaning of *scientia*, or knowledge in general; and it is less an issue in languages like French and German, both of which used terms (*science, Wissenschaft*) that are more inclusive and less tied than the English word has become to the experimental and mathematical spheres. Moreover, in the nineteenth century intellectuals could still occasionally travel between science and letters (though less easily than in previous periods), and nature importantly provided a common source of inspiration for both. Indeed, history seemed to be the quintessential amphibious activity that could straddle the boundary between the natural and social worlds. Clio had expanded her reach, and a much more comprehensive 'historicization' of outlook developed both in popular and learned culture, touching on nearly every domain of intellectual activity.

It is not going too far to say that history became the 'master discipline' of the century, simultaneously the source of material for literary fiction, the Baconian–Herodotean catch-all term for the collection and display of nature, the basis of comparative philology and the foundation of new modes of study such as sociology. When the French jurist F. F. Poncelet declared in 1820 that history was the source of all human science, he intended what we would now call social science, a term just then emerging. Ernest Renan included both philology and history within his definition of science. The English historian Henry Thomas Buckle (1821–62) was so convinced of history's importance to human achievement that he saw the state of any society's historical literature as a key indicator of its overall progress, and he included in his *History of Civilization in England* a chapter devoted to the 'history of history', intending 'to incorporate with an inquiry into the progress of the history of Man, another inquiry into the progress of History itself.' As late as 1900, when science had begun to move off in its more specialized and technological direction, it was still not unreasonable for the Byzantinist and historian of progress John Bagnell Bury (1861–1927) to declare history a science, 'no less and no more'.

For some nineteenth-century thinkers, capital-H History – a recurrent character in a work like Thomas Carlyle's *French Revolution* where the personification of History is quite literally appealed to with frequency – was above all a progressive force demanding that its own story be told. The novelist Tolstoy devoted an extended epilogue in *War and Peace* to ruminations on the grand machinations of History (which, Tessa Morris-Suzuki has noted, were a sudden leap in scale quite at odds with the rest of that novel's focus on individual emotion and vivid scenic description). Although the general thrust of nineteenth-century historiography was towards critical scholarship and away from philosophical speculation, the period nevertheless spawned a number of schemes for the comprehensive explanation of the totality of the human past, often the work of non-historians. The revelation of the ultimate direction of History would eventually be known as historical 'determinism', and while it had several cele-brated practitioners, among them Buckle, it was articulated most famously by Auguste Comte, G. W. F. Hegel and Karl Marx. The intellectual systems associated with these names were very differ-ent but they shared a belief in the inexorably forward momentum of human affairs.

Comte (1798–1857), who is credited with popularizing the pre-viously obscure term 'sociology', developed a specific philosophy that he called 'positivism', the essential features of which are straightfor-ward. Positivism assumes that progress is not only *possible* (as eight-eenth-century thinkers had believed) but *inevitable*. It ascribes such progress to forces other than providence; and it believes that human behaviour, hence History, operates according to 'laws' akin to the laws of the natural world. Comte had a training in mathematics that gave him a higher level of confidence in natural laws than possessed by many of his contemporaries who had received a more conventional humanist education. Yet he had much in common with early nineteenth-century historical thought, especially Romanticism. For Comte the key to understanding a current phenomenon (and its future development) lay in looking to its historical origins. His ideal 'positivist library' even included a section on history with a selection of authors from Herodotus to his own day. Comte's multivolume work known in English as the *Course in Positive Philosophy* (1830–42) outlined the entire history of human thought through three phases, a theological, a metaphysical and a positive age. There are echoes here of Vico's eras of gods, heroes and men, of stadialism's changing modes of subsistence and of Condorcet's nine phases of History.

Comte's 'positive' age, in which people would recognize the govern-ing power of laws on human behaviour, lay ahead, and every mode of knowledge was following a parallel path through successive stages to converge at this common destination. Aside from its socially deterministic metaphysics, Comte's theory carried with it an epistemology that viewed all forms of science (history among them) as progressive and cumulative. This has led to the application of the term 'positivist' to *any* historical thinking which assumes steady improvements in knowledge, akin to experimental progress in the natural sciences. The entire nineteenth-century Rankean approach to scholarship and its twentieth-century continuation is thus sometimes referred to as 'positivist', a highly misleading perversion of the term's original meaning (a more accurate term, though still imprecise, might be 'empiricist'). It is somewhat more justly applied to the 'cumulative and steady improvement' model of historical scholarship, but even this analogy is problematic. To some degree, 'positivism' in the study of history has become in our own time a kind of scapegoat on to which the sins of all former 'naive' views of historical scholarship, especially evidentiary empiricism, can be heaped and then driven out into the intellectual desert of discredited ideas.

Moreover, the vulgar use of the term unintentionally magnifies true positivism's actual influence. Despite their impact on certain philosophical schools such as utilitarianism, and despite, too, their natural appeal to an age that took progress almost as an article of faith, Comtean ideas acquired relatively less purchase among western European and North American historians in the nineteenth century than one might think, exceptions such as Buckle, the social Darwinist Herbert Spencer (1820–1903) and France's Hippolyte Taine (1828–93) aside, and even then only selectively. Further afield positivism had greater success. As with Ranke's version of historicism, distance from the source produced greater receptivity. In eastern Europe, positivism offered an alternative to Marx: Russia's Miliukov was an enthusiastic Comtean. The Chilean José Victorino Lastarria (1817–88) found in Comte a welcome endorsement of his own ideas. The Brazilian historian João Capistrano de Abreu (1853–1927), influenced as a young man by both Buckle and Taine, briefly pursued a positivist line in his early work, only to be convinced, once he had spent time in the Biblioteca Nacional, that German *Historismus* offered a more attractive approach.

Positivism was one school of thought about the direction of History, German idealism another, beginning with Kant and the German nationalist J. G. Fichte (1762–1914) and reaching its apogee with Hegel's philosophy of world history. Hegel chronologically belongs in our previous chapter, a creature of the late Enlightenment and post-Revolutionary period. But for our purposes, he is best studied together with his mid- to late nineteenth-century disciples and opponents. History for Hegel was the gradual self-realization of mind in time through a process of 'dialectic', the continuous conflict between thesis and antithesis and their resolution in synthesis (a triad first articulated not by Hegel himself but borrowed from Fichte). His views had roots in earlier Enlightenment thinkers, but Hegel decisively rejected the long-standing classical notion that history was 'philosophy teaching by examples'. Instead, he substituted a different relation between history and philosophy, whereby the history *of* philosophy became in itself a story of progressions in human understanding as intellectual systems gave way to superior successors, marking the movement to self-consciousness of the World Spirit. History was not, in fact, Cicero's *magistra vitae*, a teacher – or at least not a very good one. Rather, it was both a process and simultaneously a coherent narrative of that process. Moreover, though human History was itself universal, Hegel believed that attempts to write small-h universal history were problematic – ironically, what he called 'specialized history' (an approach to the whole through a particular subject such as art or law) was more likely to be fruitful. And it was the philosopher, not the historian, who had to work out History's meaning, full knowledge of which could not be realized until History itself came to an end: the 'owl of Minerva', as he put it, spreads its wings only at dusk.

In retrospect, Hegel seems now to have been to the early nineteenth century what Vico had been to the early eighteenth, a complex and often opaque academic outlier who cannot be pigeonholed: he was neither a historian in the mode of Ranke, nor did his 'absolute idealism' become the dominant thread of philosophical metaphysics. But unlike Vico, Hegel did not toil away in obscurity, to be rescued by later generations. He was famous in his own time and attracted prominent pupils or admiring disciples who became stars in their own right, often by formulating views in reaction to their master. Despite his reputation as a conservative, he had a significant number of leftward-leaning associates. This included the 'Young Hegelians', a group that under Ludwig Feuerbach's (1804–72) influence inverted Hegel's idealist philosophy into a human-centred 'materialism'.

Hegel had been received coldly by Ranke and his Berlin colleagues in 1818, and his ideas were controversial. A whole century's worth of foes would use him as the satanic symbol against which their own philosophies were formulated, from Søren Kierkegaard and Arthur Schopenhauer to Martin Heidegger and Bertrand Russell. And it is Hegel, more than any other nineteenth-century figure, who summarized two centuries' worth of European dismissal of non-Western cultures and especially their lack of historicity, in the dual senses of having neither a sense of the past nor a place in the main plot of the human narrative. Africans and certain European peoples such as the Slavs were thus both without *history* (the form of writing) and of little significance to *History* (the dialectically moving forward course of events). Only Asia (selectively) and western Europe counted, and the latter lay at the more advanced end of History's road. Not surprisingly, this position too has been a lightning-rod for modern and postmodern criticisms of Eurocentrism and Orientalism (see below, pp. 268–71), but in fairness to Hegel it should be pointed out that his reasons for adopting it were quite different from the conventional early modern and eighteenth-century ones – lack of alphabetic writing and overdependence on orality. For Hegel the key criterion of 'statehood' (which did not necessarily mean the modern 'nation-state') can alone confer status *in* History and generate the writing *of* history. It was the state, he asserted, that furnished suitable content for historical prose and the circumstances in which it could be produced, with the aim of recording its own development.

The most significant spin-off from Hegel's philosophy of history and its dialectical engine, if evaluated by sheer popular influence, must surely be its adaptation by a one-time Young Hegelian, Karl Marx (1818–83), into a materialist theory of economic and social change leading from primitive times, through feudal and capitalist phases, to communism and the triumph of the proletariat. Marx developed his philosophy of history piecemeal through early theoretical works such as *The German Ideology* (1846). He wrote at least one work that can be considered a political history, the *18th Brumaire of Louis Napoleon* (1852; in some editions, 'Louis Bonaparte'); this is the source of his famous remark, also adapted from Hegel, that historical events occur twice, the first time as tragedy, the second time as farce.

Without exception, no theory of history in modern times has had more sway, in terms of sheer numbers of adherents, especially among Marx's eventual Soviet, eastern European and Chinese admirers. Marx either alone or with his associate Friedrich Engels (1820–95) was both prolific and complex, and no attempt at a full summary of his historical thought will be made here. His theories were never actually presented as a coherent system within a single work but are scattered across his vast œuvre. Concisely stated, the Marxian theory of History runs as follows. Mankind has passed or will pass through a series of social stages beginning with a primitive state in which the first form of association is the family, through the development of property and its exploitation, then to feudalism and eventually to capitalism before ending in a socialist state which marks the commencement of 'true' History. More specifically, Marx characterizes four epochs, the Asiatic (here borrowing the well-established concept of 'oriental despotism'), ancient, feudal and bourgeois, each defined by economic and social arrangements. Only with the future fifth stage, after capitalism has collapsed, will a classless society emerge and the dialectical engine of historical change be, as it were, turned off.

The movement from epoch to epoch is not unlike that proposed by the stadialists in the previous century, but any vestigial providential or supernatural element is completely removed, and it is less modes of *subsistence* than those of *production* that simultaneously constrain social arrangements and drive History forward. Transitions from one stage to another (that aspect which stadialism had never adequately explained) do not occur everywhere at the same time, nor at the same rate. They are not even absolutely inevitable in the strict sense, since in the Asiatic epoch there was little stimulus for development. Changes will sometimes occur because of external forces. More often, however, they happen due to interior contradictions and conflicts, especially class conflicts, which for Marx produce such phenomena as alienation, class-consciousness and ultimately revolution, the cocked hammer striking home on the pistol of change: Hegel's 'dialectic' is transposed from the realm of ideas down to that of economic and material life. The culmination of every stage of human existence is the resolution of the dialectic of conflict, and the acquisition of power by a previously subordinate class. The resulting new synthesis – the next stage – is, however, but a temporary stability as the dialectic will begin anew. All the more obvious aspects of life – political, religious, ideological – are like the one-tenth of an iceberg floating above the surface. They are but a 'superstructure' whose composition is predetermined by the material and economic 'base' on which it rests. In the course of outlining this theory, Marx articulated a number of essential concepts that have now influenced social, economic and historical analysis for well over a century, several of which have survived the collapse of eastern European communism in the early 1990s: the labour theory of value, primitive accumulation, class struggle, and dictatorship of the proletariat, to name but a few.

Germany also produced other important theories concerning versions of thought about the unfolding of history, and about the nature of the historical discipline, eventually dwelling on its differentiation from the natural sciences – a position which had not, in fact, been a feature of early historicist thought (see above, pp. 158–60). The historian of Prussia and sometime theoretician J. G. Droysen, a believer in the possibility of improved historical knowledge, argued in his *Historik* (and its shorter summary, the widely circulated *Outline of the Principles of History*) for a less naive view of the historian's relationship to sources. A moderate critic of his former mentor, Ranke, Droysen thought that the cult of objectivity, along with its focus on source criticism, had taken history down the wrong path; his 'Historics' were intended to fill the role for the historical past occupied by Poetics (what today is known as literary theory) in the imagined world of fiction.

A generation later, Wilhelm Dilthey (1833–1911) provided an important revision to the very concept of historical knowledge. A turning away from the post-Rankean fetish of the document can be seen in Dilthey's assertion that historical writing presupposes historical *thinking* that itself demands a mental act of understanding (*Verstehen*) whereby the meaning of events must be derived from our own inner experience; it cannot be lifted directly from the sources. As with Droysen's distinction between the world of nature, where there could only be endless recurrence, and that of history, where progress was possible, Dilthey's position was anti-positivist, but more sharply so. Droysen had assumed that *Verstehen*, 'the most perfect form of cognition' available to humans, could still get at an objective reality. Dilthey assumed that past events could be apprehended in a way that did not at all apply to the world of science, owing to our essential humanity, shared with historical figures, and to our capacity to make sense of the world through *Erlebnis* ('lived experience'). History, which we all live through, belonged to *Geisteswissenschaften* (the human or 'moral' sciences) not to *Naturwissenschaften*, but while its methods were different, it was quite as capable of rigour as the natural sciences. In his

Introduction to the Human Sciences (1883) Dilthey identified a problematic preoccupation, in place since the Renaissance, with the application to historical phenomena of principles of analysis derived from the study of nature; this had led to an under-recognition of their differences from natural phenomena, and thus to a poverty of historical theory.

It was left to Wilhelm Windelband (1848–1915) to dismiss the naiveté of historians (earlier historicists included) who persisted in seeing their discipline as methodologically and conceptually indistinguishable from the natural sciences. In 1894, Windelband rearticulated Aristotle's ancient principle that history deals in singularities, having the status of an 'ideographic' practice (representative of the unique and singular) rather than a 'nomothetic' or law-generating one. The distinction applied only to the 'modes of investigation' not to 'the contents of knowledge itself', since both history and natural science belonged under the larger umbrella of 'empirical sciences'. In his 1933 book *Experience and its Modes*, the British philosopher Michael Oakeshott (1901–90) would develop the history/science distinction further, arguing that history and the natural sciences are alternative 'modes' by which reality is represented and that their methods are not merely different, but mutually exclusive. Influenced by Hegel, too, Oakeshott argued that the distinction between history-as-it-happened and history-as-thought (or studied) was meaningless, since no history exists outside the historian's own experience – the past itself is nothing and cannot be simply 'resurrected'.

The Cultural and Social Alternatives to Ranke

Amid all this, one wonders, what had become of the eighteenth century's approach to the history of man, to Voltaire's cultural perspective on the reign of Louis XIV and to the stadialist analysis of past societies? At first glance, it would appear that the nineteenth century's renewed focus on the political and biographical appeared to have cast these aside along with its antithesis to systematic speculation in the mode of Hegel. This is not, however, an accurate picture, for the century did present some alternatives to Ranke (Comte and Marx among them), to European state-focused historiography and to the methodological limitations of both. These alternatives provided a route for the concerns of the Enlightenment into the twentieth and twenty-first centuries.

The first major challenge to the Rankean model had appeared in the work of Jacob Burckhardt (1818–97), a Swiss historian who had once attended Ranke's lectures at Berlin but who spent most of his life in Basel and Zurich. Author of works including a 'cultural history' of Ancient Greece, Burckhardt's most famous book, *The Civilization of the Renaissance in Italy*, was a brilliant study of the art and culture of the Renaissance, of the relationship of aesthetic to political life – he treated the 'state' as a 'work of art' – and of the rise of 'individualism'. *Civilization* remains one of those rare nineteenth-century histories still in print and regularly prescribed in courses on the Renaissance. In it Burckhardt practised, if he did not quite invent, a form of historical inquiry known as *Kulturgeschichte*, and it defied the conventions of the emerging discipline by eschewing narrative for a series of reflective essays on different aspects of the Renaissance. Though well received (Burckhardt was later offered, and declined, Ranke's chair in Berlin), his masterpiece remained *sui generis* for several decades.

The great French ancient historian of the mid-nineteenth century, Numa Denis Fustel de Coulanges (1830–89) offered another alternative. An impressive scholar, he falls into a sociological tradition of history that stretches from Comte to Max Weber. A moderate positivist, in the epistemological sense of the word, Fustel de Coulanges truly believed that history, through documents, could speak for itself and was therefore an 'observational science'. He was far from averse to theory and generalization – his pupil Charles Seignobos was among those who thought his former master too devoted to systematic ideas. At the same time, he was a learned and erudite researcher, well known for his study of Greek and Roman religion, law and institutions, *The Antique City* (1864). Yet both the theorizing and the erudition were home-grown: Fustel de Coulanges remained to the end of his days quite impervious to Rankean narrative or even to Niebuhrian *Altertumswissenschaft*. Others would eventually join him: near the end of the century, after the disaster of the Franco-Prussian War, German influences became increasingly suspect, and the First World War would magnify this trend. The erstwhile French proponent of the Rankean seminar, Ernest Lavisse, even saw the development of proper training for French historians as an alternative means of 'fighting the Germans', though younger scholars like the medievalist Ferdinand Lot (1866–1952) still chafed at the inferiority of their nation's educational apparatus compared with that of the German universities.

Two different challenges to the Rankean version of Germanic historiography emerged a generation later, and this time from within
Germany itself. The first was the notorious *Methodenstreit* or 'dispute
about method' of the 1890s, set off by Karl Lamprecht (1856–1915),
which presaged some of the debates that have continued down to our
own time. More sympathetic to positivism than Droysen or Dilthey,
Lamprecht proclaimed the need for a 'new' history. He cast doubt on
the usefulness of history conceived as the account of leaders and
particular events, as opposed to larger groups, and invoked the need
for an alliance with the incipient social sciences, including psychology;
he also argued that culture was the external expression of a people's
collective psyche (*Volksseele*), and the course of history its product.
Lamprecht was a renegade in a number of senses. In 1895 he made an
unsuccessful bid for the vacant editorship of *Historische Zeitschrift*,
proposing to amalgamate it with two other journals with which he was
involved. He was outmanoeuvred by the nationalist historian
Treitschke (who would hold the post for only a year) and by the future
historian of *Historismus*, Meinecke, who would soon thereafter
achieve the editorship himself. Though marginalized by the German
historiographic establishment during his career, Lamprecht was
admired abroad; his own pupils would include the leading Romanian
historian of the next generation, Nicolae Iorga (1871–1940), and
following the Second World War a number of East German historians
saw him as having provided an alternative to Ranke. Lamprecht had
other admirers in northern Europe, in particular two medievalists, the
Belgian economic historian Henri Pirenne (1862–1935) and the Dutch
cultural historian Johan Huizinga (see below, p. 218) They, in turn,
provide important bridges from the turn of the century to later developments such as the Annales School (see below, pp. 229–32) and
modern cultural history.

Lamprecht's ideas, and the hostile response to them, were a product of
tensions left unresolved at the end of the nineteenth century between
history and philosophy on the one hand, and several newer, neighbouring branches of knowledge, including psychology, economics, anthropology and sociology – the modern social sciences. These were often
accentuated by personal rivalries and social prejudices, such as the anti-
Semitism fanned by influential public intellectuals such as Treitschke.
The full consequences of this are still being worked out today on the
borders between these subjects. Historically minded contemporaries

such as the Jewish-descended philosopher Georg Simmel (1858–1918) –
who was denied a professorial chair till late in life – the political economist Max Weber (1864–1920) and the French Jew Émile Durkheim
(1858– 1917), a former pupil of Fustel de Coulanges, were merging the
study of the past with sociology (stripped of the more speculative elements in Comte's work several decades previously). It has enjoyed
a steady if rocky relationship with its parent discipline ever since.
Economic historians were similarly turning (without the assistance of
Marx) to the history of material culture, industry and even labour; the
economist Gustav von Schmoller (1838–1917) spoke for a German
school of economics that saw historical data as the cornerstone of his
own discipline. The reception of these ideas, with their focus on 'society'
rather than the more traditional 'state', was often friendlier outside their
country of birth: in America, Lamprechtian ideas found an audience in
a generation of historians discontented with the agenda of American
historiography, and economic history soon established itself as virtually
a parallel discipline in both Britain – by William James Ashley
(1860–1927) – and eventually America. The brief assault on the supremacy of political history by Columbia University's James Harvey
Robinson (1863–1936) and the so-called 'New Historians' before and
after the First World War would open the door to North American social
history in the 1960s and 1970s.

Perhaps the most influential intellectual of the late nineteenth century, Friedrich Nietzsche (1844–1900), turned his own largely conventional humanist education into a stunning reassessment of human
nature, culture, morality and history itself. If Lamprecht, like Herder
a century earlier, might be described as the impudent schoolboy of late
nineteenth-century historical thought, Nietzsche sought to burn down
the existing school and build a new one of his own design. Nietzsche's
perspectives on history, culture and learning were the product of his
own rigorous philological training (which began, ironically, at the
same high school that had once educated Ranke) but took him to
a position that repudiated much of the four-century heritage of humanism. His 'genealogical' approach to the past, looking backwards
through time for the origins of such things as modern morality or
reason, and to their historical transitions and alterations, has deeply
affected late twentieth-century figures such as Michel Foucault (see
below, pp. 255, 258), and has been taken up (sometimes inaccurately)
by the 'postmodern' movement in historiography which we will

encounter in our next chapter. His ideas thus merit extended consideration here.

Although Nietzsche eventually grew hostile to much of the nineteenth-
century historiographical agenda, he was an admirer of classical culture
in particular and by no means indifferent to the past as a whole, which,
Anthony K. Jensen has illustrated in a recent book, suffused his writing in
one form or another throughout his career, and he admired a number of
older contemporaries such as his sometime Basel colleague, Burckhardt
(whose conservatism and distaste for mass culture he would come to
share) and the French historian Hippolyte Taine. Although he came to
believe, contrary to his philological training, that no account of the past
could 'realistically' represent that past, he did not deny that the past itself
was real, or that attempts to achieve persuasive accounts of it were
worthless. He was neither seventeenth-century Pyrrhonist nor early
twentieth-century relativist (see below, p. 217). If anything, Nietzsche's
purpose was not the denial of the possibility of history per se, or even its
utility, but simply 'to destroy belief in a historical past from which men
might learn any single, substantial truth', and to rescue the past from the
suffocating aridity of the nineteenth-century German academy on the
one hand and from unprovable metaphysical speculation of the Hegelian
kind on the other.

Nietzsche's opinions on History and history developed over the course
of several major works, perhaps most notably in a work he himself grew
to dislike, often referred to popularly as 'The Use and Abuse of History'
but more properly entitled *On the Uses and Disadvantages of History
for Life*, first published in 1874 as the second in a series of Nietzsche's
Untimely Meditations. History, Nietzsche suggested in this essay, has
witnessed cycles of progress and decay, beginning in a primitive barbarism, proceeding through the genius of pre-Socratic thought and especially Aeschylean tragedy, followed by a decline into the twin tyrannies
of religion and science that have stifled creativity. Like Vico some 150
years earlier, Nietzsche saw his own age as part of a downward trajectory towards a future barbarism. The man-made world itself springs
from the competition of two principles, the Dionysian force of chaotic,
creative energy and the Apollonian force of order: both are necessary to
the human condition and a superabundance of either is harmful. As far
as historical knowledge is concerned, it is both a tool and a burden: a tool
because it allows awareness of our debt to the past and a sense that there
is a future superior state that can be struggled towards; a burden because

it can prohibit us from living in the present and achieving great things in our own time. Against the traditional equation of history with remembrance, and memory as an essential feature of humanity, Nietzsche urges *forgetfulness* as a necessity, without which we cannot escape the endless process of becoming. In order to live, we must selectively forget, rather like putting on headphones to eliminate ambient noise; 'oversaturation' of an age with history is 'hostile and dangerous to life'. Yet we cannot live entirely without history: some of it is necessary to human existence, and distinguishes us from the animal who lives in an endless moment (though with a 'degree of happiness' and without boredom or dissimulation). History is not for the weak, for it 'can be borne only by strong personalities' while lesser beings will be overwhelmed by it.

In *Uses and Disadvantages* (though not subsequently), Nietzsche famously divided historians into three different types, respectively reflecting man's tripartite existence as a being 'who acts and strives', 'who preserves and reveres' and 'who suffers and seeks deliverance': Nietzsche calls them respectively the Monumental, Antiquarian and Critical. The Monumental historian writes the conventional history of 'great men' and their achievements. It teaches us that grand things were achievable in the past, and may be so again, but its utility as a provider of relevant examples is limited because no two instances of greatness are the same, even if historians bludgeon them into the appearance of similarity; Monumental history also neglects causes in the name of a celebration of effects. The Antiquarian form, in contrast, recovers the details of the past indiscriminately, seeking value in everything, and connections between everything. It occasions ossification or mummification if allowed to rule over the other two forms of history: it degenerates 'from the moment it is no longer animated and inspired by the fresh life of the present'. One can see in the description of these first two types of history Nietzsche's debt to earlier sceptical thought, both the Guicciardinian denial of the comparability of historical events and the eighteenth-century rejection of erudition without social purpose, though Nietzsche takes these arguments further towards their logical extremes than his predecessors.

The third form, Critical history, brings the past before the tribunal of the present, 'scrupulously examining it and finally condemning it', not according to any principle of morality or justice but out of the sheer force of life, that 'dark, driving power that insatiably thirsts for itself'. Critical history necessarily dissolves any pre-existing story or process and takes the past as a pool of elements (or to use Nietzsche's preferred analogy, musical notes) that can be pieced together as needed to serve immediate moral and aesthetic goals. But critical history is essentially a destroyer rather than a creator, a doubter of the past which, unfettered by the Monumental and Antiquarian, runs the risk of doing away with all traditions, including those out of which it itself has grown.

Here and in later works, Nietzsche attacked what he saw as the naivety of Rankean historiography in the form of its belief that reliance on legitimate sources could produce objective historiography. For Nietzsche, who knew all too well the ambiguities of source materials, the historian cannot in any case represent the past objectively since he is himself possessed of values that drive him to study one thing rather than another, and also subject to motives and psychological impulses, often unconscious, that filter his thinking in particular directions. The 'Will-to-Power' that he postulated in a late work, the *Genealogy of Morality*, as the most fundamental of all human drives, even drove, as Jensen notes, the historian's own desire to promote the superiority of his own account over those of others. And an absolute objectivity in history would not be very useful were it actually to be possible, because each individual must be free to extract what he needs from history in order to confront life, which is experienced only by subjective individuals. Therefore, if objectivity exists at all in the representation of the past, it is only ever relative and contingent. And causal sequences, the very threads that connect events in historian's narratives, are never more than the historian's own mental invention or imposition on events of connections which did not, in themselves, exist. Nietzsche's stance on behalf of subjectivity, his recognition of the irrational and his repudiation of much of the edifice of professional historiography, suggests that all was not harmonious within Clio's European temple at the close of the nineteenth century. We will explore some of the implications of this further on.

Historiographical Imperialism? The Impact of Western Methods and Models Beyond the Eurosphere

As formidable as the collective Western imperial apparatus was, it could not have converted long-standing and well-established East Asian historiographies to 'modern' (meaning 'Western') methods had there not been both an inclination on the part of reformers within those countries to adopt European practices, and a flexibility in, and variety among, those practices which made them adaptable to very different soil. Intellectuals such as China's Liang Qichao saw their countries outdistanced by a Europe now flourishing in a 'modern' era while they themselves languished in a prison-house of the past. They believed that traditional ways of doing history were part of the problem, since they neither narrated a story of social, political and economic advancement nor promoted a progressive future. In some parts of the world, the Enlightenment story of progress was embraced with enthusiasm, and even given either a Hegelian dialectic or Comtean positivist spin long discredited in its own homeland. The modern Latin Americanist Allen Woll quotes Puerto Rico's official historian Salvador Brau's (1842–1912) 1896 remarks on the historian's purpose – to use the modern tools of historical understanding as a means of defining and proclaiming his people's distinctive identity:

Yes! We have a history and we must understand it in order to march . . . with a firm and measured step to the future. We must make everyone understand this history so our regional character will distinguish itself . . . so no one will confuse us with any other people.

From the point of view of the twentieth century, it was easy for most historians of history to conclude that Western methods and European genres triumphed because the most progressive elements in Asian and African societies recognized their inherent superiority. There is plenty of evidence for this interpretation in the writings of non-Europeans themselves, who (at least initially) enthusiastically embraced Western historical methods. Legend, myth and error should be uprooted and excised from accounts of the past, and rigorous criticism applied to evidence as a precursor to narrating a forward-marching story. The spread of Clio's empire looks at first to have been quite unstoppable. Europe, after centuries of debate on how best to study and write about history, seemed at last to have put its own house in order – imposed 'discipline' on the study of the past – with the advent of Rankean scholarly practices, the secularization of historical learning and its institutionalization in universities, journals, textbooks, learned societies and book reviews. If Europe was still hopelessly divided politically, it seemed – at least to outsiders unable to detect hairline fractures – to rest on solid foundations historiographically. This was in fact an optical illusion of solidity and consensus created by distance and by language. The divisions and differences within western historiography, outlined in previous sections of this chapter, were either less visible to Asian and African audiences or, more likely, simply deemed less important than their similarities.

The transformation of historiography in India through to independence in 1947 is perhaps the most obvious case of the direct imposition and importation of historical practices from imperial 'metropole' to colonial 'periphery', in the double sense that it illustrates both a successful process of Westernization and the eventual redeployment of the tools of European historiography *against* the colonizer. One of the first of the colonial commentators to write on Indian history – without ever setting foot in South Asia – was James Mill (1773–1836). A product of the Scottish educational system, Mill was also a close associate of the English utilitarian Jeremy Bentham, and father to the more famous John Stuart Mill. In 1817 Mill *père* published the work for which he is best remembered, *The History of British India*. A critic of prior British interventions in India, Mill saw the subcontinent as a great laboratory for Benthamite social experiments; India's recent past also permitted him an opportunity to comment on the present mores and values of his own country. His lack of direct experience with the country, such as the philologist Sir William Jones had acquired a few decades earlier, or of any of Jones' extraordinary facility with languages, were to Mill a great strength since it would permit a more dispassionate, objective analysis of the subject than could be made by those who had lived in India or spoke its languages.

The History of British India both spawned a century of imperial historiography and itself influenced colonial policy quite directly; its very lack of depth and original research paradoxically made it the ideal explanatory tool of colonialism in India. It also presented an infamous dismissal of indigenous Hindu historicity, compared with that of Islam.

As all our knowledge is built upon experience, the recordation of the past for the guidance of the future is one of the effects in which the utility of the art of writing principally consists. Of this most important branch of literature the Hindus were totally destitute. Among the Mahomedans of India the art of composing history has been carried to greater perfection than in any other part of Asia. (*The History of British India*, 1817, Vol. 1, p. 648)

Mill's views on the lack of Hindu historicity were neither original nor unique. The most respected British historian of the first half of the century, Thomas Babington Macaulay (1800–59), who was among Mill's admirers, reiterated the familiar notion that measured oriental cultural inferiority by its historiographic failures, for instance claiming in 1834 that all the historical information contained in books written in the Sanskrit language was of less value than the most elementary English school textbooks. His own celebrated history of England became a major text studied in Britain's colonies overseas, carrying with it his own reformist agenda of liberal imperialism, an agenda built on notions of race, progress and the duty of the white man to 'improve' the lot of his colonial inferior.

Many of the colonial writers on India's past were historians by accident, company employees or civil servants whose careers had given them purview of India, whether or not they actually spent any time there. Mill himself was a functionary at the East India Company's London office. Among those who actually visited India, Mountstuart Elphinstone (1779–1859), governor of Bombay, authored a *History of India* (1841), widely used in Indian education (and much more sympathetic to India's past than Mill's account). In the early twentieth century, the pattern would continue with Vincent Arthur Smith (1848–1920), a Dubliner who spent thirty years in the Indian civil service. His *Early History of India* (1904) and *Oxford History of India* (1919) show the influence of a century of scholarly change in Europe, while still maintaining a firm conviction that an understanding of the past could help to solve present problems.

Smith's *Oxford History* would become a popular school textbook. However, Westernized Indian historical writing was not the exclusive property of the occupier. Indians themselves were encouraged to write their own history according to European models; as early as 1802 the Bengali scholar Ramram Basu (*c.* 1751–1813) had published the first Western-style history of India in a native language. In the course of the century, many other Indians were co-opted by imperial institutions and took up the charge of writing their own history. Some did it in order to promote Indian identity and to criticize the Raj, including the novelist Bankim Chandra Chatterjee (or Chattopadhyay, 1838–94) and the poet Rabindranath Tagore (1861–1941). Chatterjee was among a number of authors for whom fictional narratives based upon historical materials provided an opportunity to present the past in ways that appealed to embryonic national sentiment. Elsewhere, however, he would lament the apparent absence of Indian history. This deficiency had retarded India's political regeneration, and he urged a collective effort to fill the gap, and especially to create histories that stressed past heroic achievements by Indians.

Regardless of their political leanings, Indian historians mainly looked westward for models and methods. They adopted both the disciplinary practices of European historians and the civilizing pro-gramme of the British, with the former being closely linked to the promotion of the latter. It was neither necessary to endorse the colonial agenda nor even to support the Raj in order to see both history and History in Western terms. As an orientalizer, Mill had a successor of whom he might have been proud in Bankim Chatterjee's 1874 plea for an 'Indian historiography of India'. In fact, the very adoption of British historical methods and the spread of historical textbooks helped to manufacture precisely that nationalist sense of India, transcending regional or linguistic variations (and no longer dependent on myths of common descent), that would ultimately bring down the colonial edifice. The British had introduced to India the notion that there is a modern, correct way of narrating the past, derived from European models and with the nation-state as its focus, and thereby empowered Indian national consciousness in the process.

Late Victorian notions of scientific history migrated into India dur-ing the first third of the twentieth century through British-trained Indian historians returning home to teach. In part owing to the influ-ence of technically proficient scholars such as the Sanskrit philologist Sir R. G. Bhandarkar (1837–1925), his son, D. R. Bhandarkar (1875–1950), an epigrapher and numismatist, and the Mughal-period scholar Sir Jadunath Sarkar (1870–1958), the institutional apparatus of Western historiography gradually replicated itself over-seas, beginning with the Historical Records Commission of 1919 and the Indian History Congress established in 1935. Sarkar, the quintes-sential Europhile exponent of 'scientific history' in India, and an admirer of the great men who had founded states in the previous century, saw the rigorous application of Western methods as essential to national development, and opposed what he regarded as 'false patriotism'. As his recent biographer Dipesh Chakrabarty has sug-gested, the challenge by this time lay less in convincing people that history was important than in finding any agreement as to what exactly 'scientific' history meant.

Historiographical trends in Europe were replicated abroad, including challenges to the sort of political history practised by mainstream historians such as Sarkar; the success of economic history in establishing itself as virtually a parallel discipline in late nineteenth-century Britain was echoed in India by the retired Indian civil service officer Romesh Chunder (or Chandra) Dutt's (1845 or 1848–1909) *Economic History of India* (1902–4). Many of these works were written from a nationalist, even moderately anti-colonial perspective, which would flourish in the 1930s and 1940s and achieve greater prominence after 1947. India's first post-independence prime minister, Jawaharlal Nehru (1889–1964), had personally written his *Glimpses of World History* (published in 1942) in the form of a series of letters to his daughter Indira (herself a future Indian prime minister) while imprisoned a decade earlier. The production of critical editions of original texts in India also played its part in the nationalization of the past, as it had done in nineteenth-century Europe. Following independence in 1947, Ramesh Chandra Majumdar (1888–1980), directed *The History and Culture of the Indian People* (11 vols, 1951–77). History, the tool of the colonizer, had become an instrument of liberation for India's political elites, though not as yet for the massive 'subaltern' population beneath them.

The other large land mass that European colonizers believed (as with India, erroneously) to be deficient in historical literature was Africa. Modern historical writing first appears there in the later nineteenth century – not a great deal later than its establishment in Europe. Initially, it was overwhelmingly the preserve of the colonizers, especially missionaries, who were concerned to integrate African schoolchildren into the Christian and European past. There were some notable indigenous exceptions, largely unnoticed at the time, such as Samuel Johnson (1846–1901), the Yoruba son of a Sierra Leone freedman, who returned to his parents' home in Nigeria as a missionary. Johnson, strongly affected by classical historians such as Xenophon, authored a *History of the Yorubas* (published posthumously in 1921). This was based largely on Yorubaland oral historical narratives (*itàn*) and eyewitness accounts, in addition to colonial documents; Johnson's purpose, as he announced at the start of his book, was to ensure 'that the history of our fatherland might not be lost in oblivion, especially as our old sires are fast dying out'. All of these works were ethnically focused, that is, devoted to recovering and telling the past of a particular tribe. The clerical careers of most of these historians ensured a strong Christian, reformist influence. In areas colonized by Germans such as Tanganyika (part of modern Tanzania), Swahili historical works appeared in the early twentieth century, beginning with Abdallah bin Hemedi 'l Ajjemy's (*c.* 1835–1912) *Chronicles of the Kilindi* (comp. 1904) an extensive record of the dynasty that had ruled the area in the nineteenth century, derived from oral traditions and from the author's own memories of recent events.

The process of Westernizing African history-writing is well illustrated in the lengthy life and career – stretching well past the chronological boundaries of this chapter – of Uwadiae Jacob Egharevba (1893–1981) of Benin, in modern Nigeria. Educated in Yoruba territory while travelling with his trader parents, Egharevba soon abandoned commerce for a full-time literary career. In his *A Short History of Benin*, the most well known of his over thirty historical and literary works, Egharevba exploited his connections with Benin chiefs and 'court historians', including those responsible for the Benin king list, and became convinced that the future survival of his people's traditions depended on their being recorded and documented. He published the *Short History* in 1933 in the Edo language, and quickly had it translated into English the following year. The work proved so popular that several subsequent editions were published in ensuing decades, but its original oral sources were soon submerged, a recent study has shown, by an incremental addition of western writings which obliged Egharevba to reconcile conflicting narratives into a single account, eliding or distorting many of his original materials.

The importation and adoption of European methods and approaches into colonized regions such as India and Africa often came at the cost of marginalizing or outright eradicating older, indigenous forms of historical knowledge and writing. This replicated on a grander scale (and now with the benefit of mass-market printing) the process we saw previously in the early modern Americas, and unfolded similarly in the 'settler' societies of South Africa, Canada and Australasia, at the expense of the aboriginal populations' property and their pasts. Southeast Asia was slower to experience this culling of historiographical genres in favour of European models, perhaps owing at least in part to the multiplicity of languages and religions (Islam, Buddhism and Hinduism) in the area, though this had not been the case in India. A better explanation may lie in the geographic situation of the region's assorted kingdoms either on the edge of both India and China (Vietnam, Malaya, Thailand, Burma, Cambodia, for instance), or archipelagically scattered (Indonesia, the Philippines, and the South Sea island chains). Throughout the eighteenth and the first half of the nineteenth century, European administrators in parts of Southeast Asia introduced audiences at home to histories of the new colonies, while also quietly beginning the process that exploited, while simultaneously marginalizing, the indigenous histories that they were required to use as sources. As in India, local elites were eventually co-opted into the usage of Western genres. Nor was imperial occupation strictly necessary to spread European historical practices. In uncolonized, monarchical Thailand (Siam), where the historically minded Chakri king Rama IV (or Mongkut, r. 1851–68) had authorized a definitive edition of the chronicles of Ayutthaya, Western-style modern histories and school textbooks did not appear in earnest until the 1920s. At the same time, the introduction of printing expanded the circulation of historical works, including many from abroad, among the Thai learned classes. A tradition of royalist–nationalist historiography was established by Mongkut's younger son, Prince Damrong Rajanubhab, or Rachanuphap (1862–1943), a politician and educational reformer who turned to history in retirement. An admirer of Ranke and Western scholarship in general, Damrong's historical work embodied a use of source criticism while retaining the dynastic focus of an older, indigenous form of Thai historical writing called *phongsawadan*. Damrong was responsible for the publication of an extensive series of histories, the *Prachum phongsawadan* ('Collected Histories') – something like a Thai equivalent to enormous European historical-text series like the *Monumenta Germaniae Historica* or Britain's 'Rolls Series' of medieval chronicles.

A comparable process of historiographical Westernization unfolded in the Middle East, where the Western powers and the Ottoman Empire vied for influence during the nineteenth century. As Youssef Choueiri has shown in his studies of Arabic historiography, intellectuals in both the Arabic and non-Arabic parts of the Islamic world began in the mid- to late part of the century to write histories devoted to establishing national pasts, which now also included the pre-Islamic periods. Nineteenth-century Iranian historians, notes Mohamad Tavakoli-Targhi, rejected inherited, Muslim-influenced forms of historicity in favour of accounts that highlighted progress and linear development. Impressed by the apparently greater progress of Europe, they blamed their country's apparent backwardness on Arabs and Islam, they built, on a foundation of indigenous pre-Islamic literature and Western critiques of 'oriental' culture, a nationalist past that linked Persia to Europe rather than the Islamic world. In a sense, they might be said to have self-Orientalized their past.

Older pan-Islamic cultural and religious impulses remained as important as newer Arab and non-Arab nationalism: Middle Eastern peoples of various religions had to face the dilemma of coexistence with Western powers. Modern Islamic thought, influenced by Western science and technology, was also beginning to take shape in the hands of activist reformers like Sayyid Jamal al-Din al-Afghani (1838–97), the author of a history of Afghanistan. The social origins and interests of historians were also quite different than in previous ages. With the European presence had come the decline of the *'ulema'*, the transnational community of learned religious men who had influenced historical writing in the Muslim world for centuries, many of them polymaths and scientific thinkers rather than exclusively historians. Their place would be occupied by a 'bourgeois' class (doctors, lawyers, journalists), often very Western-oriented, and heirs to the medieval view of history as a branch of *adab* or belles-lettres rather than a handmaid of religion. During this period, efforts were made to print historical sources, and several learned societies with historical interests were founded.

Egypt provides a good case study. There, 'Abd al-Rahman al-Jabarti (1753–1825) had anticipated later trends with his anti-French account of the Napoleonic occupation of Egypt (1798–1801), *The Demonstration of Piety in the Destruction of the French State*, comp. c. 1801) and a longer historical account of events from the late seventeenth to early nineteenth century. Jabarti's works came at the end of a long fallow period, historical writing in Ottoman-ruled Egypt having been relatively scant and generally of poor quality, but other historians soon appeared. The political circumstances underpinning that historiography were, however, disappearing rapidly in the early nineteenth century, a period that would see rising Arab nationalism chafe against Muslim unity, notionally represented by a declining Ottoman Empire, a more objectionable foe, for the moment, than the

Europeans. Another Egyptian, Rifa'a Rafi' al-Tahtawi (1801–73), had spent five years in Paris, and he became a major channel through which modern European historiography began to enter the Arabic-speaking world. He translated into Arabic or oversaw translations of several Enlightenment works, including Voltaire's *Charles XII* and Robertson's *Charles V*. Al-Tahtawi also narrated the history of ancient Egypt in a work (1868–9) that is a hybrid of modern and classical Islamic historical forms. It continues to stress some of the long-standing values of Islamic historiography as outlined in authors like Ibn Khaldun (whose *Muqaddimah* al-Tahtawi had shepherded into print in 1857) and in the *hadith*s. While al-Tahtawi acknowledged the role of Islam in Egyptian history, his work treats the country as a distinctive national unit that had existed continuously from antiquity to modern times, celebrating Egypt as a seat of world civilization and learning (rather as contemporary Greek historians were defending their continuity with ancient Hellas). His division of history into human and sacred spheres, and periodization of the former into ancient and modern (with subject matter further arranged as either 'universal' or 'particular'), clearly shows signs of Western influence.

Al-Tahtawi was instrumental in reforming the Egyptian school curriculum, which by the 1870s routinely included history. Universities were established early in the twentieth century, and with them the academic training of scholars in history and other arts and sciences. Academic historiography began slowly in the post-Ottoman era starting in the 1920s, initially in the hands of North American- and European-trained scholars, thus extending the dominance of Western-style academic history over the Islamic world's long-distinct historiographic traditions. Shafiq Ghurbal (1894–1961) was among a group of Egyptian historians, including the Sorbonne-trained Muhammad Sabri (1890–1978), who had studied in Europe and used European sources in their research. Ghurbal had been educated in England, first at Liverpool and then at London's Institute of Historical Research, where he submitted parts of his future book for the MA degree, supervised by a young Arnold J. Toynbee (see below, pp. 218–19). Western methodological texts were also catching on in the Middle East, with a lag-effect that disseminated ideas already dated in their European home: Asad Rustum (1897–1965), a historian of Syria, published an Arabic-language manual on Western historical method in 1939, largely drawn from Langlois and Seignobos' famous textbook, the influence of which was already on the wane in its French homeland.

Nationalist and secular tendencies were also being felt in non-Arabic Islam, and nowhere more strongly than in Islam's own imperial metropole, Ottoman Turkey, where older traditions of historical writing had survived through the eighteenth and into the nineteenth century. Official historians were still being appointed through this period, and the spread of both printing and literacy stoked a public appetite for historical works. Until at least the mid-1800s, court-appointed annalists or favour-seekers continued to dominate, and truly independent historiography was rare. The outstanding historian of the period, Ahmed Jevdet (Cevdet) Pasha (1822–95), spent three decades preparing a twelve-volume history of imperial events from 1774 to 1826, the early instalments of which earned him his appointment as official historiographer. As in the rest of the Ottoman world, this was a period of transition during which interest in European culture and its history-writing grew along with knowledge of Western languages and literatures. New genres emerged, including memoirs and local histories that were more than mere biographies of local worthies. The 'ancillary disciplines' of history, such as sigillography, epigraphy and numismatics, began to appear in the second part of the nineteenth century, and Western-style academic training followed when the University of Istanbul was reorganized (1924) in close to its modern form. Following the empire's collapse at the end of the First World War, the new Turkish state's leader, Mustafa Kemal Atatürk (1881–1938), himself well read in European histories, revived the former Ottoman Historical Society as the Turkish Historical Society (1931). In 1935 Atatürk established a Faculty of Languages, History and Geography in Ankara explicitly to provide a Western-style academic institution in which young scholars could train. He aggressively supported historical writing from a nationalist perspective in an effort to displace older images of the despotic, weak, orientalized Ottomans with a 'Turkish Historical Thesis' (*Türk Tarih Tezi*) which glorified the Turkish nation and its European past; this was firmly linked to the medieval Turkish territorial occupation of Anatolia, since Atatürk wished to discourage any 'pan-Turkic' imperial adventures outside these borders, and it linked the Turks with 'white' Europe and Central Asia, whence all civilization was held to originate, rather than with 'yellow' East Asia. (This is a reminder that we should not assume that the application of a racial lens to history has ever been the sole preserve of Western imperialism.) A Turkish Historical Research Committee was established in 1931 and in the following year the *Türk Tarih Tezi* was declared to be the official doctrine of the Turkish state. While unsympathetic to the struggling empire of the previous two hundred years, republican historians nevertheless embraced the successes of the Ottoman glory days between the thirteenth and the seventeenth centuries. The academic founder of modern Turkish historiography, Mehmet Fuat Köprülü (1890–1966) began to articulate this vision in the 1930s in a series of lectures at the Sorbonne, soon published as *The Origins of the Ottoman Empire* in French and Turkish (English edition, 1992). The task of his generation of Turkish historians, sorting out legend from fact and balancing ethnicity, religion and other influences, is reminiscent of the Romantic nationalist historiographies of the early nineteenth century and, more remotely, of Renaissance debates about national origins, albeit now approached with the tools of modern scholarship.

Throughout this book East Asia has provided us with the most sustained example of a historiographical tradition, or set of traditions, distinct and separate from Europe's, and moreover one which developed and evolved in parallel rather than, except on occasion, in interaction with it. This separate development came to an end in the later nineteenth and early twentieth centuries. We must here reverse our past practice of treating the island empire of Japan after its larger Chinese neighbour, for Japan turned to modernization, and to Western influences, a full generation before China, and unlike China did not require the overthrow of its empire in order to achieve this. Long closed to the West during the Tokugawa era, Japan opened up to international influence in the years running up to and following the Meiji Restoration of 1868, which brought an end to nearly seven centuries of rule by successive bakufus on behalf of figurehead emperors. The Meiji Restoration marked a sharp break with what went before – including, soon thereafter, the historiographical practices that had underpinned the old regime.

Despite early efforts to institutionalize historical writing, the attempt to compile the *Dai Nihon hennenshi* ('Chronological History of Great Japan'), a new history along the lines of the Six National Histories, was stillborn. It was simply no longer possible to revive older forms of historical writing, or to model institutions after ancient predecessors, not least because a principal goal of the Restoration's architects was to accomplish what the shoguns had failed to do through two centuries of isolationism: deal with the inescapable presence of the West on a manifestly superior footing, and to learn from Europeans and Americans without sacrificing Japanese identity in the process. Moreover, centralized sponsorship of 'official' history (as opposed to state financial support for independent historical writing, and for the preservation and publication of sources) was itself an outdated practice in much of the rest of the world, no longer much respected in the very European countries which were supposed to provide a model for reformed historiography. There, the universities had come to the fore. A short-lived Office of Historiography established soon after the Restoration was transferred to Tokyo Imperial University in 1888, and a department of Japanese history founded there in 1889.

The solution came from bypassing the indigenous models of representing the past, along with their Chinese methods and sources, and looking to the West. As early as 1878 a young official (and in later life, influential politician) named Suematsu Kencho (1855–1920) was dispatched to London to report back on French and British historiography, several examples of which were already available in Japanese. His letters indicate a strong admiration for the classical tradition of political history from Thucydides through Clarendon to Guizot, and a healthy respect for the positivist approach of Buckle (once again either failing to see, or choosing to ignore, the critical differences). Within a decade, the director of the Office of Historiography, Shigeno Yasutsugu (1827–1910), arranged for one of Ranke's more remote disciples, the German Jew Ludwig Riess (1861–1928), to come to Japan as the first professor of history in Tokyo Imperial University in 1887. Riess retained this position till 1902, by which time he had trained a substantial number of the next generation of Japanese history professors. The transfer of the Office of Historiography to the university, as a subsidiary research institute, and the formal appointment of Kume Kunitake, Shigeno and other historians as professors followed soon thereafter. Japanese history became the subject of a separate department in 1889 and acquired its own chair in 1904. Meanwhile, reform-minded and generally pro-Western scholars such as Fukuzawa Yukichi (1835–1901), a reader of Alexis de Tocqueville, Buckle, Spencer and Guizot, formulated a theory of civilization espousing the superiority of the West and the need for Japan to catch up with the rest of the world after centuries of isolation.

As in Europe, however, not everyone accepted the value of academic historiography. Yamaji Aizan (1864–1917) was an outsider and popular historian highly critical of the sterility of scholarship at Tokyo Imperial, and – shades of Nietzsche? – of 'dead history'. He advocated the writing of narratives covering a wide range of subjects, as opposed to the government-sponsored focus on document criticism and factual verification. Yamaji coined the term *minkan shigaku* or 'private historical scholarship' to distinguish his sort of history from that generated through state sponsorship. Moreover, the scholarship generated by the source criticism that Riess' Japanese friends espoused was by no means always welcome, especially among conservative nationalists, heirs to Motoori Norinaga, who were determined to maintain the tradition of a social and moral function in historiography and the literal validity of the ancient traditions. Shigeno (who was also president of the Historical Society established in 1889) was himself reviled as 'Dr Obliterator' for his attacks on traditional verities such as the reliability of the *Taiheiki*, one of the most revered of medieval Japanese histories, and the historicity of some of its figures. His colleague, Kume Kunitake (1839–1931) was forced to resign from his position in 1892 for using scholarly methods to undermine the historicity of one of Japan's foundational myths. In 1911, a textbook controversy cost several historians their positions, and sent academic and school-level history ('applied' history to use an older category) along divergent tracks that have continued in Japan to the 'present day. In 1942, the historian Tsuda Sokichi was condemned for undermining the still-revered national mythology of the *Kojiki* in a work he had published nearly three decades earlier on the ancient imperial court. His doubts about the historicity of Emperor Jimmu and his immediate successors were entirely unacceptable in an aggressively militaristic state that had marked the founding emperor's 2,600th anniversary in 1940 with national celebrations.

Japanese experimentation would provide Western historiography with a port of entry into the rest of East Asia. In Korea this peaked during the period of Japanese occupation from 1910 to 1945, an intra-Asian episode of imperialism that broke a long chain of dynastically based Korean historiography while introducing the modern tools for a more nationalist history written on progressive lines. The most dramatic changes to East Asian historiography, however, would be felt in the very home of Confucianism, coincidental with the final decades of the Qing dynasty and of the empire itself. As noted in the previous chapter, the late seventeenth and eighteenth centuries had seen significant developments in the methods of historical research, in particular the highly empirical investigations of its philologically oriented scholars. By the early nineteenth century, moreover, Chinese historians were warming to the notion that the organization of the past primarily along dynastic lines could be abandoned or at least departed from; they knew that alternatives to the model of the Standard Histories had existed for centuries in a variety of different genres of both private and official history-writing. Understanding the circumstances behind the abrupt collapse of a twenty-two-centuries-old empire is essential to grasping why the Chinese, perhaps the most self-contained of all world civilizations (their periods of outward expansion and the importation of foreign religions such as Buddhism aside), suddenly began to absorb Western historiographical practices at the close of the nineteenth century. It is doubly important because historians such as Kang Youwei (1858–1927), and the philologist Fu Sinian (1896–1950), as well as historically minded social theorists such as Liang Qichao (1873–1929), were also at the forefront of movements for social reform or even revolution.

Western works had been trickling into China in greater numbers through the nineteenth century, and a translation bureau was established at Guangzhou in 1839. Consequently, key texts in European political philosophy and history were becoming available. In the first instance, however, Western historiography was derived not immediately from Europe but at second hand, via Japan. China's island neighbour had taken a significant head start down the road to modernization, and its recent successes were initially far more frightening to *fin-de-siècle* Chinese than those of the European powers. In 1894–5 Japan overwhelmed China in the Sino-Japanese war, largely fought over control of Korea; and in 1905 the Japanese modelled oriental success-through-modernization (*gendaika*) even more spectacularly in its stunning defeat of another ailing empire, Tsarist Russia. Chinese historical thought had long been inclined to cyclical views of history as a series of alternating periods of order and disorder, throughout which individual dynasties rose and fell. In the face of rapid political change and a sense of repetitive crisis, historians would turn instead to an explanation of the past as linear development over a series of periods, and to an understanding of their country no longer as *tianxia* ('all under heaven') but as a temporally finite, geographically circumscribed nation-state (*guojia*).

During this period, historians can be broadly divided into three groups: traditional Confucians, liberal-nationalists and, developing somewhat later, Marxists. In the last years of the Qing, a group of nationalists had founded the 'National Essence' movement, publishing historical essays and promoting the writing of a new Chinese history. More importantly, the liberal-nationalist reformer Liang Qichao was exiled in Japan and elsewhere for twelve years (1899–1911), and while in Japan he quickly acquired the language and came into contact with the views of reformers such as Fukuzawa Yukichi. It was through Fukuzawa and other Japanese authors that Liang encountered the positivist theories of H. T. Buckle, which played well in East Asia, as in Latin America, long after they had been resoundingly rejected by Buckle's fellow Britons. While in Japan, Liang authored his own articles on European thinkers such as Rousseau, Bentham, Darwin and Kant. In 1902 he published a guide to Japanese books which included a bibliography of histories then in use, a list that features Michelet and Guizot as well as various Japanese historians. Liang also looked to the West, rather than to older Chinese alternatives, for a non-dynastic periodization; he noted the commonplace division of time into ancient, medieval, modern and contemporary, which he then applied to China, though stressing that its epochs were not precisely synchronous with their counterparts in the West. Liang rejected the annalistic model of Chinese historical writing and deplored the lack of a cumulative national history. China had been a major contributor to the world's culture for thousands of years, but its story had 'never been narrated historically', having been obscured in the chopping up of the country's past along dynastic lines. He, too, believed that there could be no modern understanding of history while China continued to see itself as a world unto itself rather than a nation, and he drew an explicit comparison, derived from his reading of Gibbon, with ancient Rome: in both places, he argued, a lack of appreciation of the polity's status as a 'nation' within a wider world, compounded by a complacent sense of superiority over other peoples, had destroyed true patriotism. Interested in History as well as history – and perceiving the relation between the two – Liang came to the conclusion that it was still not too late for China to modernize itself and catch up with the rest of the world.

Liang himself was not insensitive to the role of the 'great man' in history: he dabbled in biography and used heroic figures frequently to illustrate his arguments in the manner of Carlyle, whom he quoted explicitly in an unfinished life of England's Oliver Cromwell. But if there are Germanic notes sounded here, they are Lamprechtian rather than Rankean ones, which Liang probably derived from Fukuzawa and that resembled contemporary American movements, now also creeping into Chinese historical practice. In the wake of the 'May Fourth' New Culture movement that began in 1919, James Harvey Robinson's *The New History* was soon translated into Chinese by one of Robinson's admirers, He Bingsong (1890–1946). He Bingsong had studied at Wisconsin and Princeton and would also loosely adapt (rather than translate) the much more conventional text by Langlois and Seignobos into Chinese as *New Principles of General History* (1928). Robinson's style of 'new history' seemed to offer a more attractive path to modernity than that offered by Rankean-influenced historicism. For Fu Sinian, a student leader during the May Fourth movement, these newer Western theories and methods provided an apparent solution to China's problems. As it turned out, he was overly optimistic, and China would ultimately take a very different path to modernization under the influence of another European thinker, Karl Marx, and his principal Chinese admirer, Mao Zedong.

Women and the Historical Enterprise, 1800–1945

The nineteenth century had witnessed something else not seen before historiographically, namely the far greater involvement of women in historical writing in Europe and North America. Women had of course been readers of history for many centuries, and a handful of female historians have been mentioned in earlier chapters of this book. The number of women writing popular history and biography increased after 1800 and by 1900 women had begun to enter the emerging 'profession'. The resistance that they encountered there was formidable. The research seminar (the very word itself having an obviously male etymology, as does the oft-used academic term 'seminal') remained a masculine preserve in contrast to the more open-access undergraduate lecture – Treitschke actually declared that the admission of women to his classes at Berlin would be an affront to his male pupils.

Outside the universities, women were making their mark in various ways, including the hosting of intellectual salons, as did the wives of both Ranke and Augustin Thierry. Family and social history provided a ready outlet for female historical interests, as did the physical surroundings of the home and factory: the American Lucy Maynard Salmon (1853–1927) would turn an interest in classical archaeology into pioneering work on the history of material culture. It is an open question whether women turned to such subjects because they would not be taken seriously in the more traditional areas of political and military history, or whether those older approaches simply did not interest them very much. Julie Des Jardins offers the example of Anne Wharton, who remarked in 1893 that 'to read of councils, congresses and battles is not enough: men and women wish to know something more intimate and personal of the life of the past'.

Much of the business of sorting, editing and cataloguing material in archives, and sometimes publishing summaries of them, fell to scholars on the outside of the academic establishment. In particular, women, previously confined to writing biographies (such as the English Strickland sisters' multivolume lives of queens) and children's texts, were among the most industrious (and most exploited) of research assistants – often uncredited by the male historians who used their work. Ireland's Mary Agnes Hickson (1825–99) made a name for herself editing sources for seventeenth-century Irish history, while Mary Anne Everett Green (1818–95) evolved from being a biographer of royal princesses into the author of many 'calendars' (summaries) of uncatalogued state papers. Others wrote their own works, often under a heavy male thumb. The British historian Edward Augustus Freeman commissioned a group of women (preferring them to male peers who would not 'knock under' to his will) to author several titles in a series of school texts on British history under his editorship; his friend J. R. Green referred to this as a 'historic harem'. Edith Thompson, who authored the series' volume on England, was seemingly so influenced by Freeman's distaste for anecdotes and tales that Green himself found the work dull. Green's own widow, Alice Stopford Green (1847–1929) would author several books, including a respected study of town life in fifteenth-century England, while Mandell Creighton's wife, Louise (1850–1936) published a number of history books for children.

Women began to earn PhDs in history in the early twentieth century across Europe and North America. This included a number of black

American women, who faced the additional obstacle of racism, such as the very long-lived Anna Julia Cooper (1858–1964) who defended her Columbia University thesis in her sixties. The relative lack of opportunities for academic careers inevitably caused some to abandon history for other pursuits: the Swiss historian Maria Waser (née Krebs, 1878–1939) earned a doctorate at Bern on fifteenth-century Swiss history, but soon left the discipline for a literary career. Others were more successful at carving out a niche for themselves. Within the universities, economic history, by now well established as a strong alternative to political history, would prove especially attractive to women. The American Helen Sumner Woodbury (1876–1933), though denied a professorial chair, nonetheless held university and government positions in which she became an early exponent of labour history. Cambridge-educated Lilian Knowles (1870–1926) became a successful member of the London School of Economics (LSE). Her pupils included Alice Clark (1874–1934), a prominent political activist and businesswoman who never held an academic post, but whose *Working Life of Women in the Seventeenth Century* (1919) has become a foundational text of women's history. And Clark's younger contemporary, Eileen Power (1889–1940), one of the early twentieth century's outstanding medievalists, cracked the masculine bastion of European archival scholarship when she studied at the École des Chartes as a graduate student in 1910. Like Knowles before her, Power would become Professor of Economic History at the LSE (1931), and she was a pioneer in both comparative economic history and medieval women's history. A popular lecturer, Power also had the gift of bringing seemingly dry academic topics into the public sphere, in her case through early radio broadcasts on history.

The challenges facing early women academic historians were legion and examples of their mistreatment or exploitation equally so. In France, where the Annales School (see below, pp. 229–32) was charting new directions in social and economic history, women such as Suzanne Dognon (1897–1985) contributed to scholarship; at the same time, they struggled to maintain their identity and independence in association with powerful male academics such as Dognon's much older husband, Lucien Febvre. The Jewish émigré Lucie Varga (1904–41), Febvre's sometime associate and briefly his mistress, provided a link between the world of the Annales and that of German scholarship. Recognition in their own right as academics was harder to achieve than close involvement in the work of a famous spouse. The widow of German historian Otto Hintze (1861–1940), Hedwig Hintze (1884–1942), herself an innovative specialist on the French Revolution, fled to the Netherlands because of her Jewish ancestry, committing suicide on the eve of deportation to Auschwitz. A less fatal but probably more typical case that illustrates the profession's 'glass ceiling' is that of the little-known Jessie Webb (1880–1944), an Australian who taught at Melbourne for many years, carrying a higher teaching load than her male peers and never progressing beyond the rank of lecturer.

There were certainly more women active in historical writing by the end of the Second World War than had been the case in virtually all previous eras combined, and some were especially prominent as popular authors outside the academy. Yet this success was unevenly spread and females remained second-class citizens within the profession, something borne out by examining the gender distributions of any academic department of history up to the 1960s. The American Historical Association elected only a single female president, the medievalist Nellie Neilson (1873–1947) in the first century of its existence. Nor had the study of women as historical subjects themselves developed much beyond the biographical. The comment, quoted by Anthony Gorman, of one early twentieth-century Arab woman, Zaynab Fawwaz (*c.* 1860–1914), that 'History, which is the best of all sciences, is largely dominated by men … [none of whom] has dedicated a single chapter in which to discuss women who represent half of human-kind', reminds us that real progress for women as both authors and subjects of historical writing was exceedingly slow and would only accelerate in the 1970s and 1980s.

A Crisis of Historicism? The Early Twentieth Century

Historians surveying the world at the end of the nineteenth century, from a library in France, a teacher's college in India or a study in Tokyo, might with reason feel giddy enthusiasm for their subject – now a 'discipline'. Not only had history established a set of academic codes and methodological tenets, still largely in use today; it had also achieved a global hegemony, a pre-eminence now extending to parts of the world which until then had practised modes of historicity quite different from Europe's. It is easy to overlook the fact that in order to thrive in different climates Western historiography had often been obliged to adjust to local cultural and institutional realities, and that in doing so it had not entirely escaped transformation – and appropriation – by the very peoples its apostles and missionaries had supposedly converted. This did not always unfold in the same ways, as demonstrated by the differing receptions of historians and historical theorists as varied as Ranke and Comte, Marx and Burckhardt.

A certain confidence and buoyancy was only natural at the end of the nineteenth century, but even as the West drew the extra-European world into its cultural embrace, trouble was brewing at home, and with it serious challenges to the nineteenth century's historiographical edifice. The consensus achieved by the nineteenth century on history's status, social function, epistemological superiority and methodology was both loose and fragile. Even within German historical thought, so often associated with a prescriptive role for both Europe and the rest of the world, there were already significant theoretical and methodological fissures. Within a few decades further on, three things had happened: first, within the academic profession the priority of political history and the centrality of the nation-state had been challenged; second, the door was thrown open to a seemingly endless multiplication of historical specializations and ideological interest groups (the 'fission' process alluded to above); third, the status of history as a unifying discipline among the human sciences had been decisively rejected, along with any remaining illusion that knowledge of the past could ever be perfectible, or, for some – in an apparent return to sixteenth-century Pyrrhonism – more than a fiction.

The First World War (1914–18) alone did not cause these doubts to emerge, and one must consider that they appeared amid significant intellectual and cultural developments such as the theory of relativity, the indeterminacy principle, cubism, expressionism and atonality. But the war certainly undermined the confidence of many historians in both the possibility and the point of their enterprise. The war also ruptured international ties among European historians as, with few exceptions, nationally based scholars closed ranks with their governments. The great love affair with German scholarship was chilled in western Europe and, to a lesser degree, in North America. These rifts had not healed by the time the Nazis came to power in 1933, and the isolation of German scholars continued through the Second World War, though with some important differences, including the flight of significant numbers of German and other European historians, many of them Jewish, to Britain and America, where they would become influential doctoral supervisors in the postwar era. Following Germany's second defeat, its scholarly community would be split, together with the country, into Western liberal-democratic and Eastern communist halves from 1949 up to 1990.

Notwithstanding the suspicion of some intellectuals, demand for history books and historical fiction had increased after the First World War. At universities such as Cambridge, the war changed very little in the curriculum and history enrolments actually dominated the humanities, though more students began to focus on modern history. For many, the past offered a refuge from contemporary problems. Broadly speaking, the trends outlined for the nineteenth century continued into the first half of the twentieth, though the Einstein–Planck challenges to Newtonian physics, closely followed by the horrors of the trenches and the end of the old empires, shook faith in progress, science and even objectivity. In the world of the academic historian, this uncertainty was manifested in a number of ways, including a brief flirtation in the 1930s and 1940s with 'relativism'. This became associated in particular with the American 'Progressives' Carl Becker (1873–1945) and his contemporary Charles A. Beard (1874–1948). Becker's 1932 essay 'Everyman His Own Historian' did not set out to show that there were no reliable historical facts; rather, it demonstrated that 'history' is made by the perceiving mind, recollecting events; that any individual can think historically about past occurrences, ordering them into a meaningful sequence; and that any such story is thus potentially history (something which to an early twenty-first century mind is apt to seem rather commonsensical). Beard's view was more radical. In an essay entitled 'That Noble Dream', published, like Becker's 'Everyman', in the *American Historical Review* in 1935, Beard took on the cult of 'objectivity' directly, asserting it to be an illusory and unachievable goal. Relativism in this form was not especially original, and in some ways simply the latest periodic episode of doubt about historical 'truth' within a tradition going back to Renaissance scepticism. It was scarcely a 'movement' and did not long endure, but can nonetheless be viewed as a way station on the road to later and far more intellectually formidable critiques of the possibility of historical knowledge, beginning in the 1970s and continuing up to our own time (see below, pp. 262–67).

Nationalism, and with it a focus on the national state, also loosened its grip somewhat in the wake of the 1914–18 war (despite the creation of a number of new nation-states from the rubble of several fallen empires). Some of the most ambitious works of interbellum historiography, including the great speculative ventures into world history, were devoted to taking a more internationalist, even global approach to the past. This is an understandable reaction during a relatively brief period of fragile international comity, marked by class conflict, the rise of Fascism, and the fear in the West of aggressive Bolshevism. The intellectual pessimism that followed the war's unprecedented mayhem produced some gems of cultural history, built on the themes of civilization's decline, such as the Dutch historian Huizinga's brilliant, Burckhardtesque, study of late medieval art, religion and literature, *The Autumn of the Middle Ages* (1919), which can be read today as an allegory for pre-war aesthetic and cultural decadence. For others, such as the German schoolmaster Oswald Spengler (1880–1936), the dawn of the twentieth century occasioned an opportunity to reflect at large on the entire course of world civilization. *The Decline of the West* (1918–22) was a work of reactionary generalization and extreme cultural relativism, building on then-recent revivals of cyclical theory to postulate alternating periods of growth and decay, with each culture having its own learning and forms of reason, and thus little in common with other cultures: both cumulative progress and the finding of any common ground became impossible in this scheme.

Largely completed before the war began, the first volume of Spengler's book was published to great fanfare in September 1918, a few weeks before the armistice. It would inspire an equally speculative British take on comparative civilizations, Arnold J. Toynbee's (1889–1975) *A Study of History*, which its author began in earnest in 1920. Though dismissive alike of both determinism and Spengler's variety of relativism, Toynbee saw the world in religious terms, as would another, slightly younger historian of comparable range but greater subtlety, Herbert Butterfield. Unlike Spengler, Toynbee saw nothing inevitable in the process of decline, providing more space for contingency and accident. When Toynbee's civilizations died, the causes of collapse were not 'cosmic forces outside human control' nor racial decline, but various other factors including schism in the 'body social', failures of will or self-determination and (one that looks rather prescient amid twenty-first-century ecological preoccupations) loss of command over the environment. If Toynbee had an earlier intellectual exemplar as a world historian, it may well have been Ibn Khaldun, for whom he expressed admiration.

A Study of History would grow in popularity among a general readership in the aftermath of the Second World War, and may be one of the better examples of the gap, widening since the early twentieth century, between academic historiography and a broader public readership. The academic critics of Toynbee were less exasperated by his global ambitions than by his subordination of evidence to theory. Western historians for the past two hundred years have been on the whole deeply sceptical of 'grand theory', and nowhere more so than with respect to capital-H History. This is somewhat less true with respect to small-h history as a genre of writing, a mode of explanation, a mental act, a type of narrative or, to use the most recent terms, a 'linguistic construct' or form of 'discourse'. Academic reactions to strict scientific history in the narrower, positivist sense, echoing Dilthey's earlier qualifications, can be seen first in an approach that has been called 'idealism' (which should not be confused with the German idealism of Kant's and Hegel's time). The most distinguished and influential representative of this tendency was the Italian philosopher and historian, Benedetto Croce (1866–1952). A practising historian as well as philosopher, Croce was a product of nineteenth-century historicism who had to adapt it to fit a twentieth-century world. Croce eventually called his historical outlook 'absolute historicism', to distinguish it from the German variety. Like Dilthey earlier, Croce rejected positivism, arguing instead for the autonomy of history from science, and the inseparability of history and lived experience. Records and documents, said Croce, only have significance insofar as living humans can reflect upon them and, indeed, relive them; conversely, we only make sense of life by thinking historically. The dead have another life to live in us. This is why the erection of monuments and tombs is a moral act. In his celebrated remark that 'all history is contemporary history', Croce meant not that all past events are *literally* present and coeval, but rather that every generation must select and order its past on the basis of the context and circumstances in which it finds itself – the questions the historian asks will be determined by his or her own world's requirements. Without a question or pressing problem, no understanding of the past is possible, only a replication and rearrangement of its documentary

materials. Indeed, it is precisely through writing about the past –
turning it into history – that we liberate ourselves from slavery to it.

Conclusion

Benedetto Croce's views appealed to many Europeans of the first half of
the century, enamoured by neither Marxism nor positivism. In the
archaeologist-turned-philosopher R. G. Collingwood (1889–1943),
he found a British counterpart. Collingwood's posthumously published
The Idea of History (1946) falls, like Croce's work, within a broader
tradition of historicist thought certain aspects of which can be traced
back to the eighteenth century, and indeed provides a suitable place to
conclude this chapter. Collingwood advanced the notion that 'all
history . . . is the history of thought', and he suggested that the historian
must empathize with his or her subjects, enter into the 'interior' of
a historical event (the thought of the agent behind the event) and
mentally 're-enact' it – drawing upon his or her own lived experience –
in order to retell it. This was not in itself a new notion. The debt to
Droysen's and Dilthey's *Verstehen* is obvious, and Georg Simmel had
articulated a notion of understanding through re-enactment several
decades before. But the stress on comprehending through past actions
through their resemblance to our own lived experience was
Collingwood's distinctive add-on, and has become well known in the
English-speaking world. A complicated book much studied by philosophers of history, *The Idea of History* was assembled after
Collingwood's death from lectures mainly written before the onset of
the war, and was never intended by its author to be published in the
form in which it appeared. Unsurprisingly, it is a flawed work. Friendly
critics, mainly philosophers, have noted, for instance, that it is frustrat-
ingly loose in its use of terms such as 'science', and even 'history' itself,
and that it is silent on areas that some of Collingwood's predecessors
had addressed such as the relations between history and the social
sciences. One might add, from the perspective of the present book,
that insofar as it contains an extended survey of the history of history,
The Idea of History shares with most of its nineteenth- and early
twentieth-century precursors an explicit Eurocentrism that excludes
all forms of historiography apart from the Western variety.

   In a world that had just endured two horrendous global conflicts but
not yet experienced either the polarities of Cold War thermonuclear

politics or the process of decolonization and accompanying challenges to Euro-American hegemony (literal and intellectual) that lay ahead, *The Idea of History* was in some ways a reassuring confirmation of long-held views about the nature of historical thought and writing. Oft-praised over the decades by historians who otherwise have little time for 'the philosophy of history', Collingwood remains reasonably widely read even today, and other aspects of his thought seem less dated. In particular, Collingwood's formulation of the concept of 'historical imagination' has come back into vogue over the past thirty years with the advent of postmodernism, many aspects of which Collingwood himself would have neither understood nor accepted. That, and much else that has transpired in the history of history since the end of the Second World War, is the subject of our penultimate chapter.

QUESTIONS FOR DISCUSSION

1. To what degree were historians from the mid-nineteenth to the mid-twentieth centuries the heirs of previous generations (going back to antiquity) and to what degree were they innovators?
2. What role did established institutions such as universities, schools and government play in the spread of 'modern' historical practices in Europe and beyond?
3. To what degree were the introduction of nineteenth-century historical practices and of Western notions of history to Asia and Africa an eradication of indigenous genres and beliefs? To what degree did they prove 'liberating'?
4. Nineteenth-century Asian historians of a reformist mindset sought to jettison traditional cyclical interpretations of history for ones of linear development along the European model. Did this force them to adopt, too, the Western view of progress and modernization at the expense of their own traditions and practices?
5. What were the key changes in historical thinking and in the historiographical enterprise following the First World War?
6. How were the views of Nietzsche and of other sceptics such as American relativists the heir to earlier periods of doubt in the knowability of the past? Or of its utility?
7. Was there a 'crisis' of historicism in the late nineteenth/early twentieth centuries?

8. Why did centuries-old Chinese and Japanese imperial models of historiography come to such an abrupt halt in the late nineteenth and early twentieth centuries? Was Western historiography actually, as its adherents proclaimed, an instrument of modernization?

9. Were women 'naturally' more inclined to social and economic history, to biography, and to archival endeavours, rather than military or political history (as some claimed) or was this simply because they were not taken seriously as authors of 'mainstream' history?

Further Reading

General

Bentley, Michael, *Modern Historiography: An Introduction* (London and New York, 1999)

Iggers, George G., Q. Edward Wang with S. Mukherjee, *A Global History of Modern Historiography* (Harlow, UK, 2008)

Kramer, Lloyd and Sarah Maza (eds), *A Companion to Western Historical Thought* (Oxford, 2002)

Macintyre, Stuart, Juan Maiguashca and Attila Pók (eds), *The Oxford History of Historical Writing*, Vol. 4: *1800–1945* (Oxford, 2012)

An Introductory Overview

Beiser, Frederick C., *The German Historicist Tradition* (Oxford, 2011)

Berger, Stefan and Chris Lorenz (eds), *The Contested Nation: Ethnicity, Class, Religion and Gender in National Histories* (Basingstoke, 2008)

Burrow, J. W., *A Liberal Descent: Victorian Historians and the English Past* (Cambridge, 1981)

Crossley, Ceri, *French Historians and Romanticism: Thierry, Guizot, the Saint-Simonians, Quinet, Michelet* (London, 1993)

The Great Transformer: Ranke and His Influence

Dorpalen, Andreas, *Heinrich von Treitschke* (New Haven, CT, 1957)

Gilbert, Felix, 'Historiography: What Ranke Meant', *The American Scholar* 56.3 (1987): 393–97

    History: Politics or Culture? Reflections on Ranke and Burckhardt (Princeton, NJ, 1990)

Iggers, Georg G. and James M. Powell (eds), *Leopold von Ranke and the Shaping of the Historical Discipline* (Syracuse, NY, 1990)

Krieger, Leonard, *Ranke: The Meaning of History* (Chicago, IL, 1977)

The Institutions of History and the Beginnings of the 'Profession' in Europe and North America

Baár, Monika, *Historians and Nationalism: East-Central Europe in the Nineteenth Century* (Oxford, 2010)

Berger, Stefan, *The Search for Normality: National Historical Consciousness in Germany since 1800* (London, 1997)

Boer, Pim den, *History as a Profession: The Study of History in France, 1818–1914* (Princeton, NJ, 1998)

Breisach, Ernst, *American Progressive History: An Experiment in Modernization* (Chicago, IL, 1993)

Fitzpatrick, Ellen, *History's Memory: Writing America's Past, 1880–1980* (Cambridge, 2002)

Gazi, Effi, *Scientific National History: The Greek Case in Comparative Perspective (1850–1920)* (Frankfurt, 2000)

Novick, Peter, *That Noble Dream: The 'Objectivity Question' and the American Historical Profession* (Cambridge, 1988)

Porciani, Ilaria and Lutz Raphael (eds), *Atlas of European Historiography: The Making of a Profession, 1800–2005* (London, 2010)

Porciani, Ilaria and Jo Tollebeek (eds), *Setting the Standards: Institutions, Networks and Communities of National Historiography* (London, 2012)

Ross, Dorothy, 'Historical Consciousness in Nineteenth-Century America', *American Historical Review* 89 (1984): 909–28

Sanders, Thomas D. (ed.), *Historiography of Imperial Russia: The Profession and Writing of History in a Multinational State* (London, 1999)

Stieg, Margaret F., *The Origin and Development of Scholarly Historical Periodicals* (Tuscaloosa, AL, 1986)

Torstendahl, Rolf, *The Rise and Propagation of Historical Professionalism* (London and New York, 2014)

Ziolkowski, Theodore, *Clio the Romantic Muse: Historicizing the Faculties in Germany* (Ithaca, NY, 2004)

History, Science and Determinism

Assis, Arthur A., *What is History For? Johann Gustav Droysen and the Functions of Historiography* (New York, 2014)

Ermarth, Michael, *Wilhelm Dilthey: The Critique of Historical Reason* (Chicago, IL, 1978)

Hesketh, Ian, *The Science of History in Victorian Britain: Making the Past Speak* (London, 2011)

Hirst, Paul Q., *Marxism and Historical Writing* (London, 1985)

Hobsbawm, Eric, 'Karl Marx's Contribution to Historiography', in R. Blackburn (ed.), *Ideology in Social Science: Readings in Critical Social Theory* (London, 1972), 265–83

Mazlish, Bruce, *The Riddle of History: The Great Speculators from Vico to Freud* (New York, 1966)

Morris-Suzuki, Tessa, *The Past Within Us: Media, Memory, History* (New York and London, 2005)

Perry, Matt, *Marxism and History* (Basingstoke, 2002)

Rigby, S. H., *Marxism and History: A Critical Introduction*, 2nd edn (Manchester, 1998)

Southard, Robert, *Droysen and the Prussian School of History* (Lexington, KY, 1995)

White, Hayden, *Metahistory:* The *Historical Imagination in Nineteenth-Century Europe* (Baltimore, MD, 1973)

Wilkins, Burleigh Taylor,*Hegel's Philosophy of History* (Ithaca, NY, 1974)

The Cultural and Social Alternatives to Ranke

Antoni, Carlo, *From History to Sociology: The Transition in German Historical Thinking*, trans. Hayden White (London, 1962)

Chickering, Roger, *Karl Lamprecht: A German Academic Life (1856–1915)* (Atlantic Highlands, NJ, 1993)

Hinde, John R., *Jacob Burckhardt and the Crisis of Modernity* (Montreal, 2000)

Hofstadter, Richard, *The Progressive Historians: Turner, Beard, Parrington* (New York, 1968)

Iggers, Georg G., 'The "Methodenstreit" in International Perspective: The Reorientation of Historical Studies at the Turn from the Nineteenth to the Twentieth Century', *Storia della Storiografia* 6 (1984): 21–32

Jensen, Anthony K., *Nietzsche's Philosophy of History* (Cambridge, 2013)

Richardson, John and Brian Leiter (eds), *Nietzsche* (Oxford, 2001)

Roth, Guenther and Wolfgang Schluchter, *Max Weber's Vision of History: Ethics and Methods* (Berkeley, CA, 1979)

Historiographical Imperialism? The Impact of Western Methods and Models Beyond the Eurosphere

Alagoa, E. J., *The Practice of History in Africa: A History of African Historiography* (Port Harcourt, Nigeria, 2006)

Ali, Daud (ed.), *Invoking the Past: The Uses of History in South Asia* (New Delhi, 1999)

Aung-Thwin, Michael and Kenneth R. Hall (eds), *New Perspectives on the History and Historiography of Southeast Asia* (London, 2011)

Brownlee, John S., *Japanese Historians and the National Myths, 1600–1945: The Age of the Gods and Emperor Jinmu* (Vancouver and Tokyo, 1997)

Chakrabarty, Dipesh, *The Calling of History: Sir Jadunath Sarkar and his Empire of Truth* (Chicago, IL, 2015)

Choueiri, Youssef M., *Modern Arab Historiography: Historical Discourse and the Nation-State* (London, 2003)

Cowan, C. D. and O. W. Wolters (eds), *Southeast Asian History and Historiography: Essays Presented to D. G. E. Hall* (Ithaca, NY, 1976)

Crabbs, Jack A. Jr, *The Writing of History in Nineteenth-Century Egypt: A Study in National Transformation* (Detroit, MI, 1984)

Fage, J. D., 'The Development of African Historiography', in J. Ki-Zerbo (ed.), *General History of Africa*, Vol. 1: *Methodology and African Prehistory* (Paris and London, 1981), 25–42

Falola, Toyin (ed.), *African Historiography: Essays in Honour of Jacob Ade Ajayi* (Harlow, UK, 1993)

Falola, Toyin and Saheed Aderinto, *Nigeria, Nationalism, and Writing History* (Rochester, NY and Woodbridge, UK, 2010)

Gorman, Anthony, *Historians, State, and Politics in Twentieth Century Egypt: Contesting the Nation* (London, 2003)

Guha, Ranajit, *An Indian Historiography of India: A Nineteenth-Century Agenda and its Implications* (Calcutta and New Delhi, 1988)

Hall, Catherine, *Macaulay and Son: Architects of Imperial Britain* (New Haven, CT and London, 2012)

Hama, B. and J. Ki-Zerbo, 'The Place of History in African Society', in Ki-Zerbo (ed.), *General History of Africa*, Vol. 1: *Methodology and African Prehistory* (Paris and London, 1981), 43–53

Koditschek, Theodore, *Liberalism, Imperialism, and the Historical Imagination: Nineteenth-Century Visions of a Greater Britain* (Cambridge, 2011)

Kwong, Luke S. K., 'The Rise of the Linear Perspective on History and Time in Late Qing China', *Past and Present* 173 (2001): 157–90

Majeed, Javeed, *Ungoverned Imaginings: James Mill's 'The History of British India' and Orientalism* (Oxford, 1992)

Mehl, Margaret, *History and the State in Nineteenth-Century Japan* (Basingstoke, 1998)

Reid, Anthony and David Marr (eds), *Perceptions of the Past in Southeast Asia* (Singapore, 1979)

Tanaka, Stefan, *Japan's Orient: Rendering Pasts into History* (Berkeley, CA, 1993)

Tavakoli-Targhi, Mohamad, *Refashioning Iran: Orientalism, Occidentalism, and Historiography* (Basingstoke and New York, 2001)

Wang, Fan-sen, *Fu Ssu-nien: A Life in Chinese History and Politics* (Cambridge, 2000)

Wang, Q. Edward, *Inventing China through History: The May Fourth Approach to Historiography* (Albany, NY, 2001)

Williams, Eric, *British Historians and the West Indies* (New York, 1966)

Woll, Allen, *Puerto Rican Historiography* (New York, 1978)

Women and the Historical Enterprise, 1800–1945

Baym, Nina, *American Women Writers and the Work of History, 1790–1860* (New Brunswick, NJ, 1995)

Berg, Maxine, *A Woman in History: Eileen Power 1889–1940* (Cambridge, 1996)

Davis, Natalie Zemon, 'Women and the World of the Annales', *History Workshop Journal* 33.1 (1992): 121–37

Des Jardins, Julie, *Women and the Historical Enterprise in America: Gender, Race, and the Politics of Memory, 1880–1945* (Chapel Hill, NC, 2003)

Goggin, Jacqueline, 'Challenging Sexual Discrimination in the Historical Profession: Women Historians and the American Historical Association, 1890–1940', *American Historical Review*, 97.3 (1992): 769–802

Schöttler, Peter, 'Lucie Varga: A Central European Refugee in the Circle of the French "Annales", 1934–1941', *History Workshop Journal* 33 (1992): 100–20

Smith, Bonnie G., *The Gender of History: Men, Women, and Historical Practice* (Cambridge, MA, 1998)

Smith, Nadia Clare, *A 'Manly Study'? Irish Women Historians, 1868–1949* (Basingstoke, 2006)

Spongberg, Mary, Barbara Caine and Ann Curthoys (eds), *Companion to Women's Historical Writing* (Basingstoke, 2005)

White, Deborah Gray (ed.), *Telling Histories: Black Women Historians in the Ivory Tower* (Chapel Hill, NC, 2008)

A Crisis of Historicism? The Early Twentieth Century

Bambach, Charles R., *Heidegger, Dilthey, and the Crisis of Historicism* (Ithaca, NY, 1995)

Costello, Paul, *World Historians and Their Goals: Twentieth-Century Answers to Modernism* (De Kalb, IL, 1994)

Dray, William H., *History as Re-enactment: R. G. Collingwood's Idea of History* (Oxford, 1995)

Farrenkopf, John, *Prophet of Decline: Spengler on World History and Politics* (Baton Rouge, LA, 2001)

Inglis, Fred, *History Man: The Life of R. G. Collingwood* (Princeton, NJ, 2009)

Jacobitti, Edmund E., *Revolutionary Humanism and Historicism in Modern Italy* (New Haven, CT, 1981)

O'Sullivan, Luke, *Oakeshott on History* (Exeter, 2003)

Roberts, David D., *Benedetto Croce and the Uses of Historicism* (Berkeley, CA, 1987)

Stromberg, Roland N., *Arnold J. Toynbee: Historian for an Age of Crisis* (Carbondale, IL, 1972)

1910–14	Mikhail Nikolaevich Pokrovskii's five-volume *History of Russia: From the Earliest Times to the Rise of Commercial Capitalism* is published
1929	The journal *Annales* is established
1938	C. L. R. James's *The Black Jacobins* is published, a forerunner of what would become postcolonial scholarship several decades further on
1939	Georges Lefebvre's *The Coming of the French Revolution* is published in English
1939	Marc Bloch's *Feudal Society* is published
1940	*Journal of the History of Ideas* is established
1941	Fan Wenlan's *General History of China* is published in Chinese
1946	Mary Ritter Beard's *Woman as Force in History* is published
1949	Fernand Braudel's *The Mediterranean and the Mediterranean World in the Age of Philip II* is published
1952	The journal *Past and Present* is founded
1956	Hungarian Revolution crushed; many Marxist historians depart from Britain's Communist Party
1958	Modern 'psychohistory', drawing on Freud, exemplified in E. H. Erikson's *Young Man Luther*
1963	E. P. Thompson's *The Making of the English Working Class* is published
1964	UNESCO inaugurates a *General History of Africa* (comp. 1990s)
1966	Beginning of the Cultural Revolution in China
1973	Hayden White's *Metahistory: The Historical Imagination in Nineteenth-Century Europe* is published in the United States
1974	Robert William Fogel and Stanley Engerman's *Time on the Cross* is published
1978	Edward Said's *Orientalism* is published
1982	First volume of *Subaltern Studies* published under leadership of Ranajit Guha
1986–9	The *Historikerstreit* in Germany
1988	Joan Wallach Scott's *Gender and the Politics of History* is published; beginning of Australian 'History Wars'
1989	Fall of Berlin Wall and beginnings of the collapse of the Soviet Union and Eastern Bloc; interaction between western and eastern academic communities increases
1992	Controversy in United States over celebrations of 500th anniversary of Columbus' voyage; there are subsequent clashes over textbooks, school curricula and museum displays
1996–2000	Irving *v.* Lipstadt libel trial, over allegations by Deborah Lipstadt of the inaccuracy of David Irving's writings on the Holocaust

6

Transitions: Historical Writing from the Inter-War Period to the Present

The Annales Historians; Microhistory

Perhaps the most significant historiographic phenomenon of the first half of the twentieth century, its influence still powerful after nine decades, was what eventually became known (over-stating its coherence) as the Annales 'School'. This originated in inter-war France, and is named for the journal *Annales* that began publication in 1929 at the University of Strasbourg under the guidance of Marc Bloch and Lucien Febvre. Both men were influenced by the earlier work of the sociologist Émile Durkheim and the philosopher–geographer Henri Berr (1863–1954), editor of a journal called *Revue de synthèse historique* and an early exponent of the need for a more comprehensive approach to the study of the past. Bloch and Febvre also had close connections with the Belgian medievalist Henri Pirenne. Both the journal and the practices of those associated with it have evolved through successive generations, but they remain an influential force in France and are much admired elsewhere. The Annalistes repudiated a narrowly political history in favour of an *histoire totale* that examined geography, climate, economy and agricultural and trade patterns, as well as manners, in one of the recurrent pendulum swings in European historiographical taste between the social and the political, the general and the particular, the inclusive and the selective, dating back to Herodotus and Thucydides.

Bloch (1886–1944) has become the nearest thing to a historiographical folk hero in the decades since his execution by the Nazis for resistance activities. Virtually all of his works remain in print in several languages, including *The Historian's Craft*, a posthumous collection of essays and ruminations on history. Bloch served with distinction in the First World War and then took up a post at Strasbourg before assuming a chair in economic history at the Sorbonne. His first major book, *Les rois thaumaturges* (1924) (English version, *The Royal Touch*), about the medieval practice of touching for the 'king's evil' or scrofula, has become a foundational text in the cultural history of ritual. Bloch's later works, written after he had collaborated with Febvre to found the journal *Annales*, include *Les caractères originaux de l'histoire rurale française* (1931; English version, *French Rural History*), famous for its evocative treatment of the countryside over a long period of time, and *La société féodale* (1939; English version, *Feudal Society*), which again took an anthropological and sociological approach to feudalism as not merely a military but a social and cultural system, and to the *mentalités* ('mentalities') that underlay it.

Febvre's (1878–1956) works have not aged as well as Bloch's but they were no less important in their day. In his most famous book, *Le problème de l'incroyance au XVIe siècle* (1942; English version, *The Problem of Unbelief in the Sixteenth Century*), Febvre explored the concept of atheism in connection with the Renaissance writer François Rabelais, arguing that the mental habits of a sixteenth-century European did not allow for true atheism, however irreligious or heterodox a writer may appear to have been. Febvre also became interested in print culture, planting the seeds for a subject since taken up by French *historiens du livre* such as Roger Chartier (b. 1945) and by North American scholars such as Robert Darnton (b. 1939). Febvre helped to found Paris' famous *Sixième section* of the École pratique des hautes études. The École (est. 1868) was an institution for postgraduate training only, intended to complement rather than duplicate the universities' curricula. The new section was devoted specifically to advanced research in the social sciences, and by 1975 it had become an independent institution in its own right, the École des hautes études en sciences sociales (EHESS).

The Annales approach to scholarship has changed its orientation several times in the past eight decades and is more appropriately regarded as an evolving tradition rather than a 'school'. In fact, its capacity to reinvent itself in response to new trends, symbolically reflected in several changes to the journal *Annales*' subtitle, has been a mark of its strength and a reason for its continued importance. The first major shift came almost immediately after the Second World War, driven in part by wider experimentation with the social sciences (see below). It was engineered by the 'second generation' Annalistes, a distinguished group at the head of which stood Febvre's student Fernand Braudel (1902–85). A product of the interests of both Bloch and Febvre, especially their devotion to geography, Braudel aggressively pushed the idea of the earth and the sea as agents of change. Braudel called for the subjugation of *histoire événementielle* (short-term human actions, for instance in the political world) to the study of mid-length periods of social, material and economic *conjonctures*, and to the even slower geographical and climatological changes that occurred over the *longue durée* of centuries. This last was the sphere in which natural forces ruled, providing the constraints and the structures within which the secondary and tertiary realms of change, and the individual event, could occur. While the notion of climatological influence on human events has a long history, Braudel eschewed the older link between climate and 'national character' in favour of a more complex, dynamic relationship which permitted scope for human agency. The classic expression of this layered periodization is Braudel's own study of *La Méditerranée et le monde méditerranéen à l'époque de Philippe II* (1949; English version, *The Mediterranean and the Mediterranean World in the Age of Philip II*). The degree to which the approach is in fact applicable to different subjects remains unclear. Critics of *The Mediterranean* and subsequent works such as the multi-volume study of *Civilisation matérielle, économie et capitalisme, XVe–XVIIIe siècle* (1967–79; English version, *Capitalism and Material Life*) have pointed out that Braudel was not successful in integrating the three levels of time. He was, however, extraordinarily influential in setting the agenda for future research in sub-disciplines not then fully conceptualized, such as environmental history.

The quantitative tendencies of this stage of Annales historiography, also evident in the work of Braudel's non-Annaliste older contemporary, Ernest Labrousse (1895–1988), were elaborated by historians usually considered part of Braudel's 'generation' though actually a decade or two his junior, such as Pierre Chaunu (1923–2009). In more recent decades, however, a further shift in the tradition has occurred. Many Annales historians, and others abroad who self-identify as their admirers or associates, have veered away from quantification back to the study of *mentalités* in Bloch and Febvre's mode, placing considerably more emphasis on individual and collective beliefs, and on life experienced in local settings. The medievalist Georges Duby (1919–96), initially trained as a historical geographer, turned in this direction during the 1970s, exploring issues such as the chivalric state of mind, and French perceptions of past events. Outside

France, others have worked on a deliberately smaller scale, for instance the German proponents of *Alltagsgeschichte* – literally the history of everyday life – during the 1980s, in a parallel reaction against the abstraction of German 'historical social science'.

The 'microhistory' of the late 1970s, 1980s and 1990s emerged initially in Italy, where it is known as *microstoria* and associated especially with the journal *Quaderni Storici* (est. 1966), and soon spread to France, Germany, Britain and eventually America. Early examples include works like Emmanuel Le Roy Ladurie's (b. 1929) *Montaillou: The Promised Land of Error* (a study of a medieval Cathar village) and Carlo Ginzburg's (b. 1939) *The Cheese and the Worms: The Cosmos of a Sixteenth-Century Miller*, both of which have proved highly saleable in the academic and trade book markets and have spawned numerous additional examples around the globe. Japanese practitioners of *seikatsushi* and *seishinshi*, roughly corresponding with *Alltagsgeschichte* and *histoire des mentalités* respectively, similarly drew inspiration from both German and French models. Microhistory is in fact a convenient shorthand to describe a number of different ways of studying the general through the local: one version of this examines a particular community over a period of decades or even centuries, tracing kin, social and economic relations. The more well-known version tends to a shorter chronology and sometimes a focus on a very specific story or episode, such as Robert Darnton's account of a 'massacre' of cats by French printing-shop employees, a ritual in which the unfortunate felines were a proxy for the workers' master and mistress.

The great strengths of microhistory, especially in the latter form, are that it is highly readable (typically telling a story) and it involves identifiable historical individuals whose human plights and quirks evoke an emotive sympathy, recovering a humanity sometimes lost in the grand scale of Braudel-style Annaliste history. Who could not but sympathize with the plight of Ginzburg's Menocchio, defiantly fabricating a heretical, imaginative world view on his way to the stake, or with Le Roy Ladurie's medieval Cathars? Perhaps most famous (it became a well-known film) is the extraordinary tale of the impostor 'Martin Guerre' in sixteenth-century France, chronicled by Natalie Zemon Davis (b. 1928), which tells an interesting story while painting a compelling canvas of the lives and beliefs of both villagers and judicial authorities. Microhistories are effective at providing tiny details, not especially relevant to the main points of the story, which confer on their accounts a very strong version of what the French literary theorist Roland Barthes (1915–80) once famously called the 'reality effect'. On the other side, critics have asked of some of these studies 'So what?', questioning the degree to which valid generalizations can be made about past societies and how they worked from these 'micro' examples, or challenging the evidentiary basis for the narratives themselves, or the degree of conjecture and inference that they demand. It has also been argued that by making their subjects appear familiar to us, they have the potential to elide the differences between past and present and with them a sense of distance that for three centuries has been deemed an essential element in thinking about history.

History and the Social Sciences

The Annales and microhistory are themselves both products of history's somewhat hot-and-cold flirtation with the social sciences, a phenomenon with pre-modern origins. Theoretically inclined minds during the Enlightenment had experimented with the past: the mathematician and physicist Jean d'Alembert (1717–83) thought that doubts about knowledge of the past might be solved through a scientific approach to its study. The Scottish stadialists, among the earliest European proponents of what we now call 'comparative history', had closely linked the study of the past to theories of the origins and development of society and of economic systems. We have also seen a number of non-European examples, among whom Ibn Khaldun is the most famous. Nineteenth-century historians had been mainly suspicious of the emerging social sciences, due to the dominance of Rankeanism and its emphasis on political history, to the more general historicist attention to the individual rather than society, and to the popularity of heroic biography and history among the reading public. By the end of the century, however, this began to change. In the midst of the debate over history's relation to the natural sciences, the 'human' sciences seemed to offer a compromise. Economic history had emerged by the century's end as a powerful sub-discipline, with German scholars such as Gustav von Schmoller once again influencing developments in much of the rest of the world. Marx had, of course, already outlined a particular version of the tie of history to economics, while others such as Comte had linked it with the even newer discipline of sociology. The non-Marxist late imperial Russian historian V. O. Kliuchevskii

(1841–1911) had begun to study the impact of class and geography on history, breaking with the political history mainstream. The German *Methodenstreit* had been in part a debate about the nature of history's connection to these and other disciplines, especially anthropology, geography and psychology, and James Harvey Robinson's *New History* had generated champions for it across the Atlantic (and, as we saw earlier, in East Asia).

Among the founders of modern social science-driven history, two other early sociologists stand out: the Frenchman Durkheim and the German Max Weber. Both were enormously interested in the past. Durkheim saw history as falling short of being a science itself, but nonetheless as providing a useful source of material for social science. He described collective phenomena that exist independently of individual instances of them, and encouraged an impartial, almost clinical detachment in their study, exemplified in his classic *The Elementary Forms of the Religious Life* (1912), a work remarkable also for the global span of its reference group. Weber, whom Frederick Beiser describes as a very late representative of the same historicist tradition that dates back to Herder, is best known today as a sociologist but in fact he self-identified more as a historian through much of his life. Equally ill-disposed to mainstream German historical scholarship of the late nineteenth century and to positivist critiques of it, he had nonetheless joined in the denunciation of Lamprecht during the *Methodenstreit*. Weber's sociological thought was influenced by Dilthey's clarification of the distinctions between the natural and human sciences. While Weber insisted on the rationality of the latter and their need for clear concepts and practices, he also stressed the subjective element to inquiry and the gap between actual lived reality and systematic representations of it such as 'ideal types'. Weber was also a strong comparativist, interested among other issues in explaining the differences between oriental and occidental cultures, and in exploring the connections between the economic and ideological – for instance in a famous book on *The Protestant Ethic and the Spirit of Capitalism* (1904–5). The first half of the twentieth century saw British and especially American sociologists turn to history (a traffic not always reciprocated in the other direction). George Homans (1910–89), for instance, would teach both sociology and history at Harvard, one of his earliest works being a study of *English Villagers of the Thirteenth Century*. One of his most prominent students of the next generation, Charles Tilly (1929–2008) would similarly straddle the two disciplines over the course of his long career, as has Harvard sociologist Theda Skocpol (b. 1947).

Both sociology and especially economics have become highly quantitative disciplines, and empirical measurement has always been an important component of social science-oriented history – and sometimes even of political history as the prosopographic or 'collective biography' approach of historians such as Britain's Sir Lewis Namier (1888–1960) showed. While quantification has a lengthy pedigree, it emerged most clearly as a potential 'silver bullet' for historians anxious to ally their craft to the ranks of the 'hard' sciences after the Second World War. The Braudelian generation of Annalistes was, as we saw earlier, much taken with quantification, and one of Braudel's most illustrious pupils, Emmanuel Le Roy Ladurie, once boldly prophesied that all historians would soon need to become computer programmers. Despite the subsequent ubiquity of personal computers on current historians' desks, this has, at least to date, not come to pass, though many historians have adopted quantification into their toolkit – the Annaliste historian Pierre Chaunu established 'serial history' (the collection of data for lengthy time series), and historical demographers such as Louis Henry (1911–91), Tony Wrigley (b. 1931) and Peter Laslett (1915–2001) have done so to work out not simply the size of past populations but to chart mobility, family structure, sexual relations and intermarriage, and birth and death rates. Public attention has sometimes, rather misleadingly, focused on a relatively small subset of quantifiers, principally those drawn to and often trained in advanced statistics and econometric theory. 'New economic history' or 'cliometrics' first arose in the 1960s. It often generates not only the large datasets and broad conclusions of which quantitative historians are fond, but also something additional, the use of the 'counterfactual' or 'what-if?' questions. Rather different from more qualitative and speculative forms of counterfactual thinking (see below, pp. 304–5), cliometrics involves setting up a model of how various elements within a past system interact, removing one or more of them, and seeing what, if anything, changes. Thus Robert William Fogel (1926–2013) investigated the role of railroads in America (1964) and, by eliminating them from his model of the economy, showed that other forms of transportation would have been developed or extended with very little long-term effect on prosperity. Even more controversial, because it hit on the rawest nerves in the American body politic, race and slavery, was his subsequent book, *Time on the Cross* (1974; co-authored with Stanley Engerman, b. 1936). This used plantation records to suggest that far from being a backward, economically unproductive system, southern slavery was in fact relatively efficient; unfree blacks, far from being the lazy, shiftless characters of a century of post-emancipation racism, were in fact industrious and accomplished. Leaving aside the objections that non-historians might have to any defence of the 'peculiar institution' of slavery (and the authors had been careful to declare their personal moral objections to it), the book was criticized for a range of methodological flaws and questionable assumptions. However, a number of mainstream historians began making public arguments against the use of quantification, often lumping all of it with cliometrics. As early as 1962, two years before Fogel's book on railroads appeared, Carl Bridenbaugh (1903–92), a historian of colonial America, had issued perhaps the most memorable philippic against 'the bitch goddess, quantification' in his presidential address to the American Historical Association. The very long-lived Columbia University historian Jacques Barzun (1907–2012) attacked cliometricians (along with psychohistorians) in *Clio and the Doctors* in 1974. And the German-born Cambridge historian of Tudor England, Geoffrey Elton (1921–94), a sceptic of social science-influenced quantification, debated its merits with Fogel in a jointly authored book.

The period from the late 1950s to the early 1970s marked the peak in this phase of the alliance between sociology and history, reflected in works on 'historical sociology' and in early attempts at comparison across societies in journals such as *Comparative Studies in Society and History* (est. 1958) and *Past and Present* (est. 1952). By the mid-1970s, the stock of both sociology and economics had begun to fall among historians, some of whom looked elsewhere in the social sciences, in particular to anthropology, and in the first instance the 'structuralist' variety epitomized by Claude Lévi-Strauss (1908–2009). The Oxford historian Keith Thomas (b. 1933) was among the earliest to use insights derived from anthropology, first in a 1963 essay in *Past and Present* and then in a magisterial study of early modern witchcraft and other aspects of English popular beliefs, *Religion and the Decline of Magic* (1971). This was just at the same time that European historiography was beginning to retreat from a focus on large patterns and systems and instead turn to the examination of particular, local, sometimes typical and sometimes quite atypical cases (as manifested in microhistory).

Moreover, the often exotic Asian, Latin American or African settings of anthropological investigations offered a compelling comparative dimension to Europeanists looking to generalize beyond their own immediate experience. Cultural anthropologists such as Margaret Mead (1901–78), Clifford Geertz (1926–2006), Marshall Sahlins (b. 1930) and Victor Turner (1920–83) offered a reliable touchstone for the shift from the large-scale and structural to the local and particular (and thereby provided a theoretical dimension to microhistory, discussed above). Sahlins in particular has engaged directly with the past, reinterpreting, for instance the death of the explorer Captain Cook in the Sandwich Islands (Hawaii), an episode which provided a concrete example of 'how natives think'. Geertz, an heir to Max Weber's early twentieth-century social science legacy, has been especially influential: his much-used term 'thick description' and his analysis of popular events such as a Balinese cock-fight, have become references *de rigueur* for many cultural historians and even for the 'New Historicist' branch of literary scholarship that emerged in the early 1980s.

The continuing dialogue between history and the social sciences is in part an outgrowth of that earlier, late nineteenth-century conversation about history and the *natural* sciences, a debate that survived the interventions of Windelband and Croce. It would spin off into three other areas, philosophy of history, philosophy of the social sciences, and the history and sociology of science, and from there double back into the discipline of history itself. In the former case, the German-émigré philosopher Carl Hempel (1905–97) made a critical intervention in 1942 with an article arguing that a core function of historical inquiry was to offer explanation in terms of 'covering' or 'general' laws, and that explanations which did not adduce or develop such laws were unsatisfactory. The article helped touch off a generation of debates within what is usually called the 'analytic' philosophy of history. In these exchanges, which focused on questions such as the nature and proper form of historical explanation, Hempel's views were largely rejected not only by most historians but by many members of his own discipline, including the analytic philosophers of history American Arthur Danto (1924–2013), Britain's Patrick Gardiner (1922–97) and the Canadian William H. Dray (1921–2009), the last-mentioned being an authority on the thought of R. G. Collingwood.

The other development also involved science – specifically *its* history and sociology. In 1962 Thomas Kuhn (1922–96), a physicist-turned-historian, published an unassuming little book called *The Structure of Scientific Revolutions*. Instead of trying to maintain the highly positivist and teleological notion of science's steady and seemingly inevitable progress (as epitomized by what have become known as 'internalist' histories of science), Kuhn suggested that science was conducted in two distinct modes: routinely as 'normal science', in which researchers operating under shared assumptions and rules incrementally augmented data and knowledge; and occasionally in a 'crisis' mode during which those old assumptions broke down – principally from the weight of data which now contradicted them – and new ones entirely incommensurable with the previous had to be generated. Kuhn called the collection of determinative assumptions and practices a 'paradigm', and thus bestowed that word on the social sciences forever more. In his account, paradigms determine the agenda of experiments and even of whole scientific programmes; major advances in knowledge, such as the shift from a medieval to a Newtonian universe, occur as a result not of tradition and steady, step-by-step progress, but because of their opposite – radical discontinuities between paradigms.

The impact of Kuhn's explanation of scientific change has been significant, though more so outside the scientific community than within. With respect to historiography in general, the concepts of 'paradigm shifts' and 'normal science' have had two major effects. First, within the history of science itself – which in the course of the later twentieth century has evolved into a free-standing discipline – the Kuhnian model helped bring about a different kind of history, fixed less on the detailed explication of past scientific ideas and more so on their social and cultural contexts (and the limitations and constraints these imposed on the generation of knowledge) regardless of their normative status or internal consistency. More recent historians of science such as Steven Shapin (b. 1943) and Lorraine Daston (b. 1951) have extended this approach. The second way in which Kuhn's ideas have affected historiography goes well beyond the history of science into other areas. For example, if his model helps explain scientific change, can it also be applied to our understanding of how historiography itself changes? Should the history of history itself, the subject of the present book, be told as a series of paradigm shifts where a few of the key thinkers of the past are highlighted at the expense of the rest who are deemed mere 'problem solvers', working away at plugging the holes in the dominant paradigm and thereby doing the work of 'normal' history? Such an approach would certainly draw the historian's attention towards the external social and cultural factors that lead one to embrace one paradigm over the other, but it would necessarily minimize types of historical inquiry unable to achieve the status of a paradigm – including most non-Western ones. However, Kuhn's 'paradigm' has been employed with somewhat greater success to account for the rise and fall of historical interpretations *about* particular events or problems (for instance, the French Revolution or the origins of the First World War). It is a sufficiently elastic term that allows for a great deal of variation in use, and is thus rather less closed than the term 'school'.

History under Dictatorships and Authoritarian Regimes

The philosopher Karl Popper (see above, p. 159) was deeply suspicious of ties between history and social science, believing that they had led to violent and oppressive attempts to engineer societies according to seemingly 'inevitable' historical patterns. While Popper was mistaken in conflating this with 'historicism', he was undoubtedly correct in one essential: the twentieth century has seen (and the twenty-first continues to see) both History and history turned to the service of a number of dictatorships, juntas and totalitarian regimes on the right and left of the political spectrum, and a level of control and repression practised that makes the state or crown interventions of earlier centuries seem almost amateurish and benign. The most infamous of those regimes on the right were the Axis powers, Fascist Italy, imperial Japan and Nazi Germany during the 1930s and 1940s. In Mussolini's Italy, right–left divisions in historiography were created which have never really disappeared. The anti-Fascist historian Gaetano Salvemini (1873–1957) fled the country in the 1920s, becoming an American citizen before he returned to Italy after the war. Others left for good, including the classicist and historiographer Arnaldo Momigliano, who lost his position following the Fascist imposition of anti-Jewish laws in 1938; he re-established himself at Oxford and London, and later in Chicago. But the Fascists did not stop, like some regimes, at the elimination of perceived enemies: they co-opted historians such as Gioacchino Volpe (1876–1971) to write ideologically agreeable accounts. Japan followed a similar course in the 1930s, highlighting connections to a glorious imperial past and to more recent military successes against neighbouring powers such as Russia. Dissenting historians were persecuted, for instance like Noro Eitaro (1900–34), a Marxist economic historian and political activist who died in police custody. As in Italy, the military government was also directly supported by historians of a pro-imperial inclination. The postwar response would produce both a reaction to the militarism of the past and a turn in the direction of non-Marxian social and cultural or 'people's' history. In Germany, an aggressive and nostalgic nationalism provided the ideological backbone to Nazi historiography and justified the purging of the profession and wider intelligentsia. Jewish and left-wing historians fled Germany during the 1930s, mainly landing in Britain and the United States, where they would have a profound impact on the postwar professions in both countries. Others from across Nazi-conquered Europe perished in the extermination camps. The historical writing of the Nazi period is exactly what one might expect, virulently anti-Semitic and anti-Bolshevik, and imbued with a racialism (informed by misguided beliefs about the 'Aryan' origins of Europe's Teutonic peoples) that would ultimately produce the Holocaust. It need not detain us long, though one of its outputs, *Volksgeschichte*, is of passing interest: it brought to a dreadful climax the long tradition of 'Teutonism' in historiography that began with Tacitus, was taken up by Reformation-era humanists, and was reformulated by Fichte at the start of the nineteenth century.

Of greater significance is the aftermath of Nazi historiography since 1945, the revision of German history, and the difficult, often painful process of reflection on its distinctive recent past. The major transition occurred after the war's end, as the profession's traditional resistance to social science methods broke down. A few old-guard conservative historians such as Gerhard Ritter (1888–1967), and even some rehabilitated former practitioners of *Volksgeschichte*, looked for the roots of Nazism in the failure of democracy and weakness of mass society. Others on the left, however, such as the Bielefeld social historian Hans-Ulrich Wehler (1931–2014) looked to the modernization of German political and social institutions in the nineteenth century. Wehler called for a new 'historical social science', synthesizing aspects of American and British social science with ideas drawn from Max Weber, Marx and the 'Critical Theory' of another group, just returned to Germany from exile, known as the Frankfurt School. The central problem addressed by several postwar generations of historians would be the emergence of Nazism, and their most prominent organ the journal *Geschichte und Gesellschaft* ('History and Society', est. 1975).

In the past six decades, the debate over Germany's 'Special Path' or *Sonderweg* has touched off two major historiographical tempests, the Fischer controversy in the early 1960s and the '*Historikerstreit*' of the late 1980s. The first of these episodes was ignited by the work of a reformed ex-Nazi named Fritz Fischer (1908–99) on the origins of the First World War. In *Griff nach der Weltmacht: Die Kriegszielpolitik des Kaiserlichen Deutschland, 1914/18* (1961; English version, *Germany's Aims in the First World War*), Fischer asserted German responsibility not only for the Second World War, which was now accepted by most mainstream historians, but for its predecessor, which was not. In his view, a direct line from the policies of late nineteenth-century German statesmen to the outbreak of the First World War could be drawn, and German leaders had clearly sought for Germany to become a world power well before the war erupted. Outrage was instantaneous: Fischer's publisher's office was fire-bombed, and a number of reputable historians, Ritter among them, attacked Fischer's methods and sources.

The second controversy erupted about twenty-five years later, on a separate but not unrelated topic, and ultimately on a more public stage. Whereas the Fischer affair was only indirectly concerned with the Second World War, the *Historikerstreit* focused on it directly, and especially on its single most morally defining episode, the Holocaust. The question here was whether the Holocaust was the anomalous act of a small group of criminals (the Nazi leadership) or rather something even more sinister – the appalling culmination of deep structural problems within German society. Accelerated by its rapid progress to modernization and statehood in the nineteenth century (again, along a 'separate path' of modernization from that of the western European democracies), these societal weaknesses had led to the First World War and the failure of democracy in the 1920s, and had then been exploited by the Nazis in their rise to power; they had thus, in the longer run, produced both the Second World War and, ultimately, the Final Solution. On this view, the nation as a whole (rather than just a small core of Nazi leaders and their collaborators) continued to bear a profound burden of guilt. The controversy began when Ernst Nolte (1923–2016), a conservative historian, contended that the Holocaust was (within Germany) a one-off act of a small circle of fanatical anti-Semites and that Auschwitz, for instance, was merely an answer to and imitation of Soviet gulags. The riposte to this issued principally from the left, beginning with the philosopher and social theorist Jürgen Habermas (b. 1929) in *Die Zeit* charging Nolte with attempting a 'settlement of damages', an exculpatory move to bury the unburiable. Habermas' intervention in a matter which might have been dealt with more quietly within the historians' guild transformed it from a disciplinary debate into a more widespread public spectacle.

Globally, the second half of the twentieth century has seen numerous neo-Fascist and authoritarian regimes assert control over historical writing and suppress dissent. As in the Italian and German examples, this has taken both active and reactive forms. The active consists in the energetic support by governments for ambitious, often multivolume national histories – the old tradition of official historiography, long marginalized in democratic Europe and the Americas, remains alive and well in East and Southeast Asia. The reactive side of this policing of the past is observable in those regimes, right or left, where blatant suppression and censorship occurs, the channels of publication are tightly controlled, opinion is closely monitored, and dissent is punished with loss of academic employment, exile or imprisonment. 'New Order' Indonesia of the Suharto regime (1966–98) offers an example of the two approaches combined. There, a militaristic 'official' history emerged under the direction of Nugroho Notosusanto (1931–85), a historian, soldier and minister of education. A virulently anti-communist and 'patriotic' multivolume history of Indonesia prepared in the 1970s, *Sejarah Nasional Indonesia* (1975; rev. 1984), was an uneasy amalgam of official history with the work of university-based historians. Since Suharto's resignation, nationalist historiography has been openly challenged by a number of competing visions of the past, including those representing different regions and minority ethnic groups. Despite the declaration of Indonesia's historians of their independence from state control, it remains unclear today whether the project for the 'rectification of history' (*pelurusan sejarah*) is simply going to displace one set of ideological orthodoxies with a new one. By 2007 a return to the anti-communism of the Suharto era was signalled with a confiscation of history textbooks by order of Indonesia's attorney-general.

On the far left, the conditions for historiography during much of the twentieth century were remarkably similar. The architects of Soviet Marxist historiography were in the first instance two men, one a professional historian, one not, both of whom had been at work formulating a Marxist historiography well before the October Revolution. The latter, Georgi Plekhanov (1856–1918), did not long survive the Revolution. A theoretician, Plekhanov had authored in 1891 a key text of Marxism, *The Materialist Conception of History*, followed in 1895 by *The Development of the Monist View of History*. The other key figure, more immediately influential on academic historiography, was a former pupil of V. O. Kliuchevskii, Mikhail Nikolaevich Pokrovskii (1868–1932). Pokrovskii had gone into exile after the failed 1905 Revolution, when he had got an early start on the first problem of revolutionary historiography, displacing the standard imperial account of the consolidation of Russia with a Marxist version. Pokrovskii's early take on Russian history appears in his five-volume *History of Russia: From the Earliest Times to the Rise of Commercial Capitalism* (1910–14; English trans. 1931). Politically astute, Pokrovskii tied his fortunes in the early 1920s to the ascendant Joseph Stalin (1878–1953), and by 1928 had become the dominant voice in Soviet historiography. In the next few years, as Stalin solidified his authority, opinion narrowed further still. Pokrovskii's influence at first survived his own death and in early 1934 the country's most distinguished female historian, Anna Mikhailovna Pankratova (1897–1957) defended his reputation, but by the end of the year, he had been posthumously condemned by Stalin for his lack of nationalist sentiment and for too deterministic a depiction of the impact of economic forces on events. His portrayal of pre-Revolutionary Russia as the backward land of Marx's estimation did not fit with the Stalinist encouragement of Russian pride and belief that the country had not followed, exactly, the same course of History as western Europe. With the simultaneous weakening and then dissolution (1936) of the Society of Marxist Historians, previously the engine of much debate over the past, and the establishment of the Institute of History within the Communist Academy, the moderately tolerant atmosphere of the 1920s gave way to strict Party controls, and thenceforth the state would exercise an overbearing influence on history-writing. Historians would be among the victims of the purges in the 1930s. Apart from rival party ideologues like Leon Trotsky (1879–1940), nationalist historians of non-Russian ethnicity were also targeted: the leading Ukrainian professional historian, Mykhailo Hrushevsky (1866–1934), was exiled to the Caucasus where he died suddenly under mysterious circumstances.

Rigid censorship peaked in the latter years of Stalin's rule, during which virtually any form of history in book, film or broadcast had to reflect the judgments contained in the Stalinist textbook, *History of the Communist Party of the Soviet Union (Bolsheviks): Short Course,* published in 1938, the very same year that the control of Soviet archives passed under the control of the state security agency, the NKVD. Following the death of Stalin, history remained under the oversight of the Party and the state, though not without producing a few dissenters from Marxist orthodoxy, for instance the medieval cultural historian Aaron Gurevich (1924–2006) and the literary critic and theorist Mikhail Bakhtin (1895–1975). With the arrival of the Cold War, Party oversight soon spread beyond the borders of the USSR to include its Warsaw Pact 'allies' in Romania, Poland, Bulgaria, East Germany, Hungary and Czechoslovakia, all of which imposed varying degrees of constraint on historians. During the era of Soviet dominance, historiography in its European satellites often mirrored, with variations of timing, the experience of the USSR itself. The various communist regimes kept a firm grip on the activities of historians, though this pressure was unevenly applied: Hungary, for instance, began to liberalize relatively soon after the failure of the 1956 Revolution. So, too, did Poland, which had also experienced an aborted revolution in that year. Pre-war ties between Polish and French historians were re-established, works in both languages were mutually translated, and a number of Polish historians, such as the Braudel-influenced Witold Kula (1916–88) and the theorist Jerzy Topolski (1928–98) published work in *Annales*. In other parts of the Soviet bloc, such as the German Democratic Republic (GDR), the ruling regimes proved more repressive and interventionist. In Bulgaria, for instance, a 1968 issue of the country's leading academic history journal announced that the Politburo had decided to commission a national history of the country, to be assigned exclusively to scholars who enjoyed the Politburo's confidence. The planned series, in ten volumes, would be written according to strict Marxist–Leninist principles. The first volume of this 'people's history' appeared in 1979 in a print run of 50,000 copies – the authorities were clearly determined to give the work wide circulation.

The imposition of state Marxism on historiography in communism's other major bastion, China (since 1949, the People's Republic), was complicated by the fact that Maoist dogma had to be superimposed on a society still in many ways organized on Confucian principles, and thus offers us a further example of the square peg of a western form of historical thinking having to adapt itself to the round hole of a very different receptor culture. The adaptation was not straightforward. Confucianism saw the world as a stable continuum punctuated by dynastic rises and falls, Marxism as the arena of linear progress; where Confucianism saw order and harmony, Marxism turned on class struggle and revolt. Yet China became the second major home for Marxist historiography during the twentieth century, and today remains the last superpower state to retain Marxism as official ideology despite recent economic liberalization. Although the ancient classics had lost their enormous authority rather quickly following the earlier, 1911 Revolution, neither liberal republicans nor Marxists could easily jettison the whole apparatus of Confucianism. Indeed it proved easier to adopt rather than abandon. Confucius the ancient conservative sage was refashioned into an early theorist of progress, and his very associations with class and feudalism were excused because they were appropriate for his own age, which had now vanished, along with its social arrangements.

The re-visioning of the Chinese past through European historical categories such as 'feudalism', completed the process of Westernizing Chinese historiography that had begun in the 1890s. Even more than Liang Qichao or the republican May Fourth scholars, early Chinese Marxist historians set about engineering a permanent break with the didactic and moralizing practices that had dominated two-and-a-half millennia of history-writing. An important early adherent of Marxism was Fan Wenlan (1893–1969), whose *General History of China* (1941) is considered a landmark of Chinese Marxist historiography. With the founding of the People's Republic (PRC) after the chaotic period of the Japanese occupation and the ensuing Communist–Nationalist civil war, Marxist historiography became state-sponsored orthodoxy. Fan Wenlan, a communist since the 1920s, was eventually appointed to head the Institute of Modern History.

Many of the leading historians whose careers spanned both the republican and communist periods had been trained in either Europe or America, and their scholarship transcended ideological lines. Chen Yinke (1890–1969), a distinguished authority on the Tang and Sui dynasties, was educated at Harvard and Berlin. A Columbia-trained historian (who would eventually return to the United States as his country's ambassador), Hu Shih (1891–1962), authored a history of Chinese philosophy, borrowing from such disparate European sources as Windelband and Langlois and Seignobos. Hu's pupil Gu Jiegang (1893–1980) was perhaps the most formidable mind of the group. A relentless debunker of bogus ancient texts in the great international philological tradition that includes Lorenzo Valla and F. A. Wolf, Gu published a popular school textbook situating China in world history. Sceptical towards early Chinese history before the Zhou dynasty in the eleventh century BC, he became the central figure of the early twentieth-century 'Doubting Antiquity School' (the 'doubts' of which would themselves be mitigated by the discovery of Shang oracle bone inscriptions, a new source which put the early dynasties back into historical time, and significantly reinforced faith in the reliability of early historians such as Sima Qian).

Beginning in the early 1950s and continuing into the 1970s, the focus of Chinese scholarship turned to the history of the peasantry and of capitalism, with the triumph of communism depicted as inevitable. 'Party history' (*dangshi*) was a significant subject in its own right in university curricula from the beginning of the PRC, with some universities even creating departments dedicated to it. The texts produced in connection with Party History continue to be carefully controlled and orchestrated from above in a manner that makes the bureaucrat-historians of the Tang era seem positively individualist by comparison. Since 1949, historians at various times have suffered persecution for heterodox statements, while within the Communist Party itself, different factions have sought historical support for contending political positions. The Great Leap Forward (1959–61) opened a rift among older and younger Marxist scholars and pushed academic historians towards a militant repudiation of 'feudal' or 'bourgeois' dynastic history, purging subsequent works of reference to former dynasties, emperors and events. This was accompanied by directives to subordinate past to present, history to theory, in a simplistic manner resisted by moderate academics such as Peking University's vice-president, the historian Jian Bozan (1898–1968), whose divergence from orthodox Marxist analysis would put him on the wrong side of the regime.

The Cultural Revolution had an even more terrible impact a few years later. It began with an attack on a respected historian of the Ming era, Wu Han (1909–69). Wu had written a play several years previously entitled *The Dismissal of Hai Rui*, about a real-life Ming dynasty functionary famous for populist sympathies and opposition to corruption. This was first performed in 1961, and because of its veiled criticism of the current regime and the Great Leap Forward, it quickly aroused the suspicion of hard-liners close to Mao, and sparked ten years of violent persecution during which China's intellectual and academic cohorts were imprisoned, tortured or sent into forced labour in the countryside. While some leading figures such as Fan Wenlan, a close associate of Mao, survived the purge, many others were less fortunate. Wu himself and Jian Bozan lost their lives (though both were posthumously rehabilitated after Mao's death). Since the beginning of liberalization in the late 1970s, entire eras have been opened up for examination, though a Party resolution of 1981 attempted to cut off ongoing historical discussions of the Maoist period in the name of unity. In the last quarter of the twentieth century, Chinese historiography has also begun interacting once again with the West, Chinese academicians have been trained in Western graduate schools and many Western books have been translated into Chinese (though there has been less traffic of Chinese books in the other direction). This equivalent of Soviet Russian 'glasnost' has largely continued, despite brief setbacks such as the 1989 Tiananmen Square reaction. It remains to be seen whether the recent re-emergence of the 'strong man' in the form of Chinese 'paramount' leader Xi Jinping or his Russian counterpart, Vladimir Putin, will have long-term de-liberalizing effects on historical writing in those countries – in 2009, Russia inaugurated a presidential commission to counteract 'the falsification of history contrary to the interests of Russia' and refurbish the battered Soviet image.

History from Below

One might have the impression from the foregoing section of a sharp contrast between democratic and non-democratic states insofar as freedom of historical inquiry and interpretation is concerned. But political intolerance is not the exclusive preserve of authoritarian regimes, and limitations on historians' speech and publication occur even under democratic governments, as some Marxist and socialist historians in the West would find in the 1950s and 1960s.

Without state authority to support it, academic Marxism never attained a monopoly position in the West, and its influence has waned somewhat since the 1980s, especially in North America. Marxist, socialist or broadly left-leaning historiography began to appear in the Western democracies relatively early in the twentieth century. Part of the left's resilience has derived not from rigid ortho- doxy but from its opposite, a rather broad ability to intermix with other agendas and to cross-fertilize with other approaches to history. A French socialist politician, Jean Jaurès (1859–1914), who was assas- sinated on the eve of the First World War, authored a non-Marxist *Socialist History of the French Revolution*. Similar works appeared from a number of historians born in the last decades of the nineteenth century, such as the Polish economic historian and educational refor- mer Franciszek Bujak (1875–1953) and his English counterparts, R. H. Tawney (1880–1962) and John L. (1872–1949) and Barbara (1873–1961) Hammond. Others of that generation were more radical: the leading Norwegian historian Halvdan Koht (1873–1965), for instance, was an early self-avowed Marxist (albeit one critical of Marx's strict materialism); the Greek historian Yannis Kordatos (1891–1961) narrated his country's revolution as a conflict of class rather than (as most nineteenth-century historians had done) ethnicity. The attractions of Marxism increased in the aftermath of the Wall Street crash of 1929, which seemed to bear out Marx's prediction of the inevitable collapse of capitalism. Georges Lefebvre (1874–1959) would place the French Revolution into a Marxist historical scheme, whereby it became the necessary transition to the bourgeois state. His most famous book, *The Coming of the French Revolution*, was repub- lished in 1939 on the eve of the Second World War, only to have the collaborationist Vichy government order all known copies of it to be burned following France's defeat in 1940. It would eventually become a favoured text of the postwar British left.

The dalliance of many intellectuals with both socialism and Marxism prior to 1945 provided the foundations of a broader historiographic tendency that, in the postwar era, would evolve into Labour history, 'radical history' and what is sometimes called 'history from below'. Several key Anglo-American examples of twentieth-century social his- tory such E. P. Thompson's (1924–93) *The Making of the English Working Class* (1963) and Herbert Gutman's (1928–85) *Work, Culture and Society in Industrializing America* (1977) were products of an explicitly Marxist, but more humanistic and less rigidly determi- nistic, perspective. They emphasized the daily lives of history's downtrodden, and highlighted their own agency, an aspect undervalued in classic Marxism (and, in different ways, by that other major influence on social history, the Braudel-era Annales historians). A similarly 'soft' approach to Marxism was adopted in other parts of the world, for example by the Dutch journalist–historian Jan Romein (1893–1962), who owed as much to Huizinga's brand of *Kulturgeschichte* as he did to Marx and was excluded from membership in the Dutch Communist Party because of his unorthodox opinions. A further modification of Marxism was articulated in the legacy of the Italian socialist, and victim of Fascism, Antonio Gramsci (1891–1937), whose 3,000-page *Prison Notebooks*, first published a decade after his death, has become one of the great political texts of the left. With his concept of cultural 'hegemony', the process whereby ruling powers or elites maintain authority with the willing cooperation of the subordinated, Gramsci's star has risen further in recent decades, and his ideas continue to appear in much non-Marxist historical scholarship and literary history.

France and Italy aside, no democratic country has generated so vigorous a Marxist historiography as Britain, where virtually every period from the Middle Ages to the early twentieth century has been well covered, and where socialist and Marxist historians have enjoyed a public profile quite disproportionate to their relatively small numbers. Many British Marxists, such as Christopher Hill (1912–2003), a historian of radical ideas and beliefs in seventeenth-century England), were initially active Communist Party members, but left it after the Soviet invasion of Hungary in 1956, along with several of their French counterparts. Others such as Eric Hobsbawm (1917–2012) retained their party affiliation while nonetheless taking critical stands against the excesses of Soviet expansionism. Perhaps the most important collective contribution that many of them made was the founding of *Past and Present* in the early 1950s. Quickly establishing itself as an alternative to the more mainstream political history journals, it has since then achieved the kind of international prominence that *Annales* had earlier acquired in France. Soon jettisoning its initial subtitle 'a Journal of Scientific History' (now become merely 'a Journal of Historical Studies'), *Past and Present* had become sufficiently centrist by the mid-1970s that it eventually ceded the space on its left to newer publications like the *History Workshop Journal* (est. 1976).

Left-wing British historians have largely avoided the political persecution and career disruption suffered by their counterparts elsewhere –

with a few notable exceptions such as George Rudé (1910–93), a historian of revolutionary movements who was unable to find employment in Britain, spending his career in Australia and Canada. Elsewhere, there are a number of well-known example of persecution or career blocking. In 1956, the young Australian historian Russel Ward (1914–95) had his appointment to a lectureship vetoed by the institution's leadership because of his 'seditious' and communist associations, causing the department head (who by no means shared Ward's views) to resign in protest against the violation of academic freedom. When one of Japan's most distinguished modern historians, Ienaga Saburo (1913–2002), was commissioned to write a history text in 1953, his manuscript was rejected by the authorities because it appeared to oppose the Tokugawa family system, treated peasant uprisings as legitimate and spent too many pages on the recent history of the Pacific region. On resubmitting the manuscript, without changing a word, it was passed, suggesting to him the arbitrariness of the system.

The United States has a similarly long tradition of 'left history', dating back to the Progressive and New Historians of the early twentieth century. A post-1945 recommitment to the twin ideas of America's exceptionalism and the 'consensus' on which this was built – papering over the fissures of race, class and (yet to be heard from) gender – had the effect of cooling any radical impulses at the same time that the Cold War was getting started. Those with leftist affiliations often found themselves facing tough questions about their 'loyalty' during the late 1940s and 1950s. A number emigrated to Canada, Britain and other countries. The classicist Moses Finley (1912–86), a New York-born Jew, was fired from his position at Rutgers University in 1952, subsequently moving to Cambridge where he had a long and successful scholarly career culminating in a knighthood. Natalie Zemon Davis emigrated to Toronto in the early 1960s with her mathematician husband (a victim of political persecution) though she would eventually commute to the United States and teach at Berkeley and Princeton. During the 1960s activist historians such as Howard Zinn (1922–2010) and Staughton Lynd (b. 1929) were dismissed from academic posts, the latter for visiting Hanoi in protest against the Vietnam War. As recently as 2017, legislators in the state of Arkansas were attempting to proscribe Zinn's works, including his well-known *People's History of the United States* from being used in schools; another such effort was made in 2013 by a governor of the state of Indiana, himself a former university president. (In fairness, it should be noted that fellow academics, not all conservatives, have been critical of Zinn's works on a purely scholarly basis.) The Belgian historian Antoon de Baets (b. 1955) has devoted much of his career to recording and describing known examples of political interference with the academic freedom (and sometimes literally, bodily freedom) of historians; in 2002 he published a depressing catalogue of such interventions since the end of the Second World War; there have been annual addenda to this list involving both democratic and authoritarian regimes.

Sometimes, of course, censorship could come from the other direction, as liberals fell afoul of those with more radical positions. By the mid-1960s, with Vietnam and the civil rights movement dominating public discourse, radical history emerged with a vengeance, and sometimes with polarizing violence. In an echo of the Red Guards' attacks on Chinese heritage sites and on the country's intellectuals two years previously, the liberal historian of France, Orest Ranum (b. 1933) had a year's worth of his notes destroyed by student protesters at Columbia in 1968, and soon found the climate in his department so oppressive that he relocated to Johns Hopkins University. While the radicalism of the late 1960s in America and Western Europe dissipated within a few years, it left a formidable pedagogical legacy. History from below, along with Black history, women's history and native history, had by the early 1970s established a small but firm beachhead in university history departments. By the end of that decade, the curricular position of all of these was rather more secure – just in time to resist the resurgent conservatism of the 1980s in the United States and several of its Western allies. Whether they can withstand the spread of populist anti-intellectualism, hostility to evidence and reductive thinking that has tainted public discourse in very recent years is uncertain.

Varieties of Intellectual History

Historians have studied ideas as well as events for centuries, and the German terms *Kulturgeschichte* and *Geistesgeschichte* alike embrace the content and impact of human thought in past times. Within the modern historical discipline, what is usually called intellectual history established itself by the mid-twentieth century as a distinctive sub-field under different names and in different styles: Meinecke's

Ideengeschichte was the German variant; in France the study of *mentalités* emerged with the Annales. In the United States, the 'history of ideas' as a recognizable subject of study began in earnest with Arthur O. Lovejoy (1873–1962). Lovejoy had produced in *The Great Chain of Being* (1936) a book that epitomized his method: identify a key concept or 'unit idea' and trace it forward in time as it combined and recombined with other unit ideas. Allying themselves with philosophy as much as history – in the sense that sorting out a thinker's precise arguments and their afterlife became the priority – intellectual historians produced some remarkably fine work during this period, but the Lovejoy approach began to attract criticism in the 1960s. Lovejoy founded and edited the *Journal of the History of Ideas* (est. 1940) which, though it did not adjust immediately to changes in historiographical fashion, nevertheless provides a measure of them. In the decades since its foundation it has gone through a relatively small number of editors, and in recent times it has complemented its traditional diet of 'high intellectual' history, concerned with elite thinkers, with broader 'cultural history' topics. It has also begun to abandon the almost exclusively Western focus which, along with an 'internalist' philosophical approach, had previously limited the appeal of this style of intellectual history in much of the wider world. Newer journals such as *History of Humanities* (est. 2015) and *The Intellectual History Review* (est. 2007) have been established in recent years, following the earlier-founded *History of European Ideas* (est. 1980).

Intellectual history in the European and North American context peaked in popularity in the 1950s and fell out of fashion in the 1960s and 1970s (a victim of the rapid success of social history), reinventing itself as the less elitist-sounding 'cultural history' in the 1980s, under which umbrella it has regained a good deal of ground. Lovejoy's older 'history of ideas' has been expanded at one end to include newer fields such as the histories of the book (*histoires du livre*), of libraries and of reading, and at the other into the pursuit of the meaning of terms and of texts in their linguistic and/or social contexts. The latter stream is in turn divisible into a so-called Cambridge School of the history of political thought, associated most often with Quentin Skinner (b. 1940) in Britain and the New Zealander (educated at Cambridge) J. G. A. Pocock (b. 1924) in the United States, and the *Begriffsgeschichte* (history of political and social concepts) approach advocated by the German Reinhart Koselleck (1923–2006). Koselleck's method has somewhat more in common with Lovejoy's, though its focus is not on the 'unit idea' as a kind of free-floating entity, but on the semantic usage of particular words, their signification and their connection with contemporary political and social reality. (A good example, relevant immediately to this book and already cited in Chapter 4, is the advent during the eighteenth century of 'Geschichte' in the German language, displacing the older term 'Historie', along with the development of what we have been calling capital-H History.) Pocock has examined ideas historically, within their sequential political and intellectual contexts, with major authors considered in comparison with or indebted to less well-known contemporaries and precursors. His mid-career masterpiece, *The Machiavellian Moment* (1975), demonstrates this method most fully, as it follows key political and historical concepts like 'civic humanism' and 'republicanism' backwards to ancient and early medieval thought, then examines their working out in the context of sixteenth-century Italy, before tracing them forward, via seventeenth-century English thinkers, into a transatlantic, eighteenth-century Britanno-American world. Pocock's most recent work, a six-volume study of Gibbon's *Decline and Fall of the Roman Empire*, places that book amid multiple different streams of historical thought and writing emanating from antiquity through to the various European Enlightenments (the plural is deliberate, disaggregating several different streams of eighteenth-century thought). Quentin Skinner's approach is broadly similar in insisting that great works be studied not simply to generate internally coherent meanings but within the context of other works of their time, though Skinner places a somewhat greater emphasis on particular leading thinkers such as the seventeenth-century philosopher Thomas Hobbes, and his own writing makes more explicit use of linguistic theory. (In a recent survey of intellectual history, Richard Whatmore points to a number of other significant differences in their views that need not, however, concern us here.) The Marxist scholar Raymond Williams (1921–1988) published a highly influential study of the changing meanings of particular terms, *Keywords*, in 1976 which has proved especially influential in the interdisciplinary field of Cultural Studies.

The psychoanalytic theories of Sigmund Freud (1856–1939) inspired a very different form of inquiry into the influence of the mind in history, in this case of the irrational and subconscious. In his later works, especially *Moses and Monotheism* (1939), Freud applied his theories and clinical experience to the 'diagnosis' of history. Freud had dabbled in history earlier in his career, using psychoanalysis in a 1910 book on Leonardo da Vinci and more systematically in *Civilization and its Discontents* (1930). He was known to have used archives, not relying on secondary sources, for instance in his treatment of a seventeenth-century exorcism as a type of neurosis. Freud envisaged the process of civilization as an endless dynamic struggle of love and hate, sex and death, arising from primal patricide, and carried forward by leader-figures such as Moses in conflict with the mobs whom they dominated – the resonance between the ideas of Freud and certain aspects of the thought of his older contemporary, Nietzsche (for whom an innate 'will to power' was the most fundamental drive of human action) is difficult to miss.

Psychohistory has probably aroused more passion among its most fervent devotees and contempt from its most outspoken critics than almost any other theoretical approach to the study of the past, even the 'linguistic turn' (see below). Its heyday came a generation after Freud's death, in the late 1950s, 1960s and early 1970s. In 1957, the president of the American Historical Association, William L. Langer (1896–1977), used the podium to call for historians to move on to 'the next assignment', which was the application of psychology to historical research. In the very next year, a German-born trained psychoanalyst and refugee from the Nazis, Erik H. Erikson (1902–94), published *Young Man Luther*, the first full-length attempt to psychoanalyze a particular historical figure. Like Erikson, most subsequent psycho-historians were not strict Freudians and applied their particular version of psychoanalysis to the past: in Wilhelm Reich's (1897–1957) case applying Freudian theories to an entire population, that of the lower middle classes of Weimar Germany, to account for the then-contemporary rise of Hitler and Nazism; and, in the case of American classicist Norman O. Brown (1913–2002), analyzing historical move-ments more broadly through the lens of psychoanalysis. Other variants have been applied to past social phenomena such as the early modern witch hunts. Although psychohistory has never won wide acceptance beyond a core group of admirers, and while Freudian theories and their assorted offshoots have themselves been marginalized within modern psychology by newer fields such as neuroscience and social psychology, a Freudian approach has been championed by the occasional mainstream historian such as the American intellectual historian Bruce Mazlish (1923–2016) and the German émigré Peter Gay (1923–2015) who himself underwent psychoanalytic training and wrote extensively about Freud, as well as by less conventional figures such as the theologian and historical theorist Michel de Certeau. Indirectly, it has had a significant influence on other aspects of cultural theory – Michel Foucault, for instance, formulated his ideas on sexuality in reaction to Freud's – and even on postmodernism (see below, pp. 262–67), though that approach – often associated with the French theorist Jacques Lacan (1901–81) – has also challenged the very possibility of understanding the psyche since the self (or 'subjectivity') in its own right may be both fluid and a 'constructed' feature of Western culture. At its best, in the work of a trained analyst like Erikson, psychohistory offers a plausible alternative set of explanations for individual actions.

Other forms of psychology have been brought to bear on the study of the past. The Annalistes, of course, have done so with their attention to mentalities, but more recently non-historian social scientists, including specialists in human cognition, have begun to ask whether behaviour in bygone times, and especially collective action (the behaviour of crowds, for instance), can be explained through understanding the ways in which the mind comprehends and constructs reality. This in some way is to adapt Dilthey's notion of *Verstehen*, or Collingwood's related concept of re-enactment, and try to apply it to the psychology of past groups, but using the evidence of contemporary observation and experimentation. In a sense, it provides a mirror image 'scientific' counterpart to the historicist assumption that while cultures and values may differ, elemental human thought processes are sufficiently similar throughout time as to allow for inferences about past behaviour from present evidence. To be fair, unless we assume a degree of congruence in human reactions to similar situations, it is hard to see how any conclusion about the historical motives of individuals or groups can ever be reached.

From Women's History to Histories of Gender and Sexuality

Aside from a few early twentieth-century exceptions like Eileen Power (see above, p. 214), the presence of female historians in the profession actually declined in the years following the conclusion of the First World War, a trend that continued up to the 1960s. Outside North America and Western Europe the prominence of women in the discipline was even more uneven, a pattern that has continued to the present day. In China, the profession remains today a largely masculine preserve. In Bulgaria, roughly a quarter of all its historians since the mid-nineteenth century have been female, a proportion that had improved considerably at the collapse of communism in 1989. In Finland, by contrast, very few women prior to the 1950s achieved doctoral degrees in history, though many more earned Masters degrees. The Finnish profession remained overwhelmingly male in the first decades after the Second World War, despite the activity of many women biographers and amateur historians. Practising history on the margins was one thing; entering the profession as an academic historian another – a career goal denounced by Mary Ritter Beard (1876–1958), despite her own university connections, on the grounds that the rules of academe were entirely set by men. Beard disapproved of the university career as a goal for women in part because, she suggested in her 1946 book *Woman as Force in History*, professional historians had simply chosen, being overwhelmingly male, not to see the contributions to history of half the human race.

A harbinger of the first major phase of women's history in the 1970s, Beard's book had counterparts elsewhere in the postwar world, notably Japan where Inoue Kiyoshi (1913–2001), a male Marxist historian, published *Nihon joseishi* ('Women's History of Japan', 1948) followed the next year by the feminist, journalist and later politician Kamichika Ichiko's (1888–1981) *Josei shisoshi* ('Women's History of Ideas'), a work much influenced by Beard. By the late 1960s the problem was not a lack of interest in women's history, or of significant writings about it, but rather its absence from university curricula and research agenda, along with an enduring scarcity of women in tenured faculty positions, whatever their national field of study. The eminent historian of colonial America, Mary Beth Norton (b. 1943), who was elected president of the AHA for 2018, recently recalled joining the Cornell history department in 1971 and being the only woman in the department for five years, under a department chair who began meetings by saying 'gentlemen'. For minority female historians (black and Hispanic women, for instance), the challenges of life in the academy could be even tougher as they faced both gender and racial biases.

The study of women in the past remained an occasional subject within the main streams of military, political and social history, and most often written outside the universities. The initial solution to this seemed to lie in establishing women's history as a recognizable and distinct sub-discipline without detaching it from the professional mainstream wherein lay the academic rewards and honours of which women had been struggling to gain a share for half a century. The push for women's history in the 1970s followed the growth of the Women's Liberation movement (or 'second-wave' feminism), and the development of feminist perspectives in philosophy and the social sciences, with intellectual inspiration coming from key earlier texts such as Simone de Beauvoir's *The Second Sex* (1949) and Virginia Woolf's *A Room of One's Own* (1929). There had already been sporadic courses on women's history offered at American universities, the Viennese-born Gerda Lerner (1920–2013) having taught the subject at various American institutions since the middle of the 1960s. An important factor in establishing women's history on undergraduate curricula, and in making it a research topic in its own right, may have been the decision by a number of other well-established female historians to shift interests or expand the focus of their scholarship and teaching. Natalie Zemon Davis, whose early research was on French print-workers, authored a pioneering essay on women and popular culture in early modern France in the 1970s. (Davis became only the second woman elected to the presidency of the American Historical Association, in 1987, though from then till 2018 there have been a dozen more). Gisela Bock (b. 1942), a prominent German feminist historian, had written her first book on the Renaissance philosopher Thomas Campanella before her political activities on behalf of pay equity for female workers moved her in the direction of women's history. Eileen Power, principally known as an economic historian, had begun before her death a book entitled *Medieval Women* which finally appeared in 1975. The French Africanist Catherine Coquery-Vidrovitch (b. 1935) published a history of women in modern Africa in 1987, which was translated into English a decade later. Major collaborative publishing projects on aspects of women's history have appeared over the years, such as the multivolume *History of Women in the West* edited by the French historians Georges Duby and Michelle Perrot (b. 1928).

However, arguments continued to occur during the 1970s and 1980s as to where and how the history of women fitted into 'history proper' or 'the main stream'. From the point of view of some male historians, women's history was the symbol *par excellence* of the continuing fragmentation of the discipline along 'interest group' lines. Historians of a Marxist persuasion often inclined to view women's history as a distraction from the main agenda of understanding the dynamics and impact of class; women historians responded that Marxism had entirely overlooked the contribution of women in any other sphere than the domestic. Despite its obvious intersection with family and demographic history, women's history was still often seen as of marginal importance, and 'serious' graduate students (that is males, and any female who really wanted career advancement) were steered elsewhere. Nor, for that matter, were women practitioners entirely agreed among themselves on an agenda for their subject. Was women's history simply a 'supplement' to the main agendas of historians, an addition to the pool of knowledge of achievements previously and unjustly left out? Was it sufficient simply to attribute an agency to women that had previously been attached to men, or to bring to light, as in the title of a famous 1973 work by Sheila Rowbotham (b. 1943), an entire sex 'hidden from history'? Or was this simply to fall into a historiographic analysis (and agenda) that had been established by males in the first place? In short, was it enough to write 'compensatory or contribution history' – to add women, as the saying went, and stir?

A significant shift came after 1986, in which year Joan Wallach Scott (b. 1941), an American scholar working in French history, published a seminal article, 'Gender: A Useful Category of Historical Analysis', urging a redirection of attention away from women as biologically essentialized beings and towards the study of gender and its social (and linguistic) construction. Scott was by no means the only historian thinking along these lines, but her essay struck a chord. Its impact was felt, albeit unevenly, elsewhere in the world over the next two decades, as evidenced in a multi-author forum on it in a 2008 issue of the *American Historical Review*. The eventual effect of this was to enlarge considerably the areas of potential study for both feminist and non-feminist historians. Instead of focusing on women's oppression, subordination or the converse, heroic or transgressive past agency, one could now focus on the way in which gender influenced the full scope of past human activity, including those areas such as political life in which women had been conspicuously rare. Scott herself, however, went further than simply advocating for gender's equivalency with race or class as a category. She questioned what 'gender' meant in particular contexts and how it acted as a determinant of other phenomena. Influenced by French cultural theorists such as Michel Foucault (1926–84), whose own later works focused on the history of sexuality, Scott asserted that the written discourses generated by a society are forms of power in their own right, and that they have created and constrained notions of male and female, and of masculine and feminine qualities across time. Though Scott herself has been criticized for too close an allegiance to postmodernism (see below) at the expense of more traditional feminist agendas, her article proved almost instantly catalytic.

In the past three decades women's history has been steadily augmented (some might say supplanted) by gender history, including the study of masculinity and alternative sexualities: homosexuality, for instance, has been explored in and across much of history by John Boswell (1947–94), as well as by Foucault himself; Mrinalini Sinha (b. 1960) has used Edward Said's ideas to examine 'colonial masculinity', unfolding in the interplay between gender stereotypes and British imperial power in nineteenth-century Bengal. In a similar vein, Catherine Hall (b. 1946) has studied gender's relations with class and race, and its historical connections to the relations between imperial 'metropole' and colonial periphery. Judith R. Walkowitz (b. 1945) has explored the nature of the horrific and shocking in Victorian London through narratives of 'sexual danger'. The Australian Susan K. Foley (b. 1949) has published major studies of gender and society in modern France. And well-worn subjects such as the history of witchcraft in Europe and America, previously examined from religious, psychosocial or anthropological perspectives, have been revisited through the lenses of both sexuality and gender. The changes in approach to the study of women's past lives and historical roles over the past several decades can be gauged by comparing Eileen Power's posthumous book on medieval women, conceived in the inter-war period, with more recent work on medieval gender by historians such as Caroline Walker Bynum (b. 1941) and Barbara A. Hanawalt (b. 1941), or by juxtaposing Alice Clark's classic study of seventeenth-century women's working lives with that of Marjorie K. McIntosh (b. 1940) and the same author's work on Yoruba women in Africa. The focus has shifted from recovering lost contributions and lives to exploring the ways in which gender and sexuality can be used to understand aspects of medieval life from food, to spirituality, to the human body. And some orthodoxies of early women's history – notably the thesis that modernity marked a decline in women's position and prosperity from a supposed time of more equal status in the ancient or medieval past – have been challenged by recent scholars such as Judith M. Bennett (b. 1951).

From relative marginality half a century ago, both women's history and gender history have become major sub-fields within the discipline (with strong connections to emerging interdisciplinary subjects such as Cultural Studies, Race and Ethnicity Studies and Global Development Studies) in many, though by no means all, parts of the world. As Laura Lee Downs has noted in a recent book, 'sneering dismissal' of either women's or gender history is no longer possible. And in North America at least, the population of tenured or tenure-track women in history departments has considerably grown. Norton, whose experience at Cornell in the 1970s is mentioned above, noted in 2018 that the gender split by then was much closer to even, and that more women than men occupied endowed chairs. The Department of History in the Canadian university that the present author attended in the 1970s was devoid of non-adjunct female faculty for three of my four years (an earlier, senior hire having died); I am a professor in the same department four decades later, where the ratio has also approached equality.

Postwar African Historiography

Echoing Enlightenment assumptions about the necessity of writing for the existence of historical thinking, and stadialist theories of the progress of the world away from barbarism, the British historian Hugh Trevor-Roper (1914–2003), no stranger to controversy, set off a minor firestorm. He pronounced in a 1963 set of television lectures and ensuing 1965 book, *The Rise of Christian Europe*, that it was futile to study African history prior to colonization, on the grounds both of its seeming lack of source materials and because he saw it as irrelevant to the concerns of modernity. For historians, it would be a distraction from what he considered the 'purposive movement' of History (here in the capital-H sense), a diversion on to irrelevant parts of the world that he deemed useful only as revealing a past from which modernity, largely through the dominance of Europe, had escaped.

Trevor-Roper's words were quickly rebutted by many scholars. Beginning in the 1960s, in the wake of postwar decolonization, African history began to make its way, slowly, on to mainstream history curricula within and outside Africa. With the retreat of the European colonial powers and the establishment of independent nations, a deeper interest in exploring their own past quickly emerged among African populations, stimulated by reaction to decades of education in an alien imperial historiography. With this came an urgent need to recast the historical record and to recover evidence of many overlooked pre-colonial civilizations. One consequence of the decolonization of Africa was that at first, a European-style master-narrative of progress was simply imported and converted to local purposes. The political withdrawal of Europe occurred just at the point when very new academic institutions were being created, principally as overseas extensions of European models, and highly dependent on European academic staff or affiliated universities abroad – the pattern previously seen in British India. Given this continued intellectual influence, a triumphal nationalist narrative of the advance of this or that former colony maturing, under the nurturing mentorship of a benevolent empire, into a free and full member of the international community marked much of the new African historical writing well into the 1960s. It came with most of the trappings of pre-war 'Whig' historiography, such as the steady development in the past of political institutions, the centralization of power and the improvement of administration – all the features of the modern Western state.

Foundational research in African history was done at the School of Oriental and African Studies (SOAS) in London by scholars such as Roland Oliver (1923–2014), co-founder in 1960 of the *Journal of African History*, and by the Belgian-born Jan Vansina (1929–2017), an authority on African oral tradition, which became a significant means of access to the pre-colonial past. Examining oral traditions for historicity, much less for precise chronological information, is often not very productive (there is an extensive specialist methodological literature on this that cannot detain us here). We are better off considering them for what they can tell us about contemporary values. Even the most sympathetic experts have pointed to three major complicating phenomena such as 'telescoping' (the truncation or expansion of dynastic lines to fill chronological gaps), 'feedback' (the effect of writing on spoken testimony, and specifically the risk that a tradition has been contaminated by, and is simply repeating, facts gleaned from colonial or external literary sources) and 'structural amnesia' (the collective forgetting of details of the past, and figures of history, that no longer fit with present political circumstances). On the other hand, it has also been argued that these distorting influences can be filtered out. The techniques of oral traditionalists have been applied outside Africa, in the study of Southeast Asian, Latin American and Caribbean cultures, as well as to indigenous cultures in North America and Australasia. For all its potential weaknesses as a source, there is no doubt that oral tradition has reopened a road to the past once closed off by the inherent bias of historiography towards writing which had solidified in the aftermath of early modern contacts in the Americas.

Modern African historiography has not, of course been the preserve of well-intentioned Europeans. African universities have, despite the instabilities of politics and civil war in many countries, trained their own scholars and sent many others overseas for doctoral training. They have also attracted European scholars into their teaching ranks: the 'Ibadan' school of historians (initiated in the 1950s at the University of Ibadan in Nigeria and influential into the 1970s) included both native Nigerians and transplanted Britons. The pioneering Nigerian historian Kenneth Onwuka Dike (1917–83) studied at Durham, Aberdeen and London, while SOAS has educated several leading African-born scholars, including the Ghanaian Albert Adu Boahen (1932–2006). Boahen in turn participated in an important early summary work of postcolonial historical writing, the UNESCO *General History of Africa*, inaugurated in 1964 and finally completed in the 1990s. This was directed by a 'scientific committee,' two-thirds of whom were Africans, and written by over three hundred authors including the Kenyans Ali Mazrui (1933–2014) and Bethwell Allan Ogot (b. 1929), Joseph Ki-Zerbo (1922–2006) of Burkina Faso (formerly Upper Volta) and the Nigerian J. F. Ade Ajayi (1929–2014). The development of European historiography in Africa over the past century is, again, rather reminiscent of Indian historical writing of the same period: the tools and concepts of the colonial powers were adopted by the colonized first to embrace and later to push against those powers in support of a nationalist (and more recently, a Marxian, class-oriented) goal.

The Linguistic Turn: Postmodernism

In the late 1960s, with social history in the ascendant, few professional historians were thinking much about their millennia-old relationship to the world of literature. The overwhelming majority of readers and writers of history accepted that there was a fundamental difference between works of fiction and history, which recounted a true story. In the following decade, this began to change, at the very same time that, partly as a consequence of 1960s unrest and rapid decolonization across the world, renewed questioning was occurring of the rationalist, 'Enlightenment' agenda of the previous three centuries. In short, doubts about both history and History (and, increasingly, about the connection between the two), sounded in the early years of the century but largely suppressed during and immediately following the Second World War, began to re-emerge, now in a post-atomic world and within a discipline much more fractured than it had ever been. An early challenge to strict historical 'empiricism' (a better term by far than 'positivism') came in 1961 in the form of a controversial but widely read little book by the British historian of Soviet Russia, E. H. Carr (1892–1982), entitled *What is History?*, which pointed to the role of the historian in selecting and fashioning evidence. It famously urged students to 'study the historian before you begin to study the facts'.

This seedbed of moderate scepticism, combined with disciplinary fracturing, prepared the ground within the field of historical studies for what has become known as the linguistic turn. This originated, however, quite outside the discipline, in philosophy and literary theory, and is sometimes conflated with a parallel, anthropologically influenced 'cultural turn', both being often associated with the broader theoretical movement in the humanities known as postmodernism or, with declining frequency, 'poststructuralism' (the late historiographer Ernst Breisach [1923–2016] saw poststructuralism as a subset of the postmodern, but for simplicity we shall dispense here with the former term). Postmodernism has been especially influenced by the works of the Frenchmen Michel Foucault, Jean-François Lyotard (1924–98) and Jacques Derrida (1930–2004), the German Martin Heidegger (1889–1976), his one-time pupil the hermeneutist Hans-Georg Gadamer (1900–2002), the pre-war German intellectual Walter Benjamin (1892–1940) and, further back, Friedrich Nietzsche. The philosopher Michael Oakeshott (see above, p. 190) anticipated one aspect of postmodernism when he asserted in 1933 that history could not exist outside of human experience of it – that 'the course of events, as such, is not history because it is nothing at all' and that 'the historian's business is not to discover, to recapture, or even to interpret; it is to create and to construct' (though Oakeshott, like Carr, never asserted the non-reality of historical facts). If one wants to trace its 'genealogy' (itself a favoured term in the later work of Foucault – who derived it from Nietzsche – in preference to 'causes', or to his own earlier use of 'archaeology') further, one can go back through the eighteenth-century and Renaissance debates about the merits of history versus imaginative literature, and end up back at Aristotle's *Poetics*. Although the linguistic turn has by no means exclusively been concerned with this issue, a major thrust of it has been seriously to erode conventional boundaries between history and fiction – which, Sarah Maza notes, originally meant not something false but something created and shaped. In doing so, it has challenged the superiority history has assumed over fiction for a good two centuries based on historians' claims that they portray real rather than imagined events. Leading exponents of this view include the Americans Hayden White (1928–2018), Hans Kellner (b. 1945) and Dominick LaCapra (b. 1939), the Dutch philosopher F. R. Ankersmit (b. 1945), and the British theorists Keith Jenkins (b. 1943) and Alun Munslow (b. 1947). Although its origins are Western, it has in recent years spread into Asian historical discourse, aided by the somewhat freer transfer of ideas and peoples since the late 1980s; there, it has become associated less with epistemological critiques of history than with efforts to locate Asian pasts on a trajectory leading to alternative forms of modernity, distinctive from that which has characterized the West.

The central thrust of much historiographic postmodernism has been to recast history from its nineteenth- and early twentieth-century status as a distinctive mode of *knowledge* into a form of *narrative*. In this respect, the work of Hayden White, beginning with a well-known 1966 essay entitled 'The Burden of History', has been especially influential. His 1973 magnum opus, *Metahistory: The Historical Imagination in Nineteenth-Century Europe* (the title of which borrows, for rather different purposes, a term first used by Collingwood, disparagingly, to describe the likes of Toynbee and Spengler) purports to demonstrate through close study of a series of nineteenth-century historians and philosophers from Ranke and Burckhardt through Nietzsche and Croce, that there is no fundamental difference between the writing of history, philosophy of history and fiction, arguing in effect that there can be no access to a 'real' past outside of our representation of it. White does not assert that the past has never existed or is completely imagined – merely that it is no longer directly reachable other than through texts which are themselves mediated by language; original documents do not provide direct access both because they, too, are selections from past life, mediated by *their* authors, and because they have no inherent *meaning* that is not bestowed on them by the historian's interpretation. Every narration or description of the past involves the historian in a series of mental operations that require a poetic act of imagination which in turn predetermines the story that will be 'discovered' and then fashioned into a coherent narrative. The focus on language suggests a kinship with the above-mentioned intellectual historians Pocock and Skinner. But any connection is superficial. As Michael S. Roth has observed, Skinner's hunts for a writer's intentions in writing particular texts, and Pocock's exploration of intellectual contexts within which texts are composed, are radically different from White's view that the content of texts is almost secondary to the literary form that they take, and that authorial writing decisions are largely unconscious and unintended.

Borrowing from Vico, White argued that historical narratives are constituted through four master tropes (metaphor, metonymy, synecdoche and irony) or figures of speech that create a meaningful past out of the raw materials that make up the unprocessed 'historical field'. These tropes in turn help determine the author's choices among three different strategies of narration, whereby what would otherwise be a mere temporally ordered sequence of events or *chronicle* is turned into a *story*: modes of emplotment (the kind of story that is being told), modes of formal argument (the way in which events and persons interact within the historical world, effecting events and leading to a conclusion) and modes of ideological implication (the moral to be drawn from the story). Perhaps more influential (and controversial) than the elaborate structure he erected for studying his chosen texts, however, was White's conclusion, elaborated in subsequent essays, that there is no essential difference between the writing of fiction and that of history in the sense that both tell stories – one depicts imaginary occurrences and the other events that are believed to have actually occurred in the past but which, precisely because they are past, are no longer 'real' in an existential sense. R. G. Collingwood had seemed to hint at this 'narrativist' view of history thirty years earlier, but White went much further. Influenced by the American philosopher (and critic of Collingwood) Louis O. Mink, Jr (1921–83) and by French criticism (especially Roland Barthes and his notion of a 'reality effect'), White does not quite say that history and fiction are exactly the *same* thing, nor does he suggest that a historian should simply make up documents and historical figures in the same way a novelist creates characters, but his arguments do have the effect of dissolving some key assumptions that have sustained the history–fiction distinction for centuries. Because of this, his work has become a focal point in the postmodern debate insofar as it involves history, motivating both outspoken defenders (who often take his arguments to further extremes than White himself) and equally fierce critics such as the British historians Arthur Marwick (1936–2006) and Geoffrey Elton, the latter in a much sharper tone than he had used with Robert Fogel during their earlier debate on cliometrics (see above, p. 236).

Postmodernism is often explicitly political, and at times almost fundamentalist in its antagonism to orthodoxies, master-narratives (Lyotard proclaimed suspicion of these as a hallmark of 'the postmodern condition') and power structures. It is devoted to demolishing these orthodoxies, and the knowledge foundations on which they rest, as well as to 'de-centring' those objects of learning previously deemed central, and to re-centring, at least temporarily, the previously marginal and peripheral. It is committed to dissolving essences and investigating the modes whereby objects of intellectual inquiry, analytical categories (gender, race, class) and even individuals are viewed as the product of social, psychological and even linguistic 'construction'. Rationalism is regarded with suspicion by many postmodernists, and in particular so-called 'Enlightenment' rationalism. The Enlightenment (here seen more as a set of liberal, progressivist ideals rather than the specific, eighteenth-century movement) is a convenient target for much that postmodernism resists because of its presumed tendency to universalism and essentialism, its assumption of transcendental, objectively existing values, and its faith in the direct and recoverable relationship between things and the words that signify them. 'Positivism' is to a postmodernist even more dubious and 'naive', its parallel messages of social and scientific improvement (as in Comte and Buckle) and epistemological progress being doubly suspect since they presuppose both linear forward change and the veracity of the narrative underlying and endorsing it. Thus during the 1960s Foucault (building on both Vico and Herder, and in many ways paralleling Thomas Kuhn) reconceived European intellectual history 'archaeologically' rather than as a linear development: a series of discontinuous and largely incompatible 'epistemes' (an idea he soon reconceptualized as 'discursive formations'), and not merely a tradition of great ideas evinced by brilliant thinkers, had shaped how knowledge was arranged and valued, and how it related to the exercise of power.

Like any historiographical movement, postmodernism has its flaws and extremes. In their zeal to caricature all opponents as 'positivist' (in the broader sense of that term), rationalist or simply naive, many of its adherents have, ironically, constructed their own convenient 'other', a fabricated knowledge-villain that in itself is an example of essentialization and generalization. They have also, with some exceptions, imputed a ubiquitous and omnipotent blanket-like quality to 'Enlightenment' narratives, homogenizing currents of thought from the eighteenth and nineteenth centuries that were much less harmonious and single-minded than they are represented as being, and which notably contained their own elements of resistance and counter-argument. It is worth noting that opponents of postmodernism and its focus on language have come from the traditional left as much as the right: some Marxist and labour historians have seen the fixation on language and discourse as a regrettable retreat from the main agenda of class analysis back into the airy regions of ideas and abstraction, and as a betrayal of the materialism and socio-economic analysis on which progressive or radical histories are based.

However, in spite of its occasional extremities, one must concede that postmodernism and the related 'cultural turn' have provided a salutary reminder to all historians that documents and texts never 'speak for themselves'. They are, indeed, interpreted by historians, and even the most 'neutral' document is ultimately an artefact created by a human, driven by the assumptions, social pressures and linguistic conventions of his or her own time – textual historians such as Gabrielle Spiegel (b. 1943) have applied this insight usefully to the interpretation of medieval chronicles. In other words, the sources themselves are already interpreting the past when the historian first confronts them, and few historians would now endorse Fustel de Coulanges' optimistic admonition to a group of nineteenth-century students that it was not he who spoke to them but 'history, which speaks through me'. Yet while postmodernism has been highly influential in literature and language departments, it has remained at best a dissenting voice in most history departments; it has, however, found a receptive audience among historians of gender, and among new cultural historians for whom it has provided a set of categories to replace those once derived from Marx.

De-centring the West: Postcolonialism

The postmodern project has intersected and overlapped with a contemporary intellectual movement, postcolonial studies. The two are not identical and have different origins and agendas, but they exhibit some features in common. Like postmodernism, postcolonialism is a rather broad term that includes the Indian 'Subaltern studies' approach (in its early days, more a South Asian answer to E. P. Thompson's 'history from below') and the 'Orientalist' critique of the Palestinian scholar Edward Said (1935–2003). Postcolonialism is, the Sinologist Prasenjit Duara (b. 1950) has observed, less a theory than a critique of its own 'other' – often defined as a broad 'post-Enlightenment' agenda characterized by reason, progress, the unstoppable increase of Western cultural and economic dominance, and even the false notion of the stability of the nation-state. Anticipated in mid-century by Caribbean writers such as Frantz Fanon (1925–61) and C. L. R. James (1901–89), postcolonialism is now often associated with Said (whose 1978 book *Orientalism* is a key text), and with a number of prominent Indian-born authors (many of them from other disciplines than history) such as the literary critics Homi K. Bhabha (b. 1949) and Gayatri Chakravorty Spivak (b. 1942), the political scientist Partha Chatterjee (b. 1947) and the psychologist and social critic Ashis Nandy (b. 1937).

Postcolonialism as a critical tool has been deployed most widely in Indian or Middle Eastern studies, and has overlapped with postmodernism in having the common goal of destabilizing, subverting or de-centring existing master-narratives (in particular those created and imposed by colonial powers or their indigenous elite allies) in favour of the local and previously marginalized, and reading texts and documents 'against the grain' to detect what they do not say as much as what they do. Postcolonialism has redirected scholarship concerned with former colonies such as India towards the subjected masses rather than the imperial rulers and their Indian elite political successors. The Subaltern Studies Group, a 'school' of Indian historiography founded by Ranajit Guha (b. 1922), is a prominent example of this latter trend, critical not only of pre-Independence historiography but also of the rewriting of history after 1947 into simply a counter-history with roles reversed, focused on indigenous political elites and omitting nine-tenths of the population. The Subaltern agenda prioritizes the subordinate and the voiceless, the local and regional rather than the national – 'subaltern' in this sense is a term derived from Antonio Gramsci. Spivak, among the literary theorists associated with the group (and a key link with the postmodernists as a translator of Derrida), has extended the Subaltern approach to feminist topics. In recent years, some early Subalternists such as the social historian Sumit Sarkar (b. 1939) have broken with the movement's increasing radicalism and its associations with postmodernism. A good many others, however, have shifted away from Marxist categories of analysis towards postmodern concerns with deconstructing the language of colonialism. In some cases, they reject Western historicity itself as a tool of imperial control, born of the Enlightenment's progressivist agenda, and enabling a 'dominance without hegemony' over India's (and, by extension, other colonized countries') true sense of the past, a sense that must be liberated from the seemingly inevitable Hegelian story of progress to nationhood.

This repudiation of Western historicity by Indian postcolonial critics is not entirely new. A powerful early statement of the position, long before the current discussions, came from no less a figure than Mohandas K. Gandhi (1869–1948), who rejected not only British rule but ultimately much of Western culture, including history. The Mahatma saw European modernization as part of India's problem, not its solution, and was of a view that Indians would be better off without history. 'It is my pet theory', he said, 'that our Hindu ancestors solved the question for us by ignoring history as understood today and by building on slight events their philosophical structure.' Ancient epics such as the *Mahabharata* were not, *pace* Sir William Jones, remotely like a history: they were *better* than histories, since they contained eternal truths, portrayed allegorically. In fact, said Gandhi, not just India but the world might profit from a bit less history, because history is at best a pathology of things that have gone badly wrong. History cannot record harmony, peace and love because it must necessarily focus on rupture and discontinuity rather than on the non-violence that Gandhi championed. Gandhi's position thus diverged from that of his close associate Nehru, the earlier nationalist–novelist Bankim Chatterjee, and the poet Tagore (see above, pp. 199–200), as well as pre-Independence historians in the colonial system such as Jadunath Sarkar, for all of whom history (despite their differing views on how it should be done) was an essential ingredient in the construction of nationhood. And it anticipates what Gayatri Spivak described as 'epistemic violence', the imperialist project to eradicate indigenous forms of knowledge and to Westernize and limit the very terms and conditions under which 'true' history can be written. This is the same charge levelled by Latin Americanists such as the Argentine-born Duke University scholar Walter D. Mignolo (b. 1941) at the first wave of European overseas imperialism in the sixteenth century, the decisive moment at which the Western form of 'modernity' became dominant, to the exclusion of what he preferred to call 'decolonial' alternatives. And a fellow US-based Latin Americanist, the Viennese-born anthropologist Eric R. Wolf (1923–99), argued in a 1982 book (the title of which has become virtually a catch-phrase), *Europe and the People without History*, that mainstream historiography had ignored the agency of the peoples subordinated in the expansion of Europe since the fifteenth century, and failed to take note of them in historical writing.

The postcolonial agenda has spread well beyond the regions of the world that gave it birth, overlapping with slightly older, more economically focused anti-colonial critiques such as 'dependency theory', a model adduced in the 1960s to explain the unequal relationship between a developed colonizing north and underdeveloped colonized south, especially Latin America and Africa. Later twentieth-century Latin American historians, for instance, have come to view Western historical scholarship as much more monolithic and alien than did their nineteenth-century precursors. However, fierce criticism of the imperial, Westernizing enterprise had rather older, and most often Marxist, origins, for instance in African and Caribbean 'diasporic' historiography. Parallels to the early twentieth-century Indian redeployment of European historical methods against British colonialism can be found in the writings of the Trinidadian historian–politician Eric Williams (1911–81) and in Williams' one-time teacher C. L. R. James. With an intellectual parentage going back to Michelet (whose sympathetic treatment of the French Revolution he much admired), James offered in *The Black Jacobins* (1938) a Marxist analysis of the Haitian slave revolt of the late eighteenth century and its interconnection with contemporary events in France. Revisiting his book in the early 1960s, in the wake of Fidel Castro's successful revolution in Cuba but despairing of much of the rest of the West Indies (still dominated by wealthy white minorities, American-backed dictators and cooperative black middle classes), James anticipated the Subaltern critique by nearly two decades, declaring that little had changed in the teaching of history since the European withdrawal, since it was still a propaganda tool of ruling elites rather than a means of grappling honestly with the past. A Norwegian Africanist, Finn Fuglestad (b. 1942), made a similar point with respect to African historiography, asserting that the response of his colleagues to Hugh Trevor-Roper's notorious provocation (see above, p. 260) had fallen into the 'trap' of agreeing with Trevor-Roper that only 'purposive movement' in history was worthy of study, thereby unwittingly validating his Eurocentric views and furthering the imposition of a Western-style historiography on cultures with a very different relation to the past.

History Wars, Revisionism and the Problematic Relations of 'Memory' and 'History'

In its most extreme versions postmodernism hearkens back to Renaissance Pyrrhonism in its radical denial of the fixity of any historical meaning, the existence of any external reality beyond language and the impossibility of making 'true' statements about the past. It is a variant of what historians have for a very long time called 'revisionism', with one important difference: unlike mainstream revisionist historians, who debate particular interpretations of events but generally share a common vocabulary and set of reference points (usually key events, individuals or structures), postmodernists question the very parameters within which meaningful argument can occur. A conclusion derived from this – that any interpretation of history is no more or less valid than another – while seemingly liberal, also opens the door to the legitimation of morally repugnant positions such as Holocaust denial. These are positions that most postmodernists would presumably not wish to claim, and a compromise response (articulated by Hayden White) is that the *fact* of the Holocaust is beyond dispute, but its *meaning* will shift as it is viewed over time from different perspectives and in light of current concerns such as the Palestinian–Israeli conflict. The historicity of the Holocaust – its occurrence as opposed to its significance – has come to the fore in recent years through a number of celebrated cases which had virtually nothing to do with postmodern theorizing, perhaps most notoriously the libel suit brought in the 1990s by Holocaust denier David Irving (b. 1938), a prolific writer outside the academy, against the American historian Deborah Lipstadt (b. 1947). Lipstadt had accused Irving of wilful selectivity, misreading and distortion of evidence to support his theories. The ensuing civil trial involved the historian Richard Evans (b. 1947) and a team of graduate students scrutinizing Irving's research intensively, the results of which were the utter demolition of Irving's arguments and a resounding vindication of Lipstadt and her publisher.

Holocaust denial is an egregious, hot-button example of what is at issue when perceptions of the past, heavily freighted with moral views of right and wrong, come into conflict with historians' sense of their right to 'tell the truth as they see it' – something that has been a tension in historiography virtually as long as there have been historians. Irving, and Holocaust deniers generally, rarely appeal to postmodernism or relativism in formulating their arguments: it is not a matter, in such cases, that their view may be as valid as the next person's, so much as asserting that the 'facts' as they see them support an alternative 'truth' that should displace publicly held orthodoxy. (Recent US politics, complete with the phrases 'alternative facts' and 'fake news', suggests that such views are, disturbingly, more widely held than one would like to believe.) In the Irving–Lipstadt case, historical research was adduced to explode Irving's arguments, reveal their evidentiary flimsiness and methodological flaws, and thereby sink his claim to having been libelled. Irving claimed to be telling the truth and practising proper, document-based historical method; the defendants and their expert witness accused him of deliberate sins of distortion, omission and manipulation of evidence. But other cases of prominent historiographical conflict are often less clear-cut. This can be because the issues themselves are more ambiguous and (marginally) less loaded, or because the evidence is more equivocal. These also involve conflicts between historians' statements about the past and public perceptions of what actually happened. The difference is that in these cases, the historians themselves, often in significant numbers, are either badly divided on the evidence and how to interpret it, or are ranged against powerful extra-professional interests: government, veterans' groups and nationalist or religious movements.

As noted in earlier chapters, public disagreement over history and especially over its influence in education is not especially new, having been an issue in some of the nation-building debates of nineteenth-century Europe and Latin America. University and especially school textbooks have been a site of ideological conflict for well over a century as, even in democratic regimes, both government agendas and public sensibilities change. In India during the late 1970s, several historians were criticized by the government of the day for being 'soft' on Islam's history in India and insufficiently pro-Hindu. Islamic regimes have been similarly tough on historians seen as critical of or blasphemous towards, revered figures such as the Prophet Muhammad. The governing regime of Recep Tayyip Erdoğan in Turkey conducted an academic purge following a failed coup in 2016, and as recently as spring 2017 was pursuing two historians accused of denigrating the memory of Turkey's modern founder Atatürk (somewhat oddly, given Erdoğan's apparent wish to undo much of Atatürk's secularist reforms).

The 1980s and 1990s saw a growing number of such episodes around the world. In Canada, a 1992 television series on the Second World War, which questioned the necessity of the Allies' intensive bombing campaign, enraged veterans, leading to the programme's producers and writers being condemned in Parliament. More recently, an exhibit at the new Canadian War Museum has inflamed passions once again, with veterans complaining about various aspects of its representation of the Second World War, such as the depiction of the bombing campaign, or the display of paintings showing Canadian soldiers engaged in atrocities. Museums, because of their wide accessibility to the public, many of whom will never read a history book, are especially vulnerable to popular criticism of the ways in which they present the past. They are highly visual, but their selection of exhibits, and the highly simplified, brief descriptions they must provide, can easily provoke reaction if the subject discussed has anything to do with a controversial past event. This need not be a recent episode: plans in various parts of the world to mark the five hundredth anniversary of Columbus' 1492 voyage were highly polarizing, with critics finding nothing to celebrate in the conquest and depopulation of the Americas. More often than not, however, the troublesome events are of more recent vintage, with living survivors leading the charge, as in the Canadian cases. These controversies fall into the grey zone between memory and history. A famous example occurred in the United States in 1994 around a planned Smithsonian Institution exhibit to mark the fiftieth anniversary of the dropping of the atomic bomb on Hiroshima. The suggestion in the exhibit – that the decision to drop the bomb was morally complex and perhaps even unnecessary – aroused the fury of

US Air Force veterans and conservative politicians. In vain its curators tried to tack between creating an exhibit that would make veterans 'feel good' and one that could also discuss the long-term legacy of the creation and use of atomic weapons. Unsuccessful attempts followed to rewrite the historical script, and by the time the affair was finished, advisory committee members had quit in protest against the watering down of scholarly standards, and the Director of the National Air and Space Museum had resigned. In the end, the exhibit itself was cancelled in early 1995.

Such controversies are not limited to museums. Occasionally, academic historiography, most of the time safe within its collegiate cloister, finds itself uncomfortably under the public spotlight. The above-mentioned German *Historikerstreit* is one such example. The Australian 'History Wars' are another. These began with that country's 1988 bicentennial and continue three decades later. The Australian conflicts also had a museums aspect, but went well beyond this to include a wider range of issues and historical media. The 'wars' pitted liberal and left-of-centre historians against their ideological opponents both within the profession and outside, the Liberal–Nationalist coalition government of Prime Minister John Howard becoming an active participant. In the wake of his 1996 electoral victory, Howard himself denounced what the nationalist historian Geoffrey Blainey (b. 1930) called 'Black Armband History', an 'insidious' development in Australian political life that seeks 'to rewrite Australian history in the service of a partisan political cause'. Various historians had for some time been painting a rather critical picture of the treatment of the aboriginals by nineteenth-century whites. The fear that this was going to place Australia in the same league as other countries with genocidal histories, along with comparisons to the Holocaust, induced sharp reaction. Historians such as Keith Windschuttle (b. 1942, a one-time leftist turned conservative, and also an outspoken critic of postmodernism and feminism) weighed in with alternative explanations of depopulation such as disease and internecine violence, purporting to demonstrate that the numbers of aboriginal dead at white hands had been exaggerated by propaganda, and attacking opponents' apparent reliance on aboriginal oral tradition. One Australian journalist claimed that the school history curriculum had been hijacked by left-wing, politically correct ideologues. He wanted it back with the 'community' to whom it belonged – showing no awareness of the fact that the community itself was hardly a homogeneous entity.

The Australian controversy involved a systematic attempt by a democratically elected government and the conservative press to limit discussion, and to redress the perceived liberal–leftist bias of the profession and the influence of special interests. One may agree or disagree with the perspective and at the same time worry about the control of textbooks as a worldwide threat to open historical discourse and to the training of students to think critically about the past. Yet the metaphor of 'past-as-property' is not, in itself, entirely misplaced, raising, as it does, ethical issues that ought at least to be reflected upon. What many of these disputes come down to is a variant of the questions 'Who owns the past?' or 'Whose history is it, anyway?' Do members of groups of different kinds have a stronger or even an exclusive claim to be the authentic historians of their common past? Why should the alternative views of outsiders be permitted to 'steal the voices' of the dead? Should even sympathetic outsiders be permitted to capitalize on past injustice and misery in order to sell books and achieve career advancement? Are some episodes – the Holocaust, for instance – so horrific and beyond the bounds of normal human experience that they are simply indescribable historically? And what of the conflict between the personal recollections of participants and the evidence used by historians: does Major Smith's right, as a decorated Falklands War veteran, to his own and his peers' view of the war, trump Professor Jones' academic freedom to use evidence to construct an interpretation contrary to Smith's?

Related questions apply to almost any history that is defined in terms of a particular group: to what degree must one be *of* that group in order to be able to study and render an opinion on its past? Can men legitimately do women's history, and can a white man research native or African-American history? Several white historians of slavery were attacked by black scholars in the 1960s and early 1970s: in a tragic incident, a sympathetic young white historian, Robert Starobin (d. 1971) was driven to suicide after being publicly humiliated by black speakers at a convention. The Haitian ethnohistorian Michel-Rolph Trouillot (1949–2012) once recalled teaching a class on the Black Experience in the Americas, during which a young woman had asked why he made the class read 'all those white scholars. What can they know about slavery? Where were they when we were jumping off the boats?' Scholars of race differ on this question: members of the Subaltern School, and Edward Said, have resisted the notion that the study of oppression is exclusively the property of the oppressed. Others, as Anna Green and Kathleen Troup noted in a recent anthology, regard attempts by liberal outsiders to represent that which they haven't experienced as ill-founded at best, and at worst a further form of colonization through cultural appropriation. Is 'integration' of the untold histories of the marginal and conquered into the 'main stream' nothing more than yet another form of cultural assimilation – a variant of Spivak's 'epistemic violence'?

From this perspective, the indigenous peoples of 'settler' colonial nations (in North and South America, Polynesia and Australasia principally), as well as European populations such as the Sinti or Roma, have a special claim on our historical consciences. Few subjugated populations have suffered the same degree of demographic devastation as have aboriginals, along with the purging or marginalization of their beliefs and traditions about the past – to say nothing of the general misunderstanding and mischaracterization of those beliefs. Pre-contact indigenous populations, as we saw in Chapter 3, relied heavily, if not entirely, on pictorial and oral sources, and their historical narratives appeared to text-obsessed white observers as more fantastic myth than concrete reality. The four centuries after Cortés did little to alter this view, and in 1915 the anthropologist Robert Lowie argued that '[American] Indian tradition is historically worthless'. We have come a long way since then, but there is an equal danger in the opposite viewpoint, which imposes European categories on indigenous records that superficially resemble, but are fundamentally different from, our own, and attempts to make them into the same kind of history, with the same purposes, that we commonly practise. An example of the latter fallacy occurred when a white scholar, Helen Blish, argued that Amos Bad Heart Bull's (*c.* 1868–1913) sketchbooks on the Oglala Sioux were evidence that his purpose was clearly the same as Herodotus' – that he was 'attempting to preserve the record of the life of a people' and 'consequently *earns the name historian'*. Bad Heart Bull probably had several different intentions, some of which do loosely resemble those of Herodotus (and indeed, rather more like Sima Qian, he was continuing a function his father had exercised for the tribe). But it is doubtful that he was emulating the ancient Greek pattern, even unconsciously, or that he would have seen the posthumous bestowal of 'the name historian' as a desirable honorific. In fact, Bad Heart Bull left his sketchbook to his sister, and it was buried with her when she died, following Oglala custom, suggesting that the last thing its author had in mind was the creation of a permanent record. Indigenous history, and historicity, have received considerable attention, especially from ethno-historians (often working in anthropology rather than history depart-ments) over the past generation, with greater sensitivity to its social functions, which are often of a religious or ritualistic rather than strictly commemorative or explanatory nature.

Yet a great deal of suspicion remains between the colonized and the colonizer or the occupied and occupier, manifested in the recent wave of attempts at 'truth and reconciliation'. These questions become even more complex when dealing with a past still in living memory: Japanese exploitation of Korean 'comfort women'; Apartheid-era persecution in South Africa; the 1994 genocide in Rwanda; and Aboriginal residential schools in Canada. The history wars in virtually every continent have heightened awareness of the intimate connection between history and memory, which has emerged in recent years as a subject of inquiry in its own right. This has taken various forms, of which perhaps the most well-known is the analysis of what might be called national 'memory cultures'. The work of the sociologist Maurice Halbwachs (1877–1945), who died in Buchenwald, has been fundamental in the development of concepts such as 'collective memory', 'social memory', 'shared memory' and so on. There is now a host of works on the subject, as well as a journal devoted to it (*History and Memory*, est. 1989), and memory has provided a new point of intersection for history with philosophy, anthropology, psychology and sociology. The study of memory has increasingly crossed agendas with postmodernism, particularly with respect to 'traumatic' episodes of the past such as the Holocaust, which signals not the continuity of History beloved since the eighteenth century but its discontinuities, ruptures and radical turns, emphasized alike in Foucault's 'archaeologies' of knowledge and in contemporary interest in recapturing the 'sublime' aspect of histor-ical experience, a direct, powerful, emotive and even overwhelming connection with the past that works against the cautious, 'objective' distance most historians have preferred to maintain since the end of Romanticism.

There have been useful studies on the significance of the destruction or wholesale removal of archival material on 'community' memory.

It might be assumed that every modern nation has a strong national memory, in the sense of shared beliefs about what happened in recent decades, and indeed in more remote times, and what it means. This does not, however, appear to be the case. In France, Pierre Nora (b. 1931) has emphasized the significance of *lieux de mémoire*, literally 'sites of memory', in promoting a robust sense of the past. These are locations scattered around the countryside, or in cities, marking particular events. They may be as localized as a war memorial, church or statue, or as national or global as a celebrated battlefield such as Waterloo or Gettysburg; and they can be man-made or natural. The key feature that these sites have in common is association with an event or chain of events in the past. Moreover, much of the remembered past has, over time, been rather more based on locality or community than nation, where it has intermixed with oral tradition, something that the travelling antiquaries and missionaries of the early modern era knew very well.

The precise relation between memory and history is ambiguous, and consideration of it often circles back to other and older methodological issues such as the relative value of written and oral sources, or the effectiveness of oral history as a means to capture recollections of the past from those who lived through it before they die. The most recent five or six decades prior to a historian's present have been of considerable interest at various times, and here 'oral history' has come into its own, especially in dealing with the large majority of persons, often of working-class background, who will never commit their experiences to paper. Although it shares some features in common, modern oral history is to be distinguished from the study of oral tradition that we have seen in this and earlier chapters (though the two are sometimes grouped together as 'oral historiography'). Oral tradition deals with more remote periods beyond the memory of persons still living, and thus crossing multiple generations. Oral history, in contrast, is a set of methodologies, mainly refined in the 1960s and 1970s, for interviewing human subjects and extracting from them their personal recollections about particular events in history through which they lived, or simply recording their descriptions of their own past lives and experiences. Although open to some of the same objections as oral tradition, in particular the natural human tendency to see one's own past through the prism of intervening times, or simply to misremember, oral history now has a well-established set of standards or 'best practices' for accurately and ethically coaxing testimony from living human beings. A number of important archives of oral interviews have been created around the world to preserve the testimony of particular groups – Holocaust survivors for example, as captured in the hundreds of hours of interviews conducted by Claude Lanzmann (1925–2018) for his 1985 film, *Shoah* – before their voices are permanently silenced. It can even be argued that this is the only thoroughly truthful way to represent something so horrific as the Holocaust. The Israeli-American historian Saul Friedländer (b. 1932), an early exponent of psychohistory, has proposed that the Nazi Final Solution was so distinctive and *sui generis* in both intention and implementation that it resists either narrative representation or even attempts at 'historicization'. But that sentiment will not likely endure once the event has faded entirely from living memory, as it will within one or two more decades.

Conclusion

Commenting on the writings of Michel Foucault in 1979, the intellectual historian Allan Megill (b. 1947) observed that while the French writer ought not to be taken seriously 'as a historian' (in the sense of someone committed to representing the past *wie es eigentlich gewesen*), he needed to be taken seriously 'as an indication of where history now stands'. Megill went further, noting that 'Even as orthodox historiography has been expanding the range of its subject matter and rendering its methodology more and more technical and sophisticated, two countermovements have been occurring: the higher intellectual foundations of history have been crumbling, and its accessibility and immediacy have been declining.' A generation later, these tendencies have if anything hastened in a post-Cold War, digital age.

This chapter has traversed a great deal of ground. But despite its length, it has in temporal terms addressed only a fraction of the entire period covered by this book. That is a reflection of contemporaneity – it describes a historiographical world very much with us, unlike the culture of Ranke, or Gibbon, or Motoori Norinaga, much less that of Ibn Khaldun. The comparable historical culture of antiquity is by this standard incredibly remote, though in fact many readers of this book will know much more of Herodotus and Tacitus than they do of many of the more recent names, especially those from outside the European tradition of historiography. In part this is because we stand at the end of a much longer period through most of which there were relatively few historians, and the surviving names from the most remote times have had the benefit of long circulation and familiarity. One wonders how many of the names mentioned in the present chapter (a minuscule fraction of the notables who could be referenced) will have such longevity. And that raises two bigger questions: first, what, if any is the future of these assorted sub-fields and sub-sub-fields of history; and second, is there a risk that, after twenty-five or so centuries of increasing historicity (and most recently, an increasingly *fragmented* historicity), we have simply exhausted both the past and our capacity to understand or even take interest in it? Are we close, in other words, to 'the end of history'? In our final chapter we will attempt an answer.

QUESTIONS FOR DISCUSSION

1. Are some historical topics more likely to create controversy than others? What are some of the things that have got historians into trouble over the past six or seven decades?
2. Do you accept the assertions of some postmodernists that (a) there is no ascertainable objective truth about the past that can be discerned; (b) that history is essentially indistinguishable from literature – and that the historical act of telling a story in and of itself distorts the actual reality of the past?
3. What are some of the roles that history has played in the 'decolonization' of the world since the Second World War? Do you accept the notion that mainstream academic history has been an important tool both for the imposition of empires and for their liberation?
4. Can history play a role in the 'reconciliation' of formerly conflicting nations or between rulers and historically marginalized populations?
5. In what ways does history interact with 'collective memory'? In what ways has the academic sense of 'what actually happened' conflicted with popular or official beliefs about this?
6. Is history now more fragmented into specializations than at any time in the past? Has there ever been a time when the study of the past was more cohesive than now, or when there was greater consensus as to appropriate subjects?

7. How would you evaluate the virtues of microhistory compared with national history? What about the weaknesses of each?
8. Why is Marxist historiography nearly dead in some countries and alive and well in others?
9. How have disciplines outside history interacted with it in recent decades and what have been the benefits? What are the challenges of practising 'interdisciplinary' history?
10. How important is it that historians be members of the communities or groups they are studying? Can or should a white scholar write about black history? Can a man write women's history?

Further Reading

General

Ferro, Marc, *The Use and Abuse of History, or, How the Past is Taught to Children*, trans. N. Stone and A. Brown, rev. edn (New York and London, 2003)

Green, Anna and Kathleen Troup (eds), *The Houses of History: A Critical Reader in Twentieth-Century History and Theory* (New York and Manchester, 1999)

Iggers, Georg G., *Historiography in the Twentieth Century: From Scientific Objectivity to the Postmodern Challenge* (Middletown, CT, 1997)

Lambert, Peter and Phillipp Schofield (eds), *Making History: An Introduction to the History and Practices of a Discipline* (London and New York, 2004)

Maza, Sarah, *Thinking about History* (Chicago, IL, 2017)

Schneider, Axel and Daniel Woolf (eds), *The Oxford History of Historical Writing*, Vol. 5: *Historical Writing Since 1945* (Oxford, 2011)

The Annales Historians; Microhistory

Brooks, James F., Christopher R. N. DeCorse and John Walton (eds), *Small Worlds: Method, Meaning, and Narrative in Microhistory* (Santa Fe, NM, 2008)

Burguière, André, *The Annales School: An Intellectual History* (Ithaca, NY, 2009)

Burke, Peter, *The French Historical Revolution: The Annales School, 1929–2014*, 2nd edn (Stanford, CA, 2015)

Clark, Stuart (ed.), *The Annales School* (London, 1999)

Fink, Carole, *Marc Bloch: A Life in History* (Cambridge, 1989)
Magnússon, Sigurður Gylfi and István M. Szijártó, *What is Microhistory? Theory and Practice* (Abingdon, 2013)
Tendler, Joseph, *Opponents of the Annales School* (Basingstoke and New York, 2013)

History and the Social Sciences

Barzun, Jacques, *Clio and the Doctors: Psychohistory, Quanto-history, and History* (Chicago, IL, 1974)
Burke, Peter, *History and Social Theory*, 2nd edn (Ithaca, NY, 2005)
Fogel, R. W. and G. R. Elton, *Which Road to the Past? Two Views of History* (New Haven, CT, 1983)
Hempel, Carl G., 'The Function of General Laws in History', *Journal of Philosophy* 39.2 (1942): 35–48
Mahoney, James and Dietrich Rueschemeyer (eds), *Comparative Historical Analysis in the Social Sciences* (Cambridge and New York, 2003)
Monkkonen, Eric H. (ed.), *Engaging the Past: The Uses of History across the Social Sciences* (Durham, NC and London, 1994)
Roseberry, William R., *Anthropologies and Histories: Essays in Culture, History, and Political Economy* (Rutgers, NJ, 1989)
Thomas, Keith, 'History and Anthropology', *Past and Present* 24.1 (1963): 3–24

History under Dictatorships and Authoritarian Regimes

Baets, Antoon de, *Censorship of Historical Thought: A World Guide, 1945–2000* (Westport, CT, 2002)
Barber, John, *Soviet Historians in Crisis, 1928–1932* (Basingstoke, 1981)
Berger, Stefan, *The Search for Normality: National Historical Consciousness in Germany since 1800* (London, 1997)
Brunnbauer, Ulf (ed.), *(Re)Writing History: Historiography in Southeast Europe after Socialism* (Münster, 2004)
Dirlik, Arif, *Revolution and History: The Origins of Marxist Historiography in China, 1919–1937* (Berkeley, CA, 1978)
Enteen, George M., *The Soviet Scholar-Bureaucrat: M. N. Pokrovskii and the Society of Marxist Historians* (University Park, PA, 1978)
Feuerwerker, Albert (ed.), *History in Communist China* (Cambridge, MA, 1968)
Knowlton, James and Truett Cates (trans.), *Forever in the Shadow of Hitler? Original Documents of the Historikerstreit, the Controversy*

Concerning the Singularity of the Holocaust (Atlantic Highlands, NJ, 1993)

Low, A. D., *The Third Reich and the Holocaust in German Historiography: Toward the Historikerstreit of the mid-1980s* (Boulder, CO, 1994)

Maier, Charles S., *The Unmasterable Past: History, Holocaust, and German National Identity* (Cambridge, MA, 1988)

Markwick, Roger D., *Rewriting History in Soviet Russia: The Politics of Revisionist Historiography, 1956–1974* (Basingstoke and New York, 2001)

McGregor, Katharine E., *History in Uniform: Military Ideology and the Construction of Indonesia's Past* (Honolulu, 2007)

Nozaki, Yoshiko, *War Memory, Nationalism, and Education in Postwar Japan, 1945–2007: The Japanese History Textbook Controversy and Ienaga Saburo's Court Challenges* (London, 2008)

Plokhy, Serhii, *Unmaking Imperial Russia: Mykhailo Hrushevsky and the Writing of Ukrainian History* (Toronto, 2005)

Saaler, Sven, *Politics, Memory and Public Opinion: The History Textbook Controversy and Japanese Society* (Munich, 2005)

Schneider, Laurence A., *Ku Chieh-kang and China's New History: Nationalism and the Quest for Alternative Traditions* (Berkeley, CA, 1971)

Schönwälder, Karen, 'The Fascination of Power: Historical Scholarship in Nazi Germany', *History Workshop Journal* 43 (1997): 133–53

Wang, Q. Edward and Georg G. Iggers (eds), *Marxist Historiographies: A Global Perspective* (Abingdon and New York, 2016)

History from Below

Eley, Geoff, *A Crooked Line: From Cultural History to the History of Society* (Ann Arbor, MI, 2005)

Hill, Christopher, R. H. Hilton and E. J. Hobsbawm, '*Past and Present*: Origins and Early Years', *Past and Present* 100 (1983): 3–14

Hobsbawm, Eric, *On History* (London, 1997)

Kaye, Harvey J., *The British Marxist Historians: An Introductory Analysis* (Cambridge and Oxford, 1984)

The Education of Desire: Marxists and the Writing of History (New York, 1992)

Thompson, E. P., *The Making of the English Working Class* (London, 1963)

Varieties of Intellectual History

Burke, Peter, *What is Cultural History?* (Cambridge, 2004)

Friedländer, Saul, *History and Psychoanalysis: An Inquiry into the Possibilities and Limits of Psychohistory* (New York, 1978)

Gay, Peter, *Freud for Historians* (New York, 1985)

Grafton, Anthony, 'The History of Ideas: Precept and Practice, 1950–2000 and Beyond', *Journal of the History of Ideas* 67.1 (2006): 1–32

Hunt, Lynn, 'Psychology, Psychoanalysis and Historical Thought', in Lloyd Kramer and Sarah Maza (eds), *A Companion to Western Historical Thought* (Oxford, 2002), 337–56

Kelley, Donald R., *The Descent of Ideas: The History of Intellectual History* (Burlington, VT, 2002)

Kren, George M. and Leon H. Rappoport (eds), *Varieties of Psychohistory* (Englewood Cliffs, NJ, 1976)

Loewenberg, Peter, *Decoding the Past: The Psychohistorical Approach*, 2nd edn (New Brunswick, NJ, 1996)

McMahon, Darrin M. and Samuel Moyn (eds), *Rethinking Modern European Intellectual History* (Oxford, 2014)

Megill, Allan, 'Intellectual History and History', *Rethinking History* 8.4 (2004): 549–57

Moyn, Samuel and Andrew Sartori (eds), *Global Intellectual History* (New York, 2013)

Nakamura, Hajime, *Parallel Developments: A Comparative History of Ideas* (Tokyo and New York, 1975; rev. edn 1986)

Panikkar, K. N., 'The Intellectual History of Colonial India: Some Historiographical and Conceptual Questions', in Sabyasachi Bhattachaya and Romila Thapar (eds), *Situating Indian History* (Delhi, 1986), 403–33

Pernau, Margrit and Dominic Sachsenmaier (eds), *Global Conceptual History: A Reader* (London and New York, 2016)

Stannard, David E., *Shrinking History: On Freud and the Failure of Psychohistory* (New York, 1973)

Whatmore, Richard, *What is Intellectual History?* (Malden, MA and Cambridge, 2016)

From Women's History to Histories of Gender and Sexuality

(See also titles listed in previous chapter)

Alberti, Johanna, *Gender and the Historian* (Harlow, UK and New York, 2002)

Beard, Mary Ritter, *Woman as Force in History: A Study in Traditions and Realities* (New York, 1946)

Bennett, Judith M., *History Matters: Patriarchy and the Challenge of Feminism* (Philadelphia, PA, 2006)

Bynum, Caroline Walker, *Fragmentation and Redemption: Essays on Gender and the Human Body in Medieval Religion* (New York and Cambridge, MA, 1991)

Carroll, Berenice (ed.), *Liberating Women's History: Theoretical and Critical Essays* (Urbana and Chicago, IL and London, 1976)

Downs, Laura Lee, *Writing Gender History*, 2nd edn (London and New York, 2010)

Duby, Georges and Michelle Perrot (gen. eds), *A History of Women in the West*, 5 vols (Cambridge, MA, 1992–4)

Foley, Susan K., *Women in France since 1789: The Meanings of Difference* (Basingstoke, 2004)

Germer, Andrea, 'Feminist History in Japan: National and International Perspectives', *Intersections: Gender, History and Culture in the Asian Context* 9 (2003) http://intersections.anu.edu.au/issue9/germer.html (accessed 18 April 2018)

Lerner, Gerda, *The Creation of Patriarchy* (Oxford and New York, 1986)
The Creation of Feminist Consciousness: From the Middle Ages to 1870 (Oxford, 1993)

McIntosh, Marjorie K., *Working Women in English Society, 1300–1620* (Cambridge and New York, 2005)

Meriwether, Margaret Lee, *A Social History of Women and Gender in the Modern Middle East* (Boulder, CO, 1999)

Morgan, Sue (ed.), *The Feminist History Reader* (London, 2005)

Nadell, Pamela S. and Kate Haulman (eds), *Making Women's Histories: Beyond National Perspectives* (New York, 2013)

Norton, Mary Beth, 'Numbers Matter', in 'The Awakening: Women and Power in the Academy', *Chronicle of Higher Education* 64.28 (23 March 2018), https://www.chronicle.com/interactives/the-awakening?cid=wcontentgrid_hp_6 (accessed 6 April 2018)

Rowbotham, Sheila, *Hidden from History: 300 Years of Women's Oppression and the Fight Against It* (London, 1973)

Scott, Joan Wallach, *Gender and the Politics of History*, 30th anniversary edn (1988; New York, 2018)

Smith, Bonnie G. (ed.), *Women's History in Global Perspective*, 3 vols (Urbana, IL, 2004–5)

Sonbol, Amira El-Azhary, *Beyond the Exotic: Women's Histories in Islamic Societies* (Syracuse, NY, 2005)

White, Deborah Gray (ed.), *Telling Histories: Black Women Historians in the Ivory Tower* (Chapel Hill, NC, 2008)

Zinsser, Judith, *History and Feminism: A Glass Half Full* (New York, 1993)

Postwar African Historiography

Boahen, Adu, *Africa in the Twentieth Century: The Adu Boahen Reader*, ed. Toyin Falola (Trenton, NJ, 2004)

Fage, J. D. (ed.), *Africa Discovers her Past* (London, 1970)

Falola, Toyin (ed.), *African Historiography: Essays in Honour of Jacob Ade Ajayi* (Harlow, UK, 1993)

Falola, Toyin and Saheed Aderinto, *Nigeria, Nationalism, and Writing History* (Rochester, NY and Woodbridge, UK, 2010)

Harneit-Sievers, Axel (ed.), *A Place in the World: New Local Historiographies from Africa and South Asia* (Leiden, 2002)

Temu, Arnold and Bonaventure Swai, *Historians and Africanist History – A Critique: Post-Colonial Historiography Examined* (London, 1981)

Vansina, Jan, *Oral Tradition as History* (Madison, WI, 1985)

The Linguistic Turn: Postmodernism

Ankersmit, F. R., *Meaning, Truth, and Reference in Historical Representation* (Leuven, 2012)

Appleby, Joyce, Lynn Hunt and Margaret Jacob, *Telling the Truth about History* (New York, 1994)

Breisach, Ernst, *On the Future of History: The Postmodernist Challenge and its Aftermath* (Chicago, IL, 2003)

Clark, Elizabeth A., *History, Theory, Text: Historians and the Linguistic Turn* (Cambridge, MA, 2004)

Elton, G. R., *Return to Essentials: Some Reflections on the Present State of Historical Study* (Cambridge, 1991)

Ermarth, Elizabeth D., *History in the Discursive Condition: Reconsidering the Tools of Thought* (Abingdon and New York, 2011)

Evans, Richard J., *In Defence of History* (London, 1997)

Gunn, Simon, *History and Cultural Theory* (London, 2006)

Jenkins, Keith, *The Postmodern History Reader* (London, 1997)

Jobs, Sebastian and Alf Lüdtke (eds), *Unsettling History: Archiving and Narrating in Historiography* (Frankfurt and New York, 2010)

Klein, Kerwin Lee, *From History to Theory* (Berkeley, CA, Los Angeles and London, 2012)

LaCapra, Dominick, *History, Literature, Critical Theory* (Ithaca, NY, 2013)

Marwick, Arthur, 'Two Approaches to Historical Study: The Metaphysical (Including "Postmodernism") and the Historical', *Journal of Contemporary History* 30 (1995): 5–35

McCullagh, C. Behan, *The Logic of History: Putting Postmodernism in Perspective* (New York, 2004)

Megill, Allan, 'Foucault, Structuralism, and the Ends of History', *Journal of Modern History* 51.3 (1979): 451–503

Prophets of Extremity: Nietzsche, Heidegger, Foucault, Derrida (Berkeley, CA, 1985).

Palmer, Bryan D., *Descent into Discourse: The Reification of Language and the Writing of Social History* (Philadelphia, PA, 1990)

Paul, Herman, *Hayden White: The Historical Imagination* (Cambridge, 2011)

Poster, Mark, *Cultural History and Postmodernity: Disciplinary Readings and Challenges* (New York, 1997)

Roth, Michael S., 'Cultural Criticism and Political Theory: Hayden White's Rhetorics of History', in Roth (ed.), *The Ironist's Cage: Memory, Trauma, and the Construction of History* (New York, 1995), 137–47

Spiegel, Gabrielle M. (ed.), *Practicing History: New Directions in Historical Writing after the Linguistic Turn* (New York, 2005)

White, Hayden, 'The Burden of History', *History and Theory* 5 (1966): 111–34

Metahistory: The Historical Imagination in Nineteenth-Century Europe (Baltimore, MD, 1973)

The Content of the Form: Narrative Discourse and Historical Representation (Baltimore, MD, 1987)

'Response to Arthur Marwick', *Journal of Contemporary History* 30 (1995): 233–46

Windschuttle, Keith, *The Killing of History: How Literary Critics and Social Theorists are Murdering our Past* (New York, 1997)

Zagorin, Perez, 'Historiography and Postmodernism: Reconsiderations', *History and Theory* 26.3 (1987): 263–74

De-centring the West: Postcolonialism

Chakrabarty, Dipesh, *Provincializing Europe: Postcolonial Thought and Historical Difference* (Princeton, NJ, 2000)

Chatterjee, Partha, *The Nation and its Fragments: Colonial and Postcolonial Histories* (Princeton, NJ, 1993)

Dirlik, Arif, Vinay Bahl and Peter Gran (eds), *History after the Three Worlds: Post-Eurocentric Historiographies* (Oxford, 2000)

Duara, Prasenjit, *Rescuing History from the Nation: Questioning Narratives of Modern China* (Chicago, IL, 1995)

Fuglestad, Finn, 'The Trevor-Roper Trap or the Imperialism of History: An Essay', *History in Africa* 19 (1992): 309–26

Guha, Ranajit, *An Indian Historiography of India: A Nineteenth-Century Agenda and its Implications* (Calcutta and New Delhi, 1988)

Lal, Vinay, *The History of History: Politics and Scholarship in Modern India* (Oxford and New Delhi, 2003)

Nandy, Ashis, 'History's Forgotten Doubles', *History and Theory* 34.2 (1995): 44–66

Said, Edward, *Orientalism* (London, 1978)

Trouillot, Michel-Rolph, *Silencing the Past: Power and the Production of History* (Boston, MA, 1995)

Young, Robert, *White Mythologies: Writing History and the West* (London, 1990)

History Wars, Revisionism and the Problematic Relations of 'Memory' and 'History'

Barkan, Elazar, *The Guilt of Nations: Restitution and Negotiating Historical Injustices* (Baltimore, MD, 2000)

Carey, David Jr, *Our Elders Teach Us: Maya-Kaqchikel Historical Perspectives* (Tuscaloosa, AL, 2001)

Confino, Alon, *Germany as a Culture of Remembrance: Promises and Limits of Writing History* (Chapel Hill, NC, 2006)

Friedländer, Saul, *Memory, History, and the Extermination of the Jews of Europe* (Bloomington, IN, 1993)

Hein, Laura and Mark Selden (eds), *Censoring History: Citizenship and Memory in Japan, Germany, and the United States* (Armonk, NY and London, 2000)

Henige, David, *Oral Historiography* (London and New York, 1982)

Hill, Jonathan D. (ed.), *Rethinking History and Myth: Indigenous South American Perspectives on the Past* (Urbana and Chicago, IL, 1988)

Hutton, Patrick, *History as an Art of Memory* (Burlington, VT, 1993)

LaCapra, Dominick, *Representing the Holocaust: History, Theory, Trauma* (Ithaca, NY, 1994)

   Writing History, Writing Trauma (Baltimore, MD, 2001)

Lepore, Jill, *The Whites of their Eyes: The Tea Party's Revolution and the Battle over American History* (Princeton, NJ and Oxford, 2010)

Linenthal, Edward T. and Tom Engelhardt (eds), *History Wars: The Enola Gay and Other Battles for the American Past* (New York, 1996)

Macintyre, Stuart and Anna Clark, *The History Wars* (Carlton, Australia, 2003)

Morris-Suzuki, Tessa et al., *East Asia Beyond the History Wars: Confronting the Ghosts of Violence* (Abingdon and New York, 2013)

Nabokov, Peter, *A Forest of Time: American Indian Ways of History* (Cambridge, 2002)

Nash, Gary B., Charlotte Crabtree and Ross E. Dunn, *History on Trial: Culture Wars and the Teaching of the Past* (New York, 1997)

Nora, Pierre, 'Between Memory and History: *Les Lieux de Mémoire*', *Representations* 26 (1989): 7–25

Novick, Peter, *That Noble Dream: The 'Objectivity Question' and the American Historical Profession* (Cambridge, 1988)

Olick, Jeffrey K. (ed.), *States of Memory: Continuities, Conflicts, and Transformations in National Retrospection* (Durham, NC, 2003)

Rappaport, Joanne, *The Politics of Memory: Native Historical Interpretation in the Colombian Andes*, rev. edn (Durham, NC, 1998)

Thompson, Paul, *The Voice of the Past: Oral History*, 3rd edn (Oxford, 2000)

Vickers, Edward and Alisa Jones (eds), *History Education and National Identity in East Asia* (New York and London, 2005)

Whitehead, Neil L. (ed.), *Histories and Historicities in Amazonia* (Lincoln, NE and London, 2003)

Wiener, Jon, *Historians in Trouble: Plagiarism, Fraud, and Politics in the Ivory Tower* (New York, 2005)

Windschuttle, Keith, *The Fabrication of Aboriginal History*, Vol. 1: *Van Diemen's Land, 1803–1847* (Sydney, 2002)

7 | Where Do We Go from Here? Reflections, New Directions and Prognostications

The unfortunate peculiarity of the history of man is, that although its separate parts have been examined with considerable ability, hardly any one has attempted to combine them into a whole, and ascertain the way in which they are connected with each other . . . . historians, taken as a body, have never recognized the necessity of such a wide and preliminary study as would enable them to grasp their subject in the whole of its natural relations. Hence the singular spectacle of one historian being ignorant of political economy; another knowing nothing of law; another nothing of ecclesiastical affairs and changes of opinion; another neglecting the philosophy of statistics; and another physical science: although these topics are the most essential of all, inasmuch as they comprise the principal circumstances by which the temper and character of mankind have been affected, and in which they are displayed.

> H. T. Buckle, *History of Civilization in England*, Vol. 1
> (London, 1857), pp. 3–4

Of the various words that characterize historiography in the past several decades, one would have to be *fragmentation* – or, as Jeremy D. Popkin puts it in a recent history of the Western tradition of historical writing, 'glorious confusion'. A more charitable descriptor might be *diversity*, or perhaps more neutrally, *specialization*. This is not a new concern. There have always been those across all the global traditions we have surveyed in this book who called for integration of the various pieces of history into a meaningful whole. Even Ranke, albeit with a narrower view of the proper scope of history than would be shared today, worried about specialization and spent his last years attempting a *Weltgeschichte*; so did his younger contemporary, and sometime critic, the ancient historian Theodor Mommsen (1817–1903). And Henry Thomas Buckle, quoted in the epigraph to this chapter, issued perhaps the most explicit plea of the nineteenth century for what we would now call an interdisciplinary grasp of human history, involving

290

a range of subjects from physical science and statistics to law, politics and economics.

Quite apart from any ideological differences they may have, historians now routinely self-identify variously as political, military, family, gender, economic, social, environmental, intellectual or cultural. The expansion of university history departments throughout the world, especially in the 1960s and 1970s, along with considerably greater pressure on academics, since the 1980s, to publish early and often, has encouraged a high degree of sub-specialization, together with a proliferation of journals and book series (which the relatively recent advent of the internet shows no sign of slowing down given its capacity to offer a cheap alternative to conventional print). Although Marxism is much less prominent in most North American history departments, it continues to flourish in Europe, South America and Asia. And social history has been preserved, albeit now often disaggregated into various sub-sub-disciplines. There are periodic efforts to put history together again, such as the establishment in the late 1990s in the United States of a new Historical Society by the one-time leftist-turned-conservative Eugene Genovese (1930–2012) and others to redress the compartmentalization of history and its association with identity politics. The Canadian historian J. L. Granatstein (b. 1939) has made similar pleas. But 'putting back together' is often really only a polite way of saying that the agenda ought to be re-narrowed and focused on 'traditional topics' such as political and military history, at least partly on the grounds that these are overwhelmingly more popular as subjects among casual readers than more specialist works. Inaccessible jargon has also become a target (with some cause, though this presumes that academic history should somehow be more accessible than other disciplines, the sciences especially, which have technical terminology of their own) of those who believe that university-based historians have lost the ability to communicate clearly and in sentences understandable by a reasonably educated, non-specialist reader. Stylistic complaints against historians, too, are scarcely new – recall the complaints of Liu Zhiji against the composition-by-committee of the Tang History Bureau, of many Renaissance humanists about the unreadability of medieval chronicles, or of Enlightenment philosophes with respect to the fact-laden tomes of the erudite. Both Thomas Carlyle and Sir Walter Scott imagined a fictional character, whom they called 'Dryasdust', a presenter of facts without feeling. And the Spanish

philosopher José Ortega y Gasset (1883–1955) captured these sentiments in the first half of the twentieth century, lamenting historians'
failure to maintain an audience. 'I firmly believe that God will not
forgive the historians', Ortega wrote. 'Even the geologists have succeeded in awakening our interest in dead stones; but all that the
historians, who have the most fascinating subject in their hands, have
achieved is that less history is being read in Europe than before' (quoted
in K. Weintraub, *Visions of Culture*, 1966, p. 285). More recently,
American intellectual historian David Harlan commented in the late
1990s on the 'ungovernable proliferation of new historical subjects,
new perspectives, new interpretations, new theories and styles of
presentation'.

But is fragmentation necessarily a bad thing? The continual process
of splitting-off of topics and sub-topics (and with them, the creation of
new academic journals and sub-fields) has had the effect of keeping the
discipline alive and vital. It has permitted, over the past five or six
decades, the emergence of new perspectives on the past that, while no
less contestable than those they themselves contend against, have in the
main enriched, not impoverished, our understanding of both past and
present. In the work of scholars such as Robert Rosenstone (b. 1936),
a self-proclaimed postmodernist, they have opened up the study of the
past through alternative sources such as film. Rosenstone, an advocate
of experimental and non-linear forms of historical narrative, has suggested that 'film gives us a new form of history, what we might call
history as vision', connecting it with the earliest, oral forms of story-
telling. Others have shown that mundane forms of material culture
such as textiles can give us insights into past life which documents
cannot (archaeologists, of course, are used to working primarily with
material rather than textual artefacts). History may not, in fact,
demand of us a unified approach, and indeed it may never have.
Indeed, it has been a tenet of this book that the ideal of an imagined
past consensus on 'how to do history/what history should be about',
a consensus which is sometimes nostalgically mourned, is itself scarcely
more than the creation of Western modernism in the late nineteenth
and early twentieth centuries. Ranke was an extraordinarily influential
figure, but even in the Germany of his own day his views were not
beyond dispute.

So much for fragmentation and narrowness. But what of the charge
of irrelevance? US-based historians Jo Guldi and David Armitage

published in 2014 a short book entitled *The History Manifesto*, which was rather less concerned with the narrowing of *scope* in historical research than with that of chronological *scale*, arguing against 'short-termism' (the study of very brief periods of time) and in favour of a return to something like the *longue durée* of the early Annales historians. In Guldi's and Armitage's view, historians have abandoned the capacity to speak 'truth to power' and have also eschewed any intent of prognosticating on the future based on past trends, both functions that the current state of the world seems to demand of our ivory tower. (The issue of how publicly engaged historians should actually be is one of long standing: one thinks of the attitude of the French sixteenth-century philologist Jacques Cujas who saw no connection between his study of Roman law and contemporary politics, and some members of the ensuing generation such as Jean Bodin and François Hotman who, by contrast, deliberately turned their knowledge of the past into interventions on current affairs.) However, the growth in 'public history' programmes in many institutions mitigates against this worry to some degree. So, too, does the increasing recognition by graduate students and (often more reluctantly) their faculty supervisors that there are perfectly good uses for a PhD in history out in the 'real world', including work in the non-profit and NGO sectors. Even the business sector has need of historians and, it might be added, of an awareness of past economically disastrous decision-making.

In a sense, we may be cautiously circling back to a nineteenth-century environment when historians were frequently public intellectuals who saw their role as preparing citizens first and producing scholarship (an important) second. This is a welcome development, not least in an environment where much historical research and teaching is funded from public coffers. The summons back to relevance echoes the ancient Ciceronian notion of history's role as *magistra vitae* while urging a greater sense of ethical responsibility on the part of historians, of the Crocean 'duties of the living to the dead', and of an obligation to protect the past from interference and manipulation. It is also a call to put history into service anew to rectify the world's evils, which in a world of genocides, terrorist attacks and rampant commercial greed ought to be just as compelling a reason as it was for our ancestors. Others, however, have suggested that history needs to 'lighten up' and stop taking itself so seriously. Writing in the midst of the Australian history wars (see above, pp. 274–75), Beverley Kingston commented that the risk factor of bad history is simply not high enough to justify some of the excited political rhetoric around its potential misuse. Hayden White, in an exchange with historian Dirk Moses, argued that professional historians are simply not in a position to render ethical judgments about controversial events such as the Holocaust (or contribute to resolving related modern issues such as the Palestinian–Israeli conflict) because decades of training to be 'scientific' had robbed them of the ability to determine 'meaning' as opposed to mere 'facticity'. In short, there is little consensus as to whether history (at least as practised in the academy) *can* be an educator and potential force for good in the present – even if some of its acolytes would like this to be the case.

As noted in our previous chapter, the past forty years have produced a number of reactions against the various perceived enemies of Clio – interest group history, revisionism, social theory, feminism, postcolonialism and above all postmodernism. These have been exacerbated by a growing polarization on university campuses between critics of 'political correctness'/advocates of unfettered free speech on one side, and 'social justice warriors', students and their faculty allies (most often found in the humanities and social sciences) of an agenda of diversity, anti-colonialism and 'anti-oppression'. The response of the political right to perceived challenges has been just as sharp as that of the left in advocating its interests. An ill-fated attempt in 1994 to create 'National History Standards' in the United States and address a perceived decline in student knowledge of history brought down the collective wrath of conservative talk-show hosts, former National Endowment for the Humanities' chairwoman Lynne Cheney, and eventually the United States Senate. The level of discourse in many of the exchanges is sometimes absurdly simplistic and based on a presumption that history itself is reducible to discrete 'facts' (themselves assumed never to be in dispute) the interpretation of which ought never to be revised or even questioned. A similar effort in 2013 by Britain's then Secretary of State for Education, Michael Gove, to reform the history curriculum in schools with a revived stress on dates and chronology, and focus on the national past, ran into massive resistance from teachers and academics alike.

Reductiveness of this sort has afflicted the left as much as the right, and it has been magnified in the past decade by the power of the internet and especially social media. Since 2015, several American and

Canadian campuses have experienced conflicts over issues such as 'thought police' and the shouting down or protesting of controversial speakers. Conflicts have arisen on and off campuses regarding public monuments to historical figures with controversial pasts. A particularly violent instance of this occurred in August 2017, in Charlottesville, Virginia over the statue of Confederate general Robert E. Lee. The stakes were more than historical since the conflict was provoked by far-right white nationalists emboldened by political rhetoric from Washington, DC. The incident went well beyond even the debates about 'politically correct revisionism' that had occurred a few months earlier at Oxford and Princeton Universities concerning the memorialization of two other figures seen as racist by student leaders, Cecil Rhodes and Woodrow Wilson.

Leaving aside the nefarious reasons prompting the Charlottesville alt-right demonstrators, however, questions about when to commemorate, or un-commemorate, are not *ipso facto* illegitimate. They are part and parcel of dealing with, and making use of, Nietzsche's burden of the past, and a case can be made for 'owning up' to bad aspects of our past as much as trying to consign them to oblivion. Few beyond a neo-Nazi fringe would agree now that Hitler should be given a statue or a building – though with the recent return to favour and popular admiration in Russia of his contemporary dictator Josef Stalin, and continued public homage in China to Chairman Mao, one wonders how long even this will be the case. Just as comedy is sometimes defined as 'tragedy plus time', history in the longer term seems to forgive or trivialize even the greatest crimes, and Gavriel Rosenfeld has pointed in a recent book to the 'normalization' of the Nazi past in contemporary culture. As early as 1949 the Dutch historian Pieter Geyl anticipated this development in a book highlighting shifts in views of Napoleon – from Geyl's perspective a similar figure – among historians of the nineteenth century, and the philosopher Isaiah Berlin (1909–97) feared that future historians would fail to denounce the villains of history. But most historical figures fall into a rather greyer area than a Hitler or Stalin, or even Napoleon, their otherwise worthy lives spotted by attitudes and deeds, offensive to current sensibilities but not out of line with their contemporaries. Where do we draw the line?

One reason for a degree of reductiveness and over-simplification in many such debates about the past is that the discipline of history itself is sometimes reluctant to take sides, or even to provide advice.

Historians, like other professionals, are often forced to make hard choices between the presentation of highly nuanced and qualified views of the world (past and present) that will confuse and frustrate a general audience, and the simplification of complex issues ('dumbing down') into assertions easily accessible to a reading public, and suitable for 15-second sound-bites, or 140 character tweets. Social media have provided a forum for some especially vicious historical debates. One such debate flared up on Twitter in 2017 on the issue of whether Roman Britain had a 'diverse' population. Apart from the inevitable uninformed 'trolls', the 'debate' featured an eminent Cambridge classicist, Mary Beard (b. 1955; no relation to Mary Ritter Beard), arguing that there was indeed evidence for non-white populations in Roman Britain, against opponents who (incorrectly) deemed this absurd, politically correct revisionism. The old debate between the nature of historical knowledge versus the empiricism of the natural sciences even arose when a geneticist argued that science offered the only legitimate route to understanding the past, rather than 'historian hearsay bullshit' (a position repudiated almost immediately, it should be stressed, by at least one other geneticist). The subject itself was of less moment than the manner in which the 'debate' occurred. The abuse and lack of civil discourse evident in the Twitter exchanges (eschewed, it should be said, by Beard herself, who exercised admirable dignity and restraint) and commentary elsewhere on the internet would have embarrassed the most scathing book reviewer in an academic journal. Neither the hectoring tone nor the desire to reduce complexity to the point of absurdity augurs well for the 'democratization' of history on the internet if debate cannot be conducted reasonably and respectfully.

At the same time, the internet *has* proved an enormous boon in other ways. Major international collaborative projects are occurring across borders and oceans at an impressive pace, suggesting both a new cosmopolitanism and an international commitment to large-scale initiatives. Apart from the obvious uses (near-instantaneous email communication to fellow academics half-way around the world where one once relied on the slowness and unreliability of the international post), the world wide web has made sources previously inaccessible other than by travel to remote archives much more readily available for both teaching and research purposes. There is clearly something lost in not 'going to the sources' in their physical location – not least the sensory experience of handling original documents that

Michelet thought an essential element in connecting the historian with the past – or the 'sublime' feeling derived from visiting the site of ruins and decayed monuments. In his well-known book, *The Past is a Foreign Country* (1985), written before the digital revolution, David Lowenthal (1923–2018) comments on the 'immediacy effect' of touching original documents, or visiting exact sites described, and how that in turn can enrich the historian's own account of events (though he adds further on that for most uses, collection included, a replica object or document is as good as an original). The French historian Arlette Farge (b. 1941) made a related point in a more recent book, the original title of which literally translates as the 'taste' of the archive. But it should be remembered both that not every document is readily available (very old and fragile ones in particular) and that what one finds on-line may also be subsequently visited in person: one may choose to goggle as well as google. The improvement in search engines has also helped tremendously in the location of sources or in accessing existing datasets. The hunt for relevant documents and book titles that the present author carried out as a young doctoral student in the early 1980s, hunched over card catalogues in Oxford's Bodleian Library, took three months of hard labour; a modern high school pupil armed with the latest smart-phone could come up with the same result in minutes, virtually anywhere in the world near a cellphone tower.

This is likely not the end of digital technology's ability to assist both in historical research, and in the application of methods from other disciplines. 'Big data', currently all the rage in the private and public sectors, is scarcely a new concept in historiography, as Annalistes and cliometricians of the last century have shown. But current computing capacity should allow this to progress further and unearth hitherto unseen patterns in very disparate forms of evidence. And, if we can get past disciplinary turf-protection, it has the potential to enrich historical research with newer techniques developed by geneticists (notwithstanding the recent Twitter fight regarding Roman Britain), microbiologists, environmental scientists and palaeontologists, as well as more traditional allied disciplines such as archaeology.

In this spirit, there has emerged in the past decade or so the latest episode in the ultimate form of historiographical integration, the quest to recapture a past for the whole planet, freed from the metaphysical imaginings of a Hegel or the speculations of a Toynbee or Spengler. The casual reader with little time but much curiosity instinctively gravitates to the 'big picture'. The popularity of the first modern wave of 'world history' during the 1960s and 1970s produced an early tranche of reformed introductory courses in university curricula, competing with the older, Eurocentric 'Western Civ' or 'Plato to NATO' surveys. Practitioners such as Jerry H. Bentley (1949–2012), William H. McNeill (1917–2016) and his son, the environmental historian J. R. McNeill (b. 1954), have contributed well-known texts in the field. The earliest raft of such works, in the 1960s and 1970s, coincided with the heyday of historical sociology, with the beginnings of what is sometimes called 'world systems theory', articulated by social scientists such as the Fernand Braudel-trained American historical sociologist Immanuel Wallerstein (b. 1930), and with the comparative work of fellow sociologists Barrington Moore, Jr (1913–2005) and Theda Skocpol (see above, p. 235). The same period saw the early emergence of modern medical history and an interest in biological and ecological transference (for instance in Alfred W. Crosby's classic *The Columbian Exchange*, or the elder McNeill's *Plagues and Peoples*) and an upward spike in the popularity of Latin American and African history among undergraduates (sometimes as part of interdisciplinary programmes such as International Development Studies or Environmental Studies). The International Congress of Historical Sciences, which meets at five-year intervals in different locations, routinely includes world history themes in its programmes and draws historians from around the globe. Academic journals are increasingly publishing articles devoted to transnational topics, and new journals such as the *Journal of World History* (1990) and *Journal of Global History* (2006) have appeared. Even that most insularly Western of sub-disciplines, intellectual history, is now being revisited from a global perspective. Sceptics there have been, who point to sometimes superficial similarities adduced by enthusiastic comparativists, who gloss over critical differences. R. G. Collingwood, a firm Eurocentrist, did not think much of comparison, and believed that it added nothing to our understanding of a particular event.

The resurgence in the past two decades of a reconfigured 'global history', with much of the planet now divided rather differently than during the Cold War, has lent those earlier efforts renewed relevance. A number of shifts in perspective are notable. Firstly, recent efforts at global history have profited from the work of postcolonial scholars such as Dipesh Chakrabarty's (b. 1948) efforts to 'provincialize' (that is, de-centre) Europe in historical thinking, or to sketch multiple roads to modernity and even imagine *different* modernities than the dominant Western one, many of which were foreclosed by the success of European imperialism from the sixteenth to nineteenth centuries, and which may now be re-opening as Euro-American economic and political dominance begins to wane. (The American Islamist Marshall Hodgson [1922–68], a world historian and early critic of Eurocentrism, anticipated this position when he suggested that Western dominance was not fore-ordained, China having come close to an industrial revolution in the Song era that might have resulted in a very different modernity.)

Secondly, the practice of global history in its own right has acquired a sounder theoretical underpinning, with helpful correctives to its enthusiasms provided by sympathetic critics such as the German comparativists Sebastian Conrad and Dominic Sachsenmaier and the American scholars Patrick Manning (an exponent of the use of 'Big Data' in the analysis of global history) and Pamela Kyle Crossley. Manning and Crossley have both pointed out that a truly 'global' history needs to escape from the conventional periodization, largely built on European historiography, that divides human history into chunks – many going back to eighteenth-century stadialism – such as 'pastoral' and 'agrarian', or 'feudal' and 'industrial'. The French medievalist Jacques Le Goff (1924–2014) called attention in his last book to the distorting effect that periodization has long exercised, for instance, on discussions of the transition from medieval to modern, accentuating change and minimizing continuity. And the increasing frequency of 'contact', which was a core of the late Jerry Bentley's work in world history, is itself questionable as a satisfactory explanation of change. Conrad, most recently, has questioned the degree to which civilizations of the past did in fact meaningfully interact, and under what circumstances, given the overwhelming immobility of most past populations.

Thirdly, global history has indirectly spawned two even more ambitious children whose reach extends well beyond the historian's conventional 'must-have', namely written records. The first of these offspring, 'Deep History', championed by Daniel Lord Smail, seeks to integrate history with archaeology, palaeontology and neurobiology to drive our knowledge of the past back to the origins of the human race. The second, 'Big History', reaches further back still. Its exponents, such as David Christian, an American-born Australian historian who is credited with coining the phrase, situate the blip of human history within the much longer story of the universe going back to the Big Bang, making use of the latest developments in disciplines nominally far removed from history such as astrophysics. In one sense, this is Braudel's *longue durée* extended from centuries to aeons; but it has also reorganized the human centuries in a different manner than the conventional ancient–medieval–modern, creating the notion, in particular, of an 'Anthropocene' era (from the late eighteenth century onward), defined as the age during which we humans have both existed in sufficient numbers and possessed adequate technology to effect permanent, and mainly harmful, changes to the planetary environment. (As Chakrabarty notes, it has turned us from mere 'biological' agents into 'geological' ones and, historiographically, even undone the longstanding division between 'human' and 'natural' history.) Both Big and Deep historians reject the notion that the advent of writing marks the 'beginning' of the historical era, a rupture with an unchanging, 'prehistoric' age the length of which vastly exceeds that of the recorded past.

It is amusing to think that 'Universal history' a concept and a category once used by ancient and medieval historians, and transformed during the Enlightenment into the 'history of man', has finally, with Big History, really now gone *literally* universal! But, of course, our notion of the size of the universe is itself a modern development. Within an evolving tradition of 'universal history' going back through eighteenth-century *Weltgeschichte* via such medieval writers as the Persian Rashid-al-Din (1247–1318) all the way back to Polybius, our time has contributed its fair share. In the current language of 'transnational' and 'entangled' histories (*histoire croisée*), seen by advocates as a step beyond the merely 'comparative', one can recognize a contemporary echo of that ancient historian's concept of *symploke*. While global history seems itself at the moment no more than another, wider, window on to the past, rather than a house that can bring back under one roof all the prodigal, contentious children of Clio, perhaps it may yet serve an even more important purpose in encouraging humanity, in the face of great political instability and potential environmental disaster, to recognize the things we have in common before it proves too late.

*

Since the publication in 1895 of H. G. Wells' *The Time Machine*, time travel has been a favourite device of science fiction films and sometimes of historical novelists. It is tempting to ask what would happen if either Polybius or his Han China near-contemporary Sima Qian (or perhaps even both of them) suddenly materialized in our time, and found themselves in a (post-?)modern history department. A great deal of the discussion they might hear would confuse them, as would its modern context. They would also (language problems aside) have some difficulty understanding each other's perspective on the past. But there is also a core of activity that they would share with each other, and with us: an understanding that history tells, or ought to aspire to tell, true stories about the past; a sense that whatever moral judgments the historian may intrude, he or she has an obligation to present evidence without distortion or fabrication; and a conviction that a select few among the best-written histories are not merely vessels for evidence of the past, but can become themselves (as Thucydides intended) bequests to posterity, literary artefacts to be read in future ages.

This raises the question, asked with frequency in journal articles and at learned conferences, as to what the future of history may be. The present book has described a three-millennia process through which history as an organized approach to the recapturing and representation of the past gradually evolved into a major aspect of the modern world's educational and cultural life, and then how a specific mode of historicity, that of post-Enlightenment Europe and its direct offshoots, gradually displaced the well-established alternatives developed in East Asia, the Islamic world and in many other cultures entirely unmentioned in this book. That story has been linked explicitly to the parallel 'conquest' by Europe of the rest of the world's broader cultural institutions and accompanied in many cases by a political subjugation in the form of colonization, and in others by the wish of home-grown social reformers and liberal politicians to adopt a reformed historiography as a means to 'modernize' a local civilization seen as lagging behind the West. It is no accident that the two key junctures in the suzerainty of 'modern' (or what was once termed, with nineteenth-century confidence, 'scientific') history both occurred at points of ambitious imperial expansion, first in the sixteenth and seventeenth centuries, and then again in the nineteenth and early twentieth centuries. It is similarly not coincidental that Western historicity was itself affected deeply by its engagement with historiographic 'others', not so much because it adopted those alternatives (in nearly every case, it did not) as because understanding and criticizing them obliged a level of self-consciousness about what made the Western approach to the past distinctive, and why – at least in the minds of Europeans, and their Asian and colonial admirers – it had a claim to superiority. And finally, it is no coincidence, again, that the nineteenth-century moment of Western historicity's apparent global triumph was a short one in the *longue durée* of this story, and that history's claim to an empire over knowledge of the past became, during the twentieth century, just as subject to internal dissension, rebellion, secession and democratization as the literal empires that had enabled its hegemony in the first place, and which the master-narratives spun by Clio's acolytes had both promoted and helped to sustain. If the last sixty years has seen a process of *literal* decolonization throughout the world, it has also begun to see a parallel process of *historiographical* decolonization, a breaking free from modern Western attitudes, methods and models. At the same time, academic historians remain firmly fixed in Lyotard's postmodern condition, suspicious of both past and new master-narratives, and indeed often reflexively insistent on resisting generalization through ever-smaller distinctions, qualifications and counter-examples. This cuts against the inclination of most readers who will be impatient with continuous equivocation and fence-sitting; and even the historian who compulsively cavils at the generalizations of others will of necessity generalize themselves, especially when commenting on fields more remote from their expertise. This very book has attempted to simplify, connect and generalize its subject in ways that are intended to assist the introductory reader, but has in doing so necessarily minimized nuance, elided subtle differentiation and set aside a great deal of complexity.

There are at least two reasons to be hopeful for history's future prospects. The first, already addressed, is the considerably more profound internationalization or 'globalization' of the historical discipline that has been occurring for the past three decades since the end of the Cold War. And, although few historians would now endorse Leopold von Ranke's Eurocentrism, his conservatism, or his insistence on the primacy of the state and politics, it is interesting to note that some of the values of the new global history, in particular its insistence on treating other civilizations on their own merits and as of equal value, recall at least the spirit of the great German's thoughts about history, if not much of his actual practice. Secondly, history retains a social relevance and a broad popularity in spite of what Ortega y Gasset, quoted above, regarded as our best academic efforts to deprive it of both qualities. While academic history has lost the privileged 'master discipline' position that it briefly enjoyed in the nineteenth century (when it still retained at least a vestigial tie to literature), public interest in the past has never been so evident, from television (documentary and fictional) and movies, to both literary (Hilary Mantel) and popular (Diana Gabaldon, Jean Plaidy) novels, and weekend public re-enactments. The robust sales of serious books by 'big picture' synthesizers such as Jared Diamond indicate that there is no danger, imminently, of the past being forgotten. Whether it is accurately understood, much less really relevant in the shaping of our future, are different questions.

If historical thinking has never been a truly universal feature of past cultures, there nonetheless exists in the contemporary world an almost instinctual interest in the past, whether autobiographical, genealogical or archaeological. The medieval fixation on the origins of peoples and dynastic lines has been succeeded in our own time by a seemingly unquenchable thirst (evident on the history shelves of any major bookseller, where such books sit amid the still-popular works on past wars and atrocities) to understand the origins of the contemporary world, its dangers and its preoccupations. From gun control to human rights, from technology to the threat of bio-catastrophe, and nearly every seemingly intractable world problem, we historicize current issues whether it is helpful to do so or not. Croce was right that the past is always with us and that our experience of the present is freighted with signs, legacies and traditions inherited from what once was. So, too, was Nietzsche in suggesting that all of this combined can also make for a crippling weight on the backs of living, present-day people. A little less remembering and a little more forgetting might be helpful from time to time, and understanding the chain of events that brought us to present impasses is not the same as seeing a pragmatic way forward out of them.

History occurs everywhere from family photographs and antique displays, from home videos to amateur genealogical research. It is as much a hobby as a calling. So popular is history both within undergraduate courses and in the wider world that the publication of works intended for a general audience, even if still somewhat skewed in the direction of recent events or of military conflicts, shows no sign of abating. And history is still a ready-made source of material for arguments about the origins of this or that aspect of modernity whether from the right (for whom that which is to be celebrated in the present must have respectable antecedents) or the left (for whom that which remains disturbing, wicked and in need of radical change itself has historical origins). These arguments only have appeal if one assumes on the part of the reading public a basic historical literacy or at least a wish to acquire the same.

Indeed, so successful has history been in telling a broader public *what* happened, in establishing major events and milestones that stand out in the popular consciousness, and even in persuading that public to think of modernity's emergence in historical terms, that in recent years there has been a steady flow of essay collections and novels devoted to exploring, instead, what *might* have happened. These 'counterfactual' exercises go back many centuries – the French mathematician and theologian Blaise Pascal (1623–62) speculated in the seventeenth century about the shape of Cleopatra's nose and its impact on Roman history, while no less a figure than Nietzsche considered them an important tool in evaluating causal sequences. In recent years, however, they have become almost the historian's equivalent of a parlour game. Counterfactual constructions appear to offer historians a means to reason out what would have happened, say, if President Kennedy had not been assassinated, if Charles Martel had lost to the Muslims at the Battle of Tours in 732, if Jesus had not been crucified, or – a particular favourite of some novelists and their readers – if the Nazis had won the Second World War. Richard Evans has suggested that while such speculations are amusing, and captivating to the casual reader, their value to our understanding of the past, and to proving or disproving the significance of particular events in longer chains of causation, remains dubious.

Perhaps so. But in closing, let us conduct a modest counterfactual exercise of our own. I hope to have demonstrated that, if indeed there is a natural or heritable inclination on the part of humans to recover pasts of some sort – a history 'meme' to borrow a term from the evolutionary biologist Richard Dawkins – then there is no single purpose for so pursuing such recovery, no necessary mode of its pursuit, no inherently 'correct' set of methods, theories or approaches, and no 'natural' medium, beyond the human voice, for its presentation. Given this, it is possible to imagine (as some global historians have done) an alternative version of humanity's story in which the West did not achieve its hegemony, and thus just as possible to imagine an outcome in which the types of history practised by Sima Qian and his successors gradually pushed out the modes of thinking and writing about the past with which we have been familiar for generations. Such has been the connection of history to political dominance – or, as Foucault would have framed it, to power. What, in such circumstances, would a 'modern' history department look like? Would history even be a university subject? Would it be an activity controlled by a government-employed elite? And would its narrative shape look anything like the conventional, single-narrative chronological account with which we have become comfortable? The questions and possible answers are of course endless and, like any counterfactual, entirely speculative.

What we do know, without the need of such an experiment, is that the emergence of modern historiography (and modernity, as Penelope J. Corfield reminds us, itself moves with time's arrow – the historical practices of today may not seem very 'modern' a century hence) was itself a complex story, with its own history, involving many turns, multiple engagements between cultures, numerous back-and-forth revisitations of many of the *same* questions (for instance the relation of the particular to the universal or, now, global; the boundaries between history and fiction, or the utility of history as *magistra vitae*), and of repeated experiments, in many languages, with genre and form. In short, history's own history has been intimately linked with humanity's broader past. And its successes and failures have been at least as much a function of circumstances both local and geopolitical as they have of the intellectual insight or literary brilliance of its greatest practitioners.

QUESTIONS FOR DISCUSSION

1. Has history become too specialized? Or is specialization simply a mark of the maturity of the discipline?
2. Should historians take a public role and engage in political issues of the day?
3. For centuries, most historians and readers believed that one could learn from the past. Since the time of Hegel and Ranke, there has been less agreement on this matter. What do you think?

4. Can counterfactual exercises be useful to serious historical thinking?
5. What are the strengths and weaknesses of global history? What about 'Big History'?
6. There have been movements to remove statues and other monuments to controversial historical figures, or to rename buildings bearing their names. Is this a 'rewriting of history' as some argue, or a justifiable recognition that those who held values now deemed deplorable should not be honoured, even if the values they held were commonplace in their time? Where does one draw the line? Is there a difference between a statue of an American civil war Confederate general, for instance, and one of Hitler?
7. What have been the most significant developments in historical studies since the start of the present century? Where do you see the discipline of history going in the next decade or so?
8. What implications does the 'democratization' of historical materials (for instance their ready availability via the internet) have for the future of the discipline and for the importance of traditional archival repositories?

Further Reading

Baets, Antoon de, *Responsible History* (New York and Oxford, 2009)
Bentley, Jerry H., 'The New World History', in Lloyd Kramer and Sarah Maza (eds), *A Companion to Western Historical Thought* (Oxford, 2002), 393–416
Black, Jeremy, *Clio's Battles: Historiography in Practice* (Bloomington, IN, 2015)
Blouin, Francis X. Jr and William G. Rosenberg, *Processing the Past: Contesting Authority in History and the Archives* (Oxford, 2011)
Burton, Antoinette (ed.), *Archive Stories: Facts, Fictions, and the Writing of History* (Durham, NC, 2005)
Carr, David, Thomas R. Flynn and Rudolf A. Makkreel (eds), *The Ethics of History* (Evanston, IL, 2004)
Chakrabarty, Dipesh, 'The Climate of History: Four Theses', *Critical Inquiry* 35.2 (2009): 197–222
Christian, David, *Maps of Time: An Introduction to Big History* (Berkeley, CA and Los Angeles, 2004)
Conrad, Sebastian, *What is Global History?* (Princeton, NJ, 2016)
Corfield, Penelope J., *Time and the Shape of History* (New Haven, CT, 2007)

Crossley, Pamela Kyle, *What is Global History?* (Cambridge, 2008)

Dougherty, Jack and Kristen Nawrotzki (eds), *Writing History in the Digital Age* (Ann Arbor, MI, 2013)

Evans, Richard W., *Altered Pasts: Counterfactuals in History* (Waltham, MA, 2014)

Farge, Arlette, *The Allure of the Archives*, trans. T. Scott-Railton (New Haven, CT, 2013)

Ferguson, Niall (ed.), *Virtual History: Alternatives and Counterfactuals* (London, 1997)

Guldi, Jo and David Armitage, *The History Manifesto* (Cambridge, 2014)

Harlan, David, *The Degradation of American History* (Chicago, IL, 1997)

Hill, Christopher L., *National History and the World of Nations: Capital, State, and the Rhetoric of History in Japan, France, and the United States* (Durham, NC and London, 2009)

Hodgson, Marshall G. S., *Rethinking World History: Essays on Europe, Islam, and World History*, ed. E. Burke, III (Cambridge and New York, 1993)

Iggers, Georg G., *Historiography in the Twentieth Century: From Scientific Objectivity to the Postmodern Challenge*, rev. edn (Middletown, CT, 2005)

Kaye, Simon T., 'Challenging Certainty: The Utility and History of Counterfactualism', *History and Theory* 49.1 (2010): 38–57

Kingston, Beverley, 'A Plea from the Peripheries for Modesty', in Stuart Macintyre (ed.), *The Historian's Conscience: Australian Historians on the Ethics of History* (Carlton, Victoria, Australia, 2004), 75–83

Le Goff, Jacques, *Must We Divide History into Periods?*, trans. M. B. DeBevoise (New York, 2015)

Lowenthal, David, *The Past is a Foreign Country – Revisited* (1985; Cambridge, 2013)

Manning, Patrick, *Navigating World History: Historians Create a Global Past* (Houndmills, Basingstoke, 2003)

Manning, Patrick (ed.), *Global Practice in World History: Advances Worldwide* (Princeton, NJ, 2008)

Mazlish, Bruce and Akira Iriye (eds), *The Global History Reader* (New York, 2005)

Megill, Allan, 'Fragmentation and the Future of Historiography', *American Historical Review* 96.3 (1991): 693–98

   Historical Knowledge, Historical Error: A Contemporary Guide to Practice (Chicago, IL, 2007)

Morris-Suzuki, Tessa, *The Past Within Us: Media, Memory, History* (London and New York, 2005)

Moses, A. Dirk, 'The Public Relevance of Historical Studies: A Rejoinder to Hayden White', *History and Theory* 44.3 (October 2005): 339–47

Moyn, Samuel, *Human Rights and the Uses of History*, 2nd edn (London and New York, 2017)

Munslow, Alun and Robert A. Rosenstone, *Experiments in Rethinking History* (New York and London, 2004)

Olstein, Diego, *Thinking History Globally* (Basingstoke and New York, 2015)

Popkin, Jeremy D., *From Herodotus to H-Net: The Story of Historiography* (Oxford, 2016)

Rosenfeld, Gavriel D., *Hi Hitler! How the Nazi Past is Being Normalized in Contemporary Culture* (Cambridge, 2015)

Rosenstone, Robert A., *Visions of the Past: The Challenge of Film to Our Idea of History* (Cambridge, MA, 1995)
 History on Film/Film on History (Harlow, UK, 2006)

Shryock, Andrew and Daniel Lord Smail, *Deep History: The Architecture of Past and Present* (Berkeley, CA, 2011)

Smail, Daniel Lord, *On Deep History and the Brain* (Berkeley, CA and Los Angeles, 2008)

Wallerstein, Immanuel, *The Modern World System*, 3 vols (New York, 1974–89)

White, Hayden, 'The Public Relevance of Historical Studies: A Reply to Dirk Moses', *History and Theory* 44.3 (October 2005): 333–38

Woolf, Daniel, 'Concerning *Altered Parts*: Reflections of an Early Modern Historian', *Journal of the Philosophy of History* 10 (2016): 415–34

Glossary of Terms

Where no parenthetical reference to language, e.g. Arabic, German, or culture, e.g. Hindu occurs, the term is either an English word or a loan-word now in common English usage. A few terms are included here that are not specifically mentioned in this book but which the reader may encounter elsewhere.

adab (Arabic) The study of language and literature; distinguished from *hadith*.

Altertumswissenschaft (Ger.) Literally, the 'science' of ancient times. Broad term to describe our knowledge of antiquity, without reference to discipline. As a 'scientific' (in the sense of *scientia*) method, it is associated with F. A. Wolf's *Homer* and then particularly with B. G. Niebuhr and subsequent classical scholars. Traditionally a very Eurocentric term in that it confined itself to Greece and Rome proper as the foundational cultures of modern Western progress, excluding the ancient Near East, and *a fortiori* the Far East. See also *Wissenschaft*, *Hilfswissenschaft* and *Geschichtswissenschaft*.

amátl (Nahuatl) Word used to name the surface on which graphic signs were inscribed, equivalent to *biblos* (Gk) and papyrus or *scriptum codex* (Lat.) or *vuh* (Mayan, typically tree bark).

antiquitates (Lat.) Genre of history of customs and antiquities; more than simply antiquarianism; flourished especially in the early modern period, where it was an alternative to the tradition of *narratio* or political history.

bunmeishi (Jap.) Fukuzawa Yukichi's term for 'history of civilization'.

Dichtung und Wahrheit (Ger.) Literally 'poetry [or fiction] and truth'; coined by Goethe, but useful for describing the tension between the creative and the factual sides of history.

diplomatic (Lat.) The ancillary discipline devoted to studying and classifying official documents such as charters, with special attention to their physical layout and medium, and to conventions, formulae or salutations that can provide guidance as to origin and period where no explicit evidence (or doubtful evidence, as in a forged document) is given by the actual text of the document.

epigraphy The study of inscriptions, typically on 'solid' media such as walls, stele and statues.

Erklärung (Ger.) Explanation. Distinguished in philosophy of history since J. G. Droysen and Wilhelm Dilthey from *Verstehen*, understanding.

fangzhi (Chin.) Geographically organized 'gazetteers', often containing local historical information.

Geschichtlichkeit (Ger.) Historicity, the quality of being historical. Often associated specifically, in its German usage, with the thought of Martin Heidegger.

Geschichtsbewusstsein (Ger.) Historical consciousness.

Geschichtswissenschaft (Ger.) Literally, historical science; a term first coined in the mid-eighteenth century but brought into more frequent usage after being deployed by Leopold von Ranke. See also *Wissenschaft* and *Hilfswissenschaften*.

Guoshi (Chin.) National history. Compare *kuksa* (Korea) and *kokushi* (Jap.); all three words employ the same pair of Chinese characters, indicating their common origins.

hadith (Arabic) Report of a religious authority, usually the Prophet. Essential element in early Islamic historical and religious scholarship. See also *isnad* and *matn*.

hikayat (Malay) A legend, story, biography or tales handed down from the past.

Hilfswissenschaften (Ger.) Literally 'helping sciences', i.e. ancillary disciplines to knowledge.

histoire croisée (French) 'Entangled histories', i.e. multinational histories that focus on the interconnections, cross-fertilizations and encounters between the pasts of different nations or regions.

historia (Lat.) and *'ιστορια* (Gk) History. The original Greek term more literally means inquiry, discovery, or inventory without a necessary connection to past events.

Historikerstreit (Ger.) Conflict among historians, generally; specifically used to refer to the controversy of the late 1980s and early 1990s regarding the Holocaust. Not to be confused with earlier *Methodenstreit*.

Historische Hilfswissenschaften (Ger.) Includes things such as palaeography (*Schriftkunde* or *Paläografie*), diplomatic (*Urkunden*) and historical chronology (*chronologie*; *historische Zeitrechnungslehre*). See also *Wissenschaft* and *Geschichtswissenschaft*.

Historismus (Ger.) Historism or Historicism. Term used initially to describe a particularly Germanic approach to historical study, stressing the uniqueness of particular periods or civilizations and the historian's duty to treat them all as of value. Use of the term expanded in the twentieth century to denote the broader dominant tradition of European historical thought and scholarship. It has sometimes been misused (e.g. by the philosopher Karl Popper) to denote a view that history is governed by laws and consists of a cumulative process or processes leading to a particular outcome.

huehuenonotzaliztli (Nahuatl) Expression used to refer to oral narrative of past or remote events recounted by an ancient or old person (*huehue*). See also *huehuetlatolli*, ancient discourse delivered by elders including wisdom, used for education of the young.

isnad (Arabic) One of two sections usually contained in a *hadith*; refers to the chain of transmission and authorities for the text subsequently contained in a *matn*.

istoria (Ital.) History (as used by Flavio Biondo). Often simply *storia*. Note the close etymological relation of 'story' and 'history'.

itihasa (Hindu) Literally 'thus it was'; a term from Sanskrit tradition that most closely approximates to history, while including things like legend, oral tradition and epic poetry. See also *purana*.

Jahrhundertrechnung (Ger.) The practice of calculating time in centuries; secondarily, the historiographical idea of the century as a meaningful unit of time. One of the earliest western examples deploying the latter was the *Magdeburg Centuries*, a Protestant history of the sixteenth century.

kagami (Jap.) Mirror.

Kaozheng xue (Chin.) Evidential learning.

khabar (Arabic) Literally a 'report' or 'account' of the past, but often used as meaning 'history', though a history was often an assemblage of multiple *akhbar*. One who writes or collects or transmits these is *akhbari*. See also *ta'rikh*.

ki (Jap.) Chronicle.

kitab (Arabic) History, as used especially by Ibn Khaldun in the fourteenth century in the *Muqaddimah*.

kokugaku (Jap.) 'National Learning' as in School of National Learning.

kokushi (Jap.) National history, as distinct from the history of other parts of the world. See also *toyoshi*.

maghazi (Arabic). Deeds and campaigns of the Prophet Muhammad; also the title of particular works about this.

matn (Arabic) The main text of a *hadith* following the *isnad*.

Methodenstreit (Ger.) The quarrel about method in late nineteenth-century German historiography, focusing on the cultural history of Karl Lamprecht and on the latter's efforts to introduce social science methods into history. Lamprecht was widely discredited in Germany, which stuck to traditional political history, but proved much more influential outside, e.g. in France and the United States.

Nachleben (Ger.) Afterlife, especially of a text but also of tradition or custom.

Nihonshi (Jap.) The history of Japan.

numismatics. Ancillary discipline devoted to the study of old coins and medals, with a view to their use as historical evidence.

origines gentium (Lat.) 'The origins of peoples': a historiographic theme, usually identified with western historiography from antiquity to the nineteenth century, and in particular with the late antique and early medieval writers who wished to account for the origins of the many 'barbarian' kingdoms that had emerged on the ruins of the western Roman Empire, or in the east.

palaeography Ancillary discipline (see *Hilfswissenschaften*) concerned with deciphering and classifying handwriting; apart from being indispensable in the reading of pre-modern documents, it is used to develop chronological classifications of hands (for instance early medieval 'Carolingian minuscule' or sixteenth-century 'Secretary' hands). Often associated with diplomatic.

purana (Hindu) Literally 'pertaining to ancient times' or long ago, in Hindu literature, principally written in Sanskrit. Largely written between the fourth century BC and end of the first millennium AD. See also *itihasa*.

Quellenforschung (Ger.) 'Source examination'; a variant of criticism that focuses particularly on taking one historical source (usually an earlier historian's writing) and identifying *its* sources, for instance trying to identify the histories or other sources that a Livy or Tacitus might have used.

Quellenkritik (Ger.) Literally source criticism. In the 'modern' West, it is often associated with the philologist B. G. Niebuhr's principle that the accounts of even ancient historians could not be taken at face value. However, these methods were used earlier in the West (there are medieval and many early modern examples). There are non-western counterparts, for instance in Chinese Confucian scholarship.

quipu (Quechua) Knotted cord used as a record-keeping system in the pre-colonial Andes, usually in combination with remembered and orally recited tradition.

Rekishi monogatari (Jap.) Genre of 'historical tale' in the *monogatari* (epic) form, composed between the eleventh and fourteenth centuries, and including the *Eiga monogatari* as well as later works in the 'mirror' tradition such as the *Okagami*.

Rikkokushi (Jap.) The Six National Histories.

Sattelzeit (Ger.) Literally 'saddle period' or 'bridge period'. Term used by Reinhart Koselleck for the period 1750 to 1850 in intellectual history; sometimes more specifically the period 1790 to 1830 in German literature, early Romanticism.

sejarah (Malay) History; annals; knowledge of past events.

shi (Chin.) Originally meaning a historian or more accurately 'scribe', the word later came to denote the product of the historian's work, i.e. a history.

shilu (Chin.) Veritable Records of an emperor's reign, compiled at its end; a transitional document used following the end of a dynasty in order to compile that dynasty's history; originating during the Tang dynasty.

sira (Arabic) 'Model behaviour' of an authoritative figure such as the Prophet in particular; by extension, the biography of such a person; also the title of particular works in this genre.

subaltern Term originally derived from the Italian Marxist Antonio Gramsci and now mainly associated with the 'Subaltern Studies' school of postcolonial Indian history, founded by Ranajit Guha and other Indian scholars, and the publications that appeared under that name. Subaltern means the previously ignored masses or peasantry of India; or, sometimes, the resistant or insurgent. A key concept in postcolonial thought, the subaltern studies movement is as much a reaction against elite Indian historians of nationalism as it is against the colonial historiography of Western imperial powers epitomized by G. W. F. Hegel and James Mill.

symploke (Συμπλοκή) (Gk) The interconnection of events; a concept used by Polybius in constructing the first 'universal' history. Polybius perceived the year 217 BC and the Conference of Naupactus as the beginning of a process of universal *symploke*. See also *Zusammenhang*.

tabaqa (Arabic) A class or category of men; the plural *tabaqat* denotes collections of biographies about such men.

ta'rikh (Arabic) Word denoting history in general, though often particularly meaning history organized by year, i.e. annalistically. Also used in sense of a biography providing birth and death dates of its subject. See also *khabar*.

toyoshi (Jap.) 'History of the East', i.e. mainly China, but also Korea, Mongolia, Tibet and Central Asia, as opposed to the history of Japan or history of the west.

tung shi (Chin.) Continuous narrative histories, often more specifically national histories since the nineteenth century. Sima Guang's eleventh-century *Zizhi Tongjian* (*Comprehensive Mirror in Aid of Government*) can be deemed an early example, as is Sima Qian's *Shiji*, since they transcend dynastic limits.

Tyche (Τύχη) (Gk) Fortune, or chance; first becomes a major 'character' or agent in history in Polybius, where it is not just random accident but something approaching destiny, which guides Rome to its world dominance. More or less equivalent to Latin *fortuna*.

umma (Arabic) The community of Muslim believers, transcending national or ethnic divisions; in contrast to *Al-umma al-arabiyya*, the Arab nation.

vamsas (Pali) Sri Lankan Buddhist historical traditions dating from the fourth to nineteenth centuries.

Verstehen (Ger.) Literally, understanding; often used in histories of historiography in its German form as associated with the thought of J. G. Droysen and Wilhelm Dilthey; a source of R. G. Collingwood's theory of 're-enactment'. See also *Erklärung*.

Volksgeist (Ger.) The psychic or intellectual unity of a people or 'nation'. See also the complementary notion of a *Zeitgeist*.

Volksgeschichte (Ger.) Racist form of history, popular in Germany mainly during the inter-war period.

Wissenschaft (Ger.) Science, but not in the narrow sense that word is used in English today; closer to the Latin *scientia* or French *science*; *Geisteswissenschaften* (a term associated with historicists such as Wilhelm Dilthey) now includes the 'human' or 'moral' sciences, e.g. philosophy, jurisprudence and theology. The root *Wissenschaft* is also translatable as discipline, study or learning (but see also *Verstehen*, understanding). Frequently used in connection with history: e.g. *Geschichtswissenschaft*, historical science or learning. See also *Hilfswissenschaften* and *Altertumswissenschaft*.

xiuh-amátl (or *xiuhamtl; xiuhlapohualamoxtli*) (Nahuatl) Interpreted by early post-Conquest European scholars as the equivalent of annals.

Zeitgeist (Ger.) 'Spirit' or perhaps more accurately 'mind' of the time or age. See also *Volksgeist*.

Zeitgeschichte (Ger.) History of one's own time; common in antiquity. Insofar as previous history is contained in such a work, it is usually based (prior to the eighteenth century) on earlier writers of history of *their* own times.

Zusammenhang (Ger.) 'Coherence' or 'connection', a concept similar to Polybius' *symploke* (interconnectedness); a frequent theme of Ranke's writings in the nineteenth century.

Index

For ease of reference, titles of works mentioned in the text are indexed separately from their authors, with authors' names in parantheses except in the case of anonymous or multi-authored works.